Economic Policymaking in Mexico

Related Titles in Duke Press Policy Studies Series

Modeling Growing Economies in Equilibrium and Disequilibrium
Edited by Allen C. Kelly, Warren C. Sanderson, and Jeffrey G. Williamson

No to Recession and Unemployment:
An Examination of the Brazilian Economic Crisis
Celso Furtado

Keynes' Monetary Thought:
A Study of Its Development
Don Patinkin

Essays On and In the Chicago Tradition
Don Patinkin

Theory of Spatial Pricing and Market Areas
Melvin L. Greenhut and Hiroshi Ohta

Economic Policymaking in Mexico

Factors Underlying the 1982 Crisis

Robert E. Looney

Duke Press Policy Studies
Duke University Press Durham, NC 1985

Printed in the United States of America
ISBN 0-8223-0557-7
Library of Congress Cataloging in Publication Data
Looney, Robert E.
(Duke Press policy studies)
Bibliography: p.
Includes index.
1. Mexico—Economic policy—1970- . I. Title.
II. Series.
HC135.L6138 1985 338.971 84-28739

for Ginny

Contents

Tables

Figures

Foreword

Professor Looney has performed a tour de force in using a variety of advanced quantitative tools to analyze the performance of the Mexican economy during the critical period of the seventies. Under presidents Echeverría (1971–76) and López Portillo (1977–82), the government tried unsuccessfully to cure the country's severe unemployment (labor supply grows at more than 4 percent annually) via excessive doses of the Keynesian drug. The effort ended in crisis the last year of each administration, 1976 and 1982. It seems Mexico, in contrast to other large Latin American economies, cannot maintain for long significant price and external disequilibria. Its long and semi-open border with the United States makes the adjustment urgent and unavoidable—despite the advent of substantial oil exports. Mexico knew and acted on this geoeconomic reality during the sixties, as Dr. Looney points out. It is almost certain that this fundamental premise will not be forgotten during the eighties.

Dr. Looney's multilevel analysis brings out clearly the Mexican dilemma of growth vs. stability. One only wishes that he could follow this book with his scenarios of the eighties. He might come up with fresh ideas and suggestions for refining policies or for adding new tools to the "Keynesian kit" of the Mexican authorities. They most certainly will need them to fulfill the goal of lowering the rate of growth and inflation, while increasing the rate of employment during 1983–85, if the New National Development Plan of President de la Madrid is to be reasonably successful.

Dr. Abel Beltran del Rio
Vice President and Director
DIEMEX-Wharton Mexican Project
Wharton, EFA, Inc.

Preface

Mexico's confidence in its economic system was badly shaken by the collapse of its currency in mid-February of 1982 and the specter of national default and zero economic growth by the following summer.[1] The financial crisis appears to have bruised more than economic confidence. "Let us not sink into the infertile swamp of bitterness and dispair," was the campaign slogan of the next Mexican president, Miguel de la Madrid Hurtado. He also stressed that "we must recognize the seriousness of the situation but we should analyze it soberly."[2]

The abrupt increase in both the price of crude oil and resulting increase in Mexico's oil revenues beginning in 1977 had appeared to have saved the country from near disaster. The new prosperity permitted the government to design a longer-term development strategy without the ever-present fear of a fiscal crisis. From the perspective of late 1982, however, it was apparent that this change took place within a mainly traditional economy, unprepared to absorb and cope with the expenditures the new oil revenues made possible. Inflation, bottlenecks, and severe shortages have, therefore, risen sharply.[3]

Longer-term options, viable development strategies and alternatives, were major topics of analysis and discussion only several years ago (Robert Looney, *Development Alternatives of Mexico* [New York: Praeger Publishers, 1982]). They are now largely academic, however, as the government faces the urgent need to design and implement an effective short-run stabilization program. Part of the shock of the current economic slump appears to be psychological. In recent years, many Mexicans had grown accustomed to an economic boom fed by continually rising oil prices, and now they have been caught by surprise. "I think it is part of the Mexican character to swing abruptly between optimism and pessimism," one foreign diplomat has argued. "Perhaps it is because they don't look ahead."[4]

The ultimate purpose of this study is to look ahead once again. This book considers a series of alternative and short-run stabilization programs that the Mexican economy might adopt to alleviate the current crisis. These are based on different assumptions about the effectiveness of existing policy tools and likely developments in the international economic situation. These perspectives are, in turn, largely based on an analysis of the policymaking process implemented during the Echeverría (1971–76) and López Portillo (1977–82) administrations.

There are four main sections to this volume. The first (chapters 1–3) surveys the major economic trends after 1970, with particular emphasis on the mechanisms leading up to the 1982 crisis: the increasing deterioration of the balance of payments with the resultant rapid increase in external debt, the resurgence of inflation, and the trend toward stagnation in production and employment. The second section (chapters 4–8) evaluates historically and qualitatively policymaking during the Echeverría and López Portillo administrations. Particular attention is given to the characteristics of the 1978 recovery, the high growth development strategy adopted at that time, and the appearance of new elements such as the rapid increase in oil production, hydrocarbon exports, and external debt. Chapter 8 analyzes a number of links between the country's post-1977 high growth strategy and the 1982 crisis. The third section (chapters 9–12) examines from a quantitative point of view the impact major economic policies have had on various facets of the economy. Effective economic programs particularly with regard to fiscal policy will be of obvious importance to the country's economic recovery. In this regard chapters 11 and 12 attempt to identify the mechanisms through which Mexican fiscal policy has an impact on the economy as a whole. The analytical framework in the next section (chapters 12–15) identifies the major economic interrelationships at work in the Mexican economy, among output growth, price levels, and the composition of final demand (under different assumptions about Mexican monetary and fiscal policy), and developments in the international economy. Based on this analysis, chapters 14 and 15 assess programs realistically open to the country over the remainder of the de la Madrid presidency (1983–87). The final chapter (chapter 16) draws on the preceding analysis to delineate a set of viable policy options open to the country during the de la Madrid presidency.

The main conclusion of this chapter and of the study as a whole is that the crisis of August 1982 was a cash flow problem more than a fundamental economic problem—a case of illiquidity rather than insolvency. This study contends that Mexico's main challenge is to achieve realistic adjustment at the lowest possible human cost. The challenge to policymakers internationally, and especially in the United States, is to draw the proper lessons from the Mexican experience for strengthening the international economic system. Accurate appraisal and prompt action within Mexico are all the more essential at a time when "the tides of international economic activity are too low to allow much room for faulty navigation through narrow channels."[5]

Acknowledgments

Many individuals have assisted me in conceptualizing this study. Discussions at the 1981 Eastern Economic Association Meetings in Philadelphia with Leopoldo Solis of the Bank of Mexico, Abel Beltran del Rio of Wharton Econometrics, Jeffrey Nugent of the University of Southern California, Edward Nell of the New School of Social Research, Jimmy Wheeler of the Hudson Institute, and Edgar Ortiz of the Universidad Nacional Autónoma de México provided the initial stimulus. Their comments were extremely helpful in revising my paper "Mexico's Fiscal Crisis: A Critique of the Fitzgerald Thesis," which appears as chapter 12 in this study.

A year later at the 1982 Eastern Economic Association meetings in Washington, Garry Fromm of Investment Intelligence Systems Co., Robert Kuenne of Princeton, and Louis Krauthoff of the Joint Economic Committee provided useful insights enabling me to make substantial revisions in my paper "The Oil Question and Policy Optimization in Mexico," which appears in the present study as chapter 14.

I am particularly indebted to Abel Beltran del Rio, Arthur Mann of the University of Puerto Rico, and George Feivel of the University of Tennessee for their comments on my paper "An Optimal Mexican Stabilization Program for the 1980s," presented in December 1982 at the North American Economics and Finance Association in New York. Their suggestions are incorporated in a revised version of that paper, which comprises the bulk of chapter 15.

My main intellectual debt is to Clark Reynolds of Stanford whose work on total factor productivity provided the basis for the estimates presented in chapter 2.

Redvers Opie helped focus my attention on the economy's increased inflationary tendencies and the general limitations of government policy in controlling the overall pace of economic development.

The Mexican banking community was extremely helpful in sharing their perceptions of the country's financial situation. In this regard I am especially grateful to Enrique de Bayle of Banco Nacional de México and Carlos Bracho of Banco Serfin for their time and insights. Short visits to Mexico with Eugene Mihaly, Rex Beach, and Gary Hare of Mihaly Associates International helped me gather additional information and, more important, share firsthand the views of the Mexican business community.

At the Naval Postgraduate School, Peter Frederiksen aided in some of the computer analysis and made a major contribution to chapters 10 and 11. My research assistant, Haruko Nimura, developed the optimal control programs from the original programs developed by Garret Vanderplaats. I am particularly indebted to Dr. Vanderplaats for sharing his original optimal control programs.

Albertine Potter was most helpful in typing part of the final draft. I am grateful to the Research Foundation at the Naval Postgraduate School for its financial assistance during the spring and summer of 1981, enabling me to complete the empirical sections of the book.

Finally, special thanks goes to my wife, Pam, who persevered through the final editing with patience and good cheer.

The responsibility for any errors or shortcomings is solely mine. Also, this study does not necessarily reflect in any way the views of the Research Foundation of the Naval Postgraduate School or the Department of National Security Affairs.

I. Historical Trends and Sources of Growth

Introduction

Mexico is now classified as a newly industrializing nation.[1] The country's gross domestic product of 121.3 billion dollars in 1979 made it the world's eighteenth largest economy, and a per capita GNP of $1,640 in 1979 (see Appendix, table A.1) was sufficient to place the country slightly ahead of North Korea in the group of newly industrializing countries (see Appendix, table A.2). The absolute value of manufacturing in Mexico falls below the level of Brazil but considerably above those of Singapore and Korea (table A.2). With 71.91 million inhabitants (mid-1980), Mexico is the world's eleventh most populous country.[2]

Chapter 1 presents an overview of the Mexican economy. It examines the main factors in Mexican economic performance, the role of economic policy in the country's recent growth, the manner and degree to which exports have contributed to the country's growth, the major lessons from Mexico's growth experience that are pertinent for policy formulation in other developing or newly industrializing countries, and the internal dynamics of Mexican economic development. Chapter 1 and the two following chapters provide the background for understanding the factors responsible for Mexico's recent economic crisis and serve as a framework for the analysis that follows.

1. An Overview of the Mexican Economy

Long-Run Growth Patterns

From a long-run perspective Mexico's growth performance has been quite remarkable.[1] After 1930, real GDP increased at a rate of 2.9 percent per annum between 1930 and 1940,[2] accelerating to 6.9 percent annual growth from 1940 to 1950, then leveling off at 5.6, 7.0, and 5.5 percent growth rates for the 1950–60, 1960–70, and 1970–80 periods, respectively. Increases in employment and growth in industry have followed this same pattern (tables 1.1 and 1.2). The resulting structural changes have shifted (table 1.3) the economy from one largely oriented toward agriculture (20 percent of GDP to 9 percent, 1930–80) to one which is becoming increasingly industrial (25 percent GDP to 39 percent 1930–80). However, the Mexican economy still depends on services as the major source of income (55 percent to 52 percent, 1930–80). Recent growth (table 1.4) has been (1978–81) in the 8 to 9 percent per annum range, led by mining, construction, and transportation.

In addition to achieving relatively high overall GDP growth rates, the Mexican economy has also generated relatively high levels of savings and capital formation; the latter had been at about 20 percent of GDP during the 1960s and had risen to 28 percent by 1979. Still, these figures were somewhat below the 39 and 55 percent experienced by Singapore and Korea, respectively, in 1979 (table 1.5).

A World Bank study of gross marginal or incremental capital output (ICOR) offers a broader comparative perspective on Mexican growth.[3] This measure relates the change in capital stock to the change in GDP (at constant prices) with a one-year lag. The Bank's calculations yielded an ICOR for Mexico of 3.2 for 1951–60 and 2.7 for 1961–67. To be sure, these figures are not very high when Mexico is compared to the more advanced countries, where the introduction of labor-saving technology commonly produces ICOR values of 4 to 6. However, Mexico's ratio is well above those of many of the recent success stories among the developing countries such as Taiwan, Hong Kong, and South Korea, and even above those of slightly less rapid growth cases such as Thailand. Each of these countries has growth that was about as fast as in Mexico, but their incremental capital output ratios averaged around 2.0. Admittedly a low incremental capital output ratio does not necessarily indicate successful labor-intensive development. However, given the relative abundance of labor in most of these countries, a low incremental output ratio does imply an efficient allocation of resources.

In terms of a simple capital coefficient (the rate of growth in gross domestic product divided by the rate of growth in gross domestic investment), Mexico

Table 1.1. Mexico: population, gross domestic product, employment, and production, selected years, 1910–80

	1910	1911	1930	1940	1950	1960	1970	1975	1978	1979	1980
Population (in millions)	15.2	14.3	16.6	19.6	25.8	35.0	50.7	60.2	66.9	69.4	71.9
Gross domestic product (billions 1975 pesos)											
Agriculture	20	20	17	24	39	61	88	96	106	106	112
Industry	14	18	21	27	60	112	262	355	425	464	503
Services	39	41	47	63	123	211	410	545	595	634	678
Total	74	80	85	114	223	384	760	996	1,126	1,204	1,293
Gross domestic product per capita (1975 pesos)											
Agriculture	1,350	1,430	1,050	1,230	1,530	1,750	1,735	1,594	1,584	1,527	1,558
Industry	920	1,260	1,250	1,400	2,330	3,210	5,168	5,897	6,353	6,686	6,996
Services	2,600	2,880	2,850	3,190	4,770	6,040	8,087	9,053	8,894	9,135	9,430
Total	4,870	5,570	5,150	5,820	8,630	11,000	14,990	16,544	16,831	17,348	17,983
Employment (thousands)											
Agriculture	3,596	3,490	3,626	3,831	4,824	6,097	5,004	5,676	6,098	6,241	6,384
Industry	906	660	773	909	1,319	2,144	3,083	4,011	4,683	4,929	5,187
Services	762	734	752	1,118	2,129	3,033	5,256	6,647	7,641	8,002	8,380
Total	5,264	4,884	5,151	5,858	8,272	11,274	13,343	16,334	18,422	19,172	19,951
Employment/population ratio (percent)	34.6	34.1	31.0	29.9	32.0	32.2	26.3	27.1	27.5	27.6	27.7
Productivity (GDP per worker, 1975 pesos)											
Agriculture	5,700	5,870	4,790	6,280	8,190	10,100	17,700	16,913	17,382	16,984	17,543
Industry	15,400	27,300	26,800	30,200	45,500	52,500	84,800	88,506	90,753	94,136	96,973
Services	51,800	56,100	63,000	56,000	57,800	69,700	77,900	81,991	77,869	79,230	80,907
Total	14,000	16,300	16,600	19,500	26,900	34,200	56,900	60,977	61,122	62,799	64,808

Sources: International Monetary Fund, International Financial *Statistics*; Nacional Financeria, *La Economía Méxicana en Cifras*; Bank of Mexico, *Mexico Statistical Data, 1970–80*; and Bank of Mexico, *Informe Anual, 1981*.

Table 1.2. Mexico: average annual growth rates in population, gross domestic product, employment, and productivity, selected periods, 1910–80 (percent per year)

	1910–21	1921–30	1930–40	1940–50	1950–60	1960–70	1970–75	1975–80	1970–80
Population	−0.6	1.7	1.7	2.8	3.1	3.8	3.5	3.6	3.6
Gross domestic product (billions 1975 pesos)									
Agriculture	0.0	−1.8	3.3	5.1	4.6	3.7	1.8	3.1	2.4
Industry	2.3	1.6	2.9	8.1	6.5	8.8	6.3	7.2	6.7
Service	0.4	1.6	2.8	7.0	5.6	6.8	5.9	4.5	5.2
Total	0.7	0.8	2.9	6.9	5.6	7.0	5.6	5.4	5.5
Gross domestic product per capita (1975 pesos)									
Agriculture	0.5	−3.4	1.6	2.2	1.4	0.0	−1.7	−0.5	−1.1
Industry	2.9	−0.1	1.1	5.2	3.2	4.9	2.7	3.5	3.1
Services	0.9	−0.1	1.1	4.1	2.4	3.0	2.3	0.8	1.5
Total	1.2	−0.9	1.2	4.0	2.5	3.2	2.0	1.7	1.8
Employment (thousands)									
Agriculture	−0.3	0.4	0.5	2.3	2.4	−1.9	2.6	2.4	2.5
Industry	−2.8	1.8	1.6	3.8	5.0	3.7	5.4	5.3	5.3
Services	−0.3	0.3	4.0	6.6	3.6	5.6	4.8	4.7	4.8
Total	0.7	0.6	1.3	3.5	3.1	1.7	4.1	4.1	4.1
Productivity (GDP per worker, 1975 pesos)									
Agriculture	0.3	−2.2	2.7	2.7	2.1	5.8	−0.9	0.7	−0.1
Industry	5.3	−0.2	1.2	4.2	1.4	4.9	0.9	1.8	1.4
Services	0.7	1.3	−1.2	0.3	1.9	1.1	1.0	−0.3	0.4
Total	1.4	0.2	1.6	3.3	2.4	5.2	1.4	1.2	1.3

Source: Computed from table 1.1.

Table 1.3. Mexico: composition of product and employment, selected years, 1910–80 (in percent)

	1910	1921	1930	1940	1950	1960	1970	1975	1980
Gross domestic product (1975 pesos)									
Agriculture	27	25	20	21	17	16	12	10	9
Industry	19	23	25	24	27	29	34	36	39
Services	53	51	55	55	55	55	54	54	52
Total	100	100	100	100	100	100	100	100	100
Employment									
Agriculture	68	72	70	65	58	54	38	35	32
Industry	17	14	15	16	16	19	23	25	26
Services	14	15	15	19	26	27	39	40	42
Total	100	100	100	100	100	100	100	100	100

Source: Compiled from table 1.1.

fares relatively better. During the 1960s and 1970s (table 1.6), Mexican GDP tended to grow about 75 percent as fast as investment, lower than Brazil for both periods and considerably below Singapore and Korea for the 1960s, but considerably above the latter two countries' respective 41 and 44 percent in the 1970s.

Major Economic Trends and Developments

Despite this seemingly rosy picture, a number of structural imbalances have also characterized Mexico's development, particularly in the interconnections between the economy, social classes, and the political system. These have been noted at length in the literature[4] and can be summarized as follows:[5]

1. The growth of the economy over the last three decades has been promoted through a strategy of industrialization. Agriculture was deemphasized after having financed the industrial take-off. Economic growth has been very unbalanced and has sharpened the inter- and intrasectorial inequalities as well as the regional differences in Mexican society.
2. Industrialization through import substitution has ultimately led to an increasing dependence on foreign imports.
3. The agricultural sector has experienced structural change as a result of the emergence of modern agricultural corporations in the 1940s, producing export crops on most of the best irrigated lands in the northern regions of the country.
4. The small property owners and subsistence farmers who made up the remainder of the agricultural sector were largely neglected and subsequently have seen their relative standards of living decline.
5. Declining relative incomes together with strong population pressures in rural areas have induced large segments of the rural population to migrate to the

Table 1.4. Mexico: rate of change in gross domestic product by sector, 1971–81 (in percent)

Economic activity	1971	1972	1973	1974	1975	1976	1977	1978	1979	1980	1981
Agriculture, livestock, forestry, and fishing	5.7	0.7	4.1	2.5	2.0	1.0	7.5	6.0	−2.1	7.1	6.4
Mining	−0.4	4.6	6.6	13.8	5.8	6.1	7.6	14.3	14.7	22.3	16.6
Extraction of petroleum and gas	−0.6	4.0	3.5	21.0	17.5	6.7	16.6	24.7	21.9	32.6	n.a.
Manufacturing	3.9	9.8	10.5	6.3	5.0	5.0	3.5	9.8	10.6	7.2	7.4
Construction	−4.5	12.7	14.6	6.8	5.9	4.6	−3.5	12.4	13.0	12.3	11.5
Electricity	5.4	13.7	12.3	12.8	5.4	12.2	7.6	7.9	10.3	6.5	9.0
Commerce, restaurants, and hotels	3.9	10.0	8.7	5.0	5.2	3.2	1.8	7.9	11.7	8.1	8.9
Transport, storage, and communications	7.8	14.5	15.5	13.2	10.0	5.1	6.6	12.5	15.5	14.1	11.0
Financial services	4.5	7.3	6.9	4.9	4.9	4.0	3.7	4.4	5.3	4.6	5.1
Community, social, and personal services	6.4	7.9	4.4	6.5	8.5	5.7	3.8	6.7	7.9	7.5	6.8
Government services	10.5	12.2	7.7	8.9	16.2	3.4	−1.8	8.1	8.4	10.3	n.a.
GDP (billions)											
1970 pesos	4.2	8.5	8.4	6.1	5.6	4.2	3.4	8.2	9.2	9.3	8.1
1960 pesos	3.4	7.3	7.6	5.9	4.1	2.1	3.3	7.3	8.0	7.4	—

Source: Constructed from Bank of Mexico, *Informe Anual*, *1980*, *1981*.
Note: 1980, 1981 figures preliminary; n.a. = not available.

Table 1.5. Mexico: comparison of structure of production with selected countries

	Newly industrializing countries				Developing countries			
	Mexico	Brazil	Singapore	Korea	Cameroon	Tunisia	Sri Lanka	Philippines
Percent of GDP								
Public consumption								
1960	6	12	8	14	—	17	13	8
1979	12	10	11	11	10	16	9	9
Private consumption								
1960	76	67	95	84	—	76	78	76
1979	72	69	63	61	80	61	77	67
Gross domestic investment								
1960	20	22	11	11	—	17	14	16
1979	28	23	39	35	25	29	26	29
Gross domestic savings								
1960	18	21	−3	1	—	7	9	16
1979	26	21	26	28	10	23	14	24
Exports								
1960	10	5	163	3	—	20	43	11
1979	12	7	187	30	25	38	34	19
Resource balance								
1960	−2	−1	−14	−10	—	−10	−5	0
1979	−2	−2	−13	−7	−15	−6	−12	−5

Average annual growth								
Public consumption								
1960–70	9.5	3.5	12.6	5.5	6.1	5.2	—	5.0
1970–79	10.0	8.6	6.4	8.7	5.4	9.8	—	8.4
Private consumption								
1960–70	6.6	5.1	5.4	7.0	2.7	3.2	2.1	4.7
1970–79	3.8	9.1	7.2	8.0	5.3	8.2	3.0	4.7
Gross domestic investment								
1960–70	9.6	7.0	20.5	23.6	9.3	4.2	6.6	8.2
1970–79	6.9	10.1	6.0	14.9	7.9	11.4	6.4	10.6
Exports								
1960–70	2.8	5.1	4.2	34.1	7.1	4.2	4.7	2.2
1970–79	10.9	7.0	11.0	25.7	0.5	4.8	−3.0	6.2
Imports								
1960–70	6.4	4.9	5.9	20.5	9.2	1.9	−0.2	7.1
1970–79	5.0	5.6	8.0	13.5	7.0	11.2	−0.6	3.7
Terms of trade (1975 = 100)								
1960	97	114	100	99	106	64	203	112
1979	84	94	101	94	144	81	116	107

Source: Compiled from World Bank, *World Development Report*, 1981.

Table 1.6. Mexico: comparison of capital coefficients, selected countries

	Newly industrializing countries				Developing countries			
	Mexico	Brazil	Singapore	Korea	Cameroon	Tunisia	Sri Lanka	Philippines
Average annual growth								
(1) Gross domestic investment, 1960–70	9.6	7.0	7.2	8.0	9.3	4.2	6.6	8.2
(2) Gross domestic product, 1960–70	7.2	5.4	8.8	8.6	3.7	4.7	4.6	5.1
(3) Gross domestic investment, 1970–79	6.9	10.1	20.5	23.6	7.9	11.4	6.4	10.6
(4) Gross domestic product, 1970–79	5.1	8.7	8.4	10.3	5.4	7.6	3.8	6.2
Capital coefficient								
1960–70 (2) − (1)	0.75	0.77	1.22	1.08	0.40	1.12	0.70	0.62
1970–79 (4) − (3)	0.74	0.86	0.41	0.44	0.68	0.67	0.59	0.58

Source: Compiled from World Bank, *World Development Report*, 1981.

cities in search of better income and living conditions. In most cases migrant rural workers have added to urban underemployment problems as they become part of the reservoir of cheap unskilled labor for the urban industries.

6. The accumulation of capital has occurred increasingly at the expense of consumption. The extreme inequalities in income distribution have added to what was at times an inflationary environment. In addition, the relatively low rate of taxation has permitted high profit rates.
7. The poverty of the lower income groups has hampered the expansion of the domestic market, while the middle classes that grew with the expansion of the diversification of the economy and the government bureaucracy generate insufficient demand. Further industrial growth, especially of those industries dependent on large markets, may therefore depend on changes in income distribution (which in turn would require drastic changes in the power relations within the political structure).
8. The Mexican economy has become more and more dependent on direct and indirect foreign (mostly U.S.) investment. Foreign economic interests have become a powerful pressure group. They do not dominate the country directly, but impose sharp limits on external and internal economic policies.
9. The import and export trade has been directed toward the United States. The importance of U.S. tourism and border transactions has further increased the dependence of the Mexican economy, with obvious political consequences.
10. From the structural reforms of the 1930s, the government has changed to measures for economic and social growth, which do not basically affect vested interests such as national or foreign entrepreneurs, or organized labor.

Several of the more important of these trends are elaborated in the following sections.

The Agricultural Sector

Half the population of Mexico lives in rural areas. About 40 percent of the labor force is engaged in agricultural occupations paying less than the minimum subsistence wage.[6] The share of agriculture in total production declined from 22.5 percent in 1950 to 9.0 percent in 1980, and most of the decline took place in the production of basic food crops. Rates of growth of overall production have also fallen off dramatically, from 5 percent per annum (1960–65) to around 1.0–1.5 percent per annum since 1966 (indicating a decline by 2.4 percent per annum in per capita agricultural production).

The large numbers of Mexicans who live off the land are the most impoverished, and therefore have the greatest propensity to migrate (internally to the cities or externally to the United States as undocumented workers). The majority of Mexico's farms are small. Over half of them are less than five hectares (twelve acres), and only 7 percent to 8 percent can really be considered as modern operations. The remainder follow traditional practices and many are in actuality subsistence farms.[7]

While Mexico's overall agricultural trade balance was positive until 1980, the country is quite dependent on imports to provide basic food items. The slow growth of agriculture combined with one of the world's fastest growing populations has caused the country to shift from a net exporter of basic grains (as late as the 1960s) to a net importer.

Basic socioeconomic and political conflicts have tended to emerge in Mexican agriculture. The majority of Mexico's export crops are grown on irrigated land by the more knowledgeable farmers. Corn and beans, the basic ingredients in the Mexican diet, tend to be concentrated on rainfed terrain. Among the main import commodities, only oilseeds and wheat are grown on irrigated land.

The government thus faces a difficult choice in agricultural policy: whether to take irrigated land out of export crops to strive for food self-sufficiency, or encourage exports to generate rural employment opportunities to pay for the country's growing import food bill.

These trends in agricultural income and production can be traced to the general physical conditions under which production is undertaken, land ownership and land use patterns, and government policies toward the sector.[8]

Mexico's agricultural resources are not abundant. Of the almost 200 million hectares of land in Mexico, only about 30 million are considered suitable for agriculture, while only 10 to 12 million hectares are actually planted. Total harvested land area is estimated at 14 to 17 million hectares (taking into account double planting).

Most of Mexico's agricultural land is rainfed, with only 15 percent irrigated. Water is the key constraint to increased production; only 17 percent of the agricultural land area receives sufficient rainfall to be considered drought-free. Overall the runoff of all the rivers in Mexico combined is less than that of the Mississippi.

An important factor contributing to low agricultural output in recent years has in fact been poor rainfall, combined with the limited extent of irrigation. All during the 1970s, rainfall has been significantly below its historical average. In the 1978 and 1979 agricultural years, the situation was particularly bad with rainfall 15 to 18 percent below normal.

A related problem stems from the imbalance between the location of the country's water resources, 40 percent of which are in the underpopulated southeast and only 10 percent in the central plateau around Mexico City, the area accommodating half of Mexico's population and the greatest concentration of small individual farms. The larger, more productive holdings are generally on irrigated land in the dry northwestern coastal plain in Sonora and Sinaloa states.

With regard to land ownership and land use patterns, most authorities on Mexican agriculture now concede that production has been impeded by the highly uneven distribution of land ownership.[9] Holdings with an average of 100 hectares or less account for 74 percent of all farms, but include only 1.6 percent of the farmed area, while the 7 percent of the holdings with an average of 100 hectares or more comprise 94.6 percent of the land. This pattern is mirrored in the ownership of cropland where 3 percent of the holders own 63 percent of the land, while 85 percent of the holdings account for only 16.0 percent of the land.[10]

These patterns have developed as a result of Mexican politics and the Mexican Revolution of 1910. In practice, these forces have led to the development of *ejidos*, or communal holdings, farmed either individually or collectively, that cover most of Mexico's agricultural land area, the redistribution of land by breaking up large estates and farms, which goes on even today, and limits imposed on the size of landholdings (100 hectares of irrigated land or agriculture or 300 hectares for orchards are permitted, or the equivalent necessary to run 500 head of cattle).

Government policies have reduced the share of agriculture in public sector investment. These policies led to concentrated investments in large-scale irrigation projects in the northern regions, and have maintained a system of guaranteed prices, thus protecting urban consumers and large-scale producers at the expense of the small farmer. All of these policies contributed to the decline in the rates of agricultural production.

More specifically, public sector investment in agriculture declined from 20.0 percent in 1940 to 13.1 percent in 1979. More than 90 percent of the government's investment was used to develop the large irrigation schemes in the northwestern zones of the country—zones with the highest concentration of land ownership. Clearly, the government's agricultural strategy has focused on expanding the irrigated area and providing large-scale producers with a supportive infrastructure, cheap and abundant credit, and modern farming technology. At the same time, the government has left the more traditional agricultural regions largely to fend for themselves. Subsidized input prices and government-guaranteed prices have minimized risks and ensured profits in the modern agricultural sector. In addition, the structure of relative prices has favored the production of crops for cattle feed (soya, sorghum, and alfalfa) and crops for export (tomatoes, strawberries, and flowers) instead of production of the corn and beans consumed by the majority of the population.

The government's disequilibrium pricing policies in agriculture, together with directly subsidized inputs, are given credit for much of the sector's early postwar growth, at rates of 6.5 percent per annum between 1952 and 1956 and 5.0 percent per annum between 1956 and 1966. However, as many developing countries have discovered, growth induced by these means tends to be self-terminating once it becomes difficult to bring new land under cultivation or irrigation. Thus, as the area under cultivation failed to increase after 1966, increases in production have been largely due to the shift to higher-value crops.

While new lands were being opened in the north, the rainfed area under cultivation declined from 12.5 million hectares (1965) to 10.8 million hectares (1974), due largely to traditional agriculture's stagnant productivity, which has not been able to keep ahead as costs have risen faster than prices. The decline in the area under cultivation in these rainfed districts is one of the principal causes of the drop in the rate of expansion of basic food items such as corn and beans.

A second factor responsible for this decline (in the rate of expansion of basic food items) is the shift to higher-value crops in the irrigated areas. Only 8 percent of the area growing maize is permanently irrigated.

Increases in domestic food production will require a change in agricultural support policies that in the past have given low priority to producing basic foodstuffs. The guaranteed prices of corn, wheat, and beans remained constant in nominal terms between 1963 and 1972. Despite recent increases, the real price of maize in 1976 was still below the 1965 level. The real price of sorghum, in contrast, was 36 percent higher than it was in 1965. It is little wonder then that the area under cultivation in maize and beans actually declined after 1965, while the areas devoted to soya, sorghum, and alfalfa (non-price-controlled crops) expanded dramatically. In addition, sorghum, alfalfa, and tomatoes all receive highly subsidized inputs, increasing their profitability even further.

An analysis along comparative advantage lines therefore provides few insights into the development path followed by Mexican agriculture over the past several decades. The productivity of the small farmers is low and the domestic price of corn is also higher than the price of corn exported by the United States, but little has been invested in raising the productivity of the small farmers. More important, farmers in the rainfed areas cannot shift to producing the higher-valued crops. They are mostly subsistence producers who have too little income to buy imported food and few have nonfarm alternative employment opportunities.

The Industrial Sector

The structure of production of Mexican manufacturing by type of product, and its level relative to the size of the country, resembles that of other countries in comparable circumstances—at least at the two-digit level of aggregation.[11] Mexico's industrial structure and output per capita are quite similar to Brazil's. Both countries are somewhat more industrialized than Turkey but lag behind Spain, countries of roughly similar size and level of overall development (table 1.7).

In general, the scale of operation of the average producing unit is fairly low. The economic meaning of such a structure for productive performance is evident. Industrial groups with establishments of above average size are largely in the fields of basic metals, rubber, tobacco, beverages, petroleum derivatives, textiles, and to a smaller extent in paper and allied products.

In 1970, labor productivity in Mexican manufacturing was behind that of both Brazil and Turkey, and similar to that of Spain (tables 1.8 and 1.9). However, Mexico's labor productivity rose considerably between 1970 and 1975 (as measured by the industrial census).

Comparison to an international pattern based on income level, population, and economic structure shows that in 1970 the Mexican manufacturing sector was smaller than the predicted level. The only subsectors larger than expected were food, beverages, and tobacco; chemicals and petroleum products; and metal

Table 1.7. Mexico: comparison of industrial structure, selected countries, 1970 (in millions of 1975 U.S. dollars)

Sector (ISIC)	Mexico		Brazil		Turkey		Spain	
	Value added	Percentage distribution	Value added	Percentage distribution	Value added	Percentage distribution	Value added	Percentage distribution
20–22. Food, beverages, and tobacco	2,213	22.7	2,920	17.1	1,274	32.6	1,275	13.5
23. Textiles	773	7.9	1,595	9.3	757	19.4	870	9.2
24. Clothing, footwear	424	4.3	571	3.3	14	0.3	478	5.0
25–26. Wood products	245	2.5	788	4.6	31	0.8	521	5.5
27. Paper	325	3.3	438	2.6	58	1.5	301	3.2
28. Printing, publishing	325	3.3	628	3.7	52	1.3	296	3.1
29. Leather, leather products	54	0.6	110	0.6	8	0.2	139	1.5
30. Rubber products	221	2.3	333	2.0	51	1.3	235	2.5
31–32. Chemicals	1,442	14.8	2,871	16.8	753	19.3	1,576	16.6
33. Nonmetallic minerals	515	5.3	1,004	5.9	156	4.0	795	8.4
34. Basic metals	865	8.9	1,974	11.6	313	8.0	241	2.5
35–38. Metal products	2,219	22.7	3,483	20.4	426	10.9	2,699	28.5
39. Miscellaneous	137	1.4	360	2.1	15	0.4	46	0.5
20–39. Total	9,758	100.0	17,074	100.0	3,908	100.0	9,472	100.0

Source: World Bank, *Mexico, Manufacturing Sector: Situation, Prospects and Policies*, pp. 95, 96.

Table 1.8. Mexico: comparison of industrial value added per capita, selected countries, 1970 (in U.S. dollars per person)

Sector (ISIC)		Mexico	Brazil	Turkey	Spain
20–22.	Food, beverages, and tobacco	43.67	31.47	36.16	37.90
23.	Textiles	15.26	17.19	21.48	25.85
24.	Clothing, footwear	8.37	6.15	0.40	14.20
25–26.	Wood products	4.84	8.49	0.88	15.49
27.	Paper	6.41	4.71	1.65	8.95
28.	Printing, publishing	6.41	6.77	1.48	8.80
29.	Leather, leather products	1.07	1.18	0.23	4.13
30.	Rubber products	4.36	3.58	1.45	6.98
30–32.	Chemicals	28.46	30.95	21.37	46.84
33.	Nonmetallic minerals	10.16	10.82	4.43	23.63
34.	Basic metal	17.07	21.28	8.88	7.16
35–38.	Metal products	43.79	37.55	12.09	80.21
39.	Miscellaneous	2.70	3.88	0.43	1.37
20–39.	Total	192.00	184.06	110.93	281.53

Source: World Bank, *Mexico, Manufacturing Sector: Situation, Prospects and Policies*, p. 97.

Table 1.9. Mexico: comparison of value added per worker, selected countries, 1970 (in thousands of 1975 U.S. dollars)

Sector (ISIC)		Mexico	Brazil	Turkey	Spain
20–22.	Food, beverages, and tobacco	5.83	8.51	10.70	4.65
23.	Textiles	5.00	5.06	6.30	4.10
24.	Clothing, footwear	3.40	4.02	2.80	3.88
25–26.	Wood products	3.24	4.12	3.10	3.72
27.	Paper	8.65	7.66	5.27	6.27
28.	Printing, publishing	5.71	8.72	5.77	4.70
29.	Leather, leather products	4.51	1.52	2.66	6.61
30.	Rubber products	9.93	11.89	5.66	6.52
31–32.	Chemicals	10.06	18.64	20.91	9.43
33.	Nonmetallic minerals	5.64	5.45	4.33	4.91
34.	Basic metal	12.36	8.69	6.02	2.34
35–38.	Metal products	6.81	9.02	3.00	4.87
39.	Miscellaneous	4.86	7.05	5.00	3.83
20–39.	Total	4.09	7.86	7.04	4.95

Source: World Bank, *Mexico, Manufacturing Sector: Situation, Prospects and Policies*, p. 98, 99.

products. A similar analysis for 1975 using preliminary results of the 1975 census shows manufacturing again below its expected value; those groups above predicted levels are the ones just mentioned. Metal products, however, dropped to 5 percent below predicted size (table 1.10).

Thus, deviations from the international pattern increased from 1970 to 1975.

The sector most above its predicted level in 1970 is also the one that grew most relative to its predicted growth (food, beverages, and tobacco). Two of the other three sectors above or near predicted values in 1970 ranked second and third in relative growth (chemicals and paper). The exception is metal products, which fell from slightly above to slightly below its predicted level. All sectors below predicted levels in 1970 were even further below predicted levels in 1975. The rapid growth in food products was a response to Mexico's natural advantages in these lines, and probably to strong growth in domestic demand. Growth in chemicals and in paper also responded to natural advantages, but in these sectors import substitution and export markets were the major sources of growth in demand.

There seems to be a relationship, albeit a weak one, between labor productivity and growth, and also between labor productivity and Mexico's deviation from the international pattern. Sector 27 (paper and paper products) and sectors 31–32 (chemicals, chemical petroleum products, and coal products) show high labor productivity, high growth rates, and are large relative to other Mexican sectors when compared to values predicted by the international cross section.

At the other extreme, sectors 23 (textiles), 24 (clothing), 28 (printing and publishing), and 29 (leather and leather products) show low labor productivity, low growth in output, and large negative deviations from international patterns. These differences are shown to some extent in the export share of each sector.

Chemicals, petroleum refining, and wood products export more of their production than Mexican manufacturing on the average, while clothing and leather export at above average levels. The textile sector, with an above-average export share, is not consistent with this pattern. This tendency, as well as the export figures in general, suggest that Mexican manufacturing performs well in products that are capital-intensive, high-technology, and/or based on mineral resources, while it performs less well in traditional, low-technology, labor-intensive processes.

Certain factors in the Mexican setting seem particularly to have influenced and in a sense induced or hastened the expansion of manufacturing during the postwar period: (1) The national market in general, and for manufactured goods in particular, enlarged significantly as a result of the rapid increase in the country's population, the growth of urban centers and the development of the internal transportation network, and the extensive land reform of the 1930s.[12] The land reform changed the distribution of agricultural assets and produced shifts toward intensive commercial crops and livestock production. (both of these changes in agriculture favored industrial expansion, at least from the point of view of a demand for manufactured goods). (2) Intensified population pressure was a motivating productive force. Manufacturing activity that would replace imports offered to absorb at least part of a rapidly increasing labor supply. (3) The strong protection against foreign competition was partly the result of a deliberate government industrialization policy, and partly and no less importantly the result of persistent difficulties that Mexico experienced through this period with the

Table 1.10. Mexico: actual and normal value added in manufacturing, 1970 and 1975

Sector (ISIC)		1970 Actual (in millions of pesos)	1970 Predicted (in millions of pesos)	1970 Percentage deviation	1975 Actual (in millions of pesos)	1975 Predicted (in millions of pesos)	1975 Percentage deviation	Average annual change in percentage deviation 1970–75
20–22.	Food, beverages, and tobacco	17,948	15,721	14.0	43,110	36,299	19.0	6.3
23.	Textiles	6,266	13,187	−53.0	12,126	35,141	−65.0	−4.2
24.	Clothing, footwear	3,441	8,237	−58.0	5,869	22,159	−74.0	−5.0
25–26.	Wood products	1,985	5,511	−64.0	4,698	15,188	−69.0	−1.5
27.	Paper, paper products	2,633	2,650	−1.0	6,803	6,882	0.0	12.9
28.	Printing, publishing	2,633	6,496	−59.0	5,109	17,253	−70.0	−3.5
29.	Leather products	434	853	−49.0	895	2,102	−57.0	−3.1
30.	Rubber products	1,783	3,703	−52.0	3,869	9,240	−58.0	−2.2
31–32.	Chemicals	11,697	10,834	8.0	30,507	27,872	9.0	2.4
33.	Nonmetallic minerals	4,180	6,647	−37.0	10,011	17,355	−42.0	−2.6
34.	Basic metals	7,019	11,767	−40.0	18,677	34,306	−45.0	2.4
35–38.	Metal products	17,996	16,969	6.0	45,449	47,720	−5.0	−12.9
20–38.	Total (excluding Miscellaneous)	78,025	102,575	−24.0	187,123	271,517	−31.0	−5.3

Sources: Actual values: Secretaria de Industria y Comercio, *Industrial Census*, 1970, 1975. Estimated predicted values computed from normal patterns estimated by H. B. Chenery and L. J. Taylor, "Development Patterns: Among Countries and Over Time," *Review of Economics and Statistics* (November 1968), pp. 391–416.

balance of payments. The country's endowment of natural resources, and certain economic and social factors, have fundamentally shaped the pattern of industrial development.

Prior to World War II, narrow savings margins and serious deficiencies in the financial system resulted in limited capital formation and a poor allocation of investment funds. In particular, the 1930s found the possibilities of financing industrial investment from domestic sources somewhat restricted, with conditions of political and economic stability that prevailed throughout the 1920s and 1930s making Mexico relatively unattractive to foreign venture capital.

Such conditions greatly influenced both the technology used in industry and the failure to form larger manufacturing units even in industries with no direct market limitations. Reliance upon low-productivity equipment and labor-intensive production methods seems to have been the rule even in large industrial plants.

Supply of labor does not appear to have ever been a limiting factor in the development of Mexican industry, though specific industrial skills were in short supply, particularly at the supervisory and managerial level.

Indigenous entrepreneurship and risk-taking in industrial ventures were also rare in Mexico until the postwar period. Venture investment under such conditions was limited mostly to borrowed funds.

Evidently, the low income of the country and its uneven distribution offered a very small and narrow market for manufactured products and a rather skewed pattern of demand. The size of the market for industrial products was further affected by the country's transport and communications systems, whose inadequate auxiliary development kept large geographical areas outside the national market, and by the sizable segment of agriculture that operated outside the money economy. Such conditions reduced the market for manufacturing goods even below the size dictated by population and income levels.

Low productivity and low incomes in the sectors of primary activity were thus the major determinants of the market open to Mexican manufacturing industry. The uneven distribution of income added further to this unfavorable situation by concentrating the demand of the relatively small high-income group on luxury or quality products not easy to produce locally because of scale limitations, or the lack of skills or technical knowledge.

On the other hand, a system of tariff protection, with high tariffs and without specific purposes, combined with foreign exchange or fiscal difficulties, led to the establishment during the interwar period of a large number of highly inefficient manufacturing units. This resulted in a considerable waste of capital resources and gave rise to many structural and economic problems now facing Mexican manufacturing industry.

In more recent times, similar developments have also come about as the result of ill-applied government interventions, beyond those arising from monetary and foreign exchange problems. Thus, measures aimed at import substitution, agricultural price-fixing, and the excessive regulation of rail transportation have all helped to generate more such problems.

In addition, the many administrative controls on the establishment of new industries were not guided by clear criteria or specific goals. Instead, these laws gave wide discretionary power to the administering government officials, and fostered political nepotism and abuses in directing industrial investment.

Government administration has often frustrated and distorted Mexico's industrial growth instead of assisting it. The authorities have tended to protect and preserve established interests and old inefficient plants, to impose job security for labor at the expense of industrial firms, or to interfere directly with the administration of enterprise and its cost structures. The present structure of Mexican industry seems to have been affected considerably by such past government practices and consequent administrative inefficiencies.

Finally, inadequate development in tertiary activities serving industry has hampered the growth of Mexican industry. Power, transport facilities, and commercial activities have all fallen short of industry's needs. Efficient trade and product distribution seem to be a crucial prerequisite of manufacturing industry. A poorly developed commercial sector forces industry to undertake some of the distribution functions and to carry unduly high stocks of materials and finished products. These side effects are even greater under an industrial structure of small establishments like that of Mexico.

In sum, while the manufacturing sector has been quite dynamic, registering growth rates of 9 percent per annum in the 1960s and 7 percent per annum through the 1970s, the sector does not appear capable of sustaining growth in output and employment, or of improving the country's balance of payments position significantly.

The industrial base, although highly developed, is characterized by a number of structural imbalances. First, the skewed distribution of income has severely limited the domestic market. The half of the labor force earning less than the minimum wage has no effective demand for the wide range of consumer durables, beverages, cigarettes, and cosmetics—major areas in which Mexican industry is concentrated.

Excessive reliance on protection and government subsidies has fostered an inefficient and high-cost industrial structure. Historically, the main instrument of protection has been import licenses. These are currently being replaced by tariffs on a large number of items, but licenses still cover the bulk of the goods produced. Average price levels in the manufacturing sector increased from 15.6 percent to 19.0 percent above international levels between 1970 and 1975. Furthermore, while the average efficiency of Mexico's industrial sector compares well with other newly industrializing countries, a number of products are clearly noncompetitive in international markets. In 1975, 78 out of 394 products, or 20 percent, had prices that were 50 to 100 percent above international levels (World Bank, 1979).

Government subsidies to industry have increased over the years to the point

Table 1.11. Mexico: production and employment by sector, 1960 and 1970

	1970 Shares (Percentage)		1960–70 Average annual rate of growth	
Sector	GDP	Employment	GDP	Employment
Agriculture, forestry, fisheries	11.7	50.2	3.7	2.4
Mining and petroleum	5.2	1.3	7.6	3.9
Manufacturing (total)	22.8	14.2	8.9	3.5
Light	12.7		7.1	
Heavy	10.1		11.8	
Construction	4.6	5.0	8.3	6.6
Services	55.7	29.3	7.0	3.9
Total	100.0	100.0	7.0	3.2

Source: Derived from S. Watanabe, "Constraints on Labor-Intensive Export Industries in Mexico," *International Labor Review*, (January 1974), tables 1 and 2.

where the estimated cost to the government of subsidized energy alone was U.S. $10 billion in 1980. Subsidies also prevail in many other aspects of Mexican life, providing, for example, cheap food, housing, and transportation to the urban labor force. Government subsidies and protection are often cited as partly responsible for the evolution of a dualistic domestic industrial structure, where a few large producers account for the bulk of manufacturing production, while a large number of smaller producers provide for the remainder.

Backward linkages between industry, agriculture, and labor remain weak. In principle, agriculture should provide a market for industry, food for its workers, raw materials for production, and a surplus for investment. The low level of agricultural incomes in Mexico, however, has reduced effective demand for domestically produced manufactures. In addition, the relative decline in food production after the mid-1960s has raised the urban cost of living while the slowdown in production of agricultural raw materials has increased the country's reliance on imports of producer goods. The other weak backward linkage is the capital intensity of production. In large part this deviation from what might be optimal from a comparative advantage point of view results from a combination of cheap capital, cheap energy, and regulations prescribing the minimum wage and nonwage benefits.

The working population has increased at an average annual rate of around 3 percent between 1960 and 1980.[13] In 1950 and 1960 more than 50 percent of the total labor force was still employed in the agricultural sector, but in 1970 agricultural employment share fell to 39 percent with a further drop to 37 percent in 1979 (table 1.11).

Industrial employment in contrast shows a sharp increase of about 50 percent as the relative employment share increased from 20 to 26 percent between 1960 and 1979. Also, the combined sectors of commerce and services experienced a rapid increase in employment, with their share in the work force increasing from

25 to 37 percent between 1960 and 1979. The increase in service employment is not a healthy phenomenon, as most of the increases in employment during this period were in activities that must be considered marginal. A large proportion of the newly created jobs are really disguised unemployment or severe underemployment rather than employment.[14]

Therefore, although the decline in the country's agricultural employment might normally be regarded as a healthy phenomenon, the reverse might be the case. A clearer picture of the actual forces at work is obtained by aggregating employment in agriculture, commerce, and services. Looking at these three sectors as a whole, it is clear that the declining employment share of agriculture has simply been absorbed to a large extent by the service and commerce sectors. One must assume, based on comparisons of productivity by sector, that the marginal product of workers shifting into services and commerce has not increased appreciably over what it was in agriculture. In fact, their standard of living may have fallen due to increased expenses incurred in their new urban setting. Furthermore, the increased cost of providing the urban social overhead facilities for these migrants reduces considerably the net social benefits the economy may be deriving from this type of rural-urban migration. In short, rural-urban migration based on the expectation of better living conditions in the urban centers may produce a net loss in both private and social terms. This would be the case especially for those migrants who left agriculture as a result of increased mechanization in that sector.

Many agricultural migrant workers have undoubtedly been absorbed by the construction sector, which has increased its relative employment share rather rapidly during this period. The government has stimulated much of the employment in this sector by backing the tripartite housing program in which employers, employees, and the government participate. Shifts of agricultural workers into the construction sector therefore appear to impose fewer social costs than the shift to services and commerce. The employment shares of mining and petroleum, of electricity production, and of transport services appear to have remained more or less constant during the 1950–80 period.

In Mexico's case, the growth of GDP, technology, the educational system, and output mix all contribute importantly to employment creation.[15] Rapid growth of the economy tends to increase the overall demand for labor, albeit at a rate lower than the overall growth rate. Obviously because labor is not a homogenous unit, maximizing employment requires that the structure of labor demand be met as closely as possible by a corresponding supply structure. Despite an overall excess supply of labor, labor shortages have created production bottlenecks in certain key sectors. The result was overcapitalization and mechanization in these sectors. On the other hand, overpricing of essentially unskilled or poorly qualified labor by institutional factors has caused a disproportionate capital-intensive structure or at least levels of capital intensity greater than the country's comparative advantage would warrant.[16]

In terms of overall productivity, the labor coefficient declined by almost a third

Table 1.12. Mexico: incremental capital/labor ratio, Mexican industries, 1971–74 (in U.S. 1970 dollars per additional worker)

Industry	Incremental capital-labor ratio
Iron and steel	36,500
Rubber products	34,800
Chemicals—industrial	26,300
Food products	26,000
Paper and paper products	25,500
Mineral products (nonmetallic)	24,200
Glass and glass products	21,200
Textiles	17,300
Beverages	10,200
Metals—nonferrous	9,900
Electrical machinery	8,900
Motor vehicles	5,600
Metal products	1,800
Tobacco products	(negative)
Wood products	(negative)

Source: Edwin Reubens "Surplus Labor, Emigration, and Public Policies: Requirements for Labor Absorption in Mexico," in Barry W. Poulson and T. Noel Osborn, eds., *U.S.-Mexico Economic Relations* (Boulder, Colo.: Westview Press, 1979), p. 136.

during the 1950–80 period, indicating that labor productivity nearly tripled. The labor coefficients were reduced very substantially in electricity production, in manufacturing, and also in construction and agriculture.[17]

Relatively labor-intensive sectors continue to be agriculture, construction, transport, and services, along with manufacturing (table 1.11). A good case could be made that further increases in the labor force should be absorbed in these sectors, because increased employment in the services sector almost certainly reflects disguised unemployment or underemployment.

Labor coefficients vary considerably from sector to sector. It seems useful to group together those sectors that are about equally capital intensive or labor intensive. Such groupings make clear (table 1.12) a huge difference in the employment potential among sectors. Those sectors with a very low labor coefficient—iron and steel, rubber products—can be easily classified as capital intensive, with the cost of job creation considerably above the national average. The capital-intensive sectors may have only a limited choice of technology with imported capital equipment providing the bulk of new investment.

Everything else being equal, the labor-intensive industries undoubtedly have more scope for selecting among alternative technologies. However, the labor-intensive sectors may or may not actually adopt highly sophisticated and capital-intensive technology, depending on wage and interest rates, sales, and size of production runs. These considerations make it clear that the distinction between labor- and capital-intensive industries is not a very meaningful one. A more realistic classification would be between technology-choice sectors and capacity-choice sectors. The latter include many of the capital-intensive sectors, but all have control to one extent or another over their capacity. Thus, capacity adoption by means of scaling down the capacity is a meaningful concept in Mexico.

The choice of technology in the technology-choice sectors in part depends on the variables listed above. In some instances, the firm has some control over the values these parameters take. For example, firms can decide on their annual production volume and lot sizes, although variables are also determined partly by the size of the total market.

Initial Assessment of the Overall Mexican Economy

Despite the prospect of oil wealth, the future of both industrialization and the role of the state in the Mexican economy is still uncertain in 1984. In fact, an ongoing debate has been taking place since 1978 over the role of the state and of oil in the country's industrialization process. The main participants in this political struggle have been bureaucrats of different tendencies, bankers, the trade unions, and the industrialists themselves. The two major themes or lines of argument are best articulated by the Mexican Ministry of Industry on the one hand and by the World Bank on the other.[18]

The Ministry of Industry maintains in its Industrial Plan that (1) Nearly all of the oil income (that is, the foreign exchange generated by oil and gas sales) should be used to strengthen the country's industrial structure. (2) A high rate of growth (9 or 10 percent per annum) of aggregate demand (from both internal demand and the export of manufactures) can be maintained throughout the 1980s if the plan is implemented. (3) High growth will bring the foreign exchange constraint to bear again by generating a current account deficit on the balance of payments of around 2 percent of GDP—that is, the average for the 1960s. (4) The country's import coefficient can be reduced by substituting domestic production for capital goods imported (that is one of the priorities of the plan). (5) Agricultural output is unlikely to grow at more than 2 percent per annum, substantially less than the rate of population growth (3.5 percent). Thus, food imports will grow rapidly even though the real wage rate is not projected to rise as fast as output per head. (6) Considerable public enterprise involvement is foreseen: the overall rate of gross capital formation (as a proportion of GDP) is planned to rise from 22 percent in 1975 to 29 percent in 1985 (of which at least 11 percent would be in the state sector). (7) Import control should be maintained, higher prices charged for petroleum products, and an effort made to decentralize industrial production from the Mexico City area.[19]

The plan implies continuing import substitution while building up domestic industry behind tariff barriers, without too much regard for comparative advantage in the short run. The plan assigns the government a prominent role in financing industrial development either indirectly or directly through state enterprises. With the government enjoying sufficient external earnings (Pemex exports) and internal revenues (Pemex profits) to avoid the fiscal and balance of payments crises that undermined earlier (1970) attempts along these lines. Finally, the plan attempts to maintain wages at or below the level of manufacturing productivity. This is necessary if manufactured exports are to be maintained with an overvalued exchange rate supported by oil income and a low rate of investment in (and expansion of) agriculture.

The World Bank in sharp contrast advocates an industrial strategy based on the "opening" of the economy together with a reduced role for the government.[20] According to this strategy a first priority would be paying off the external debt, which the Bank estimated at U.S. $27 billion by the end of 1978. The Bank recommends building up a fairly high level of reserves; making available large amounts of foreign exchange to the banking system to finance investment in industry; allowing the peso to float; and reducing barriers to imports. This strategy is clearly in opposition to the Industrial Plan, which would increase the debt and periodically devalue the peso, to keep exports competitive.

The expected effect of the World Bank strategy would be to eliminate or at least halt the expansion of those industrial branches that are not competitive in international markets while reducing considerably the country's (and government's) external capital requirements. In short, the World Bank advocates a strategy whereby oil revenues would be used indirectly to support the balance of payments or channeled through the development banks to fund private accumulation in the most profitable branches rather than to finance state enterprises or the expansion of government investment. The World Bank's analysis indicates that strategies such as that proposed in the Industrial Development Plan would actually require higher tax rates in order to contain domestic demand.

Clearly the two plans differ largely over the role played by the state in the country's industrialization process. In essence, the World Bank advocates that that economy should return to the "stabilizing development," the 1955–70 strategy that is criticized extensively in the introductory chapter of the Industrial Plan.[21] The outcome depends upon political developments both within and without Mexico, with the bank's view seemingly having a better chance of being adopted in light of the oil glut and financial crisis facing the government as of mid-1982.

At this stage in our study, our conclusions can only be tentative and brief. Broadly, the main theme would seem to be that in any process of capital accumulation in Mexico, involving the state to a significant degree will only be successful if the state has financial and political independence. In the Mexican case, the state appears to have possessed both kinds of independence at the outset of the modern industrialization period (1940), but the very process of industrialization itself increasingly restricted the state both politically and financially and prevented it from completing in 1970–76 the import substitution process begun by private capital in 1954–60. These developments underlie and are the direct causes of the broad movements of Mexican economic growth, which the following chapter presents quantitatively.

2. Mechanisms of Mexican Economic Growth

A number of controversies have developed in the literature concerning the nature of the development process in Mexico.[1] One particularly important controversy concerns whether the country's post–World War II growth has resulted from a steady accretion of capital or from the progressive transformation of old ways into new.

This study argues that the acceleration of growth in the 1960s and relative slowdown throughout most of the 1970s can be explained in large part by movements in total factor productivity. At the aggregate level this argument requires quantifying the relative contribution labor, capital and land have made to the country's economic expansion. The objective of this chapter is to determine how total factor productivity has grown during periods of quite different patterns of employment, investment, government policy, and land use.

Total Factor Productivity Growth

The basis of the calculations is a simplified production function along the lines suggested by Denison[2] in which output is expressed as a function of labor (L), capital (K), land (R), and a total factor productivity term (c^T), and the form of the production function is of the Cobb-Douglas type: $Y = e^T L^a K^b R^c$. The advantage of this formulation is that its logarithmic form $\dot{Y} = \dot{T} + a\dot{L} + b\dot{K} + c\dot{R}$ (where · signifies rate of growth of the respective variable) permits one to use information on observed growth of labor, capital, and land and gross domestic product to derive total factor productivity (T):

$$\dot{Y} - a\dot{L} + b\dot{K} + c\dot{R} = \dot{T}$$

The three factor inputs, land, labor, and capital, are weighted according to the constant returns to scale assumption implicit in the Cobb-Douglas production function; the coefficients with respect to each input (a, b, and c, respectively) sum to unity, with the coefficient representing the respective share of that factor in value added. In Mexico's case, the shares of factor incomes during the 1960–80 period were approximately:

a = labor share = 0.60
b = capital share = 0.35
c = land rent share = 0.05

and thus these values are used in the sources of growth computations.[3]

The relatively high capital share of 0.35 in Mexico during this period, compared to 0.30 or 0.25 often found in the more advanced countries, can be explained in part by Mexico's stage of industrialization, where there were numerous and obvious "gaps" in the capital structure to be filled. To a considerable degree investment has represented efforts to fill in these gaps. In contrast, investment in countries with an already extensive capital structure is usually replacing and duplicating existing capital, hence the generally lower rate of return in these areas.

Second, Mexico's import substitution policy—the policy of eliminating entirely the importation of certain products to encourage their domestic production—has also created gaps that in turn provided possibilities for profitable investments. The monopolistic position of many of the import substitution plans has often maintained prices at levels sufficient to assume relatively high returns on capital. In the present study, it is this latter explanation of Mexico's relatively high marginal product of capital that is particularly relevant.[4]

The following calculations of factor productivity take their figures on the growth of output from the International Monetary Fund's *International Financial Statistics* deflated to constant 1960 prices using the GDP deflator. Figures on investment are also taken from the *International Financial Statistics*, and deflated to constant 1960 prices by using the wholesale price index. Growth of the labor force is based on the International Labor Office's figures for five-year intervals; intervening years are derived by extrapolation. The capital stock was calculated beginning with Reynolds' estimate for 1959.[5] A hypothetical rate of depreciation (5 percent) was then applied and gross investment for the year (in constant prices) added in order to derive the capital stock (K) at the end of the year (table 2.1). The figures for land are taken from Reynolds and are probably the least reliable. Land per se, however, probably has played a relatively minor role in the country's recent growth; the margin of error is not critical to the overall results.

Using the assumed factor weights, the relative importance of direct factor inputs together with the residual or unexplained productivity were estimated. The results (table 2.2) confirm the general trends found in earlier studies and indicate that these have continued through 1980: (1) growth in real GDP has gradually decelerated from 8.2 percent per annum in 1960–65 to 6.8, 5.9, and 5.5 percent per annum for the 1965–70, 1970–75, and 1975–80 subperiods, respectively; (2) the rate of capital formation has continued to accelerate during the 1960–80 period, from 3.1 percent per annum in the 1960–65 period to 5.9, 6.8, and 7.4 percent per annum for the 1965–70, 1970–75, and 1975–80 subperiods, respectively; (3) similarly, the contribution of capital to overall growth has increased during this period as has that of total factor inputs; (4) it follows that pure productivity growth (the unexplained growth factor) has continued the decline observed for earlier periods, falling from 5.3 percent for the 1960–65 period to 2.9, 1.4, and 0.8 percent per annum, respectively, for the 1965–70, 1970–75, and 1975–80 subperiods; (5) investment has expanded at a rate faster than GDP, and thus its share in GDP has risen progressively since 1940. Similarly, the internal rate of savings has almost doubled since the 1940s. Still in-

Table 2.1. Mexico: investment, capital, GDP, and capital output ratios, 1960–80

Year	Gross investment (billions of current pesos)	Gross investment (I) (billions of 1960 pesos)	Capital stock (K) (billions of 1960 pesos)	Change in capital stock (ΔY)	Gross domestic product (Y)	Change in gross domestic product (ΔY)	Capital-output ratio (K_{t-1}/Y_t)	Incremental capital-output ratio $\Delta K_{t-1}/\Delta Y_t$	$I_{t-1}/\Delta Y$
1959	19.6	—	331.1	—	—	—	—	—	—
1960	23.2	23.2	337.8	6.7	150.5	—	2.2	0.9	—
1961	24.1	23.3	344.2	6.4	157.9	7.4	2.1	0.9	3.1
1962	24.8	23.3	350.3	6.1	165.3	7.4	2.1	0.5	3.1
1963	32.6	29.7	362.5	12.2	178.5	13.2	2.0	0.6	1.8
1964	41.0	35.4	379.8	17.3	199.4	20.9	1.8	1.3	1.4
1965	44.2	37.2	398.0	18.2	212.3	12.9	1.8	1.2	2.7
1966	50.2	40.7	418.8	20.8	227.0	14.7	1.8	1.5	2.5
1967	59.6	46.9	444.8	26.0	241.3	14.3	1.7	1.3	2.8
1968	65.7	50.5	473.1	28.3	260.9	19.6	1.7	1.7	2.4
1969	72.8	53.9	503.4	30.3	277.4	16.5	1.7	1.6	3.1
1970	82.3	58.3	536.5	33.1	296.6	19.2	1.7	3.2	2.8
1971	81.6	55.4	565.1	28.6	306.8	10.2	1.7	1.3	5.7
1972	97.8	62.8	599.6	34.5	329.1	22.3	1.7	1.4	2.5
1973	126.4	72.2	641.8	42.2	354.1	25.0	1.7	1.4	2.5
1974	173.6	80.0	689.7	47.9	375.0	20.9	1.7	2.0	3.5
1975	235.6	91.9	747.1	57.4	393.0	18.0	1.8	2.7	4.4
1976	288.4	92.0	801.7	54.6	401.4	8.4	1.9	6.8	10.9
1977	363.3	82.1	843.7	42.0	414.5	13.0	1.9	4.2	7.1
1978	492.4	96.2	897.7	54.0	444.7	30.2	1.9	1.4	2.7
1979	718.4	118.6	971.4	73.7	480.2	35.5	1.9	1.5	2.7
1980	1,032.9	136.9	1,059.7	88.3	520.2	40.0	1.9	1.8	3.0

Sources: Gross Investment and Gross Domestic Product computed from data in International Monetary Fund, *International Financial Statistics*; capital stock 1959 figure, Clark Reynolds, *A Shift-Share Analysis of Regional and Sectoral Productivity Growth in Contemporary Mexico* (Laxenburg, Austria: International Institute for Applied Systems Analysis, 1980).

Note: Capital stock 1960–80 computed for each year by using a depreciation rate of 5 percent to previous year's capital stock and adding the current year's gross investment.

Table 2.2. Mexico: sources of growth, 1960–80

	Average annual rate of growth (percentage)				Contribution to GDP growth (percentage)				
Year	GDP	Capital	Labor	Land	Capital	Labor	Land	Total inputs	Unexplained
1960	13.4	2.0	2.6	3.2	0.7	1.6	0.2	2.5	10.9
1961	4.9	1.9	2.6	3.2	0.7	1.6	0.2	2.5	2.4
1962	4.7	1.8	2.6	3.2	0.6	1.6	0.2	2.4	2.3
1963	8.0	3.5	2.6	3.2	1.2	1.6	0.2	3.0	5.0
1964	11.7	4.8	2.6	3.2	1.7	1.6	0.2	3.5	8.2
1965	6.5	4.8	2.6	−0.5	1.7	1.6	—	3.3	3.2
1966	6.9	5.2	3.0	−0.5	1.8	1.8	—	3.6	3.3
1967	6.3	6.2	3.0	−0.5	2.2	1.8	—	4.0	2.3
1968	8.1	6.4	3.0	−0.5	2.2	1.8	—	4.0	4.1
1969	6.3	6.4	3.0	−0.5	2.3	1.8	—	4.1	4.2
1970	6.9	6.6	3.0	2.0	2.3	1.8	0.1	4.1	2.8
1971	3.5	5.3	3.3	2.0	1.9	2.0	0.1	4.0	−0.5
1972	7.3	6.1	3.3	2.0	2.1	2.0	0.1	4.2	3.1
1973	7.6	7.0	3.3	2.0	2.5	2.0	0.1	4.6	3.0
1974	5.9	7.5	3.3	2.0	2.6	2.0	0.1	4.7	1.2
1975	4.1	8.3	3.3	2.0	2.9	2.0	0.1	5.0	−0.9
1976	2.1	7.3	3.3	2.0	2.6	2.0	0.1	4.7	−2.6
1977	3.3	5.2	3.3	2.0	1.8	2.0	0.1	3.9	−0.6
1978	7.3	6.4	3.3	2.0	2.2	2.0	0.1	4.3	3.0
1979	8.0	8.2	3.3	2.0	2.9	2.0	0.1	5.0	3.0
1980	8.3	9.1	3.3	2.0	3.2	2.0	0.1	5.3	3.0
1960–65	8.2	3.1	2.6	2.6	1.1	1.6	0.2	2.9	5.3
1965–70	6.8	5.9	2.9	−0.1	2.1	1.8	—	3.9	2.9
1970–75	5.9	6.8	3.3	2.0	2.4	2.0	0.1	4.5	1.4
1975–80	5.5	7.4	3.3	2.0	2.6	2.0	0.1	4.7	0.8

Sources: Computed from data in GDP, Investment, International Monetary Fund, *International Financial Statistics*; Labor—International Labor Office, *Labor Force 1950-2000*, vol. III, Latin America (Geneva, 1977); Land—Clark Reynolds, *A Shift-Share Analysis of Regional and Sectoral Productivity Growth in Contemporary Mexico* (Laxenburg, Austria: International Institute for Applied Systems Analysis, 1980); Capital—table 1.

Note: Following Reynolds (above reference), the weights used for computing capital's, labor's, and land's contribution to growth were 0.35, 0.60, 0.05, respectively.

vestment opportunities appear increasingly to have outstripped domestic savings capacity, leading to a growth of foreign borrowing. External borrowing (imports over exports) has risen sharply as a share of GDP, from 0.2 percent in the 1940s to 1.8 percent and 3.1 percent in the 1960s and 1970s, respectively. As a share of total investment, external borrowing rose from under 2 percent in the 1950s to 10 percent in the 1960s and 15 percent in the 1970s. This is consistent with the decline in net productivity growth and implies that the domestic surplus available for savings and investment is expanding at a lower rate, thus forcing increased dependence on foreign borrowing and foreign direct investment.

These trends obviously reflect the higher growth rates of labor and capital in recent years. The slowdown in productivity is especially serious since the capacity of the market to transmit productivity gains from leading to lagging sectors depends on net productivity growth. The results also suggest that the Mexican economy may have reached a watershed in the early 1960s. The previous pattern of development is now giving way to a new set of structural forces that imply slower output growth per unit of input.

This process of deceleration has been occurring simultaneously with mounting pressures for wage increases, greater social outlays, more equitable agrarian policies, and other reform measures. Therefore, it is especially critical to stop the decline in productivity growth. At the same time, the acceleration in demographic growth and urbanization in recent decades makes it imperative that the economy increase its ability to absorb new entrants into the work force.

Reynolds found (table 2.3) productivity gains at the national level rising steadily from the 1940s through the mid-1950s, only to level off in the mid-1950s.[6] They reached a high of 3.4 percent per annum in the period 1960–65, falling to 2.9 percent per annum in the second half of the decade, and further declined to 1.6 percent per annum in the 1970–75 period.

The study by Henry Bruton indicates (table 2.4) that product growth not caused by increases in the productive factors of labor and capital amounted to 6.75 percent a year in 1940–45, 1.25 percent in 1946–53, 2.05 percent in 1955–59, and 2.85 percent for 1960–64.[7] According to Bruton, the rate of production increase has slowed in all of Latin America, including Mexico to a lesser extent. Bruton explains this slowdown of any rise in productivity not attributable to the increase in productive factors (capital and labor) as a result of the inefficiency of the process of "forced" industrialization undertaken by these countries. In Europe and the United States, a very high percentage of any increase in production is a result of increases in productive factors; in Latin America this percentage is very small. In other words, the growth attributable to technological or residual change in Latin America has been very limited and declining, because the "forced" replacement of imports in these countries has not developed the economies of scale and other types that could be expected under other conditions of the growth process. It should be noted that Bruton assumes a functional distribution of production amounting to 50 percent for the capital factor and 50 percent for labor. He omits changes in the area cultivated as a productive factor.

In an earlier work, Clark Reynolds makes the same calculations for 1940–50 and 1950–60.[8] For the first period he estimates an increment of 3.3 percent a year in the product not attributable to increase in capital and labor factors. For 1950–60, growth not resulting from these productive factors drops to 2.5 percent of the product. Although Reynolds differs somewhat from Bruton methodologically, his work implicitly accepts Bruton's hypothesis. Furthermore, Reynolds estimates "social accounting equations" of the Denison type for farm and industrial sectors and concludes that in the agricultural sector the percentage of product growth rate not accounted for by increase in productive factors is comparatively much higher than in the industrial sector. Accordingly, during 1940–50, only 0.2 percent of sectoral growth in the industrial sector can be attributed to factors other than labor and capital, while for 1950–60 only 0.7 percent is attributable to these causes. This compares with a growth for the same periods of about 1.2 and 1.9 percent in agriculture. In other words, the calculations of

Table 2.3. Proximate sources of productivity growth in the Mexican economy, 1940–75 (average annual growth)

	1940–50	1950–60	1960–70	1960–65	1965–70	1970–75
Output						
(1) Gross domestic product	5.8	5.9	6.8	6.9	6.7	5.5
Input						
(2) Man-years of labor	3.5	2.0	2.4	2.4	2.4	2.5
(3) Capital stock	2.8	5.5	6.0	5.3	6.7	6.7
(4) Hectares of land in cultivation	3.6	1.0	2.1	3.2	−0.5	2.0
(5) Rate of growth attributable to idirect factor inputs (2–4 above)	3.3	3.2	3.6	3.5	3.8	3.9
(6) Rate of growth unexplained by above inputs	2.5	2.7	3.2	3.4	2.9	1.6

Source: Clark W. Reynolds, *A Shift-Share Analysis of Regional and Sectoral Productivity Growth in Contemporary Mexico* (Laxenburg, Austria: International Institute for Applied Systems Analysis, 1980), p. 6.

Table 2.4. Mexico: sources of growth, 1940–64

Period	Average annual growth (percentage)			Contribution to growth (percentage)		
	GDP	Capital	Labor	Capital	Labor	Productivity
1940–45	9.0	1.7	2.8	0.9	1.4	6.7
1946–53	5.0	4.9	2.6	2.5	1.3	1.2
1955–59	5.7	4.2	3.1	2.1	1.6	2.0
1960–64	6.2	4.2	2.5	2.1	1.3	2.8

Source: Henry J. Bruton, "Productivity Growth in Latin America," *American Economic Review* (December 1967), pp. 1099–1116.

Note: Capital and labor rates of growth are weighted by (0.50) each to derive their contribution to the rate of growth of GDP.

Reynolds imply that production factors are much more profitable or generate a relatively higher percentage of technological or residual change in the farm sector than in the manufacturing sector. Seen from one standpoint, Bruton and Reynolds agree in explaining product growth in Mexico along similar lines. They both believe that the productivity of productive factors is much higher in the farm sector than in industry.

The third study, by Marcelo Selowsky, includes adjustment of the labor force for improvement of education.[9] The findings of this study are most interesting on two counts. On the one hand, Selowsky indicates that improvement in education tends to increase steadily the weight of this factor in economic growth. Thus, in 1945–50 improvement in education accounted for only 0.1 percent of the annual growth rate. Subsequently, in 1950–55, it accounted for 0.21 percent a year, in 1955–60 for 0.20 percent, and in 1960–64 for 0.51 percent. In other words, improvement in education tended to become increasingly important as a component of economic growth. Once the necessary adjustments have been made, the product remainder tends to diminish. Accordingly, the 1940–45 remainder accounted for 5.92 percent out of a growth rate of 7.37 percent. In 1945–50 it represented 2.18 percent out of 5.84 percent, and finally in 1960–64 out of a rate of 6.22 percent for the gross domestic product, the remainder came to only 1.47. This tends to confirm the hypothesis explicit in Bruton's work, implicit in Reynolds' study, and defended in this study: that basic inputs are being used in an increasingly less profitable manner as a result of their diversion from agriculture to industry.

Along these lines, several possible explanations are consistent with the results obtained in the current study. Clearly, the increasing size of the work force may have begun to place a significant drag on productivity growth. This could have occurred as early as the mid-1960s as the supply of available workers began to outstrip demand growth, thus causing labor productivity growth to fall. Coale has hypothesized that the acceleration in population growth beginning around 1940 eventually led to a lower rate of productivity growth and social progress than would have been obtained under more moderate demographic conditions. Through detailed shift-share analysis, Reynolds has provided additional evidence to support this view.

Another hypothesis, while acknowledging the influence of rapid growth on productivity, stresses the contributions of government policy to the decline in productivity. Development policies that created profitable opportunities for investment, especially after 1955, also made it extremely difficult for technological reasons to achieve as high a rate of productivity increase and created an economic environment in which Mexican entrepreneurs had little incentive to raise productivity.

During the 1940–45 period (the war years), both technological and incentive factors worked in favor of a relatively high growth in productivity. In particular, World War II provided protection without distortion by cutting off consumer goods imports from the advanced countries. The import substitution approach to development has provided protection, but has also imposed severe distortions. These distortions create the two effects outlined above.

During the 1940–45 period the growth of capital was much lower than in later periods, due largely to the curtailment of imported capital goods. From 1940 to 1945 there existed a strong and obvious demand in both the internal markets and for exports. Consequently, there was simultaneously a great incentive for firms to increase output but an inability on their part to obtain new plant and equipment, spare parts, and replacements.

The flow of many raw material imports was also irregular and unpredictable during the 1940–45 period. Foreign supplies of capital equipment were difficult to obtain. In order to take advantage of the favorable market, firms were forced to use their existing capital stock with increasing effectiveness. Improvisation and adaptation of existing equipment were common. One can find many examples in Mexican industry during this period of indigenously devised machines producing various items for household and business use. World War II then not only provided "protection" from foreign competition but, more important, helped to create an environment within which Mexican entrepreneurs had incentives to use resources at hand with increasing effectiveness. Mexican industry during this period changed techniques to fit the domestic supply of inputs complementary to capital, including labor of various skills and quality, raw material imports, and managerial ability. Domestic producers also adapted their techniques to fit the country's market size, and their products to fit the nation's unique profile of demand.

Although the growth of the labor supply was not thwarted the way capital inputs were, the wartime isolation had some effect on labor's use. One of the consequences of the efforts to use physical capital more effectively was the adaptation of local tools and equipment to fit the quality of the available labor. Thus, Mexico's capital stock became increasingly appropriate for the country's relative factor endowments (and thereby raising its productivity). Strong and obvious demand in a situation where availability of new imported capital was recognized to be almost nil forced entrepreneurs to strive for a relatively high productivity.

The wartime experience contrasts clearly with the post-1955 period. In this latter period, a large sector of the domestic economy was again isolated from foreign competition, but this time by high tariffs and other forms of import impediments, particularly import licenses. As the war had created profitable opportunities for increased output of a wide range of manufactured goods, so also did the government's strategy of import substitution, particularly as applied on an increasingly large scale in the 1960s. The period of import substitution obviously created a much different environment for industrialization than periods of relatively free trade (1945–55) or the war years (1940–45). The high rates of productivity that responded to these opportunities during 1940–45 seem to be absent in the latter period. In comparing the later periods with the war period, three characteristics seem especially relevant.

The most obvious difference has to do with the supply conditions of imported capital goods. As noted, capital goods imports were virtually unavailable during the 1940–45 period. After 1955 the almost universal and continuous overvaluation of the peso made capital imports cheap relative to domestic inputs. Mexican entrepreneurs not only knew that foreign-made capital was available but had a major incentive to use it intensively in their production. Based on a number of studies of developed and developing countries, there is no real evidence that capital formation tends to incorporate the sources of productivity growth. On the labor side, a variety of social welfare policies in the 1960s may have added somewhat to the cost of employing labor.

There is no doubt then that prevailing market prices for capital and labor reflected the real factor supply situation much more accurately in the 1940–45 period than they did in the later periods. In a very general sense, the capital equipment imported from and designed for capital-rich, labor-scarce countries was more nearly appropriate for the individual producer in its unmodified state than was the case in the war years. In this sense, Mexican entrepreneurs had less incentive to modify or adapt and thereby raise the productivity of their imported capital than they had in the earlier period. Indeed, their incentives worked in the opposite direction: they were encouraged to meet any demands for increased output by acquiring more capital from abroad. It is important to emphasize that the misleading factor prices arose largely from specific policy measures, not from some endemic characteristic of the economy. Similarly, note should be taken of the fact that "entrepreneurial response" did not change; i.e., entrepreneurs reacted to market signals from both periods with considerable rationality.

Another difference between the 1940–45 and later (especially post-1965 periods) has to do with the composition of output. Although industrialization was underway in Mexico before 1940, it was not until the 1950s that an explicit import substitution policy of industrialization became effective. In the present context the most relevant characteristic of this policy is the haphazard and ad hoc manner in which trade barriers were applied. There is no evidence of a careful review leading to the protection of individual industries or activities on the basis of expected productivity growth or special considerations for infant industry. Rather, import limitations were initiated largely either to relieve balance of payments difficulties or in response to pressure from specific interests wishing to expand into new activities.

This policy has reduced current income in accordance with the conventional free trade model, perhaps directly accounting for the continuous deceleration in overall growth throughout the 1960–80 period. More important, these policies have created an industrial structure that is quite incapable of creating a significant number of new jobs due to the capital-intensive nature of capital good imports. Furthermore, profit rates on invested capital remained high, even with considerable underuse, and thus offered opportunities for further investment. As foreign loans have become easily obtainable and are usually given for increasing capacity rather than for using existing capacity, the rate of capital growth has remained high. Consequently, an economic structure has emerged that when subjected to strong pressure on the demand side has produced rising prices rather than rising productivity.

Conclusions

In sum, the rate of growth of productivity in Mexico has continuously decelerated, as a result of the following processes: (1) an increasingly inappropriate mix of productive inputs caused in large part by interest and wage rate policies that undervalued foreign exchange; (2) an increasingly inappropriate composition of output, in the sense that productivity activity was not based on costs or potential costs, but rather has evolved in response to the incentives generated by protectionist policies; (3) declining competition; and (4) a rapidly growing labor force.

These longer-run trends have built up a series of pressures, which finally caused Mexico's economic experience during the 1970s to depart significantly from the pattern of the 1960s. During the 1960s the country still sustained a high growth rate and a considerable degree of internal and external stability. In the 1970s, however, the rate of growth fluctuated greatly and decelerated for several years following the 1976 devaluation. Moreover, the Mexican economy in the 1970s has been characterized by inflation and unemployment together with a growing disequilibrium in the balance of payments.

3. External Sources of Instability

As a result of the accelerated decline in factor productivity discussed in the previous chapters, Mexico's balance of payments deteriorated dramatically. By 1982, the country found itself in the midst of its worst economic crisis in forty years, a crisis that spurred speculation about the continued viability of the country's entire political system.

Reserving discussion of the specific policies of the Echeverría and López Portillo administrations until later in the book, this chapter traces the major trends in the external sector. It emphasizes the deteriorating balance of payments, manifested overtly in massive capital flight, several major devaluations of the peso, the provision by the United States of interim credits, and Mexico's agreement to a stabilization program proposed by the International Monetary Fund.

The Balance of Payments

Several of the more important longer run trends characterizing Mexico's balance of payments show that Mexico's trade patterns have fluctuated considerably.[1] For example, merchandise trade as a percentage of gross domestic product (GDP) varied between 31.6 (1954) and 16.5 (1975) percent from 1951–80, with a slight downward trend through most of this period. Only the impact of petroleum in the late 1970s reversed this trend, with merchandise trade rising to 26.1 percent of GDP by 1980.

Both exports and imports have been remarkably steady as a percentage of GDP throughout the 1951–80 period, averaging around 9–12 percent of gross domestic product. Petroleum exports, which were nonexistent in the early 1970s, were around 3.5 percent of GDP in 1980. Nevertheless, Mexico ran a trade deficit that year. Trade patterns were thus fairly stable throughout the postwar period, with a notable decline in trade in the late 1960s to early 1970s.

The U.S. share of Mexican foreign trade, apart from the short-term factors associated with oil nationalization in the late 1930s and World War II, has remained remarkably stable. The U.S. share of Mexican commodity exports has ranged between 70 and 80 percent each year from 1951 to the present, with no particular trend evident during those years. Mexico's imports have gradually diversified away from the United States. Whereas the U.S. share of Mexican commodity imports was never below 80 percent from 1941 to 1954, it was never over that figure after 1955. The merchandise export pattern also remained stable from 1960 to 1980 (table 3.1). The high proportion of Mexico's new crude petroleum exports that went to the United States in the late 1970s raised the overall U.S. share of Mexican exports briefly: 88 percent of Mexican crude petroleum exports in 1977, and 85 percent in 1978, went to the United States. The U.S.

Table 3.1. Mexico: direction of trade (in percent)

	1960	1965	1970	1975	1977	1978	1979	1980
Exports								
United States	61.5	62.6	69.7	61.9	59.3	69.5	70.2	61.9
West Germany	2.4	2.1	2.0	3.1	2.2	2.0	2.4	1.7
Japan	6.0	8.1	5.9	4.6	2.0	1.8	2.8	3.7
England	1.6	0.8	0.9	1.0	0.8	0.9	0.5	0.5
France	0.8	1.4	0.4	0.8	0.9	0.7	0.8	1.8
LAFTA	—	—	1.9	9.4	8.9	6.6	4.7	4.0
CACM	—	—	0.6	2.8	2.7	2.4	1.6	1.5
USSR	0.1	0.0	0.0	0.1	0.1	0.1	0.1	0.0
Other	27.6	25.0	18.6	16.3	23.1	16.0	16.9	24.9
Total	100.0	100.0	100.0	100.0	100.0	100.0	100.0	100.0
Imports								
United States	72.1	65.7	63.7	62.8	63.5	60.7	60.3	62.3
West Germany	6.2	7.8	7.5	7.3	5.7	6.7	6.2	5.0
Japan	1.5	2.5	3.5	4.7	5.4	8.0	5.8	5.1
England	4.9	2.9	2.9	2.9	2.3	2.6	2.0	2.1
France	2.0	3.1	4.3	2.5	2.9	3.7	4.0	2.6
LAFTA	—	—	2.6	6.3	4.4	4.3	4.3	3.4
CACM	—	—	0.5	0.3	0.3	0.1	0.1	0.2
USSR	0.0	0.1	0.0	0.1	0.0	0.1	0.0	0.1
Other	13.3	17.9	15.0	13.1	15.5	13.8	17.3	19.2
Total	100.0	100.0	100.0	100.0	100.0	100.0	100.0	100.0

Source: International Monetary Fund, *Direction of Trade*, various issues.

Note: LAFTA = Latin American Free Trade Association; CACM = Central American Common Market. *Maquiladoras* (border industries) excluded.

share of Mexican crude petroleum exports fell, however, to between 50 and 60 percent in the early 1980s, bringing the overall U.S. share of Mexican exports down to the levels prevalent from 1960 to 1975.

The remaining geographic distribution of Mexican foreign trade is also very stable. The Latin American share of Mexican trade rose in the early 1970s, but that was not sustained in the late 1970s. The share of Mexican exports going to Japan declined, but Japan's share of imports into Mexico has risen. In the end, these changes are quite modest. Trade with the Soviet Union has always been economically insignificant.

The regional origins of Mexico's exports has been fairly stable over the years. At least seventeen states have each provided over 1 percent of Mexico's exports in every year except 1975 when that figure fell to sixteen.[2] In 1970, twenty states each had over 1 percent of total exports. Through the 1960s, each of nine states contributed at least 4 percent of Mexican exports but this figure fell to seven in the 1970s. (These numbers exclude the border *maquiladoras*.) Six states were above the 4 percent threshold throughout the 1960–80 period. There are no major changes in the identity, distribution, and importance of exporting states during these years. The Federal District of Mexico contributed 29.9 percent of exports in 1960 and it still contributed 26.4 percent in 1975. A change did take place with the increased importance of oil, however. The state of Veracruz, which had historically accounted for 4 to 8 percent of export value, increased its share to 20.3 percent in 1975. In short, the same areas have generated Mexico's exports continuously in the long term, but the number of significant exporting states has recently decreased, and the regional impact of petroleum exports has grown.

As might be expected Mexico's merchandise exports have contained a high percentage of fuels, minerals and metals compared with other newly industrializing countries (table 3.2). On the other hand, it has lagged somewhat behind them in exports of textiles and clothing, machinery and equipment, and other manufactures. Between 1960 and 1978 machinery and equipment exports from Mexico increased from 1 to 10 percent, but the same category of exports rose from 2 to 20 percent for the other newly industrializing countries. As late as 1966, agriculture and cattle accounted for around 50 percent of Mexican exports. By 1974, these sectors had declined to 37.1 percent. On the other hand, manufactured exports increased from 37.7 percent to 53.8 percent during the same period. Before 1974, petroleum's share remained more or less constant at around 0.5 percent. By 1980, however, petroleum and natural gas had risen to 67.3 percent of Mexican exports, manufacturing had fallen to 16.5 percent, and agriculture and cattle fell to 9.9 percent. As might be expected, Mexico imports a proportionately higher share of its machinery and equipment than do the other newly industrializing countries or developing countries, for that matter.

Trends in the Trade Balance

Mexico's changing trade picture also reveals several significant trends.[3] While manufacturing exports were achieving their highest growth rates between 1967 and 1974, their coefficient rose in 16 cases, and the import coefficient rose in 17 of the 23 major manufacturing groups. In 1967, the import coefficient was higher than the export coefficient in 17 out of 24 cases. In 1974, despite rapid industrial growth, the import coefficient was still higher than the export coefficient in 16 of the 24 major industrial sectors. The inability of industry to reduce its import coefficient helps explain why the country has had difficulty in reducing its overall trade deficit. Since World War II and before the oil boom, no single product, except cotton in the late 1950s and early 1960s, has accounted for over 10 percent of Mexican exports. Manufactured exports declined in constant prices from 1974 to 1977. After a recovery in 1978–79, the real value of manufacturing exports fell again in 1980, thus ruling out for the time being a return to Mexico's characteristically diversified export profile before the oil boom. The real value of agricultural exports also declined from 1973 to 1976 and from 1979 to 1980. These declines in manufacturing and agricultural exports reflect the increasing inability of the Mexican economy to remain competitive in international markets.

The border industries' rapid expansion in the late 1960s to early 1970s generated a trade surplus. From 1965 to 1973, the balance of border transactions (in 1974 dollars) grew in Mexico's favor from $376.1 million to $666.3 million.

Table 3.2. Mexico: composition of trade, comparison with selected countries, 1960–78 (in percent)

	Fuels, minerals, and metals		Other primary commodities		Textiles and clothing		Machinery and equipment		Other manufactures	
Percentage of merchandise exports	1960	1978	1960	1978	1960	1978	1960	1978	1960	1978
Newly industrializing countries										
Mexico	24	39	64	31	4	3	1	10	7	17
Brazil	8	11	89	55	0	4	0	15	3	15
Singapore	1	31	73	23	5	5	7	25	14	16
Korea	30	1	56	10	8	32	0	21	6	36
Average	16	21	71	30	4	11	2	19	8	21
Developing countries										
Cameroon	19	6	77	90	0	1	2	1	2	2
Tunisia	24	44	66	18	1	20	1	3	8	15
Sri Lanka	0	1	99	81	0	4	0	0	1	4
Philippines	10	14	86	52	1	6	0	2	3	26
Average	11	16	82	60	1	8	1	2	4	12
Percentage of merchandise imports										
Newly industrializing countries										
Mexico	4	13	2	3	10	7	52	45	32	32
Brazil	14	10	19	33	13	6	36	26	18	25
Singapore	21	10	15	24	38	9	7	29	19	28
Korea	10	8	7	16	25	17	12	33	46	26
Average	12	10	11	19	22	10	27	33	29	28
Developing countries										
Cameroon	20	10	8	7	3	2	17	39	52	42
Tunisia	20	12	9	10	4	27	23	31	44	20
Sri Lanka	17	15	10	15	1	2	18	22	54	46
Philippines	15	8	10	21	5	7	36	27	23	37
Average	18	11	9	13	3	10	24	30	46	36

Source: Derived from data in World Bank, *World Development Report, 1981*.

During this period, the ratio of Mexican income from border transactions to income from exports increased only slightly (from 0.50 in 1960 to 0.54 in 1975). This ratio fell to 0.10 in 1980.[4]

Mexico's devaluation of the peso in September 1976 was a definite stimulus to the country's border transactions. These increased in Mexico's favor from $444.7 million in 1976 to $719.9 million in 1977 and to $870.5 million in 1978. Apparently, much of this gain was achieved at the expense of the U.S. border region; the latter's income fell by 34 percent in constant dollars from 1976 to 1977. The favorable Mexican balance fell, however, to $604.2 million in 1980, giving further evidence of the weakening of Mexico's nonoil economy.

Border transactions declined in relative importance from 30 percent in 1970 to 18 percent in 1979, largely as a result of increased oil exports. Yet border transactions continue to be an important link between the Mexican and U.S. economies. Unfortunately, recent increasingly severe short-term swings in this relationship have worsened tensions between the two countries.

The border industrialization program grew most rapidly after 1966 when Mexico began permitting the importation of machinery, equipment, and materials to manufacture products that were to be reexported. Mexican regulations harmonized with U.S. Tariff Schedules 806.30 and 807.00, which permit certain U.S. products to be processed or assembled abroad and then returned to the United States duty-free (except for taxation of the value added abroad). Obviously, the major advantage of these processing plants, called *maquiladoras*, is access to less expensive Mexican labor.

Several further tariff reductions for materials and equipment imported into Mexico have stimulated expansion in the border industrialization program. As a result, the number of *maquiladoras* has increased from 20 in 1966 to 120 in 1970, 476 in 1974, and 595 in 1980 (526 of these on the border), employing 118,261 workers.

As might be expected, the 1976 devaluation of the peso also stimulated the border industries (albeit only significantly after 1977). The ratio of *maquiladora* net income (international receipts minus payments) to Mexican exports, however, also fell from 0.16 in 1976 to 0.05 in 1980 as a result of the increase in petroleum exports. In 1978, Mexico accounted for 73 percent of the net income of Latin American and Caribbean countries from these "offshore" exports to the United States. Eighty percent of *maquiladora* income depends on the U.S. market.

Mexico's net income from tourism grew substantially faster than Mexican merchandise exports from 1960 to 1975. The U.S. share of tourist expenditures in Mexico had fallen from 88 percent in 1970 to 75 percent in 1980. When Mexico voted in the United Nations on 10 November 1975, to condemn Zionism as a form of racism, Jewish groups in the United States organized a tourist boycott of Mexico. This boycott cancelled about 30,000 hotel reservations within days as the peak tourist season was opening. Mexico's net income from tourism had been growing virtually without interruption for many years, but it fell by 21 percent from 1974 to 1975. The 1974 level was not surpassed until 1978.

The structure of the Mexican economy has important implications for the country's pattern of trade. In part, the underlying economy has provided an environment of stability and continuity. The same states of Mexico consistently account for the country's exports, for example. Mexico's international economic transactions are, however, disproportionately weighted toward the United States. Trade, external debt, border transactions and industries, direct investment, and tourism all depend directly on the state of the U.S. economy. In the 1970s, increasingly sharp fluctuations in both economies tended to create instability in Mexico's pattern and level of foreign trade.

However, several long-term trends have persisted. Most important, Mexico has reduced its trade dependence on the United States, especially for imports, over several decades. Mexico has also begun to depend less on government-to-government loans, relying increasingly on private bank borrowing. These developments have increased the number of options available to the Mexican authorities. Yet Mexico's trade is still dependent on the United States, on a limited number of products, and on a few regions for their supply.

Recent Developments in the Balance of Payments

Until 1981, Mexico's balance of payments has deteriorated at an alarming rate. The Bank of Mexico has given five major reasons for this development: (1) the fall in the real price of oil and difficulties exporting it caused receipts to drop by nearly $5 billion; (2) the low rate of growth in the countries that are Mexico's traditional markets caused nonoil exports to contract in real terms; (3) the widening of the differential between inflation in Mexico and abroad together with the appreciation of the dollar during 1981 adversely affected trade in goods and services; (4) the persistence of unprecedentedly high interest rates in international money and capital markets increased the cost of foreign borrowing; and (5) the depression in the world silver market lowered the value of silver exports.[5]

Specifically in 1981 the current account deficit (goods and services) increased (table 3.3) by 73.1 percent to −$11,704.1 million. The trade deficit (goods only) increased by 17.2 percent to −$3,725.4 million. Thus the deficit grew in spite of the lower than expected increase of 40 percent in the value of petroleum exports to $13,827.5 million, which raised the share of oil in total exports from 64.5 percent in 1980 to 71.4 percent in 1981.

The deterioration in the service items was even greater, with an increase of 122.7 percent in the deficit, to −$7,978.7 million. This decline in the service account reflected reduced surpluses in border transactions (−84.2 percent) and tourism (−66.0 percent), items that suffered severely from the overvalued peso; and the reduction of −52.8 percent in nonmonetary transactions in gold and silver. The most important cause of the decline in the service account was the 53.5 percent increase in the financial services deficit, which reached −$7,601.5

Table 3.3. Mexico: balance of payments, trade balance, 1976–81 (in millions of dollars)

	1976	1977	1978	1979	1980	1981
Trade balance (goods only)	−2,714	−1,391	−1,854	−3,162	−3,179	−3,725
Services balances (services only)	−355	−159	−839	1,714	−3,582	−7,978
Current account (goods and services)	−3,069	−1,550	−2,693	−4,876	−6,761	−11,704
Receipts	7,371	8,437	11,653	16,283	25,021	30,556
Exports of goods	3,316	4,451	6,063	8,818	15,308	19,379
Processing services	536	525	452	638	772	982
Nonmonetary gold and silver	160	186	249	488	936	520
Miscellaneous transportation	177	200	251	320	448	497
Tourism	836	867	1,121	1,443	1,671	1,759
Border transactions	1,637	1,506	2,364	2,919	3,722	4,709
Receipts from investments	123	169	403	695	980	1,335
Other services	414	345	524	707	866	1,014
Transfers	173	189	226	256	319	360
Payments (−)	10,440	9,987	14,346	21,159	31,782	42,260
Imports of goods	6,030	5,842	7,918	11,980	18,486	23,104
Insurance and freights	—	—	419	610	945	1,089
Nonmonetary gold	42	31	74	152	65	109
Miscellaneous transportation	204	192	2,358	521	987	1,293
Tourism	423	396	519	693	1,045	1,547
Border transactions	1,193	786	1,632	2,246	3,130	4,615
Payments related to investments	2,002	2,158	2,787	4,072	5,933	8,936
Profits remitted	328	172	214	335	496	720
Interest—public sector	1,266	1,542	2,023	2,888	3,958	5,507
Other interest	408	444	549	849	1,479	2,710
Other services	530	560	612	854	1,148	1,510
Transfers	17	21	29	33	44	56

Source: Bank of Mexico, *Informe Anual*, various issues.
Note: (−) indicates outflow of foreign currency.

Table 3.4. Mexico: balance of payments, capital account, 1976–81 (in millions of dollars)

	1976	1977	1978	1979	1980	1981
Capital account (net).	5,202	2,513	3,145	4,521	9,799	18,153
Long-term capital (net)	4,641	4,380	4,652	4,594	6,476	14,092
Public sector (net)	4,216	3,872	4,063	3,147	4,059	11,530
Credits and bonds	5,418	6,232	8,343	10,415	7,771	n.a.
Credits and bonds amortization	−1,155	−2,295	−4,264	−7,280	−3,723	n.a.
Credits to other countries (net)	−47	−65	−16	18	11	−391
Private sector (net)	436	508	589	1,447	2,418	2,563
Foreign direct investments	299	327	385	782	1,071	1,142
Purchase of foreign companies	−12	−1	−21	−40	−10	—
Liabilities to foreigners (net)	202	213	223	756	1,488	1,469
Companies foreign owned (net)	291	214	−191	239	664	587
Other companies (net)	−89	−1	417	517	824	881
Security transactions	−54	−31	2	−51	−132	−48
Short-term capital (net)	551	−1,867	−1,507	−72	3,322	4,061
Liabilities (net)	1,253	−1,182	−1,032	1,697	4,188	5,664
Public sector (net)	878	−950	−1,489	206	68	2,976
Private sector (net)	375	233	457	1,491	4,120	2,688
Assets (net)	−702	−685	−475	−1,769	−865	−1,604
Special drawing rights	•	•	•	70.0	74	70
Errors and omissions	−2,454	−459	−18	703	−1,961	−5,506
Changes in Bank of Mexico Reserves	−321	504	434	419	1,151	1,012

Source: Bank of Mexico, *Informe Anual*, various issues.
Note: (−) indicates outflow of foreign currency. n.a. = not available.

million and constituted 95.3 percent of the total deficit in services. The financial part of the services deficit resulted (table 3.4) mainly from payments related to investments, which rose the increase to $8,936.4 million. These comprise −$719.5 million of profits remitted by foreign owned companies, which rose by 45.0 percent but still constituted only 8.1 percent of the total; −$2,709.6 million of interest paid by other private sector companies, an increase of 83.2 percent to 30.3 percent of the total; and −$5,507.3 million of public sector interest payments, an increase of 39.2 percent to 61.6 percent of the total.

The deficit in "errors and omissions" (short-term capital outflows not otherwise recorded) jumped by 180.8 percent to −$5,506.4 million. This amount must be added to the current account deficit of $11,704 million to reach a total deficit of −$17,201 million, an enormous increase of 97.3 percent over 1980 to be financed by foreign capital.

To provide the necessary financing, the capital account rose correspondingly by 85.3 percent to $18,153.1 million. The foreign borrowing consisted of $14,092.3 million of long-term capital (an increase of 117.6 percent) and $4,060.8 million of short-term capital (an increase of 22.2 percent). The net total of long-term capital borrowed by the public sector increased by 184.1 percent to the staggering amount of $11,529.5 million. The private sector long-term capital account increased by only 6.0 percent to $2,562.7 million, but this followed a very considerable increase of 67 percent in 1980. The total long-term capital included $1,142.1 million of foreign direct investment, the equity capital brought in by multinational corporations. This nominal increase of only 6.6 percent was actually a decline in real terms.

By early summer 1981, the peso exchange rate with the dollar was depreciating by about four cents a day (twenty centavos a week). The rate is obviously fixed each day by the Mexican monetary authority. The middle rate for the conversion of documents on 14 May 1982 was 46.48 pesos. Starting from the rate of 22.70 pesos to the dollar at the beginning of 1981, the government attempted to devalue the peso gradually. By 1982, the peso had been devalued by a total of almost 105 percent, defined by the increase in the number of pesos needed to buy one dollar.

The balance of payments did not appear to be seriously deteriorating before 1981 thanks to the increasing receipts from oil exports after 1978. Owing to the oil boom, Mexico had no difficulty whatever in borrowing to finance the deficit. Nevertheless, the peso was becoming increasingly overvalued. This was demonstrated in 1979–80 by the declining surpluses in tourism and border transactions, and by the rapid rise in total merchandise imports. This was the inevitable result of the accelerating rise in domestic prices. From mid-1978 to November 1981, inflation (measured by the consumer price index) increased by 44.5 percent in the United States, by far Mexico's leading financial and trading partner, but it increased by 107.5 percent in Mexico. As for the exchange rate, the Mexican peso was devalued against the dollar by only 0.3 percent in the twelve months to December 1979, by 2.0 percent to December 1980, and approximately by another 12.5 percent to the end of 1981. The differentially higher rate of inflation in Mexico was not matched by the adjustment in the exchange rate.

Exchange Rate

Traditionally, the Mexican peso has been pegged to the U.S. dollar. Its value is largely determined in the long run by the relative inflation rates between the two countries and Mexico's trade deficit with the United States. Pressure on the peso stems from the mutual free convertibility of the two currencies and the lack of any other restrictions on currency flow. The so-called dollarization of the Mexican economy has made it difficult for Mexican authorities to implement monetary restrictions.[6]

Recently, inflation has been high and probably increasing in Mexico. The rate was about 30 percent in 1980, over 28 percent in 1981 and probably considerably higher—perhaps up to 60 percent—in 1982. In short, the peso was becoming increasingly overvalued up until the February 1982 devaluation. Still, some Mexican officials were arguing against devaluation as late as January 1982, when one dollar was buying 22 to 23 pesos. In support of their positions they suggested: that a rate of 30 pesos to the dollar would accommodate at most only one-half of the difference between Mexican and U.S. inflation rates over the past few years; that petroleum exports would make devaluation unnecessary in balance of payments terms; that devaluation would produce even higher inflation rates since so much of Mexico's food, capital goods, and consumer goods were imported; and that without even more massive food price subsidies, high levels of basic food imports would impose most of the cost of devaluation on the poor.

In the end it was clear, however, that without devaluation Mexican industrial exports would be squeezed between rapidly rising domestic costs and sluggish exchange rates. By August 1982, the rate had fallen to 90 pesos per dollar. At even a 25 to 30 percent inflation rate, the minimum that could be expected under present policies, the cost structures of individual firms would most likely change more than their profit margins. To increase earnings from manufactured exports, the country had to reduce inflation or devalue its currency in the short run and increase productivity in the manufacturing sector in the long run. Of course, many firms might not experience much of a cost squeeze in light of a devaluation because the overvalued peso in effect subsidized imported inputs. These exchange rate subsidies, combined with oil-financed production subsidies, could then maintain effective profit rates at high levels. Thus, as with other forms of import protection, it is always in the interest of some firms or industries to maintain an overvalued peso.

As in many other policy areas, the government has always sided with the protectionists. In fact, no Mexican president in the past several decades has devalued the peso unless the outflow of funds into dollar accounts or abroad has been sufficient to threaten the ability of the central bank to support the peso. Immediately before both the 1976 and 1982 devaluations, Mexico suffered capital flight of several hundred million dollars per day.[7] Devaluation may be becoming a bit easier in light of two major devaluations in the last six years. Yet it is still very difficult politically for a Mexican president to devalue the peso and maintain his nationalist credentials in the absence of a balance of payments crisis. For a while, the López Portillo administration got around this problem by making a series of mini-adjustments of only a few percentage points per year. These were expected to resolve the problem of keeping Mexican manufactured exports competitive. However, in light of Mexico's inflation differential with the United States, these small adjustments were insufficient, and in fact only encouraged the further dollarization of the Mexican economy.[8]

External Debt

As a result of these trends, Mexico's external public debt has grown, so that the country is now one of the world's most indebted.[9] The country's debt service as a percent of gross domestic product increased from 2.1 percent in 1970 to 8.8 percent in 1979. In terms of exports the country's debt service increased from 24.1 to 64.1 percent during the same period (table 3.5).

Along with Mexico's rapidly increasing foreign debt, both public and private, direct foreign investment in Mexico has increased sharply. Such investment

Table 3.5. Mexico: balance of payments and debt service ratios, selected countries, 1970 and 1979

	Current account balance before interest payments on external public debt (millions of dollars)		Interest payments on external public debt (millions of dollars)		Debt service as a percentage of			
					GNP		Exports of goods and services	
	1970	1979	1970	1979	1970	1979	1970	1979
Newly industrializing countries								
Mexico	−844	−1,672	216	2,874	2.1	8.8	24.1	64.1
Brazil	−704	−7,600	133	2,865	0.9	3.1	12.4	34.6
Singapore	−566	−1,091	6	86	0.6	2.5	0.6	1.3
Korea	−553	−3,216	70	937	3.1	4.4	19.4	13.5
Developing countries								
Cameroon	−26	−1,945	16	146	0.6	1.0	3.3	4.2
Tunisia	−35	−134	18	163	4.5	4.8	18.5	11.8
Sri Lanka	−47	−203	12	28	2.0	2.3	10.3	6.5
Philippines	−23	−1,266	25	298	1.4	2.7	7.5	12.6

Source: Derived from World Bank, *World Development Report, 1981*.

quadrupled from 1979 to 1980. Direct foreign investment amounted to $200 million in 1970, rising to $196 million in 1971, $295 million in 1975, $665 million in 1979, and $1,661 million in 1980. In 1981, it reached $3 billion, fifteen times what it was in 1970. Total investment by the end of 1981 was estimated at around $11.5 billion.

The aggregate foreign debt of the public sector was $4.262 billion in 1970, rising to $14.266 billion in 1975, $29.599 billion in 1979, and $34.1 billion in 1980. Estimates are that it exceeded $40 billion by the end of 1981. Cumulative foreign debt of the private sector amounted to $10 billion in 1979. The rate with which it expanded in 1980 and 1981 is alarming, with estimates that it will total about $20 billion by the end of 1981.

Adding up aggregate direct foreign investment and the cumulative foreign debt of the private sector produces a total figure of $71.5 billion by the end of 1981. This is the equivalent in domestic currency of 1.7 trillion pesos (about the size of the Mexican federal budget in 1980). Foreign banks held about 40 percent of the credit in the Mexican market in 1981 compared with just 25 percent in 1976.

The composition of the external public debt has changed considerably in recent years. In the mid-1960s official bilateral and multilateral agencies and banks accounted for 45.1 percent of Mexico's external public debt. By the mid-1970s official lending sources accounted for only 27.1 percent of the debt. Multilateral banks also increased their share of the official debt from 63.7 percent in the mid-1960s to 70.8 percent a decade later. During these same years foreign private banks increased their share of the external debt from 21.5 percent to 56.1 percent and then to 80 percent in 1978.

In early 1980, 77.6 percent of the external public debt was contracted with private financial institutions and 9.5 percent with multilateral banks, 8.4 percent consisted of bonds, 3.2 percent of bilateral loans, and 1.4 percent of suppliers' credit.

Assessment of Recent Trends in the External Sector

While the expanded oil revenues were a major contributor to growth, they also represented a source of distortions, disequilibrium, and instability. Thus, even though in 1978 the economy entered a stage of rapid and sustained growth, by 1981 it was becoming apparent that this expansion was self-terminating due to the buildup of strong inflationary pressures and an increasing external disequilibrium. Thus, in 1981 while real GDP grew by 8.1 percent, consumer prices increased by about 29 percent and the current deficit of the balance of payments reached $12 million.

Mexico's current economic problems therefore clearly stem from both external and internal factors.[10] The external causes were a weakening world oil market since 1981 and higher world interest rates beginning in 1980. Oil constitutes three-fourths of Mexico's exports. Yet last year Mexico's oil exports amounted to only $14 billion instead of the $20 billion government planners had anticipated.[11] In addition, higher international interest rates combined with rising debt drove Mexico's interest burden from $5.4 billion in 1980 to $8.2 billion in 1981.[12] Together these external forces helped cause an unusually high external deficit relative to exports. In 1981, the current account deficit was $11.7 billion compared with exports of $19.4 billion.

Internal factors aggravated the situation. Although the country's ambitious growth policy held real economic growth at an average of 8.2 percent in 1978–81, long-term capacity growth of the economy was only about 6 percent. The result was an overheated and increasingly inflationary economy, out of step with slow growth internationally. The government's inability to reform the tax system resulted in increasing budget deficits reaching 16 percent of gross domestic product in 1982. The overvalued peso also aggravated the problem. Determined to maintain a fixed, or nearly fixed, exchange rate, the authorities during 1977–80 held the peso at 23–25 per dollar in spite of 23 percent annual domestic inflation. This artificial exchange rate caused nonoil exports to stagnate.

In fact, exports of hydrocarbons increased more than five times between 1978 and 1981. Exports of manufactures increased at an annual average rate of only 2.2 percent in the same period; in 1981, they fell by 10 percent.[13] The deterioration of manufactured goods exports was due partly to increased domestic demand, but resulted largely from the increased overvaluation of the peso reducing Mexico's competitiveness in the international market. The relative share of hydrocarbon exports rose from approximately 21 percent in 1977 to 71 percent in 1981, whereas that of manufactured goods fell from 46 percent to 17 percent.

This growth policy was extremely vulnerable to external change. In 1981 approximately 15 percent of the available goods were financed with external inflows, 70 percent of which were generated by exports of a single commodity. The high inflation rate in Mexico, approximately three times higher than the world inflation rate, led to a gradual overvaluation of the peso that was only partially eased by mini-adjustments in 1980 and 1981. To keep the exchange rate under control, the monetary authorities were forced to use interest rates to strengthen the balance of payments and support the peso.[14] In December 1981, the normal interest rate on time deposits (90–179 days) denominated in pesos was approximately 32 percent, 19 percentage points higher than the London Interbank Offered Rate (LIBOR).[15]

Conclusion

The 1982 economic crisis in Mexico was the result of an unfavorable balance of payments in 1981, accelerated inflation and the high level of external debt. Inflation reached 5.1 percent monthly in early 1982. The external debt included $11.4 billion of long-term public debt; $4.5 billion of short-term public debt, and $19.1 billion of total private debt. Both of these factors undermined efforts to keep the exchange rate under control. Financial flows denominated in dollars as a percentage of total flows of the banking system rose from 27.0 percent in December 1981 to 60.4 percent in January 1982. As noted above, the Bank of Mexico withdrew from the dollar market and allowed the peso to float freely. Beginning 18 February 1982 the dollar began to be traded at 38.5 compared with 27 pesos to the dollar on the previous day. In other words, the peso had been devalued by approximately 30 percent overnight. A second devaluation of 18 percent increased the value of the dollar at the end of May, and by the end of the year the rate stood at 160 pesos to the dollar. These developments stemmed in large part from a series of ill-fated policies undertaken during the Echeverría and López Portillo administrations. These policies will be examined in detail in part II.

II. Economic Policymaking, 1971–82

Introduction

Between 1971 and 1982, the Echeverría and López Portillo administrations substantially increased the state's participation in the Mexican economy, financing growth through external borrowing and a rapid increase in the internal money supply. When Luis Echeverría became President in 1970, government contribution to the GNP was about 30 percent, the foreign debt was about 6 billion dollars and the inflation rate was about 5 percent. Twelve years later, the debt had climbed to 80 billion and inflation was running at about 100 percent a year.

As Echeverría took office, 1 million pesos were worth 80,000 dollars. As López Portillo left office, 1 million pesos were worth 6,666 dollars. Five years prior to the date when Echeverría took office, the Mexican minimum wage was equivalent to about three dollars. In April 1982, five months after López Portillo left office, the minimum daily wage of the Mexican worker was still equivalent to only three dollars.

The following five chapters trace the major developments in economic policy under presidents Echeverría and López Portillo, leading to the 1982 crisis.

4. Policymaking during the Echeverría Administration, 1971–76

In his final presidential message, President Echeverría repeatedly referred to his administration's efforts to improve Mexico's inequitable income distribution. Two other themes stand out in Echeverría's recapitulation of his objectives while in office. First, he emphasized his administration's efforts to correct deficiencies in the provision of education, housing, nutrition, and health services to the lower-income groups, and to compensate for shortfalls in private sector investment. Second, Echeverría recalled his government's efforts to maintain the value of the Mexican peso with respect to the dollar.[1]

Mexico's policy objectives under Echeverría may be briefly outlined as follows: (1) to increase job creation capacity; (2) to maintain the recent high growth rate in industry; (3) to earn through exports of manufactured goods the foreign exchange needed for the expansion of industry; (4) to achieve a more balanced geographical distribution of industry and create new development in backward areas; (5) to orient industrial production more strongly toward the needs of the great majority of the population; (6) to reduce Mexican industry's dependence on foreign capital and in particular on the services of transnational enterprises; and (7) to develop the Mexican capital goods industry to insulate the country from cyclical fluctuations in the world economy.[2]

Javier Marquez pointed out some basic dilemmas in Mexican economic policy under Echeverría.[3] These included the desire to use fiscal policy to reform the social structure, but then doing this without creating an adequate tax base; the desire to raise exports, but seeking to do this while maintaining a fixed exchange rate in the face of accelerating inflation; the desire to strengthen public sector enterprises while trying to maintain their prices at unrealistically low levels; and striving for greater industrial efficiency under a policy of protectionism. Mexico was forced to address these dilemmas when it embarked on its stabilization program in 1977.[4] The following sections attempt to show how these policy dilemmas combined with several of the longer-run structural trends identified in the previous chapters to produce the financial and economic crisis of 1976.

Public Sector Expansion

The critical destabilizing decisions of the Echeverría administration appear to be attempting to expand and rely on the public sector as the main vehicle for economic growth, and rectifying social inequalities before developing an adequate tax- and revenue-generating base. Early in his administration, Echeverría attempted to increase taxes but failed under sharp opposition from the country's commercial banks and the private sector. His decision to expand public expenditure despite this setback resulted in an overall public sector deficit that averaged 2.5 percent of gross domestic product annually between 1965 and 1970, increasing to an average of 5.7 percent of GDP in the 1971–76 period. By 1976, the deficit was 9.5 percent of gross domestic product.

Public sector revenue in relation to GDP increased but not commensurately with expenditures, growing from an annual average of 11.3 percent in the mid-to-late 1960s to 17.0 percent in the 1971–76 period.

One of the more interesting facets of the federal budget during the Echeverría years was the role of the so-called decentralized agencies. In the period 1970–76, 65 percent of total budgeted revenues came from these organizations, as well as from enterprises with state participation. The government organized these companies to promote economic development. The public sector depended on them heavily for revenues. Therefore, with very few exceptions, such as the National Railways System and Conasupo, the prices charged for the goods and services produced and sold by these companies must be economically sound, that is, high enough to cover current costs and provide funds for expansion.

Current public sector expenditures increased from an annual average of less than 6.5 percent of GDP in the mid-to-late 1960s to more than 17 percent of GDP in the final two years of the Echeverría period. Public sector investment expenditures increased from an annual average of less than 6 percent of GDP in the first year of the Echeverría term to more than 12 percent in the last year. Private sector gross fixed investment remained fairly constant at 12 to 13 percent of GDP between 1971 and 1976. As a result, total gross fixed investment (public plus private) increased to an annual average of 21.3 percent of GDP, compared with the average of 18.2 percent from 1965 to 1970. By contrast, public sector savings as a percentage of GDP declined from the annual average of 3.3 percent during the mid-to-late 1960s to 2.6 percent during Echeverría's term.

In the federal budget, the balance of current receipts over current expenditures covered 76 percent of capital expenditures in 1971, but only 24 percent in 1975. The ratio of current expenditures to current revenue, which had averaged 84 percent in the 1965–70 period, averaged 90 percent between 1971 and 1976. Since current revenue tends to constitute from 97 percent to more than 99 percent of the federal government's total budgetary revenue, the decline in savings forced the federal government to use growing deficits to finance investment that was itself growing.

The largest increases in current federal government expenditures in the Echeverría period were for transfers, most of which went to public enterprises. The most important of these under budgetary control are the oil company (PEMEX), the electricity companies, and the railways. Clearly, the government substantially subsidized (and still subsidizes) many of these enterprises, resulting in a significant drain on the federal budget.

In fact, transfers to these enterprises increased from 2.3 percent of GDP in the period 1960–68 to 3.4 percent in 1973–76. The largest subsidies were geared toward reducing energy prices (oil, fuel, and electricity), operating the railroads, and lowering food prices. Subsidies from the central government to public sector enterprises, and to the private sector in the form of reduced prices, averaged 5.3 percent of GDP in the 1973–76 period, compared with 3.5 percent of GDP from 1969–76.

As a consequence of the spending-savings disparity, the annual borrowing requirement rose from about 3 percent of GDP in the previous presidential administration to 8 percent in the final years of the Echeverría period. Of this, more than two-thirds came from internal sources and less than one-third from external sources.

One of the best descriptions of the government's economic strategy was given in July 1977 by the Mexican Ministry of Finance and Public Credit:

> The policy of public indebtedness which has been followed by the Government of Mexico is based on the desire to expand productive activities and on an effort to improve the standard of living of and offer a more equitable life to a population growing at a considerable rate.
>
> As is the case with most developing countries, internal savings in Mexico are insufficient to meet the levels of investment required. Furthermore, our export-derived income does not cover the foreign currency requirements generated by our import needs. The complementary resources (i.e. from international financial markets) are required by our struggle to achieve a rate of capital formation that will enable us to attain a high rate of economic growth and a sustained increase in the levels of our exports.[5]

Between 1971 and 1976, Mexico's federal government budget went from 4.8 billion pesos (1 percent of GDP) to 57.4 billion pesos (3.8 percent of GDP). In the same period, public sector investment expressed in 1960 prices more than doubled during that period while private investment increased only 16 percent. The number of state-owned corporations expanded from 86 in 1970 to 740 in 1976. By the end of the Echeverría period, public enterprises dominated the oil, electricity, steel, petrochemicals, banking, transportation, and communications industries, with the public sector accounting for around 45 percent of GDP.

In short, Echeverría's budgetary decisions and the emphasis on increasing the public sector produced massive budget deficits, considerable crowding out of the private sector from bank credit, rising inflation, a growing internal and external debt, and eventually massive capital flight, reflecting the lack of confidence in government policy.[6]

The decline in private sector confidence was reflected in capital flight estimated at $4 billion in the eighteen months preceding the devaluation. From December 1975 to December 1976, the peso liabilities of the banking system increased by only 10 percent, less than half the percentage increase of the previous twelve months, whereas liabilities denominated in foreign currencies increased by 72 percent, more than double the percentage increase in the previous twelve months. Reserve requirements on dollar deposits were 100 percent, compared with about 40 percent for peso deposits. The lack of confidence is apparent from data starting in 1972, but the process accelerated in 1976. The quantum increase in "dollarization" in 1976 reflected the crisis mentality in the country.[7]

Balance of Payments Deterioration

As noted in the previous chapter, the key elements in Mexico's balance of payments after 1965 were the growing deficit in merchandise trade during the later 1960s and the growth of the deficit beginning in 1974. This pattern was definitely associated with Mexico's accumulating inflation, leading to the overvaluation of the peso. The money supply (*M* 1, cash plus demand deposits) also increased by considerably more in the 1970-76 period (by 19 percent annually) than in the late 1960s (11 percent). Clearly, much of this demand spilled over into imports.

In addition, the recession in the United States and elsewhere dampened demand for Mexican exports. Still, Mexico's total merchandise exports grew by 37 percent in 1974, but this was offset by the almost 60 percent increase in imports. Exports did not grow at all in 1975.

The current account deficit averaged 2.4 percent of GDP between 1965-70 and 3.7 percent during 1971-76. In the final two years of the Echeverría administration, 1975 and 1976, the current account deficits were 5.1 and 4.3 percent of GDP. This deficit was financed by growing capital imports.[8]

Over the five-year period 1971 through 1975, manufactured exports grew by 30 percent per year, of which about 12 percent per year was attributable to price increases and 16 percent per year represented real growth. In relative terms, however, industrial exports were still a small proportion of total manufacturing output in Mexico compared with a number of the newly industrializing countries. In a sense even the relatively low aggregate export figures give a somewhat inflated picture of the overall competitive position of the country's industrial exports. In the early-to-mid 1970s, nearly half of Mexico's manufactured exports came from plants that assemble products for the U.S. market. These border industry plants rely on inputs imported in bond from the United States, taking advantage of special provisions in the U.S. tariff that limit import duties for such products to value added outside the United States. About two-thirds of assembly plant exports consisted of items such as electronic parts and television and communications equipment, while clothing is a distant second.

Exports outside of the border areas were considerably more diversified, with nonelectrical machinery, electrical machinery, and transport equipment exports amounting to $270 million (25 percent of nonassembly plant manufactured exports) in 1975. Most of these exports consisted of parts or components, with automobile engines and parts the most important. Chemical exports were worth $204 million in 1975—19 percent of nonassembly manufactured exports. These chemical products were largely based on natural resources such as sulphur, lead, and zinc. These went mostly to the United States and Latin American Free Trade Area (LAFTA) countries. Textile exports based on locally produced henequen and cotton, and food product exports led by molasses and simply preserved fruits and vegetables were also important. In spite of the concentration of exports within a few sectors, however, many sectors were exporting 10 percent or more of their output in 1974, the last year for which these comparative data are available. These sectors included basic chemicals, fertilizers, and pharmaceuticals—all principally based on natural resources. Despite some promising signs in the manufacturing area, however, exports from this sector were not sufficient to offset the general erosion of the country's balance of payments.

The rapid deterioration in the balance of payments in the 1970s stemmed from a number of interrelated factors. In summary, these factors exhausted the internal sources of finance needed to sustain the industrialization that began in the 1960s. The deterioration of industrial funds, and the accompanying increased dependence on foreign financial sources are reflected in the rapidly growing industrial trade deficit as a proportion of manufacturing production, the growing inability of the agricultural, oil, and service sectors to generate the external surpluses needed to finance that deficit, and the resulting expansion of the residual deficit that in turn had to be financed by external sources.

Mexico's import substitution strategy was based on the premise that the resulting industrial trade deficit was an inevitable side effect of modernization and rapid development. The government assumed that this deficit was manageable and likely to be incurred only during the early stages of industrialization. These policies also presumed that at least initially foreign trade surpluses generated by the more traditional sectors such as agriculture could finance the deficit, and that eventually a declining import ratio and in increasing ability to export would turn the deficit into a surplus.

Import substitution growth did imply high annual rates of growth in industrial output: 8 percent on the average over the period 1950–70, without a rapid deterioration of the balance of payments. Nevertheless, industrialization continued to depend on the importation of capital equipment. As a result, the foreign trade deficit persisted and showed no significant tendency to decrease as a proportion of manufacturing output.

Deterioration Due to Import Substitution

Many of Mexico's problems in the 1970s can be traced back to the import substitution strategy initiated in the 1950s. This section examines this process in greater detail, in an attempt to throw more light on the overall decline in Mexican economic activity in the early 1970s.

Although the level of tariffs in Mexico is generally low in comparison with other developing countries, quantitative controls account for most of the protection afforded domestic producers from foreign competition. Of the quantitative controls, import licenses introduced in 1948 are by far the most important. By 1970, around 65 percent of the value of imports and a similar number of import items were covered by some form of import licensing requirement.[9]

These protective structures made raw materials, intermediate goods, and capital goods fairly easy to import and imposed lower import duties on these goods. Over time, therefore, effective protection for manufacturing final consumer goods became higher than the nominal tariff protection. The pattern of relative prices created by commercial policy gave producers incentives to shift gradually toward production of consumer goods for the domestic market. Nondurable consumer goods decreased their relative share in total imports, and imports of machinery and equipment increased their share from 23 percent in 1940 to 36 percent in 1970. The infant industry argument was consistently applied and protection was never removed, once imposed, despite the fact that in principle import licensing could be granted only for periods of three to five years.

Unquestionably, protectionism raised the profit rate in manufacturing. In so doing, commercial policy discriminated against other sectors where expansion might have produced higher economic benefits. Import substitution policies seem to have protected final consumer goods rather than intermediate or capital goods. These policies especially aided manufactures, which generally satisfied total domestic demand.

After the initial period of import substitution of nondurable consumer goods and certain intermediate goods in the 1940s and 1950s, industrial development in the 1960s tended to shift to new lines of production such as durable consumer goods. In part, this shift was a response to the demand profile created by an increasingly unequal distribution of income. The rapidly growing incomes of the upper income groups created new markets for a variety of new consumer durables. Yet the absence of broad-based middle-income groups inhibited the normal pattern of industrial development experienced by the industrial countries at comparable levels of per capita income. The high levels of capital goods imports required by the new industries tended to counterbalance the reduction in the trade deficit made by their direct contribution to import substitution. Moreover, the new durable consumer goods industries were developed largely by foreign capital. Because many of these companies repatriated profits, they had an additional negative impact on the country's balance of payments. Of course, the underdevelopment of a capital goods industry all through this period contributed directly to the growing industrial trade deficit.

The relative underdevelopment of the capital goods sector was critical in affecting the country's trade balance.[10] The low rates of domestic expansion observed in this area cannot be explained simply in terms of the rapid expansion in demand for consumer durables and thus the relative attractiveness of investment in these areas. Government policy was also a contributing factor. The government established a structure of protection much more favorable to consumer than to capital goods industries, subsidized capital goods imports, and maintained an overvalued exchange rate. In combination, these three policies were largely responsible for the high import ratio and income elasticity characterizing the capital goods sector during this period.[11]

As a result of these developments, the capital goods sector made a major contribution to the expansion of industrial imports and the trade deficit. This pattern occurred despite an overall declining ratio of imports to total supply. Finally in the 1970s, the stage of relatively easy domestic substitution for industrial imports had been completed. At this point, the decline in the import ratio could not be sustained.

This interpretation of the Mexican trade deficit stresses the pattern of structural change. This emphasis is consistent with the more orthodox interpretation attributing economic distortions to the structure of tariffs and quotas used by the government to promote industrialization. These protectionist measures made it even more difficult for Mexican industry to reduce its trade deficit. The orthodox position stresses that the excessively high level of protection is the chief contributing factor to inefficiency and thus a loss of competitiveness in world markets. Admittedly, industrial exports did grow rapidly after 1965. Between 1967 and 1974, when there was an acute deterioration in the balance of payments, the rate of growth of manufactured exports increased by 15 percent. However, most of this increase was from the new border industries and thus did not reflect the overall competitive position of Mexican industry at this time.[12]

Contribution of Agriculture to the Balance of Payments Deterioration

Agricultural output increased rapidly in Mexico between 1940 and 1965 due largely to increases in productivity. Improved water control methods, land reform, and increased levels of agricultural extension services and agricultural research helped to raise productivity. During the 1940–65 period, agricultural production expanded at an average annual rate of over 6 percent per annum in real terms.[13]

In marked contrast, output fell to only 1.2 percent in the second half of the 1960s, and agricultural exports mirrored the decline in production. In fact, the country was importing many of its basic grains and oilseeds by 1970. The causes underlying agriculture's poor showing are somewhat controversial. Lower public investment in the sector, credit policies, and changes in relative prices clearly contributed to this decline.

In particular, the reduction in the proportion of public funds budgeted for agricultural investment seems to have played a critical role in agriculture's weak performance. The share of agriculture in public investment fell from about one-fifth in 1950 to less than one-tenth by 1960. Not until the late 1960s, when agricultural stagnation was evident, did the government devote a greater proportion of its capital allocations to agriculture. The decreasing public investment in agriculture was particularly serious because it appears to have induced private investment in the sector to fall as well. The net result of these trends was that investment in agriculture fell from 14.0 percent of gross fixed capital formation in 1960 to 4.5 percent in 1970. The share of agriculture in value added decreased from 15.9 percent to 11.6 percent of the GDP during the same period.

From all accounts, the government's diminished role in agriculture was not so much a result of deliberate discrimination. Rather, agriculture was simply the victim of circumstances. A series of developments drained government funds away from agriculture. As the nationalized sector expanded, the income elasticity of tax collection was reduced; the prices of products supplied by state-owned enterprises, which required more government support, remained rigid; and the public utilities, which charged fixed rates, required increasing transfer payments from the government.[14] The drain on the government's budget caused by these factors, together with the pursuit of monetary stability, led the government to treat agriculture's allocations more and more as a residual after other, more pressing claims had been met.

Agricultural producers also faced serious adverse price effects from the import substitution strategy. Protectionism resulted in an anti-export bias, since export prices were governed by world markets and import substitutes were overpriced compared with world prices. For example, in 1970 the effective protection rate of export activities had a minus 5 percent level, while import substitutes had a plus 39 percent. The decreasing share of manufactures exported is thus not surprising. Price changes due to protectionism contributed to worsening relative agricultural prices. Effective protection for agriculture was 1 percent, while for manufacturing it was over 20 percent.

The decline of agriculture had a number of ramifications. In addition to increasing rural poverty, agriculture's decline also worsened the balance of payments. During 1961–65, the agricultural foreign trade surplus financed almost half of the industrial deficit. By 1974, the sector's trade surplus had deteriorated so badly that it had ceased to be of any significance. In fact, there is a close correlation between the decline in the agricultural trade balance and the narrowing gap between production and per capita consumption of agricultural goods. Per capita consumption of agricultural goods remained practically unchanged between 1964–65 and 1972–73, while per capita agricultural production during the same period decreased 15 percent.

The decline in per capita agricultural production continued into the 1970s, averaging 12 percent during 1965–70 and 8 percent in 1970–75. The effect on agriculture's trade balance at constant prices was also at least as important in the late 1960s as the early 1970s. However, deteriorating terms of trade during the latter period brought about a more rapid decline of the trade balance between agricultural imports and exports, calculated in current prices.

Over the 1965–72 period, the effect of the decline in the agricultural surplus was concealed somewhat by international export prices that were growing faster than import prices. Between 1972 and 1975, however, this pattern was reversed. Combined with the continued deterioration in trade balance at constant prices, the surplus in the trade balance measured at current prices was nearly eliminated.[15]

Other Factors Responsible for the Balance of Payments Deterioration

The increase of the industrial deficit, together with the erosion of the agricultural surplus, account for a large part of the growing disequilibrium in the trade balance. Another contributing factor was the slowing down of oil production, so that substantial deficits began to appear in the oil trade balance. Finally, a number of incentives provided for the service sector did not stimulate development in this sector, or enable it to offset the declining ability of agriculture to continue financing the industrial deficit.

As expected, the growing inability of internal sources to finance the expansion of industry resulted finally in a rapid increase in foreign debt. Between 1961 and 1965, foreign loans financed only 7 percent of the industrial deficit. By 1975, this proportion had increased to 66 percent. As a result, net income paid abroad increased from 29 percent of the deficit on current account in 1960–64 to more than 50 percent in the 1974–77 period. It appears that the foreign debt was incurred mainly to finance the growing deficits in the balance on current account. As noted above, however, these deficits originated with the decline in the trade balance. Current account deficits, therefore, created an equivalent deficit in the balance of net income paid abroad. By the mid-1970s, Mexico was falling into a vicious cycle whereby the deficits tended to determine the rate of foreign borrowing, while the accumulation of debts in turn partly caused the deficits.

Thus, industry failed to generate exports while simultaneously absorbing increased amounts of foreign exchange in the importation of capital and intermediate goods. This problem was obvious by 1975, when the income from the export of manufactures and minerals was not enough even to cover the interest payments on the foreign debt. Between 1960 and 1975, net property income paid abroad as a percentage of manufacturing and mineral exports had doubled.

To summarize, the country's industrialization program created a set of economic forces tending to cause a deterioration in the trade balance and in the balance of payments on current account. The deterioration became progressively worse in the 1960s and clearly implied the occurrence, sooner or later, of an exchange rate crisis.

While the country's development strategy created the environment conducive to foreign exchange instability, the actual peso crisis of 1976–77 was precipitated by the resurgence of domestic inflation, the international economic recession, and finally by a rapid acceleration in capital flight.[16]

Efficiency of Policy Instruments

A survey article on Mexico in the *Economist* contained the following harsh judgment on the Echeverría period:

> Enter in 1970 President Luis Echeverría, a man whose political instinct far outran his political abilities, whose economic ambitions outran his economics,

and whose populism outran his popularity. Exit in 1976 three months after he devalued the peso, following 22 years of financial stability, and thereby giving rise to fear for the stability of the whole Mexican system.[17]

In evaluating the Echeverría administration, however, particular attention should be drawn to a number of developments in the 1960s that made the economy less stable and more difficult to manage. The first factor was the growing substitution of domestic consumption for exports, with a major proportion of manufactured goods exported as residuals or surplus only after supplying domestic demand. A similar situation was developing in the minerals and agricultural sectors. The increased substitution of internal for external demand was caused by export diversification into new commodities, and the stagnation of traditional exports such as sugar, coffee, hard fibers, and minerals. Thus, changes in domestic activity had a significant influence on the current account deficit. Imports of capital goods expanded with domestic output, and expanding domestic consumption tended to divert exports toward the home market. Clearly, the more exports became substitutes for domestic goods the greater the chance of external imbalance.

The other factor contributing to instability was the gradually decreasing effectiveness of monetary policy. All through the 1960s, the public sector deficit had fluctuated, with a tendency to increase as a percentage of GDP. A part of the deficit had to be financed domestically, leading to a gradual upward trend in the central bank's reserve ratio until the usefulness of that instrument was greatly diminished. By 1970, deposit banks in Mexico City, which handle half of the country's financial assets, had 50 percent of their liabilities turned in as reserve requirements. The reserve requirements for banks outside Mexico City was 25 percent. The overall ratio was 30 percent for savings banks and 20 percent for financial banks.

There were some other ominous trends in Mexican banking and finance at this time. From 1965 to 1970, public savings decreased from 5.6 percent to 3.8 percent of the GDP. Public investment, on the other hand, rose from 6.7 percent to 7.3 percent in the same period. Savings in financial institutions also increased on a share basis from 4.4 percent to 5.7 percent of the GDP, with half of these being channeled by the central bank into financing the public sector.

Monetary policy was quite effective all through the 1950s and 1960s in controlling the level and composition (between public and private) of credit. In general, there was excess demand for funds in this period. Thus, as John Koeler has demonstrated, any additional funds made available by the monetary authorities were immediately either borrowed or invested. At the beginning of the 1960s, monetary policy still was an effective antirecession instrument. By the end of the decade, it had largely lost that capacity, assuming that the rapid expansion of financial assets had eliminated any excess demand for loanable funds.[18] At the same time, the reserve requirements were gradually increasing to the point where they could retard inflationary pressures. In short, the management of macroeconomic activity was becoming much more difficult through loss of monetary policy as an effective stability tool.

The following sequence of events illustrates the increasing incompatability between domestic and external equilibrium that the Mexican government faced at this time: (1) an increase in public spending raises aggregate demand and gross domestic product; (2) productive capacity becomes strained, imports increase, and exports are reduced by growing domestic demand with the current account deficit expanding; (3) the current account deficit thus expands; (4) prices start increasing more rapidly; (5) to restore control of the balance of payments, the government reduces or slows its expenditures, decreasing the GDP growth and thus slowing the upward movement of prices and imports; (6) the rate of growth of imports decreases, but the new absolute level of the current account deficit in the balance of payments either stabilizes or expands at a slower rate; (7) even if exports resume their expansion after the stabilization of aggregate demand, they may only prevent the deficit from getting bigger, because an enlarged absolute deficit is necessary to support the higher level of output. Monetary policy, which had been so successful as a stabilizing tool in the 1950s and 1960s, had little power to offset these developing trends in the early 1970s. As Solis has noted: ". . . from this perspective it becomes clear how damaging the 1964 failure of tax reform was, not only because it failed to add a new instrument to the arsenal of policy tools, but also because it accentuated conditions that would eventually cancel the flexibility of reserve requirements, the most powerful existing instrument.[19]

Conclusions

In retrospect, it seems clear that any fair evaluation of the Echeverría government's attempts to make development less unequal must see that the tendencies toward inequality, disequilibrium in the balance of payments, and a slowdown of agricultural growth are in many ways a logical result of the policies followed in the postwar industrialization period. Analysis should start not in 1970 but much earlier. In addition, this analysis can only ignore at serious risk the political elements that gave rise to or even forced some of the key decisions during the period under discussion. Finally, much more empirical work is needed on the short-term dynamics of the Mexican economy to prove fully the assertion that government investment displaced private investment activity.

On the other hand, the fact remains that most of the Echeverría administration's objectives were not met. If anything, income distribution became more unequal between 1970 and 1976. In this regard, therefore, the Echeverría policy of shared development (*desarrollo compartido*) was no more successful than the policies of his predecessors. The decline in agricultural production was not reversed, nor did Echeverría fundamentally alter the substitution strategy of industrial development with its inherent subsidization of industry at the expense of other sectors.

Echeverría's policies created no more jobs than had been created during the 1960s. Indeed, the problem probably worsened because of the lower rates of economic growth combined with demographic trends of the previous two decades. Perhaps the achievement of the Echeverría administration that will have the greatest long-term consequences was the institution of a population program. Except in the last days of the administration, there was no attempt to change the land tenure pattern significantly.

In retrospect, it appears the economic strategy adopted in the early 1970s responded to a number of urgent political rather than economic concerns. Mexican leaders have some grounds for their belief that by preserving their established political system, they are enhancing the country's long-term capacity for effective economic management and development. In this light, Echeverría's economic strategy is best evaluated not as a mere product of arbitrary and irresponsible personal leadership but as a rational attempt to reinvigorate that political system at the price of a certain loss of short-term economic equilibrium. Clearly, the short-term economic consequences were far more extensive than anticipated.

5. Policymaking in the Early López Portillo Years: Devaluation and Stabilization

On 13 September 1976, approximately two weeks after it had devalued the peso from 12.5 to nearly 23.0 per dollar, the Mexican government applied to the IMF for financial assistance in tackling its acute balance of payments difficulties. It required immediate assistance to replenish official foreign exchange reserves, and longer-term support while it implemented a three-year plan of economic stabilization intended to restore external and internal balance to the economy.

In his letter of intent to Director Witteveen of the IMF, on 13 September 1976, Treasury Secretary Mario Ramón Beteta explained the causes of Mexico's economic crisis as follows:

> The Mexican government maintained the level of national economic activity in the face of international recession by raising public expenditure. This caused pressures on the public finances despite the strong increase in government and public sector incomes. Unfortunately the combination of international inflation and recession and the financial costs of our efforts to reinforce key sectors of the economy with the consequent effects on the national price level, produced an adverse effect on our balance of payments. These disequilibria, both internal and external, accentuated the erosion of Mexico's international competitiveness. This loss of competitiveness began an economic upswing in which our economy did not participate to the degree we had anticipated.[1]

The Fund initially agreed to grant assistance, but insisted that many of the country's economic problems were largely the Mexican government's own doing, rather than of the adverse international developments blamed by that government. The Fund estimated that of the $2.4 billion added to Mexico's current account deficit between 1973 and 1975, only one-third could be attributed to factors beyond the responsibility of the government. The Fund also estimated that between 1973 and August 1976, Mexico's competitiveness had declined by 40 percent, implying that the equilibrium exchange rate was around 17.5 per dollar at the time of the devaluation. Clark Reynolds' analysis, however, indicates that the devaluation was more or less by the correct amount.[2]

While they differed as to the cause and extent of the exchange crisis, both the Mexican government and the Fund agreed that it would require at least several years to correct fully the imbalances that had been allowed to accumulate over the years. The following sections offer a preliminary evaluation of Mexico's experience with stabilization, and assess the apparent change in Mexico's development strategy.

The Stabilization Period

Judging the stabilization program on the basis of its limited objectives, it was mostly but by no means fully successful. The program aimed broadly to restore conditions conducive to higher rates of sustained growth, reduce inflation, and lower the current account deficit in the balance of payments to some level deemed acceptable in terms of external financing.

The Mexican government's agreement with the IMF imposed conditions on Mexico's external borrowing, its international reserve buildup, the deficit of its nonfinancial public sector, the net domestic assets of the Bank of Mexico, payments for current transactions, and the use of import restrictions for balance of payments purposes.[3]

This was only the second time any country had made use of the IMF extended facility. This facility, established in September 1974, was designed to mitigate the impact of stabilization measures by extending the time for implementation. Under the facility, Mexican repurchases (prepayments) would take place quarterly over four years, with the first repurchase beginning four years after the purchase (drawing).[4]

More specifically, the three-year (1977–79) agreement was made under the IMF's extended facility. Total IMF resources potentially available to Mexico under the agreement amounted to Special Drawing Right (SDR) 837.125 million ($965 million). In addition, the government could also draw on considerably larger reserves than even this amount. The October 1976 agreement with the Fund had been preceded in September by a bridge loan from the United States of up to $600 million. In addition, the Bank of Mexico and the Federal Reserve had a swap arrangement of up to $300 million.

As in all agreements of this nature, the Fund imposed a number of stipulations on the Mexican government, some of which had already been undertaken by the authorities. The list included the imposition of export taxes to prevent windfall profits from the peso devaluation and to augment government revenue, the suspension of many export incentives or tax rebates under the Mexican system of CEDIs (which had averaged 15 percent ad valorem before devaluation), and some dismantling of import license requirements. The Fund permitted subsidies and price controls for essential consumer goods and raw materials to remain in effect.

More importantly, however, the new program limited public borrowing from abroad during 1977 (including debts with maturities of less than one year) to $3 billion over the level of the disbursed public debt as of the end of 1976. Mexico's disbursed public debt with original maturity of more than one year was about $16 million at the end of 1976. If short-term debt is added, the total debt at that time was nearly $20 billion. Since Mexico's debt had been growing by about $4 billion a year for the previous three years, the $3 billion ceiling was clearly intended as an austerity measure.

Many observers felt the external borrowing limit would be less in 1978 than the previous year. However, the limit was maintained at $3 billion in both 1978 and 1979 largely to facilitate the massive borrowing needed for PEMEX's expansion.

As a result of these measures, Mexico's external public debt, including short-term debt, was $26.3 billion at the end of 1978 (about 35 percent of GDP). While this ratio was high by most standards, the country's expanded oil discoveries seemed capable of servicing such debt. As usual with Fund agreements, Mexico was obliged progressively to reduce the overall deficit of the public sector, increase public savings, increase its international reserves, and limit the increase in net domestic assets of the central bank.

To date, these guidelines seem to have been met more or less. Although the country has undertaken to moderate both public expenditures and foreign borrowing, the economy remains heavily dependent on state intervention, financed by large amounts of foreign borrowing. Thus, in 1978, the public sector's fiscal deficit was 162 billion pesos of which 69.7 billion (43 percent) was financed by borrowing abroad. The government's autonomous agencies, including most of the public industrial enterprises, obtained 86.8 percent of their financing from abroad. By the end of 1979, the Mexican government reported a net external debt of nearly $30 billion, the vast majority of which was owed to private sources.

The gross international reserves of the Bank of Mexico declined by about $300 million in 1976, to $1.3 billion, then recovered in 1977 and 1978 to about $2 billion. The public sector deficit declined from 9.5 percent in 1976 to 6.6 percent in 1977 but increased again to 7.5 percent in 1978. On the other hand, public sector savings increased from 0.3 percent of GDP in 1976 to 4.5 percent in 1978.

Immediate Effects of the 1976 Devaluation

One of the first and more direct impacts of the peso devaluation was a sharp increase in the price level. The money supply increased at an annual rate of 97.8 percent from September to December 1976.

In October 1976, shortly after the devaluation, there was a 22 percent emergency increase in minimum wages to compensate workers for the increase in import prices. However, minimum wages were increased by only 10 percent in 1977 and 12 percent in 1978, compared with inflation rates of 30 percent in 1977 and 17 percent in 1978. Price controls were liberalized substantially in February 1978.

The stabilization program seemed to be relatively successful in achieving its planned objectives at first. The inflation rate fell from 30 percent in 1977 to 17 percent in 1978. The deficit on current account was reduced by approximately U.S. $1,260 million in 1977. Finally, economic growth recovered and reached a rate of 6.6 percent in 1978.

But the devaluation together with the stabilization program also brought about a severe contraction of aggregate demand in 1977. There was a decline in investment together with a decrease in capital goods imports. In addition, the volume of real assets in the banking system contracted. Part of this decline was due to inflation, but investor apprehension also played a significant role.

Overall, the growth in GDP remained positive but small in 1977, recovering in 1978. There was an increase in industrial production of about 10 percent in 1978 compared with an average of around 7 percent in the previous decade. On the negative side, however, agriculture remained depressed. Inflation, though decelerating, remained above the levels targeted for the stabilization program. More than anything else, oil exports helped reduce the current account deficit as a percentage of GDP during the first several years of the program. Workers appear to have borne the brunt of the programs, as real wages declined in 1977 and 1978.

Employment

One of the central goals of the Mexican administration's development policy is to stimulate economic growth that will absorb the increase in the economically active population in productive employment and also lower the unemployment and underemployment rates. The long-range objective is to eliminate unemployment and underemployment. These objectives guide the country's industrial development strategy, and play a primary role in government policies on agriculture, livestock development policy, public sector investment, and the design of the overall economic policy system.

A comparison (using three-quarter moving averages) of the pattern of unemployment with that of the Industrial Production Volume Index for 1973-III to 1978-IV provides a number of insights as to the working of domestic labor markets. The longer-term trend in the volume of industrial production is especially important for these comparisons. In general, open unemployment tends to decrease as the industrial production index rises above the long-term trend and vice versa. From 1976-III to 1977-II, industrial production slowed down, causing the open unemployment rate to increase from 6.7 percent to 8.4 percent.[5]

While these figures seem to establish a link between industrial demand and employment, there is some evidence that the industrial sector's demand for labor is not excessively sensitive to changes in production, at least in the short term. One explanation is that institutional rigidities may prevent rapid adjustment of the supply of workers to increasing demand. Another explanation stresses the fact that businesses may anticipate that any variation in production significantly outside the trend will last only a short time. The result of these factors was an elasticity of labor demand.

Based on several surveys taken in 1977, it appears that almost a third of the country's 11.1 million households had underemployed workers, defined as economically active workers employed less than 40 hours per week. This proportion is much higher among households in the less urbanized areas (municipalities of less than 2,500 inhabitants). In the municipalities of more than 100,000 inhabitants and in the three major metropolitan areas, the proportion of households with underemployed workers decreases considerably, and in the metropolitan areas of Mexico City and Monterrey about 5 percent of the households had an underemployed worker.[6]

By 1979, the crisis was for all purposes over. President José López Portillo has since commented that his administration's initial plan was to devote two years to overcome the crisis, two years to consolidate the economy, and then the final two years to economic growth.

Monetary and Credit Policies

Beginning in 1977, the Mexican government designed its monetary and credit policies largely to reduce inflationary pressures, stimulate savings in Mexican currency, and expand credit to the private sector to stimulate overall economic recovery.[7] By and large, these policies achieved their credit objectives, increasing the flow of funds to the private sector. These funds played an important role in the recovery of investment activity.

Also in 1977, the Bank of Mexico initiated several measures enabling private and mixed banks to increase their lending capacity (in Mexican currency) to small and medium-sized firms. Four million pesos were earmarked under this plan to finance new fixed asset investment.

The López Portillo administration introduced a major program in 1978 to provide financial support to Mexican industry. The program included roughly 85 percent of the country's industry and entailed technical assistance, preinvestment studies, straight credit for working of investment capital, credit guarantees, stock participation, and loans for physical facilities. Technical assistance included the provision of information on the program itself, a diagnosis of whatever problems the company or the project may have, and the training of technical and professional staff. Two hundred and seventy million pesos were allocated for technical assistance over the first three years of the plan.

In addition, credit lines were to be extended for the purchase of equipment, the expansion of existing facilities, and the replacement of aging machinery. Although a good start, this total credit of 1.2 billion pesos is far from the amount currently needed by industry. To provide additional aid to industry, therefore, the government is also attempting to promote a larger and more efficient stock exchange.

Historically, the Mexican Stock Exchange (Bolsa de Valores) has not functioned as a major mobilizer of capital for Mexican enterprises. The volume of trading on the exchange has been small and has been concentrated in a few issues. Lack of secondary trading has made it difficult for companies to raise capital by selling stock to the public. Companies have received the bulk of their capital from bank credits and private investments, while individuals seeking to invest have preferred fixed income securities to equities.

Beginning in the early 1970s, however, the government announced the goal of developing the Bolsa, and steps have been taken in that direction. The government interest in building a viable stock market aimed at democratizing capital, diversifying the sources of capital for corporations, broadening the range of investment instruments, easing the raising of capital for Mexican companies at reasonable costs, and encouraging the process of "Mexicanizing" industry by increased participation of the public as stockholders.

Along these lines the government, acting through the Bank of Mexico, the Treasury Department, and the National Securities Commission, instituted in 1971 a formal program for developing and strengthening the securities market. The program aimed to diffuse corporate securities among the public by withdrawing advantages from other financial instruments (such as higher yields, lower taxes, and quasi-money liquidity), to reorganize the exchanges, to review the intermediary role of banks and finance companies in their competitive aspects with dealers and brokers, particularly in the field of underwriting, and to reorganize the regulation of the capital markets by strengthening the National Securities Commission and granting it new powers and resources, with a view to improving the quality of securities supervision over transactions and protection of the investing public.

López Portillo continued the trend toward stock market reform. During the first two years of his administration, the government moved to reactivate the market while fostering new issues of stocks and bonds, as well as their wider distribution among the public. At this time (1978), earnings of individuals made through buying or selling shares at the stock exchange were exempted from income tax. New issuing instruments, such as underwriter bonds, Petrobonds, and Federal Treasury certificates (to replace finance and mortgage bonds, which were scheduled to disappear from the market by October 1979), could be added to the market. In addition, credit institutions were induced to devote more resources to purchasing shares and to financing stockbrokers and their clients. The stockbrokers were given the necessary leeway so they could efficiently assume and fulfill their responsibilities within the stock market. Finally, legal modifications permitted the establishment of marketing institutions such as the Instituto para el Depósito de Valores (Securities Deposit Institute).

Clearly, the government intended to make the stock market an essential element in the country's economic development. With this goal in mind, the Law of the Stock Market was revised in May 1978 and amended for the purpose of defining public offers in stocks, bonds, and shares, stock brokerage, the Registro Nacional de Valores (National Stock Register). At the same time, the Instituto para el Depósito de Valores was established to satisfy the needs of the general public in the safekeeping, management, compensation, buying, selling, and other transactions of stocks, shares, and bonds.

The institute was granted the power, upon demand by stockbrokers, companies, or credit institutions, to become the depository of stocks, bonds, and shares of other securities issued; to manage the securities entrusted to it; to provide various services such as transfer, compensation, and selling of the securities deposited with it; and to carry out all operations in which it becomes a guarantor of the securities deposited with it.

Most observers believe that the 1978 law has promoted and strengthened the securities market. More and more companies are now able to meet their financial needs by placing shares on the exchange. For example, in 1979 thirty-three issues were placed on the market with twelve blocks coming from newly listed firms. Of the other twenty-one issues, one was a conversion while the remaining twenty were secondary placings (or issues made by corporations already listed on the exchange). The thirty-three offerings had a total face value 94 percent greater than that of the twenty-three public issues placed on the market in 1978. In 1979, overall increases of 47 percent and 70 percent, respectively, were obtained for value of shares and the volume of trading.

Of the thirty-three corporations that placed shares on the exchange during 1979, seven increased their capital by 100 percent of the sum total of issues; twenty-two sought to spread out their capital by offering shares to the public; one made a conversion; and three placed miscellaneous issues. Only 15 percent of the 85 billion pesos in shares placed on the exchange in 1979 belonged to the primary placement category. These 112,151,249 shares accounted for 13.2 percent of the total. While the stock market has greatly expanded in recent years, it still plays a very limited role in aiding small and medium-scale industry.

Luis R. Luis found that government policies during this period may have been well conceived, because the gradual stabilization approach followed may have avoided a considerable amount of unemployment that harsher measures might have caused.[8] Two policy simulations of the economy were carried out by Luis to demonstrate the impact of alternative programs. Simulation I describes a drastically contradictory monetary-fiscal policy, amounting to a 10 percent annual reduction in the growth of the nominal money supply. In essence, that assumption means either a drastically reduced consolidated public deficit or an unlikely significant increase in net foreign public sector borrowing, given no changes in the tax structure. Simulation II is what Luis refers to as a "crawling peg" simulation. It assumes the exchange rate is adjusted (starting in 1973-I) at a quarterly rate equivalent to the overall devaluation that took place between 1976-II and 1978-IV. In other words, it is not identical to the government's programs but undoubtedly more gradual than that suggested by the IMF. It is the most gradual of the drastic exchange rate adjustments of the last four months of 1976. In this simulation, a gradualist monetary policy smooths out the fluctuations in the money supply trend, consistent with the same long-term expansion rate that actually occurred.

The drastic stabilization implied in Simulation I does achieve the twin objectives of reducing the inflation rate and eliminating the current account deficit in the balance of payments. The average inflation rate was reduced to 13.9 percent (from 23.6 percent in Luis's basic simulation), and the current account balance was always positive. Real income growth averaged 1.1 percent annually compared to 4.9 percent in the basic simulation. Simulation I, however, reached a maximum rate of open unemployment of 10.4 percent, one full point above the basic simulation, reflecting the adverse effect of the implied drastic monetary slowdown.

Simulation II lowered the average inflation rate as well as its maximum value in relation to the basic simulation. It also reduced the maximum value for the current account deficit. More importantly, it lowered the maximum level for the open unemployment rate to 8.5 percent (from 9.4 percent in the basic simulation results). Average real income growth was not affected.

The "crawling peg" simulation reduced the variance of both the current account balance and the unemployment rate vis-à-vis the two other simulations. The drastic stabilization scheme in Simulation I did best, on the other hand, in reducing the variance of prices.

In the present context, it is particularly important that the two significantly different policies simulated both had relatively low short-term effects on labor demand and the open unemployment rate. While this result should be interpreted with the greatest caution, it nonetheless provides some evidence as to the likely cost of stabilization programs for an important labor market indicator. On the other hand, the larger impact on real income may have important implications for other labor market indicators that strive to measure underemployment. In that broader sense, the results do indicate that the costs of drastic stabilization programs may be quite high in Mexico.[9]

Assessment of the Stabilization Effort

Luis's results suggest that the stabilization program itself was generally effective. Yet it is extremely difficult at this point to quantify the extent to which its apparent success was due to the government's sound policies and how much was simply the result of fortuitous events such as the oil discoveries and the fall in international agricultural prices.

It may well be that the deceleration in the rate of inflation was largely due to the declines in international agricultural prices. The drop in inflation and wage increases may therefore be largely unrelated to the fiscal and monetary policies implemented by the government. The net effects of the peso devaluation on the level of prices and on the distribution of income may have reinforced rather than compensated for the negative effects of the government's fiscal and monetary policies on the level of economic activity. The increase in export profit margins and size of the foreign debt stemming from the devaluation could be partially responsible for the inability of the country to eliminate its balance of payments disequilibrium. In any case, devaluation due to the low elasticity of demand for agricultural products with respect to relative prices and real aggregate income, together with the importance of agriculture's surplus in the balance of payments, would not be expected to correct the disequilibrium completely.

The main effect of the devaluation may have been on industrial goods. The reduction in the industrial trade deficit in 1977 could have stemmed from the relative price changes between imports and exports caused by the devaluation. In addition, the effects of devaluation were most likely only temporary. By 1978 inflation may have eroded away the competitive price advantages devaluation had created in the first place. If this is true, by 1978 the trade deficit had reached the level it probably would have attained without devaluation (leaving out oil).

While admittedly speculative, this interpretation does provide useful insights into the basic mechanisms at work in the Mexican economy. The nonoil deficit in the trade balance (as a proportion of GDP) resumed its upward trend in 1978, in contrast to the overall deficit. It is worth noting that in 1978 the nonoil trade deficit (as a proportion of GDP) was far greater than in 1971, and this occurred despite the fact that the 1977–78 recession was more severe than the 1971 downturn.

These developments suggest that the economy is prone to a growing imbalance in the current account of the balance of payments, slow growth of output, and high rates of unemployment and inflation. Orthodox policies—such as monetary, fiscal, or exchange rate policies—are often incapable of dealing with the interaction of these three factors.

Oil exports may provide the country with the best means of breaking this vicious cycle. Oil revenues enabled public investment to expand by 18 percent in real terms in 1979. Private investment partly stimulated by this increase rose at a similar rate. In 1980, public and private investment grew by 17 and 15 percent, respectively. Large industrial projects are being implemented with Mexican capital and also with foreign capital (especially from the United States, Japan, Sweden, Germany, France, and Canada). Mexico is not only using its oil to earn foreign exchange, but also to acquire modern industrial technology. The government appears committed to expanding the country's industrial base with foreign technology so as to create sufficient employment in nonoil activities. The government's goal is to eliminate unemployment and underemployment by the end of the century.

Unfortunately, this whole process increased already strong inflationary pressures. In large part, investment has increased without generating sufficient domestic savings. Thus, by 1980 the country suffered from a Keynesian inflationary gap. The public sector deficit began increasing, and by 1982 it was around 16 percent of GDP, clearly approaching dangerous levels. By 1980, consumption expenditures as a whole began increasing at about 5 percent per year in real terms. Inflation has also encouraged anticipatory spending and has discouraged current savings. High bank interest rates have had an adverse effect on small industry, agriculture, and housing. Several studies have suggested that foreign firms may not provide much direct competition for domestic producers.[10]

Impact of Devaluation on Labor

In recent years, the Mexican government has made a number of special efforts to strengthen the dialogue between workers and management. The National Tripartite Commission (a consultant agency created by the Echeverría administration and made up of labor, management, and federal government representatives) has played a leading role in the effort to achieve a national consensus on major problems in housing, wage protection, productivity, employment, manpower training, nationwide management of human resources, and the general improvement of working conditions.

In this context, a number of agencies were established in the early-to-mid-1970s including: the National Joint Wage Protection Committee, the National Development and Guarantee Fund for Workers' Consumption, the National Labor Information and Statistics Center, and the National Institute of Labor Studies and Labor Legislation.

In general, Mexican labor organizations have been characterized by their overlapping jurisdictions.[11] Mexican law has never regulated the structure of the labor movement. As a result, no one labor group—whether organized on a craft, industrial, or geographic basis—has ever had a complete jurisdictional monopoly. Local organizations are affiliated with regional or national federations and confederations. For example, Mexico's largest labor group, the Mexican Workers' Confederation (CTM), incorporates no less than 59 to 70 percent of all union members. Unions have a considerable impact on the day-to-day work environment in Mexico. They negotiate collective agreements, enforce them, present grievances, and represent workers in Mexico's labor courts. In addition, unions control hiring through the operation of closed shops, which prevail in virtually all Mexican collective agreements.

The unions use collective bargaining as a major means of exerting their power. Mexico's Revised Labor Law expressly requires employers to bargain collectively with a union if it has membership among their employees and if it demands such bargaining. With over 50 percent of the country's nonagricultural labor force organized at this time, collective bargaining is therefore very common. If more than one union claims representation at a plant or firm, the Revised Labor Law designates the body with the largest representation as labor's bargaining agent.

In recent years, the CTM has campaigned vigorously for two major reforms. The first is a reduction of the work week from 48 to 44 hours. Until this change is incorporated in the body of Mexico's labor laws the CTM has urged its affiliates to press for a reduced work week in collective bargaining sessions.

The second and more recent reform desired by the CTM is a change in Mexico's federal labor laws so that escalator clauses can be incorporated officially in labor contracts. The government, however, has not been receptive to suggestions for wage indexing, arguing that such measures would make it more difficult to control inflation. Employer groups are also not enthusiastic about this scheme, arguing that indexing would deprive them even more of any control over wage negotiations and wage cost movements.

Management associations also exist in Mexico. Firms capitalized at 500 pesos or more are legally obliged to join an official national chamber of commerce. These groups, such as the Confederation of Industrial Chambers (Confederacion de Camaras Industriales, CONCAMIN) and the Confederation of National Chambers of Commerce (Confederación Nacional de Cámaras de Comercio, CONCANACO) have also cultivated close government ties, although they have much less power than their labor counterparts.

The government is increasingly concerned with the growth of splinter labor groups in Mexico and with the CTM's weakening influence on the country's labor movement. These concerns may eventually lead the government to meet both of the CTM's current demands. The CTM itself, however, is beginning to lose some control over Mexico's rank and file. Inflation and the 10 percent wage increase ceiling in effect from December 1976 to August 1977 seriously tarnished the CTM's reputation as labor's top bargaining agent.

The changing influence of the CTM is best evidenced by increased worker restlessness during the last several years.[12] Beginning around 1978, workers in general have shown an increasing tendency toward independent action and veering away from the CTM. Apparently, many workers feel that the CTM agreed too easily to government restraints during this period, particularly to limits on wage increases, to the detriment of labor interests.

The result was an increasing number of strikes. In large part, the strikes were over purely economic issues. In light of an annual inflation rate of around 20 percent, many of the country's workers were unsatisfied with the CTM-government agreement limiting wage increases to 12 percent, an integral part of the government's post-1976 devaluation-stabilization program. Workers were particularly unlikely to accept this policy given that wages and salaries had increased by only 10 percent in the previous year (1977) while inflation was increasing to 20 percent.

One of the most dramatic labor disputes in 1978 was in the textile industry, which negotiates on an industrywide basis. After a strike that lasted twenty-one days, workers were able to obtain a wage increase of 23 pesos a day, the equivalent of an 18.1 percent for those earning the sector's minimum wage of 127 pesos per day and more than 15 percent for the rest of the industry's workers.

The political connotations of labor stoppages that ostensibly centered on economic issues were undoubtedly the most worrying aspect of these developments for the government and the CTM. The unions outside the CTM gained strength from the disparity between inflation and wage increases, which eroded the purchasing power of workers. Workers—spurred on by the dissidents—claimed that excessive collaboration between their leaders and the government was detrimental to labor interests. Other factors contributing to political conflict were the tactical and strategic reorganization of some independent groups; the political reform carried out by the López Portillo administration, which allowed into the country's political system groups such as the Mexican Communist party (PCM) and the Workers' Socialist party (PST); the lack of cohesion within the traditional labor structure; the often incoherent way in which the CTM's leaders handled attacks by independent groups; and the apparent lack of concern within the López Portillo administration over the rise of the independents.

Labor unrest carried over into 1979 with collective bargaining sessions characterized by increasing union militancy, unwillingness on the part of many labor groups to compromise with employers, and strong demands to increase wages and fringe benefits. In general, labor tended to regain some of its purchasing power lost in 1977 and 1978. The trend toward increased fringe benefits also continued, with subsidized food and housing the most sought-after goals. The traditional labor syndicates, particularly those associated with the CTM, showed a certain weakness. The López Portillo administration did not—as expected—step up its efforts to control the independent labor groups, in part because of its desire to pacify workers after two difficult years. However, the administration showed itself most anxious to avoid excessive wage demands, ostensibly to prevent them from adding further to inflationary pressures. This attitude was one of the major causes of unrest throughout the year.

In short, the labor sector confronted the major problem characterizing the economy in the postdevaluation period— inflation at around 20 percent, coupled with a governmental insistence that wage increases be held to 13.5 percent. The result was numerous conflicts with the inevitable strikes. Many large private companies had to grant wage increases of 17–18 percent to maintain labor tranquility. Smaller firms were unable to match these settlements and suffered prolonged strikes before reaching agreements closer to the government's guideline.

In the late 1970s, therefore, the labor movement and its indispensable pillar, the union organization framework, were under a two-dimensional attack. In addition to the problems brought about by the overall economic situation, labor leaders also had to face internal pressures resulting from discontent within their own ranks. The main internal problem of the labor movement was the continued gaining of ground by the independent unions against the more traditional organizations.

In addition, the infiltration of dissidents into the ranks of the CTM, with the resultant weakening of its member unions, began to create a serious problem for firms. With increasing frequency, managers were becoming involved in negotiations with union leaders who did not represent a majority of the workers. The end result was an increasing tendency for strikes to linger on even after a new contract had been signed.

The changing nature of the country's industrial relations is illustrated by the 1979 telephone workers' strike, the third in a year. This strike was unusual since it involved a state company traded on the stock exchange and offering a public service of social and economic importance and a union comprised of relatively elite groups of workers who, along with the petroleum and electrical groups, were also state employees. Thus, the telephone workers' union was not isolated from the country's institutional political structure, as were the independent unions. On the contrary, it was a leading member of the Congreso del Trabajo from which it had received a good deal of political support.

The conflict was aggravated by the controversy about the legality of the government's takeover of the telephone system, which the government justified as necessary to preserve some semblance of operating service. The strike took place precisely at the climax of an election campaign for federal deputies (the first under the new election reform). In the end, a presidential exhortation was required on Labor Day to end the dispute.

By 1980, the country's industrial relations were still strained by the tensions accumulated during the previous three years of declining real wages. Developments during that year suggest the basic trends in the country's industrial relations system. First, workers felt a drop in their purchasing power more intensely than in previous years. This was in turn translated into strikes and increased union political activity. In addition, an attempt was made to create two important new labor unions: that of the university workers, who wanted a single organization to represent their interests, and that of the bank workers. Neither one of these efforts was successful, but both were supported by the rank and file of the country's labor unions and by the leader of the Congreso del Trabajo, the country's top labor organization.

In sum, the Mexican labor force is more or less divided into two equal blocs—the great majority of the half that has full employment is unionized, particularly in the public sector; the other half is without work and therefore not organizable. It is in the interest of the fortunate half to maintain its position, and many of the actions of the CTM and other established unions can be understood in this context.

The reasons for labor stability become even clearer when the position of unionized workers is contrasted with that of the great mass of the poor. Millions of poor live in squalid conditions, which have changed little over the centuries. They depend for their livelihood on such activities as cleaning shoes, selling chewing gum, and tilling a patch of parched land. Few of the employed workers are going to risk their jobs when there are so many willing replacements.

In the last several years, the salaries of unionized workers have not kept pace with inflation, but they have fared far better than the millions of unemployed Mexicans who do not even receive the legal minimum wage on the rare occasions when they can find some regular work. Union members, on the other hand, have seen their wages increase every year in line with the rise in the minimum wage, if not by even greater amounts. Skilled workers in particular are in great demand and can negotiate even higher increases.

In general, the real living standard of workers covered by labor legislation appears to have improved from 1960 to 1976; during that time nominal daily minimum wages increased from 9.89 to 78.81 pesos. Between 1960 and 1972, salaries increased at an annual rate of 9.5 percent, an amount considerably above the rate of consumer price inflation. During 1972–77 nominal salaries increased 21.9 percent a year, an annual increase of about 3.1 percent in real salaries. While the nominal minimum salary doubled between 1974 and 1977, it is likely this was more in response to price increases rather than reflecting real income gains.

In September 1976, before the stabilization effort began, there was a general emergency wage adjustment of 23 percent to maintain purchasing power following the devaluation. Thereafter, wage policy became part of the adjustment, with workers bearing the brunt of the reduction in domestic demand. On 1 January 1977, minimum wages were adjusted upward by only 10 percent; the September 1977 (covering work in 1978) pay increase for government employees had a ceiling of 10 percent. The government wage guideline for contractual settlements was set at 12 percent. Minimum wage increases differentiated by urban and rural areas and by level of wages averaged 4.5 percent nationally in 1978, and 18.6 percent in 1979. Actual wage and salary increases did not greatly exceed these norms in 1978.

The disadvantaged groups in Mexico surely were the unemployed and underemployed rather than waged or salaried workers. Although real wages declined during the first two years of the stabilization program, they had increased during the previous years of growing inflation.

The share of total income going to the lowest income group deteriorated during the Echeverría period. This change indicates the plight of unorganized Mexican workers all through the 1970s. Clearly, the underemployed and unemployed, particularly in rural areas, benefited least from educational and health services provided by the state.

Conclusions

Among the major criticisms of IMF stabilization programs in the past have been that the conditions imposed by the Fund required too rapid an adjustment, were applied indiscriminately to all countries without sufficient regard to domestic political circumstances, and imposed too great a burden on the poorest groups in the society.[13] The Mexican stabilization program scores well on the first two points. The stabilization effort was spread over three years by the agreement with the IMF. While some rapid policy shifts were required, particularly in slowing expenditure growth in the public sector, this gradual program permitted Mexico to reduce the hardships suffered in the society generally. In this sense, the program did not ignore the country's political realities. In addition, the program was altered once it was clear that oil discoveries had changed Mexico's balance of payments position.

It is much more difficult to assess the third point since there is no standard of comparison showing how well or badly the poorer groups would have done in the absence of the program.[14] Clearly, unemployment (and underemployment) were severe before the stabilization program, as was income inequality. For those who had jobs, wage and salary increases reduced their burden somewhat. In addition, stabilization measures permitted subsidies of vital consumer goods to continue, in order to mitigate the hardships on the lower-income groups.

Mexico was fortunate in the timing of its program. The program coincided with the discovery of large oil and gas reserves and the beginnings of increased earnings from petroleum exports. Imports of goods and services grew as a percentage of GDP (from 13.5 percent in 1976 to 14.0 percent in 1977), but exports increased at an even greater rate (9.2 to 11.1 percent). The timing of the program also coincided with periods of high growth in the United States, facilitating Mexico's export growth. Contrary to anticipations, the balance of payments constraint under the program did not impose a great hardship.

Again, whether Mexico came through this period as a result of good luck or good planning (or both) is a question not yet resolved. The 1982 devaluation of the peso has swung some opinion toward the good luck explanation.[15]

6. Industrial Policy under López Portillo

Until 1981, the López Portillo administration had developed what seemed to be a fairly coherent set of economic plans and policies to achieve goals upon which nearly all of Mexico's political elites agreed. In large part, López Portillo's industrial policies were simply an extension of past objectives and approaches. These policies had evolved within the general context of Mexico's nationalism vis-à-vis the United States, and reflected the view prevalent within the country that as a newly industrializing country Mexico suffered severe trade and other economic disadvantages for which petroleum might provide at best a temporary solution.[1]

Assumptions Underlying Mexican Industrial Policy

Mexican development policies have been based on the beliefs that, first of all, Mexico does not have the industrial capacity to compete with the United States on an equal basis. It lacks the technology, infrastructure, and trained technicians to compete except in a few very specific areas.[2] Second, Mexico is also vulnerable to decisions of foreign investors, capital flight of the kind that forced devaluation in 1976, and the general weakness of the peso vis-à-vis the dollar, given free currency convertibility between the two countries. Third, high unemployment and high inflation also make Mexico dependent on the United States for temporary employment.

Nearly all Mexican policymakers agree on a series of general economic objectives.[3] They see an urgent need to reduce the unemployment and underemployment rate, which may be over 40 percent. The Mexican economy must create 525,000 new jobs every year simply to stay even with the 3 percent-plus population growth rate. Planners also agree on the need to ease what is one of the most inequitable income distribution patterns in Latin America. These goals require a sophisticated manufacturing export base to provide jobs and take on the burden of maintaining economic growth as petroleum reserves decline over a twenty-year period, and a much more solid base for agriculture, both for food self-sufficiency and for export.

To meet these goals the López Portillo administration presented a series of development plans laying out in detail targets and strategies to guide government and private sector activity through the end of that administration (1982) and beyond. This action was unprecedented, as no prior Mexican president had ever made an effort to set out policy guidelines for his successor. The planning documents included a Global Development Plan, eight sectoral plans, state plans, and the Mexican Food System (SAM). These documents were not of equal importance. One of the sectoral plans, called the 1979–90 National Development Plan (NIDP), and the slightly more recent 1979–82 Global Development Plan, which compiled various sectoral targets and strategies, were the two key documents. The Mexican Food System emphasized the agricultural sectors of the GDP.[4]

Both the NIDP and the GDP emphasize employment as a key goal. Both rely on very rapid economic growth rates of 8 percent per year through the 1980s to achieve their employment goals. Growth is to be led by exports; principal exports for the present are expected to be petroleum and petroleum derivatives, but manufactured exports are planned to account for an increasing share of foreign exchange earnings. An industrial growth rate of 11 percent is projected by the GDP; this in turn is expected to require a 15–20 percent growth in exports through 1982. The 8 percent overall growth rate is seen as necessary to achieve even a modest growth of 4 percent in employment, (enough to keep slightly ahead of population growth).[5] The NIDP deals almost entirely with industry. It sets targets for 83 industries, with particularly high growth rates planned for oil, petrochemicals, construction, electricity, and manufacturing.[6]

In short, by 1980 it was apparent the the Mexican authorities anticipated that they would be able to achieve a series of related objectives: (1) increase employment through rapid growth; (2) increase labor participation in economic growth through significant increases in real wages; (3) rejuvenate rainfed agriculture and achieve food self-sufficiency through government investment, tax and other incentives, and bureaucratic reforms; (4) diversify exports away from petroleum and primary materials by increasing domestic manufacturing and by penetrating international markets; (5) diversify export markets, thus reducing dependence on the United States; (6) create a strong capital goods industry through selective import substitution; (7) use petroleum as a fundamental instrument not only to achieve internal economic goals but as a key tool in international commercial and other negotiations with the United States and other industrialized countries; (8) decentralize the economy by developing major growth in regions of the country outside the Mexico City and Guadalajara region through government investment and more decentralized private investment; and (9) use foreign investment policy and regulation of technology transfer as another fundamental instrument to achieve employment, industrialization, and export goals, while maintaining indigenous managerial control over firms with foreign capital participation.

The National Industrial Development Plan

The National Industrial Development Plan (1979–82) represented the government's attempt to move the economy to the next stage of industrialization.[7] The major strategy of the plan involved integrating petroleum revenues into general industrial development so as to ensure more enduring benefits from the development of the hydrocarbon sector. The fundamental objectives of the plan were to eliminate unemployment and underemployment, in addition to improving the general welfare of the population.

The principal objective of the plan was to implement an industrial investment strategy consistent with increasing employment in the country by 5 percent a year over the period 1979–82.[8] This would itself be consistent with a rate of increase in real GNP of between 8 and 10 percent for the same period. The plan anticipated that industry would absorb 30 percent of the yearly employment increase in the economy.

The plan's strategy is to revise the present trends of Mexican industrialization by increasing the production of basic consumer goods, developing industries capable of exporting or efficiently substituting imports, integrating the industrial structure to more efficiently use the country's natural resources, promoting capital goods production, decentralizing economic activities, and supporting medium- and small-scale enterprises.

To these ends, the plan establishes an order of priorities for subsectors, regions, and small enterprises. The criteria for establishing the subsectoral priorities are type of products (basic consumer or strategic products), origin of inputs, and macroeconomic effects. On this basis, seventy priority industrial branches are identified and classified into two groups. The first includes agro-industry, capital goods, and strategic inputs such as cement and steel. The second includes other basic consumption goods and industrial inputs that are widely used. The plan calls for massive state investments and numerous incentives to private investors.

More specifically, the National Industrial Development Plan projects investments in those sectors likely to make efficient use of the country's relatively abundant labor and natural resources. As a result, the plan allocates significant funds for investment in labor-intensive activities. However, to use the country's hydrocarbons efficiently, a number of capital-intensive projects are also planned. In general, basic consumer goods (mainly food) and energy constitute the main thrust of the plan, with machinery and equipment manufacture also receiving high priority.

One of the plan's important objectives is to modify market structures to generate more competition in a number of key industrial areas by reducing as much as possible existing oligopolistic power. The plan stresses access to markets for greater numbers of large firms in those sectors where economies of scale result in more efficient production. On the other hand, the plan will attempt to stimulate the growth of small- and medium-sized enterprises through fiscal and financial incentives, so that they can fulfill an important role as suppliers to larger enterprises and in the direct production of final consumption goods.

The National Industrial Development Plan stresses the need for industrial decentralization, and in this sense is consistent with the government's stated (1977) goal of territorial decentralization. A series of fiscal, credit, and administrative ordinances and guidelines for executing federal government projects are intended to encourage the development of priority zones. These include the four industrial ports of Coatzacoalcos, Lázaro Cárdenas, Salina Cruz, and Tampico, and their surrounding municipalities as well as other industrial cities. Other zones whose industrial development will be encouraged have also been designated in agreement with state governments. Finally, the metropolitan area of Mexico City has been declared an area of controlled growth.

The main policy instruments to be used in stimulating the private sector include fiscal incentives, financial supports, industrial promotion mechanisms, development and regulation of technology, and promotion of investment projects. The price system for basic energy resources should provide a strong incentive for industrial development in priority geographic areas. The maintenance of energy resource prices and tariffs below their international cost should also provide an incentive to industrial development.

Industrial development measures in the plan follow sectoral, regional, and seasonal criteria. Differential energy resource pricing is based on regional criteria, while fiscal incentives take into account the need to stimulate labor demand and other social considerations. The structure of protection, based on duties rather than licenses and quantitative discretional controls, only takes into account the policies established for each industrial activity. A central aspect of the plan involves stimulating manufactured exports. The plan favors those sectors where use of the country's national and human resources is likely to give firms a comparative advantage.

Enterprises with foreign capital play an important role in the plan, particularly when they provide access to foreign markets and to technologies available abroad. The plan anticipates identifying areas where foreign participation should be encouraged. Each foreign investment project will be negotiated according to existing legislation and will stipulate the type of technology transfer and conditions for the eventual transfer of capital to Mexican nationals.

Mexico's future growth patterns are closely linked to the potential surplus earnings from the export of hydrocarbons. These resources give the country the means to greater financial independence. More important, oil revenues may enable the government to revitalize the economy while addressing a number of the structural problems that built up in the 1950s and 1960s.

The strategy contemplated by the government consists of three phases. The first stage calls for a solution to the 1976 crisis by lifting restrictions enforced after the peso devaluation. By 1980, this phase was completed. Economic activity had recovered, due largely to increased government investment and wage restraint on the part of the working classes.

The second phase of the strategy consists of consolidating past development gains while striving toward increased economic self-sufficiency. Achievement of this goal should facilitate accelerated growth during the last two years of the López Portillo administration. The third phase would be a prolonged one—at least for the duration of the 1980s where hopefully high rates of economic growth would eventually enable the economy both to absorb the annual increases in the labor force and to eliminate the existing residual unemployment and underemployment.

A basic premise of the plan was that there should be no social or political justification for an economic strategy that did not aspire to end unemployment, the most serious of the national problems. This strategy required the achievement of higher economic growth rates in ways compatible with increasing employment. In this way, the government hoped to achieve another fundamental objective of the plan: guaranteed minimum welfare for the whole population.

Government planners felt that complete realization of the above goals would require reorganizing production toward basic consumer goods, which provide the mainstay of adequate remunerative work, together with the development of high-productivity sectors for export and efficient import substitutions. In addition, they argued that the nation's industrial structure should be reorganized to take greater advantage of the country's natural resources, to develop sectors such as plant and machinery manufacture, to decentralize economic activity by directing investment toward the coasts, frontiers, and other selected locations seen as viable alternatives to the existing industrial centers, and to balance market structures by attacking oligopolistic tendencies in the most dynamic industries and amalgamating the larger firms with medium- and small-sized firms.

To enable the strategy to work, its objectives would have to be translated into specific, consistent aims in phases. This would be Mexico's first systematic effort at planned economic development.

Assessment of the Plan

The National Industrial Development Plan presents an ambitious program aimed at effectively using the country's increased foreign exchange earnings. The plan to move industrialization into the domestic production of capital goods and export of intermediate goods seems realistic in light of the country's stage of industrialization and development requirements. The plan is also realistic in aiming to strengthen long-term trends rather than proposing a radical redirection of the economy. The decision to support the private sector, but to expand state intervention as a substitute if no private response is forthcoming, is quite consistent with the tradition of Mexican economic policy since the revolution. It is not realistic in that it underestimates the inflationary impact of the government's expenditures and overestimates the country's likely oil revenues during the plan period.

Of course, the success of Mexico's industrial development will not hinge completely on the plan. The attitudes of foreign firms and U.S. policymakers will also be critical in shaping the country's pattern of growth.

In addition, the parity of the peso and the real wage rate will be crucial for the development of manufactured exports. Clearly, the relative rise of both the value of the peso and the wage rate would depress the profitability of labor-intensive exports. Unfortunately, this has been common in oil-exporting countries. Finally, the scope of Mexico's manufactured exports will depend in large part upon the farsightedness of the U.S. government and the capacity of the United States to restructure its economy away from traditionally labor-intensive items such as textiles and automobile parts, or resource-intensive items such as steel and cement, toward technologically advanced branches of industry. There is little indication, however, that U.S. policymakers are capable of implementing a policy along these lines.

Obstacles to Industrial Policy Reform

Mexico's economic and political system underwent a considerable change in the 1970s. The slowing down of growth in the early 1970s, and the student movements and their repression by the police in 1968 and 1971, were crucial political events that made it imperative to reform the system as quickly as possible. The main objective of political reform was to open up the power structure to new groups that had been kept outside until then—especially middle class intellectuals—and to commit the government to solving political problems by political means, not by force or administrative decisions.

By the end of the 1960s, it was clear to most observers that growth per se could no longer be Mexico's economic objective. Changes were needed to spread benefits more widely while maintaining steady economic expansion. In other words, a consensus was growing among Mexican economists that structural changes would have to be made to meet these objectives. In trying to achieve such objectives, a number of political and social forces had to be dealt with, many of which actually thwarted the government's efforts.[9]

Both political and economic changes were undertaken at the same time (mainly 1972–76) and were so closely connected that they cannot be judged as two separate processes. Any evaluation has been made even more difficult by the results not coinciding in time. An important initial step in describing these attempts to modify the country's industrial strategy is the identification of the forces that were opposed to change, and in very general terms the major reasons for their opposition.[10]

National Entrepreneurs' Organizations

Domestic producers' associations have often formed one of the most important impediments to changes in industrial policy in Mexico. Proposals for import liberalization have traditionally aroused entrepreneurial opposition and threats of harsh retaliation against the government, especially from small producer groups. The first line of opposition usually emerges from within the administration where the private sector's case is represented by the governmental agencies with authority over the affected groups of firms. The agencies often have dealt with representatives of these firms on a daily basis and in many cases have become quite sympathetic to their problems. Government officials who are ideologically identified with entrepreneurial attitudes also tend to defend what they perceive as the private producer's best interests.

While not strictly an industrial matter, the ill-fated tax reform of 1972 illustrates the forces at work most vividly. After the government announced its intention to press for changes in the structure of taxes together with an increase in their level, it appears the first opposition actually came from within the agencies in charge of financial institutions and policies. The officials argued that the tax reform would damage financial stability and growth, might provoke an attack on the peso, and would make it difficult to defend the peso. The private financial sector repeated these arguments almost verbatim. In addition, the private sector representatives pointed out the adverse impact of the tax reform on investors' confidence, which at that time barely was recovering from the impact of the 1971 recession. Within a short time, the private sector prevented any change whatsoever.

An industrial matter illustrating the constraints on government action came in 1980 with the decision of the government not to join GATT. The Mexican government had favored membership and had extensive discussions with GATT officials in Geneva. The government maintained that it had negotiated liberal terms of entry, for the country would be allowed to eliminate its system of import licenses over 12 years, except on some agricultural goods. In anticipation of membership, the government had even begun supplanting import permits with tariffs in an effort to conform with GATT protocol.

The government's thinking on seeking GATT entry centered on two alternatives: either Mexico must use its oil revenues to develop just internally, or the country must use its oil to strengthen the already strong industrial base but weak agricultural base in such a way as to develop both internally and externally. The government felt GATT membership was an important starting point in the country's greater involvement in international affairs.[11]

Mexico was obliged to accept certain conditions on joining GATT. The country would have to continue eliminating import permits, which it probably would have done in any case. More important, import concessions would have to be given to 300 products already imported (worth about $504 million a year). The country would then have received similar concessions on 260 of its export items (worth about $656 million).

The protocol for GATT membership specified that Mexico would not be subject to the general obligations contained in part two of the GATT code, which deal with dismantling the protective apparatus. The only danger was that "if Mexico did not make an effort to eliminate the official prices for customs valuation of imports, then the contracting partners would examine the question in 1985."[12] Mexico's only obligation was to inform GATT every two years about its program of substituting tariffs for import permits. Twelve years after the protocol entered into force the contracting parties would examine the remaining restrictions.

The 300 items on which Mexico would have to give concessions represented 8.6 percent of the country's total imports. On 152 of them (representing 3 percent of imports), permits would have been eliminated immediately, but 90 of these would have carried import tariffs higher than they had immediately prior to the debate over membership.

Clearly, joining GATT would barely have affected the degree of protection granted Mexican industry. Faced with these facts, the reasons given for not joining GATT are quite weak. Critics of GATT cited limits to the "flexibility" of the nation's development, but these objections do not hold up in view of the wide exceptions established in the protocol. The objection to "imprecisions in the norms derived from the so-called codes of conduct" is invalidated by the same exceptions made for Mexico's benefit. The argument that Mexico would be impeded from reducing petroleum exports if it did not also reduce internal oil consumption is weakened because Article 20 of the protocol nowhere obliges Mexico to follow that line of behavior.[13] Four members of OPEC and seven net petroleum exporters belong to GATT, and that membership has not stopped them from reducing their exports when convenient. This history undermines any criticism of possible membership based on control of oil exports.

Opponents of GATT membership, however, include such influential organizations as the National College of Economists, elements of the Labor Congress —the trade union umbrella organization of the Institutional Revolutionary Party (PRI), various parts of the private sector, and left-wing political parties. These groups argued that Mexico is not sufficiently developed to join GATT and that membership would place industry at a great disadvantage. They also argued that small companies would be put out of business, unemployment would increase, and Mexico would be subjected even more to the interests of multinationals. The left put forward this latter argument as a way of playing on anti-U.S. feelings inherent in the Mexican character.[14]

The Mexican private sector was about equally divided on the question of membership, with the powerful Employers Confederation (COPARMEX) and the private sector coordinating council in favor of membership, and the Manufacturing Industries Chamber (CAMACINTRA) vehemently opposed to membership.[15]

COMPARMEX and the council maintained that GATT membership would eliminate the protectionism under which Mexican industry had developed, and was inadequate to make the nation's products really competitive in international markets. CAMACINTRA's position was that GATT entry would deprive the country of the chance to legislate its own future and could make it into a chronic exporter of natural resources rather than manufactured goods. CAMACINTRA claimed that more trade liberalization would make Mexico totally dependent upon imports of all kinds because domestic industry would not be able to compete with foreign products. CAMACINTRA argued that GATT membership would discourage protection and Mexico would have to rely more and more on its oil exports, which is what in fact the GATT members wanted. CAMACINTRA also felt that GATT membership would mean the massive bankruptcy of small and medium-sized industry in Mexico.

As one observer has noted:

> The months before the decision were characterized by a vociferous publicity campaign launched by protected industry which has lived for three decades

> or more outside the competitive international standards accepted by the 85 nations with whom Mexico maintains 99 percent of its foreign trade. The campaign against the GATT made it look as though Mexico would cease all protectionism at once, allowing a flood of imports to drown its own industry, destroying millions of jobs, obliging the nation to exist on petroleum exports alone.[16]

In sum, much of industry was opposed to the move, arguing that the country would be swamped by imported goods and as a result many workers would lose their jobs. The government position was that with the captive domestic market already largely satisfied, industry could only continue to grow—and create more jobs—by learning to export. They argued that South Korea and Brazil among others had previously chosen this path out of underdevelopment.[17]

After the government decided not to join GATT on 18 March 1980, Alan Robinson noted that "everyone with any official standing in Mexico has spoken in fulsome terms of the president's political wisdom in staying out of GATT, even those who clearly supported entry in the first place."[18] He concludes:

> So Mexico has rejected GATT, chosen SAM and opted for an oil fed economy with clear intimations that the petroleum production platform could rise when necessary in future. While thousands cheer the president, some few articulate and intelligent specialists are already questioning the common sense of that "superior political wisdom."

Labor Unions

Labor unions, especially in capital-intensive areas in both the public and private sectors, have been accused of constraining government policy. Several times their actions have undermined government income policies.[19] Labor groups have learned that they can share in the income of oligopolistic and natural resource industries, and often reap the profits of nationalized industries. In response to these wage and fringe benefits, the labor unions of nationalized enterprises form the backbone of the labor sector of the PRI and systematically offer support to the government. As a result, labor's recommendations become part of the PRI's platform and part of government policy. The labor movement also opposed joining GATT.

Political and Bureaucratic Elites

Perhaps no other groups can hold back reform in Mexico as effectively as the bureaucracy itself, a fact that is seldom mentioned in the economic literature. The bureaucracy especially influences spending. As a matter of analytical convenience, bureaucratic elites can be considered together with political elites in analyzing Mexican decision making because appointments of public officials are often the result of political patronage. The authority legally vested in bureaucrats is enhanced by the administrative power they gather, because policymaking traditionally relies on the exercise of judgment and discretionary decisions. The scope for personal judgment in routine work makes the goodwill and cooperation of key bureaucratic personnel essential for the success of any major policy proposal such as GATT. Attempts at reform not previously negotiated with them are doomed to fail. The bureaucrats have countless opportunities to impede a policy of change, even when they seem to have accepted it in principle.

As in most countries, the bureaucratic elites in Mexico appear to pursue interests of their own, regardless of their functions in the departments and official agencies where they operate. They tend to adapt their functions to personal or group interests. Their links with their clientele or with that sector of society they are supposed to regulate lead to a tacit pact of reciprocal support, which more often than not has meant maintenance of the status quo. It should not be forgotten that a bureaucracy owes its first loyalty to itself. Administrations come and go. Bureaucrats stay; they work for self-maintenance and survival. Any policies of reform that may endanger their position, change their routine patterns, or disturb their relations with their clientele will arouse suspicions, passive or active resistance, or even antagonism and conflict. The bureaucrats' participation in the design of plan objectives and their involvement in plan implementation are thus essential prerequisites for obtaining their cooperation in any policy of reform.

The Middle Class

Recently, it has been suggested that the Mexican middle class represents an obstacle to modernization in the country, and that the middle class has built a social structure that by itself constitutes an obstacle to reform, especially on the spending side.[20] This argument points to middle class pressure for public services and other demands on the budgets. Requests for new and better urban services, for tariff subsidies and service changes, and for allocations in general may cut down other projects and programs that may be more important for both growth and distribution. Luxury consumer goods, urban transport facilities, automobile services, and many types of public services—education, water, fuel, police, and the like—have tilted the allocation of social funds toward meeting the demands of the middle class and away from other things such as the manufacture of mass consumer goods, public transport, rural works, and social welfare. In this way, the middle class has supported imported consumption patterns, and its behavior has often become embedded in the social structure.

Conclusions

During the first half of the 1970s, the government began to deal with many of the country's long-term growth problems. However, no attempt was made to deal simultaneously with the entire range of post-import substitution problems with equal vigor. In fact, one can roughly divide the 1970s into two periods. The first half (during the Echeverría administration) concentrated on problems related to equity, and the second half (during the López Portillo administration) shifted emphasis more to efficiency and growth maximization.

All in all, it is apparent that equity problems were given lower priority. Little was done to counter increases in the concentration of income. In addition, the pursuit of a more equitable tax system and the amelioration of regional inequalities were only half-hearted at best. Finally, since the government did not perceive market size to be a problem, it was not particularly concerned about the success of the Latin American Free Trade Association.

On the other hand, substantial attempts were made to make the economic system more modern and efficient, and to use it to stimulate investments in priority sectors. The López Portillo administration also was favorably inclined to encourage further foreign investment to expand the productive capacity of the industrial sector.

Disillusionment with the import substitution industrialization strategy has taken various forms and a host of post-import substitution policies have appeared together with the National Industrial Development Plan. It is impossible, however, to pinpoint any one problem that has dominated official concern, or to discover any real consistency between the government's budgetary process and its development objectives. Nor is it clear that the authorities have created an institutional environment conducive to the implementation of its industrial strategy.

In terms of equity, the country has long been plagued with a highly concentrated distribution of income. The import substitution process undoubtedly aggravated this problem. One of the primary causes of disillusionment has been the failure of industrialization to expand employment opportunities sufficiently while creating a new group of small and highly profitable capital-intensive industries. The inequitable geographic concentration of economic activity is another unfortunate result of the import substitution strategy.

It may well be that in Mexico's case many problems developed not because of the import substitution strategy and its aftermath but because the country's industrialization policies were poorly planned. Import substitution in Mexico began with piecemeal responses to the requisites of individual producers, without any real official strategy or overall framework for evaluating decisions. In this regard a recurrent theme in the literature on Mexico is the need for more rational and consistent economic policy.[21]

The following three chapters illustrate various aspects of the government's industrial strategy: the regional impact of public expenditures, the impact of increased defense expenditure, and the inflationary impact of government expenditure. The purpose of these chapters is to illustrate the complexity of economic forces within the Mexican economy while at the same time demonstrating the need for overall coordination of economic policies as a prerequisite for the attainment of the government's major development plans and objectives.

7. Fiscal Policy under López Portillo: Prelude to the 1982 Crisis

In the sixth and final Report to the Nation of his administration (the *Informe*), delivered on 1 September 1982, President José López Portillo stunned both his country and the international banking community by announcing two historic decrees: one to nationalize Mexico's private banking system, the other to institute strict exchange controls on all foreign currency transactions.

On several occasions, the president, clearly under pressure to discuss his government's direct role in the country's economic and financial crisis, did "admit" to his administration's "responsibility" for Mexico's financial difficulties. In his more detailed Complementary Report, he stated, "they still have not invented crystal balls" capable of foreseeing the sudden changes in the world economy. "If the crisis had been foreseeable, there never would have been a crisis."

Throughout his 1 September 1982 report, the president was especially critical of neoclassical economic critiques and analyses (the mainstream interpretation of Mexico's current economic problems articulated by representatives of the developed world). Consequently, the president also was extremely defensive of his Global Development Plan. He repeatedly pointed to the massive industrial base and infrastructure growth that developed after 1977 as the result of the implementation of the Industrial Development Plan. When he identified the causes of the current crisis, the president refused to "occupy himself" with the following "opulent and offensive" phrases that he said "stereotyped" these critiques: "inefficient public investment," "excessive, wasteful and inflationary public spending," "excessive and alienating foreign debt," "petrolized economy," "mistaken political economy," and "undefined and corrective measures." He later added that his government had never "confused realism with the hypocritical puritanism of simplistic orthodoxies." The present situation was often said to be the result of a "trap" set by the developed world.[1]

A detailed examination of movements over the last several years in the budget and its composition, however, reveal a somewhat different picture. This analysis suggests that, however well-intentioned, the government must assume major responsibility for the crisis.

Changing Role of the Government

The government's new growth model outlined in recent budgets requires an increase in the socioeconomic infrastructure, including the areas of technology and education, to satisfy the rapidly growing demands for public sector services.

The government has indicated that this does not mean displacing private sector activities. It involves rapidly modernizing public sector activities to make them more efficient. The private sector is expected to show "a harmonious response" by channeling its investments into the high-priority branches of industry and areas complementing and making use of the new social and physical capital created by the state.

This way of looking at private sector–public sector relations in a mixed economy after the state has chosen its priorities does not raise, and therefore leaves unresolved, the vital question of who determines the decision-making and -implementing mechanisms by which private capital is channeled into specific investment projects. However, the political philosophy of President López Portillo, the Global Plan, and various statements by his ministers imply that the mechanism evolves from consultation—that it is voluntary and not coercive. Therefore, it should not destroy market forces or block their operation.

Fiscal policy implemented by the Treasury has generally sought to harmonize total investment and the balance of payments deficit with the volume of domestic savings, adjust total public sector expenditure with expected income in line with the country's borrowing capacity, and strive for greater balance in the distribution and allocation of resources.

In pursuit of the third aim, the government is attempting to revise the income tax to make it more progressive. During 1977–80, tax remissions for incomes at the lowest end of the scale cost the treasury 34 billion pesos. In spite of these remissions, total taxes collected increased by 65 percent in 1980, partly the result of better enforcement and collection procedures.

Close to 50 percent of total budgeted revenues between 1970 and 1980 came from firms wholly or partly owned by the federal government. Twenty-eight of these companies are budget-controlled.

The public sector's heavy dependence on its business operations has left a deep mark on the country's economy. In all cases, the government either created or bought into these firms with the basic purpose of furthering economic and social development. Dependence on them for such a large portion of federal revenues means that, with few exceptions, the prices of goods and services supplied by the companies should be economically justifiable; that is, they should cover operating and expansion costs. This point provides an insight into the workings of the Mexican economy and clearly defines the government's role in the economy, particularly through the nature of the firms it operates.

Many experts claim that the overall deficit generated by the public sector companies coupled with high outlays by the federal government are the chief causes of the country's recent inflation. In their view, what has not been achieved by controlling the finances and administration of state-owned firms can hardly be achieved by limiting the credit available to productive activity via the legal reserves of the banking system. Government use of these funds, it is argued, only keeps production from meeting growing demand and thus contributes further to inflation.

As a result, government officials have been expressing their conviction that, even though public sector companies may have "social" objectives, they should nevertheless be efficient by the test of profitability. Goods and services provided below cost for social reasons should be acknowledged to be receiving subsidies, the magnitude of which should be revealed.

Recent Budgetary and Fiscal Developments

The tax system must support government activities at three levels: the federal, the state, and the municipal.[2] It is being simplified, and rationalized, and at the same time a bigger share is being given to the states and municipalities. The extent of the simplification can be seen in several areas. Many indirect taxes have been reduced throughout the country. The number of special taxes is now only 10 instead of 52 (as formerly). Ad valorem taxes have been reduced from 119 to 23, and the specific taxes from 338 to 59. Taxes on products such as tobacco, sugar, and alcohol have also been simplified. Also, taxes are now being used to reduce "consumerism," especially "sumptuary" expenditures, as is illustrated by the 40 percent tax on the purchase of new automobiles.

The fiscal system is also being used to channel (or direct) private sector activities into the priorities of the Global Plan. Priority is given to the encouragement of small and medium-sized firms, the production of capital goods and of "strategic" industrial inputs, the promotion of exports, the support of tourism, and the production of basic consumer goods.

The system of subsidies has been improved with increasing reliance on CEFROFIs (Certificados de Promoción Fiscal), certificates that are acceptable in payment of federal taxes. The use of CEFROFIs has increased so that in 1980 they stimulated investment of 19 billion pesos in 110 municipalities. Preferential zones received 63 percent of this investment, with only 8 percent going to the overcrowded zone in which new industrial activity is in principle being discouraged.

Perhaps more important, the capital goods industry has received a considerable amount of CEFROFIs. These were responsible for 6.8 billion pesos of new investment in the sector. In addition, more than 700 small and medium-sized businesses have received CEFROFIs. The tourist industry has received 170 million pesos in CEFROFIs, which in turn produced tenfold that amount of private investment in the sector. Finally, the system has been used to encourage the purchase of technology. In 1980, the special tax incentive for the employment of additional workers led directly to the creation of 65,000 new jobs and indirectly to 120,000 new jobs in associated activities.

Specifically, the 1981 budget was designed to achieve a rate of growth of 7.5 percent to 8.0 percent in GDP in real terms, while generating 750,000 jobs. This increase in output was expected to allow private consumption to grow at an average annual rate of between 6.5 and 7.0 percent in 1981.

The government anticipated that its total revenue would be three and a half times the 1977 amount and the amount of borrowing 3.8 times that in 1977. Similarly, the 27 state organizations and enterprises were expected to have revenue 3.9 times and borrowing 2.8 times their 1977 levels. The revenue of the whole public sector in 1981 was projected to grow to 3.2 times that of 1977, and borrowing to 2.8 times, on the assumption that the 27 entities would borrow absolutely less than in 1980.

The 1981 budget's assumption that state entities would borrow less in 1981 than in 1980 was overly optimistic, given that these entities had often failed to meet budget targets before. This assumption may have deluded officials into an unrealistic sense of security about the level of the deficit.

In fact, with the exception of federal government borrowing in 1977, actual borrowing since 1973 has always exceeded planned borrowing. And even though the federal government reduced its own borrowing below the budgeted level in 1977, it did not have enough control over the state entities to do any more than reduce their overruns. As a percentage of the forecasted budgeted amounts, overruns have fallen from their high point of 106.2 percent in 1975 to 43.1 percent in 1977. Combined with the discipline introduced in federal government expenditure to reduce inflation, this decrease in overruns reduced the excess in total public sector borrowing to 4.9 percent, a record low. While excess borrowing of the state enterprises was held to 15.2 percent over budget in 1978, it increased to 71.9 percent in 1979 and 38.1 percent in 1980. The federal government's excess over planned borrowing (and consequently the public sector total) has also increased continuously from its 1977 low point.

Nearly 94 percent of the 1980 estimated total revenue of the federal government was derived from six taxes (table 7.1). And these were expected to provide 97 percent of the tax revenue in the 1981 budget. The large increases in the revenue of the state entities in 1981 is mostly due to PEMEX's anticipated increase in oil revenues (export taxes).

The 1981 Expenditure Proposals

The detailed spending proposals of the 1981 budget reveal the administration's priorities and the direction the administration would take in its last two years in office. The creation of employment was given the highest priority. The 1981 budget proposed to create 750,000 new jobs, an addition of 4.2 percent to the total number employed.

The funds allocated to social welfare were to increase by 40 percent over the 1980 amount. Within this sector, the appropriation for education was to increase by 42 percent, thereby absorbing more than 50 percent of the total social welfare allocation. The percentage coverage of preschool education was to be raised from 32 percent to 45 percent of the number of this age group; the present 100 percent coverage in primary education was to be maintained; and provisions were to be made for more than 4 million pupils to receive secondary and middle

Table 7.1. Main sources of revenue and borrowing requirement, 1980–81 (billion pesos and percentage changes)

	1980			1981		
	Budget	Estimated	Change percent	Budget	Change over 1980 Budget	Change over 1980 Estimated
I. Federal government						
Total revenue	646.9	680.4	5.2	955.5	47.7	40.4
Income tax	198.7	241.9	21.7	307.6	54.8	27.2
Export taxes	150.5	147.5	−2.0	265.7	76.5	80.1
Value added tax (VAT)	80.4	114.7	42.7	157.0	42.7	36.9
Social security taxes	67.0	67.0	0.0	91.9	37.2	37.2
Import taxes	33.5	37.6	12.2	60.1	79.4	59.8
Petroleum tax[a]	n.a.	29.7	—	44.8	—	50.8
Others[b]	116.8	42.0		28.4	−75.7	−32.4
Borrowing requirement	259.2	329.2	27.0	485.2	87.2	47.4
Total receipts	906.1	1,009.6	11.4	1,440.7	59.0	42.7
II. Organizations and state enterprises						
Total revenue	571.0	616.0	7.9	845.9	48.2	37.3
Borrowing requirement	206.6	285.4	38.1	213.2	3.2	−25.3
Total receipts	777.6	901.4	15.9	1,059.1	36.2	17.5
III. Total public sector (I + II)						
1. Revenue	1,217.9	1,296.4	6.4	1,801.4	47.9	39.0
2. Borrowing requirement	465.8	614.4	31.9	698.4	49.9	13.6
3. Total receipts (1 + 2)	1,683.7	1,910.8	13.5	2,332.7	38.6	22.1
Percent of total receipts borrowed (2/3)	27.7	32.2	16.2[c]	29.9	7.9[c]	−7.1[c]

Source: Budget documents, 1980 and 1981.

a. The presentation of Secretary Ibarra in November 1980 to Congress (*El Mercado de Valores* [December 1, 1980], p. 1196) gives 44.8 billion for 1981, but Secretary de la Madrid (*Exposición de Motivos*, table on p. xxxv) gave 41.2 billion for 1981 and 29.7 billion for 1980. I assume that *Hacienda* is the responsible authority on revenue.

b. Includes nontax current income and 2 billion pesos of capital receipts.

c. The percentage change in the percentage share borrowed.

education. Medical and other health services were to be extended to more than 60 percent of the population, largely by concentrating on children and rural inhabitants.

Special emphasis was to continue on various programs to provide food, basic commodities, and services. Specifically, continued support was to be given to the 200 regional warehouses for the distribution of such products to 6,000 rural centers in order to assure supplies to 14 million agricultural workers, of whom 12 million were in isolated rural areas. New roads would continue to be given priority for these rural groups in the government's ongoing attempt to bring them into contact with the commercial and cultural life of the nation. Other programs were to provide technical advice and training to encourage cooperative organizations, which were to create 60,000 new jobs.

The budget appropriation for the agricultural sector, including livestock raising, was to increase by 53 percent. This increase was to enable the sector to achieve 69 percent of its 1980–82 goal for bringing new rainfed land into cultivation, 62 percent of its total for extending the irrigated areas, and 72 percent of its goal for rehabilitating irrigated zones. Other goals for the 1977–82 period are to bring an additional 2.1 million hectares of rainfed, 1.2 million of irrigated, and 1.4 million of rehabilitated irrigated land into cultivation. To put these increases in perspective, the total area of cultivable land in Mexico is 30 million hectares, or about 15 percent of the total area of the country. The 1977–82 budget targets are therefore very significant additions to the less than 20 million hectares that have been under cultivation in any one crop cycle.

The budget appropriation for the industrial sector was to increase by 34 percent, with the aim of enabling it to achieve the specific goals set for six major subsectors: The petroleum sector was to maintain the platform, defined as "satisfying domestic requirements and fulfilling the international commitments of Mexico." The capacity to produce electric power was to be expanded to 74.769 gigawatt hours (1 giga $= 10^{12}$). The mining industry was to add .8 million tons to its extraction and refining capacity, although the amount of the necessary appropriation was not stated. In addition, the goal for sugar production in the 1980–81 crop cycle was 2.6 million tons, which was intended to bring the country near to the goal of self-sufficiency. Fertilizer output was to increase to 3.2 million tons, also in a move toward self-sufficiency. The steel industry was to increase its output of flat and nonflat products and seamless pipe by 18.6 percent to 3.7 million tons.

In sum, the budget was intended to achieve five general objectives, all of which are derived from the strategy of the Global Plan. Of these, two are growth targets—the 750,000 jobs and the increase of 7.5 percent to 8.0 percent in GDP. Two are of a social nature—raising the standard of living and strengthening group programs for functional and geographical priorities. The fifth goal is the control of inflation.

Public Sector Expenditure and Borrowing

A comparison of the budgetary recovery record of the federal government with that of the 27 decentralized organizations and state enterprises (or the "state entities") indicates that these two sections were almost equal in size up to 1981, but now the federal government will spend 36 percent more than the gross budget of the state entities, and 62.9 percent more than their budget excluding transfers (table 7.2).

The country's overall economic performance has been very much affected by the extent to which total expenditure was financed by borrowing (loans), and the excess of budgeted over actual expenditure. The first is directly relevant to the problem of inflation, especially in the case of the federal government because its borrowing at the Bank of Mexico may be financed by methods that the bank itself admits are inflationary. The second or actual overbudgeted expenditures indicate a high degree of financial indiscipline. Fiscal indiscipline is also relevant to the problem of inflation, because the excesses are sure to increase the need for additional governmental borrowing, and therefore the danger of inflationary financing by the central bank.

Clearly (table 7.3), the percentage borrowed has been high in both parts of the public sector over the last seven years. However, it was at a higher level and has shown a greater tendency to increase in the state entities than in the federal government. With the exception of 1977, the excess in the federal government of actual over budgeted expenditure has been greater in the expenditure financed by borrowing than in total expenditure, and it has been very much greater in the case of the state entities.

Except for 1977 and 1978, when a concerted effort was made to stop inflation, indiscipline has characterized the Mexican budgetary process. The excess of actual over planned total public spending reached a low point of 4.9 percent in 1977, judged by the difference between the planned and the actual percentage of the total budget financed by borrowing (32.6 percent planned and 34.2 percent actual). But the low points of the excesses in the absolute amounts of public sector expenditure, both in the total (2.7 percent) and in the loan expenditure (8.8 percent), were reached in 1978. In the next two years, the excesses of planned over actual borrowing rose to the high level of 42.1 percent and 31.9 percent, respectively.

It is also clear (table 7.2) that the main source of indiscipline has been in the state entities, because in their budget the excess of actual over planned percentage of expenditure financed by borrowing is enormously greater than the excess in the federal government. Only the loss of discipline in 1980 by the federal government, when the excess of borrowing surpassed the high point of 21 percent in 1975, brought the degree of inequity in the two spending sections closer together.

The division between current and capital items in expenditure and revenue together with the reliance on borrowing and the burden imposed by the amorti-

Table 7.2. Public sector expenditure and borrowing 1975–81 (billion pesos and percentages)

Year	Federal government			State entitles			Total public sector		
	Total expenditure (1)	Borrowing (2)	(2)/(1) Percent (3)	Total expenditure (4)	Borrowing (5)	(5)/(4) Percent (6)	Expenditure (1) + (5) (7)	Borrowing (2) + (5) (8)	(8)/(7) Percent (9)
1975									
Budget	186.1	54.2	29.1	160.6	32.2	20.1	346.7	86.5	24.9
Actual	200.5	70.5	35.2	200.2	66.6	33.3	400.7	137.1	34.2
Excess actual percent	7.7	30.1	21.0	24.7	106.2	65.7	15.6	58.5	37.3
1976									
Budget	238.0	83.2	35.0	201.6	33.8	16.8	439.6	117.0	26.6
Actual	275.1	112.2	35.5	271.0	65.5	24.2	530.2	157.4	29.7
Excess actual percent	15.6	34.9	1.4	34.4	93.8	44.0	20.6	34.5	11.7
1977									
Budget	349.8	135.4	38.7	327.6	85.6	26.1	677.4	221.0	32.6
Actual	355.1	127.5	35.9	375.5	122.5	32.6	730.6	250.0	34.2
Excess actual percent	1.5	−5.8	−7.2	14.6	43.1	24.9	7.9	13.1	4.9
1978									
Budget	434.3	141.5	32.6	478.1	149.9	31.4	912.5	291.4	32.0
Actual	442.0	144.7	32.7	495.4	172.7	34.9	937.4	317.4	33.9
Excess actual percent	1.8	2.3	0.3	3.6	15.2	11.1	2.7	8.8	5.9
1979									
Budget	571.7	213.8	37.4	552.6	129.5	23.4	1,124.3	343.3	30.5
Actual[a]	650.1	265.1	40.8	657.6	222.6	33.9	1,307.7	487.7	37.3
Excess actual percent	13.7	24.0	9.1	19.0	71.9	44.9	16.3	42.1	22.3
1980									
Budget	839.0	259.2	30.9	844.4	206.6	24.5	1,683.4	465.8	27.7
Estimated	875.8	329.2	37.6	901.4	285.4	31.7	1,777.2	614.6	34.6
Excess[a] percent	4.4	27.0	21.7	6.8	38.1	29.4	5.6	31.9	24.9
1981									
Budget	1,273.6	485.2	38.1	1,059.1	213.2	20.1	2,332.7	698.4	29.9
Change 1981/1980[a]	45.4	47.4	—	17.5	−25.3	—	31.3	13.6	—
Change 1981/1980 budget	51.8	87.2	—	25.4	3.2	—	38.6	49.9	—

Source: Constructed from tables in the 1975–80 budget documents.
a. Estimated.

Table 7.3. Budgeted public sector expenditure, revenue, and borrowing, 1977–81

						Percentage increase			
	1977	1978	1979	1980	1981	1978/ 1977	1979/ 1978	1980/ 1979	1981/ 1980
I. Expenditure (billion pesos)									
(1) Current	435.4	497.2	622.1	989.1	1,328.8	14.2	25.1	59.0	33.8
(2) Capital	147.8	257.1	327.0	450.0	694.4	74.0	27.2	37.6	54.3
(3) Percentage (2)/(4)	25.4	34.1	34.5	31.3	34.4	—	—	—	—
(4) Total	582.2	754.3	949.1	1,439.2	2,018.3	29.3	25.8	51.6	40.2
(5) Amortization of debt	94.3	158.2	175.1	244.2	314.5	67.8	10.7	39.5	28.8
(6) Gross total	677.5	912.5	1,124.3	1,683.4	2,332.7	34.7	23.2	49.7	38.6
II. Revenue (billion pesos)									
(1) Current	451.7	601.3	759.4	1,189.6	1,630.9	33.1	26.3	56.6	37.1
(2) Capital	4.7	19.8	21.6	28.8	3.4	321.3	9.1	29.6	−87.9
(3) Total	456.4	621.1	781.0	1,217.7	1,634.3	36.1	25.7	55.9	34.2
(4) Financing	221.0	291.3	343.3	465.8	698.5	31.8	17.9	35.7	50.0
(5) Gross total	677.4	912.5	1,124.3	1,683.4	2,332.7	34.7	23.2	49.7	38.6
(6)Percentage (4)/(5)	32.6	31.9	30.5	27.7	29.9	—	—	—	—
(7) Percentage I(5)/II(4)	42.7	54.3	51.0	52.4	45.0	—	—	—	—

Source: Budget documents on expenditure.

zation of debt have been growing over the last few years. The share of capital expenditure in the total was at its low level of 25.4 percent (table 7.3) in the postcrisis and anti-inflation year of 1977. It rose to 34.1 percent in 1978, when the fight against inflation was more or less abandoned, and it continued to rise in 1979. It fell again in 1980 to 31.3 percent. Also in 1980, there was a correspondingly large increase in the absolute amount of current expenditure—59 percent. The 1981 budget planned to increase the capital proportion to 34.4 percent, with corresponding increases of 54.3 percent in the absolute amount of capital expenditure and of only 33.8 percent in current expenditure.

Of total revenue, the capital proportion was very small and even negligible, at 0.2 percent in 1981. The difference between total revenue and total expenditure, plus the amortization of debt, is the amount of financing required (table 7.4). Amortization as a percentage of total financing was relatively low in 1977 at 42.7 percent, but it was more than 50 percent in the following three years, and was budgeted to fall to 45 percent in 1981. Amortization is treated separately in the budget because it is not considered to be a part of the current inflationary forces arising out of public sector spending, although it may have originated in earlier inflationary expenditures. The reliance on financing in the 1981 budget was expected to increase to 29.9 percent of total spending, and its absolute amount was forecast to increase by 50 percent, despite the increase of only 28.8 percent in debt amortization. The latter is the smallest increase since 1979 when the low of 10.7 percent reflected an increase of 67.8 percent over 1978.

Gross financing was budgeted at 86.1 billion pesos (table 7.4) in 1981. Amortization of debt was deducted from gross financing in order to arrive at the final concept of net financing, which is the definition of the budgetary deficit. The public sector deficit gives a summary expression of the inflationary forces emanating from expenditure and borrowing. It fell to 94.6 billion pesos in 1978 during the short-lived effort to stop inflation. After a moderate increase in 1979, it rose spectacularly in 1980, and in 1981 it was budgeted to increase even further, by 63.8 percent to 297.9 billion pesos.

Sectorial Composition of the Budget

Another important classification of public sector expenditure is according to economic sector, or at least of the part of it that can be divided into sectors. More than 25 percent of the budget, however, cannot be so divided. The designation "special attention" is given to four sectors (table 7.5), which received more than half the sectorizable expenditure in both years. Commerce receives special attention because it includes the activities of CONASUPO, which subsidizes the production and distribution of food and other basic commodities.

Except for the 42 percent in commerce, in 1980 the excesses of estimated over budgeted expenditure were very small, and the total estimated was only about 7 percent above budget. By way of contrast, all the other sectors showed very

Table 7.4. Budgeted public sector expenditure by borrowing, 1977–81 (billion pesos and percentage changes)

	1977	1978	1979	1980	1981	1978/ 1977	1979/ 1978	1980/ 1979	1981/ 1980
Total gross financing	221.0	291.4	343.3	465.8	698.5	31.9	17.8	35.7	50.0
Less payments in the next year	19.6	22.0	45.0	5.0	16.0	12.2	104.5	−88.9	220.0
Less payments not includable[a]	—	33.6	45.0	34.7	70.1	—	33.9	−22.9	102.0
Gross financing	201.5	235.8	253.3	426.1	612.4	17.1	7.4	68.2	43.7
Less amortization of debt	74.7	141.2	145.1	244.2	314.5	89.0	2.8	68.2	28.8
Net financing	126.8	94.6	108.1	181.9	297.9	−25.4	14.3	68.3	63.8

Source: Budget documents 1977–81.

a. Beginning in 1978, the item "less payments in the next year" was replaced by two items: "increment of payments pending" and "estimate of expenditure not includable in the accounts."

Table 7.5. Comparison of expenditure in 1980 and 1981 by economic sector (billion pesos and percentages)

	1980 budget				1981 budget			Change 1981	
			Total						
	Current (1)	Capital (2)	Budget (3)	Estimated (4)	Current (5)	Capital (6)	Total (7)	Budget (7)/(3) (8)	Esti-mated (7)/(4) (9)
Special attention sectors									
Agriculture	49.1	96.5	145.6	146.1	76.1	147.8	233.9	60.6	60.1
Communication and transportation	54.7	42.4	97.1	104.0	75.5	83.1	158.6	73.0	52.5
Commerce	56.1	6.4	62.5	88.5	97.0	13.0	110.0	76.0	24.3
Social welfare	259.8	22.8	282.5	291.5	353.7	53.0	406.7	44.0	39.5
Subtotal	419.7	168.0[a]	587.6	630.1	602.3	296.9	899.2	53.0	43.0
Industrial	189.7	165.7	355.4	428.9	243.4	330.9	574.3	61.6	33.9
Administration	38.2	2.3	40.5	52.2	61.8	14.8	76.6	89.1	46.7
Human settlements	6.6	9.5	16.0	37.1	17.8	37.5	55.3	245.6	49.1
Defense	16.5	2.4	18.9	24.7	30.5	7.4	37.9	100.5	53.4
Tourism	2.2	1.9	4.2	5.9	3.0	4.1	7.1	69.0	20.3
Legislative and judicial	1.6	0.8	2.4	2.8	3.4	0.9	4.3	79.2	53.4
Subtotal	254.8	182.6	437.4	551.6	359.9	395.6	755.5	72.7	37.7
Total sectorial	674.5	350.6	1,025.0	1,181.7	962.2	692.5	1,654.7	61.4	40.0
Nonsectorizable[b]									
Participations and fiscal incentives	113.2	0.0	50.0	113.2	152.5	0.0	152.5	205.0	34.7
Public debt	137.7	327.8	357.7	465.5	186.1	314.5	550.6	39.9	7.5
Other	16.8	—	36.9	16.8	23.0	1.9	24.9	−32.5	48.2
Total Nonsectorizable	267.7	327.8	658.4[c]	595.5	361.6	316.4	678.0	52.5	13.9
Total budget	942.2	678.4	1,683.4	1,777.2	1,323.8	1,008.9	2,332.7	38.6	31.3

a. Includes 21.7 billion pesos for PIDER-CUC-COPLAMAR, which is not a part of the 1981 breakdown of the figures.

b. Only the estimated expenditures in the breakdown between current and capital are available for 1980.

c. Includes 165.8 billion pesos of "PEMEX taxes" listed separately in the 1980 but not in the 1981 budget documents. The nonsectorizable total is arrived at by subtracting the sectorial from the total budget (1,683.4 billion pesos).

Table 7.6. Distribution of budgeted expenditure on industry, 1980 and 1981 (billion pesos and percentage changes and shares)

	1980	1981	Change 1981/1980	Share in total 1980	Share in total 1981
Total industrial	355.4	574.3	61.6	100	100
Federal government	52.7	67.3	27.7	14.8	11.7
Patrimony and industry	1.5	2.1	40.0	0.4	0.4
CONASUPO	48.1	65.2	35.6	13.5	11.3
Others	3.1	0.0	—	0.9	0.0
Organizations and enterprises	302.7	507.0	67.5	85.2	88.3
Petroleum (PEMEX)	171.3	294.4	71.9	48.2	51.3
Electricity (CFE)	64.1	119.1	85.5	18.1	20.7
Light and power company	17.1	19.0	11.1	4.8	3.3
Fertilizantes Mexicanos	14.7	25.3	72.1	4.1	4.4
DINA (motor vehicles)	16.5	25.4	53.9	4.7	4.4
National steel	1.9	2.6	36.8	0.5	0.5
Las truchas (steel)	7.0	13.2	88.6	2.0	2.3
National rail cars	5.9	7.0	18.6	1.6	1.2
PIPSA (paper)	4.1	1.0	−75.6	1.1	0.2

Source: Statistical Appendix of the 1980 budget and Proyecto de Presupuesto de Egresos de la Federaction, 1981. *Exposicion de Motivos*, Passim.

considerable excesses; particularly the 124 percent in Human Settlements, while the total of all six of the special sectors spent 26 percent more than budgeted. For 1981, increases are higher in the ordinary than in the special attention sectors. In the latter, the 1981 increase is 53 percent, but the increase is 72.7 percent for the other group. The higher proposed increase of 43 percent in the special attention group, compared to an increase of 37.7 percent in the nonspecial group, is largely a result of the comparatively large amount by which the latter overspent the budget in 1980.

The industrial sector dominates sectorizable expenditure, especially in capital spending. In 1980, industry was budgeted to receive 28.1 percent of the current budget, 47.3 percent of the capital budget, and 34.7 percent of the total sectorial expenditure. In fact, it received 36.3 percent of the estimated total sectorial expenditure. This was an excess of 20.7 percent or 73.5 billion pesos over the budget, a comparatively moderate percentage but the largest absolute amount. In the 1981 budget, industry accounted for 25.3 percent of the current, 47.8 percent of the capital, and again 34.7 percent of the total sectorial expenditure.

In view of the preponderance of the industrial sector in the budget, the breakdown among the different components of the public sector productive apparatus is of interest (table 7.6). The bulk of the direct federal government expenditure went to CONASUPO—91.3 percent in 1980 and 96.9 percent in 1981—although these figures represented a diminishing share of the industrial total. As would be expected, spending in the industrial sector is carried out mainly by the state entities; 85.2 percent in 1980 and 88.3 percent in 1981.

Also as would be expected, PEMEX is dominant among the state enterprises. On the average it accounted for about 50 percent of the total industrial expendi-

Table 7.7. Comparison of budgeted and actual public expenditure and borrowing, 1971-81 (percentages)

	Total expenditure			Gross borrowing		Net borrowing: the deficit	
	Increase over previous year		Increase in same year	Increase over previous year	Increase in same year	Increase over previous year	Increase in same year
	Budget/ budget (1)	Budget/ actual (2)	Actual/ budget (3)	Budget/ budget (4)	Actual/ budget (5)	Budget/ budget (6)	Actual/ budget (7)
1972	54.7	6.1	19.5	n.a.	35.9	n.a.	n.a.
1973	41.0	18.1	17.3	81.5	24.4	n.a.	n.a.
1974	32.8	13.2	19.7	14.6	33.3	n.a.	n.a.
1975	50.1	25.4	15.6	50.7	58.5	n.a.	n.a.
1976	26.8	9.7	20.6	35.3	34.5	n.a.	77.4
1977	54.1	27.8	7.9	88.9	13.1	n.a.	−1.2
1978	34.7	24.9	2.7	31.9	11.4	−25.5	17.5
1979	23.2	19.9	16.3	17.8	42.1	14.4	15.6
1980	49.7	28.7	—	35.7	31.9	68.3	8.1
1981	49.9	13.6	—	49.9		63.8	

Source: Constructed from tables in the budget documents, 1972-81.

ture, and for over 57 percent of the "own resources" of the state entities. The two electric companies together received the next highest allocation, in accordance with government policy of giving high priority to energy. This priority is also evident from the high rates of increase for PEMEX and the electric companies in the 1981 allocation. By the same test (of rates of increase in the 1981 budget), fertilizers and steel are also given priority, again in accordance with declared policy.

Budgetary Discipline

The preceding discussion has measured the budgetary discipline achieved in past years by the size of the gap between budgeted and actual expenditure, which is obviously a factor in determining the size of the public sector deficit and the borrowing requirements. Clearly, there has been a very large annual intended increase in total public sector expenditure (table 7.7), whether over budgeted or actual. The degree of indiscipline in the excess of actual over budgeted spending is reflected in the gross borrowing and also in the net borrowing, which is the budget deficit as defined in table 13.2. In 1980–82, gross borrowing exceeded budgeted borrowing by the same order of magnitude as in 1974–77; and the excess of the net borrowing over budget has been particularly high from 1979–82.

The Budget and Prospects for Inflation

The significance of the budget figures in current prices can be revealed more fully by relating them to changes in gross domestic product (table 7.8). This is a substitute for deflating all the figures by the implicit price deflator (IPD). As

Table 7.8. Actual public sector expenditure, borrowing[a] and GDP 1972–81 (billion current pesos and percentage)

Year	GDP (1)	Increase percent (2)	Expenditure (3)	Ratio percent (3)/(1)	Gross borrowing (4)	Ratio percent (4)/(1)	IPD[b] (5)
1972	512.3	13.2	137.2	28.7	37.5	7.3	5.6
1973	619.6	20.9	204.0	32.9	62.3	10.1	12.4
1974	813.7	31.3	276.5	34.0	76.5	9.4	24.0
1975	988.3	21.5	400.7	40.5	137.1	13.9	16.7
1976	1,228.0	24.3	530.2	43.2	157.4	12.8	21.7
1977	1,674.7	36.4	730.6	44.6	250.0	14.9	32.1
1978	2,122.8	26.8	937.4	44.2	317.4	15.0	18.1
1979	2,767 [b]	30.3	1,307.7	47.3	487.7	17.6	20.7
1980	3,862.7[b]	39.6	1,777.2	46.0	614.6	15.9	30.0[c]
1981	5,801.9[c]	50.2[c]	2,332.7	40.2	698.4	12.0	41.0[c]

Source: Constructed from Bank of Mexico annual reports and budget documents 1971–81.

a. The actual total gross borrowing is given, except in 1979 and 1980, when it is the estimated actual, and in 1981, when it is the budgeted.

b. IPD is the implicit price deflator of GDP.

c. Estimated by the author.

percentages of GDP, public sector expenditure and its borrowing requirement have risen drastically since 1972 when inflation began—from 28.7 percent to 46 percent and from 7.3 percent to 15.9 percent, respectively. While the borrowing requirement as planned in 1981 would decline from 15.9 percent to 12 percent of GDP, that was still a proportionate increase of 64 percent over 1972.

Concomitantly with the increase in borrowing, the implicit price deflator rose from an annual rate of 5.6 percent in 1972 to 30 percent in 1980, a total increase of 436 percent.

In sum, the expenditures budget for 1981 indicated that the government was continuing its expansionist policy, despite the impact of inflation. At the beginning of 1980 the country seemed headed toward another period in which accelerated growth took precedence over any hope of eliminating inflationary pressures in the short term.

Thus, the projected budget for 1981, which amounted to $2.5 trillion pesos, represented an increase of 48.5 percent with respect to the 1.68 trillion pesos originally planned to be spent for 1980. With respect to the $1.9 trillion pesos actually spent in 1980, 1981 expenditures grew by 30.8 percent. Clearly, the federal government decided to continue its effort to maintain an accelerated rate of economic growth.

Conclusions

The oil euphoria that developed in Mexico in the late 1970s encouraged a sense of economic omnipotence. Carried away by the oil prospects, the state sector embarked on an investment spree of massive proportions. By the year

2000, energy output was projected to grow tenfold, steel fivefold, petrochemicals more than sevenfold. Taken in isolation, perhaps a case could have been made for any of the mammoth projects on the drawing boards. Swallowed whole, however, they were guaranteed to give the country development indigestion. And some of the projects, prestige apart, were hard to justify.

As Basil Caplan has noted:

> The productivity of [Mexico's] steel industry is less than half that of EEC and the world steel industry has been begging for customers and offering bargain basement prices. Yet a massive investment programme was launched aimed at quadrupling the state owned steel sector in this decade. In parallel, PEMEX undertook a huge petrochemical expansion program, boasting that one in eight petrochemical plants in the world were under construction in Mexico. Nobody, it seems, thought to ask why. In parallel too, the government launched a $30 billion program to create four new industrial ports. And with the cheapest, massively subsidised gasoline (50 cents a gallon) encouraging the nation's motorists to burn up the country's oil, plans were laid for a $30 billion nuclear power program, conceived on an heroic scale.
>
> Mexico was becoming a building site where much was under construction, but little as yet finished and paying for itself.[3]

In addition, until mid-1982, government efforts to rein in expenditure were far stronger in intention than achievement. Thus, it is not too difficult to see that the country was becoming vulnerable to an oil revenue shortfall.

8. Policymaking in López Portillo's Final Year: The 1982 Devaluations and Aftermath

The 1982 devaluations of the peso and their consequences have tended to overshadow the industrial gains made in the last years, have raised questions as to the wisdom of the government's development strategy, and have introduced an element of great uncertainty as to the country's industrial progress during the next few years.[1]

The following sections are a chronology of events, intended to convey the flavor of the government's thinking concerning the current crisis and its longer-term policy response. An in-depth analysis of the government's stabilization efforts is given in chapters 14 and 15.

The February 1982 Stabilization Program

As a result of the 1982 devaluations of the peso, inflation was anticipated to rise above 90 percent during 1982, up from about 30 percent in 1981. The government's evolving austerity program was expected to slow down economic growth, which had been previously estimated at 6.5 percent a year, to around one percent. Early in 1982 the government's official position was that a devaluation of the peso was necessary because the reserves of the Bank of Mexico had eroded rapidly at the beginning of 1982, as loans were renewed and capital transferred. For this reason, as well as to maintain adequate reserves, the Bank of Mexico was forced to withdraw from the exchange market. The peso crisis arose as a result of the ever increasing dollarization of the domestic market and the acceleration of purchases abroad; "this was what hit the reserves of the Bank of Mexico."[2]

The government expected the February 1982 float of the peso to prevent an excessive increase in the value of the peso as well as speculative transactions in foreign exchange. After taking this measure, the government announced a number of significant modifications of past policies.

The general orientation of the government's programs was outlined on 20 February 1982:

1. Exchange policy was to aim at preventing Mexican goods and services from becoming more expensive and less competitive abroad. The exchange rate was also to be set at a level preventing foreign goods and services from becoming more attractive than national products.

2. In the future, financial authorities would make sure the exchange rate was adjusted to other currencies in a timely manner; daily adjustments were to be made to avoid a burdensome overvaluation.

3. Budgetary policy was to give preference to spending on high priority activities or activities most closely tied to the public welfare. For this purpose, the budget was to be more carefully controlled than in the past.
4. Financial policy was to keep domestic interest rates at a level competitive with foreign levels, in real terms. Interest rate levels were to discourage the dollarization of the national banking system and any tendency for capital to flee abroad.
5. Interest rates were to minimize obstacles to production and investment. Higher rates should encourage increased domestic savings. Private enterprises that in good faith were forced to contract debts in dollars were to be supported to avoid decapitalization.
6. Incentives for exports and tourism were to give Mexican businessmen full guarantees against the loss of competitiveness due to inflation, and to establish a solid foundation for agreement on investment or increased supply. In the case of basic consumer goods or products that were deemed indispensable for production, tariffs and permits were to be liberalized.
7. Indispensable increases in prices were to be authorized if justified by movements in costs. However, such increases were not to exceed wage increases.

The April Stabilization Program

The government quickly began working on the specifics of these broad objectives. By late April, it had developed a comprehensive stabilization program to deal with the foreign exchange crisis in particular and the increasing lack of confidence in the economy in general.

The 21 April 1982 stabilization program was in essence a fairly rigid set of guidelines for the adjustment of public sector financing—to be expanded to the private sector—ultimately aiming at rapid economic recovery and reduced inflationary pressures.

According to the 21 April 1982 program, the total financial deficit of the public sector was to be reduced by 3 percent. For this purpose, a new adjustment was to be made in the budget of the federal government and the Department of the Federal District, totaling 8 percent. Public spending schedules were to be drawn up. There were to be no advance payments, and semigovernment programs were to be handled in accordance with revenues, expenditures, and the deficit. All undertakings not directly related to the production process were to be set aside and new investments postponed.

In addition, an attempt was to be made to get $150 billion pesos through increases in prices and rates on goods and services supplied by the public sector. The public sector's net borrowing abroad was to be strictly limited to a maximum amount of $11 billion. No bills (promissory notes) were to be issued unless they were guaranteed by an equivalent income in foreign exchange and unless they were backed by money reserves.

The deficit in the current account of the country's balance of payments was to be reduced in 1982 to between $3 and $4 billion. Public sector imports were to be reduced by $3 billion and private sector purchases abroad limited to $3 billion. The Bank of Mexico was to avoid creating excess liquidity in the financial system and any surplus funds collected were to be deposited under the control of that institution.

The government intended to adopt a policy of passive interest rates in keeping with the development of foreign rates and changes in the rate of exchange. A bonus in favor of investments in pesos was planned. With regard to credit, the government intended to strengthen the policy of giving preferential treatment to the social-economic sectors. To private enterprises requiring dollar financing, the Bank of Mexico intended to grant better terms for contract negotiations, exemptions, and reduced costs. There were to be no restrictions on foreign exchange transactions. Interventions on the exchange market were to be undertaken if necessary. Exchange policy aimed at maintaining the Mexican economy's competitiveness, while preventing the excessive valuation of the Mexican peso at all times.

When the stabilization program was announced, Miguel Aancera Aguayo, general manager of the Bank of Mexico, noted that:

> It is under no circumstances advisable to have foreign exchange control in Mexico because that would not be the way to prevent the flight of foreign exchange; it would promote corruption and foreign exchange smuggling; it would increase the cost of living; it would create massive unemployment; it would slow down imports, and it would paralyze broad sectors of the economy.[3]

This conclusion was based on a study undertaken by the Bank of foreign exchange control in other semi-industrialized countries. In each case, foreign exchange control had been a failure with serious consequences for long-run growth. On this basis, the Bank concluded, "that system would fail in Mexico."

By mid-1982, the official Mexican interpretation of the 1982 crisis was that in large part the foreign sector of the country's economy has been seriously harmed by the adverse development of the international economy in recent years. This situation was reflected in a noticeable drop in worldwide demand and prices for Mexican export products, especially petroleum, as well as an extraordinary rise in interest payments on the public sector's foreign debt, due to the devaluation of the currency.

The Twelve-Point Recovery Program of the Department of Patrimony and Industrial Development

On 25 March 1982, the Secretary of SEPAFIN (Department of Patrimony and Industrial Development) announced a twelve-point economic program. The intent of the plan was to "keep us away from the dangers of instability and preserve to the extent possible the employment policy."[4]

The measures announced included certificates known as CEPROFI (Fiscal

Incentive Certificates) equivalent to 15 percent of the monthly payroll.[5] The payroll figures were to be calculated as an average for the year 1982 and based on minimum wage rates. Businesses that could prove they maintained their level of jobs would be entitled to the certificates. The PRI estimated that benefits might reach 15 billion pesos, thus significantly helping businesses to meet their obligations resulting from previous wage adjustments.

Additional incentives were also proposed to create jobs. A five-year CEPROFI was to be issued, equivalent to 80 percent of the business payroll increase. An incentive was to be granted to businesses that maintained or established specific training programs for their workers.

Businesses were to be allowed to anticipate their tax deductions for exchange losses for up to one fiscal year. This meant that businesses with liquidity problems might make additional resources available to themselves to meet their debts contracted in dollars, and those that resulted from wage adjustments. Businesses with exchange losses might reduce their profit coefficient in order to determine their estimated taxes. This was intended to help a good number of businesses avoid income tax payments during 1982.

Businesses were to be allowed to defer a third of the total taxes withheld from their workers for salaries paid during March 1982. The deferred tax was to be payable in three equal installments in September, October, and November 1982, bearing interest at the rate of 1.5 percent per month. "It has been estimated that this deferment might amount to 4.5 billion pesos. This provision is designed to help businesses to meet obligations resulting from the salary increases, by providing greater liquidity and some benefits in their financing costs."[6] The Mexican Social Security Institute was willing to support to the fullest extent possible business compliance with obligations resulting from wage adjustments.

The resources administered by state funds for the development and promotion of priority activities were to be increased, especially for medium and small industries, to support these activities with more favorable financial terms and rates. "This provision is designed to enable the hardest hit businesses to rebuild their working capital, thus helping to avoid a reduction in jobs and in supplies of basic goods, caused by liquidity problems."

The above measures, added to those announced earlier (on 10 March), expanded the criteria governing aid to small and medium industries, provided from the appropriate fund established by the federal government. At the same time, a mechanism was set up jointly with the commercial bank of Mexico to back priority industries that had been hurt by the exchange modification. "In addition, the Bank of Mexico has expanded and improved access conditions for the instrument known as 'deposit-credit' for encouraging investment in machinery and equipment not produced in Mexico. This incentive consists of converting foreign currency used for this purpose into Mexican currency."

In the case of basic products, the mechanisms already provided by the federal government for wage-price agreements were to be adapted and made more flexible. The government intended the prices of basic products to decline relative to wages, in order to guarantee a steady rise in the workers' standard of living. "In implementing these mechanisms, a number of additional criteria will also be considered, such as the financial aid of 35 billion pesos for basic products already approved by the executive, as well as the fiscal incentives listed above, in order to avoid having the full burden of the adjustment fall on price changes. We will also have to determine more precisely the appropriate profit margins." The prices of controlled items could be revised on the basis of the estimated impact of the devaluation and the wage adjustment costs in seventy-two areas of production. The system of import permits continued to govern foreign trade. However, a tariff reduction was approved shifting rates to levels existing in June 1981 for 1,500 basic products, raw materials, and capital goods.

Presumably, these measures were intended to shift demand toward the domestic market and to increase national production, in addition to providing businesses with sufficient liquidity and cash flow to get them through the post-devaluation period.

The 1982–88 Basic Plan and Electoral Platform of the PRI

The PRI's Basic Plan Design for 1982–88 (and the Electoral Platform derived from it) outlined the government's philosophy of economic planning, the proposals from the PRI's various sectors and organizations for the next six years, and recommendations from the IEPES (Institute of Political, Economic and Social Studies) commissions. The document was issued in October 1981 and represented a semi-official statement of likely changes in economic policy and procedures during the 1982–88 period. The document is largely political and therefore represents the best statement available to date as to the government's longer-term response to perhaps the most serious economic crisis facing the country since the 1930s.

The plan covers a number of areas—political, social, philosophical, and economic. In its economic objectives, the plan stressed several policy alternatives. The plan noted that a number of sectors were lagging and inadequate, including transportation and the production of certain basic products and raw materials. These sectoral maladjustments caused distortions in productive activity that were "intolerable over the medium term and incompatible with the fundamental goals to meet the basic demands of the popular majorities and to generate jobs." The plan aimed to eliminate these distortions and to reduce monopolistic practices in the industrialization process.[7]

The plan called for agrarian reform, which did not mean merely redistributing land, but also "a distribution of resources farmers should receive along with the land and for their collective and communal organizations." Clearly a supply of productive resources for farming (presumably provided by the government) is a major priority of the PRI. The plan even foresaw reforming the fishing industry to diversify the popular diet and increase the country's self-sufficiency in food.

In the future, the industrial sector was to continue to play a leading role. However, it was to "create more well-paid jobs (than recently) in addition to continuing the high rate of growth in production during a period of slow world growth." Industry must achieve greater production of goods for popular consumption, and do so "with more efficiency so as to raise the population's level of prosperity and improve the purchasing power of wages." There was a disturbing trend toward oligopolistic concentration in the most dynamic industries. To overcome this, "associations of big business with small and medium-sized business will be encouraged. Small industry will be strengthened through a total development program that will afford it greater access to the mechanisms available for fiscal, financial and technological backing."

The state enterprises were to play a basic role in these qualitative changes in the economy. They must "contribute to capital formation in strategic branches of industry and to the supply of popular consumer goods (that must be fostered to support the living standards of Mexicans)." Programs to expand public enterprises should encourage investment in other priority sectors "by offering a greater supply of goods which they manufacture, bringing about a greater demand for national machinery and equipment."

An improvement in the standard of living of Mexicans and the nation's development would be possible "if commerce is transformed into a more effective distribution system, providing consumers with necessary goods at prices within the reach of the majority." The country needs a massive supply of basic products at low prices and "an elimination of excessive middlemen, thus reducing to a minimum the gap between producers and consumers."

The plan declared that science and technology should not be confused with autarchy, but rather should be interpreted as the fostering of a national capacity for generating, desseminating, selecting, adapting, and applying scientific and technical knowledge, consistent with the possibilities and requirements of a self-sufficient development strategy.[8]

Finally, tourism was to be redirected "primarily toward an improvement in the living standard of the working class and making the right to recreation a reality." The plan asserted that the public sector would have to assume a greatly expanded role in implementing the above objectives. Public spending was to be the key to attaining Mexico's national goals, "because it is one of the most active and effective instruments for guiding and regulating the process of economic and social development."

A chief concern of the plan's designers was that in recent years public spending had not been completely and exactly adapted to the national goals. To rectify this, they noted that productivity and efficiency in public spending must be intensified through improvements in budget programming and with greater attention to follow-up and evaluation. Furthermore, control of spending must be improved with a more efficient regulatory and accounting system.

A major premise of the plan document was that public enterprises constitute the most important economic, social, and political legacy the state has given to the people of Mexico, and that the major increase in the state's participation (mainly through its enterprises and agencies) has to a great extent determined the country's socioeconomic evolution. The plan argued that the selective control of credit should be reoriented to bring credit allocation more in line with the priorities of national planning.

Anti-inflationary policy must seek the causes of inflation in the structural problems of the economy and the society; in the time lag between a growing public and private aggregate demand and the supply of goods and services that has not progressed at the same rate; in the effects of international inflation on the economy; in the burdensome nature of the commercial system; and in the current maladjustments leading to speculative activities that bring wealth to a few to the detriment of the many. Anti-inflationary policies must draw on all the tools at the state's disposal, preferably promoting internal supply and modulating demand, and use forceful measures in trade policy to prevent and combat speculation to correct regional and seasonal shortages of supply. The problems of inflation clearly require a participatory planning system as a means of controlling inflation effectively.

In the international area, the plan argued that Mexico's balance of payments problems required rationalizing protection and imports to promote exports, to implement an international strategy for Mexican foreign trade, to use the public sector's purchasing power in relationships with other countries, and to stimulate the commercial development of the border areas and free trade zones. Mexico should continue its policy of diversifying trade relations with different parts of the world, avoiding dependence on the United States, seeking to increase its relations with all countries, and striving for a revaluation of raw materials and greater equity in world trade. Priority would continue to be given to intensifying economic and commercial relations with Central America and the Caribbean and to pursuing the economic integration of Latin America.

Foreign investment was to be subjected stringently to the legal provisions and priorities for development. Three criteria should govern all foreign investment subject to Mexican laws: it must generate new jobs, it must provide new technology, and it must support the opening of markets for Mexican exports.

Policy Miscalculations, 1978–82

In assessing the country's development strategy under José López Portillo, Carlos Ramirez writing in Mexico City *Proceso* (22 March 1982) commented as follows on the resignation of David Ibarra Muñoz, the secretary of finance:

> The years of Ibarra Muñoz—1978–82, central years in the term of President López Portillo—were times of particular economic strategy: growth at all cost, but based on petroleum and not on the wealth of the few who got rich in the oil boom, even at the price of inflation and of reduced standards of living for the majority of the nation. These were also years of postponements: submerged in the oil euphoria, there were plans to achieve a surplus in the current account of the balance of payments—the key to the 1982 devaluation—at the very time when demands for social justice, such as a tax reform to

redistribute wealth, a monetary reform to obtain sound financing sources, an anti-inflation policy to avoid harmful social consequences, and reforms of the subsidies given the private sector in order to avoid augmenting privately held wealth, were going unheeded.

"This is 'neo-developmentism,' neoAlemanism," Deputy Arturo Salcido Beltran told Ibarra Muñoz in 1980, but Ibarra Muñoz did not recognize his policy in this description. Ever since his appearance before the first Chamber of Deputies of the political reform in March, the then secretary of finance had disregarded criticisms and questions about the quality of the economic recovery, terming them ideological attacks and on matters of national concern. He believed in economics as a pure science and in his view, the nation's development was independent of prior commitments or ideological views. It was neo-developmentism that brought the nation to a formidable period of economic growth which did not redistribute wealth, but instead helped to concentrate income even more sharply. In the chamber, confronted with a secretary of state who was hostile to criticism, there was a revival of the concept of two separate Mexicos: one wealthy, based on oil, living side by side with a Mexico of poverty and misery.[9]

Each of Ibarra Muñoz's years in office was perceived to reflect a bias against labor:

1978: the promotion of the multiple banking system, oligopolies, and incentives for production in the private sector; salary limitations
1979: tax adjustments that instead of reforming the system left taxes on capital virtually unchanged
1980: the initiation of a value-added tax placed an additional burden on consumption
1981: an inflationary upsurge that affected the income and standards of living of the vast majority of the people
1982: monetary devaluation as a consequence of the failure of recent economic policies.[10]

On the whole, it is apparent that López Portillo's economic policy as handled by Ibarra Muñoz was not sound. For the purposes of growth, the treasury policy impeded consumption while discriminating against labor but not against capital. While inflation leveled off at about 25 percent, domestic credit became more expensive, the foreign debt evolved into one of the highest in the world, the government's deficit got out of control, subsidies to businessmen were multiplied, and the private sector was pampered even more than in the past to encourage investment.

While real GDP growth accelerated to 9 percent in 1979, the increased output was not more equitably distributed. Despite the overall development plan calling for income created through the oil-investment-output mechanism to be distributed through the multiple wage-price-profits mechanism, nothing of the sort happened. In fact, SPP (Secretariat of Programming and the Budget) data indicate that average profits were increasing between 80 and 200 percent a year in the late 1970s to early 1980s, while salaries were increasing by an average of 22 percent a year. The Treasury did not cut taxes for low incomes but adjusted taxes to these inflationary rates. In essence, then, the cost of growth was reflected in a decline in real salaries of approximately 30 percent over a five-year period.

Fiscal policy, therefore, continued to favor the concentration of wealth, impeded national consumption, and did not touch the wealth that grew with the oil boom. Financial policy was in no better condition. By the end of 1981, Mexico's foreign debt amounted to $60 billion. In 1981, Mexico paid $12 billion in interest and debt service charges, and in 1982 the country would require over $18 billion to finance its development costs. The federal budget for 1982 dramatizes the limitations of this policy: a third of the budget was financed from loans, while the treasury contributed barely another third. Mexico needed about $30 billion in 1982 to pay interest charges and finance the government's debt. Clearly, these financial developments are the result of miscalculations made by the government over the last several years.

The February and April 1982 programs constituted an effort by the Mexican government to effect adjustment through self-discipline. The program was styled after International Monetary Fund programs but did not involve the IMF as an outside source of discipline and finance.

While well structured, the programs were never fully implemented, particularly in the key area of public finances.[11] The deficit/GDP ratio for 1982 was about 16.5 percent. In addition, by July it became apparent that Mexico would not be able to raise sufficient funds in international capital markets to meet the net external borrowing target in the 20 April program. Confidence in Mexico was also affected by broader problems not associated with Mexico such as the Falkland Islands crisis, the external debt, and declining levels of liquidity in the international banking system.

More specifically, recent reports show that in spite of austerity measures taken following the first devaluation, federal expenditure in 1982 was about 0.9 billion pesos higher than the budget in December 1981, and 65 percent more than actually spent in 1981.[12] The original budget required outlays of 3,021 billion pesos that were reduced by 150 billion in April. However, with wage rises decreed after the first devaluation adding 179 billion pesos and the debt service demanding an extra 392 billion, the total rose to 3,742 billion pesos. The Secretariat of Planning and Budget also estimated that increased costs owing to inflation, other charges, and pressures on the investment program would bring the bill to 4,250 billion pesos, against 2,575 billion in 1981. Developments in the exchange markets since then have increased the budgetary excess further.

The resulting deficit was expected to be financed partly from greater income from personal taxes because thresholds have not been raised along with wages and salaries, but later measures may have precluded any significant increases in revenues.[13] Also, subsidies were modified in mid-1982 on several products, doubling the price of the staple tortillas and bread. These changes raised gasoline prices by 50 percent, and the cost of electricity and gas by 30 percent and 11.8 percent, respectively, for domestic users and increased the cost of electricity and fuel oil by 50 percent and 62 percent for industry. However, these increases are likely to be offset by a fall in income from corporate taxes after the devaluations and an insufficient contribution from foreign trade or tourism. In short, authorities had to implement further austerity measures to avoid a large measure of inflationary financing and in this regard followed the IMF recommendations agreed to at the end of the year.

Ironically, the spark that ignited the financial panic in early August was an austerity measure.[14] After a sound election victory in July for the official government party—Partido Revolucionario Institucional (PRI)—on 1 August the government decreed price increases of 100 percent for bread and tortillas and 50 percent for gasoline. Anti-inflationary in the long run, these measures meant short-run corrective inflation. More significant, though, they provoked the public—already shocked by a 60 percent annual inflation rate—frantically to convert pesos to dollars. With sharply declining foreign exchange reserves, the government declared domestic dollar deposits in banks redeemable only in pesos, instituted a dual exchange rate, and temporarily closed the exchange markets.

The withdrawals from the Mex-dollar accounts (dollar-denominated checking and time accounts held in the Mexican banking system) were significant because they carried a 70 percent reserve requirement. The Bank of Mexico therefore lost $70 in reserves for every $100 transfer of a Mex-dollar account to a foreign bank. To counteract a possible run on these accounts, which would quickly deplete the Bank of Mexico's foreign currency reserves, the government declared that all withdrawals from Mex-dollar accounts must be in pesos at a new exchange rate of 69.5 pesos to the dollar.[15]

On 5 August, a dual exchange rate system was announced. The dual rate system involved a preferential rate of about 50 pesos to the dollar for the payment of public sector external debt obligations, private sector interest obligations, and imports of "basic goods." A general or "freely floating" rate was established for all other transactions requiring foreign exchange. This latter rate fluctuated between 65 and 85 pesos per dollar until 12 August when the government announced two unprecedented decisions: the forced conversion to pesos of withdrawals from dollar-denominated (Mex-dollar) accounts in Mexican banks and a temporary closing of the foreign exchange market.

Seven days later, the U.S. and Mexican governments arranged an immediate financial assistance package for Mexico. The package included a $1 billion advance payment for petroleum exports to stock the U.S. Strategic Petroleum Reserve, up to $1 billion of U.S. government guarantees issued by the Commodity Credit Corporation to support U.S. commercial bank loans and purchases of U.S. agricultural products, and a $1.5 billion short-term "swap" loan involving the U.S. Treasury, the Federal Reserve, and Bank for International Settlements, representing a group of central banks from Mexico's other creditor nations. This "swap" loan was later increased to $1.85 billion.[16]

The next development came on 1 September when to the surprise of most observers President López Portillo nationalized the private banks and imposed complete exchange controls. The full impact of both decisions has yet to be determined. The bank nationalizations will probably expand significantly the government's influence on the investment and production decisions of the private sector through the allocation of credit. The subsequent decisions to lower interest rates may lead to less growth in bank deposits than would otherwise be the case.

The impact of exchange controls was more immediate. Two exchange rates were established: the preferential rate at 50 pesos to the dollar for interest and principal payments on the public and private sector external debt and all authorized imports, and the ordinary exchange rate at 70 pesos to the dollar for all other allowable foreign transaction as defined in the decrees of 1 and 14 September, plus supplementary regulations. Access to either exchange rate depends upon the availability of foreign currency and all purchases of foreign exchange require prior government approval. The decrees made pesos the only legal currency in Mexico and banned the import or export of either pesos or foreign currencies except in amounts of less than 5,000 pesos or the foreign currency equivalent.[17]

The theory behind the September measures appears to be that by imposing complete exchange controls no internal savings will escape the country. As a result, interest rates can be determined more or less independently of world interest rates. The Bank of Mexico reduced peso interest rates for both loans and deposits. The government hoped that the lower interest rates would reduce inflationary pressures.

In addition, the authorities clearly expected that the centralized allocation of credit would channel savings so as to maximize the increase in output and social well-being, in contrast to their perceived previous inefficient uses. The 1 September measures and their implementation may constitute the beginnings of a significant structural change in the Mexican economy.

Entering the final quarter of 1982, the Mexican crisis appeared to be subsiding. Nevertheless, a severe recession seems inevitable, and the inflation rate for 1982 was approaching 90 percent. Although a voluntary conversion of short- to long-term debt remained possible, the probability increased that Mexico would have to request a formal debt rescheduling from its creditors. Rescheduling would tarnish Mexico's credit record in the medium term. It would also further discourage foreign banks from lending significant amounts of additional money to the country in the near future, forcing adjustments to compress further the external deficit.

The future seems to hold austerity for Mexico and inconvenience for the international financial system.[18] In fact, on 10 November 1982, the Mexican government reached an agreement with the IMF that would provide Mexico with $3.84 billion in credit over the next three years on the condition that the country adopt austerity measures. The agreement diminished the risk that Mexico would enter a temporary debt moratorium.[19]

Conclusions

The economic pattern of the 1970s can be characterized as one with lagging public sector savings, import substitution policies aggravating the overvaluation of the peso, and export growth and agricultural production lagging behind GDP. In these circumstances, foreign debt tended to be treated as a slack variable. It complemented domestic credit in financing the public sector deficit and kept the exchange rate stable, regardless of the growing current account deficit.

The current account deficit was widened in steps, but the trend of growing dependence on foreign savings has been strong. The foreign public debt, which was $1,327 million in 1962, increased to $4.2 billion by the end of 1970, and reached over $60 billion by 1982.

Given the conditions as of early 1983, therefore, future expansion of the economy is likely to be curtailed by either of two mechanisms: (1) Given that the rate of increase in the level of national income seems to govern the current account deficit in the balance of payments, a boom might be choked, the deficit might become unsustainable, and/or foreign credit might be unavailable. (2) The inability to generate domestic savings in line with investment demands at high rates of growth will narrow the possibilities for domestic noninflationary financing of the public sector deficit.

III. Empirical Examinations of Policy Impact

Introduction

The design of policies for economic stabilization in Mexico is complicated by the dynamic structure of that country's economic system. It may well be that in the Mexican context certain types of "intuitive" stabilization policies can result in undesired instabilities. Furthermore, policy measures in Mexico encounter a complicated lag structure—the existence of several policy instruments may only complicate forecasting the actual timing of policy impact.

These considerations lead to the conclusion that the only useful way to study the response of the economy to various governmental policy measures is to work from a complete macroeconomic model. This section is a first attempt at building the macroeconomic model developed in part IV. Part III is divided into four main chapters. The first attempts to determine the empirical nature of the inflationary process in Mexico—with implications for the relative effectiveness of fiscal, monetary, and structural reform policies in controlling the Mexican price level. The final three chapters examine the controversies surrounding the use and impact of various fiscal measures open to the government for such purposes as stimulating private investment, increasing employment and the overall rate of growth, and bringing the balance of payments into equilibrium.

The empirical relationships identified in the following four chapters, therefore, form the starting point of the macroeconomic policy forecasting model developed in part IV.

9. Scope for Anti-Inflationary Policy

Inflation poses not only a serious obstacle to the achievement of the Industrial Development Plan's targets but a grave threat to Mexico's economic and political system as well. It does so because it succeeds in touching the lives of the ordinary citizen—not some, but all—in a way in which the government's development expenditures rarely do. Whether inflation operates at the double-digit rates of the last few years or the more gradual increases of the late 1960s to early 1970s, the damage done to the individual and society is evident. By creating an atmosphere of insecurity and futility, by permitting wholesale economic injustice, and by giving rise to abject poverty, inflation creates an environment that makes for irrationality in politics.[1] This in turn deeply affects the nature and effectiveness of subsequent stabilization measures.

This chapter addresses three main questions. First, what role did accelerated government expenditures play in increasing inflationary pressures? Second, to what extent was the recent inflation imported rather than domestically induced? Finally, did the underlying mechanism of inflation change during this period so that the inflation experience in the mid-1970s was fundamentally different from that in prior periods?

The following empirical analysis will show that, in general, accelerated government expenditures have contributed significantly to the country's inflation, particularly during periods when stepped-up expenditures resulted in rapid increases in the money supply. While potentially an important source of inflationary pressure, changes in external price levels actually contributed rather little to such pressure. In other words, the country's recent inflation was largely domestically induced. The underlying inflationary mechanism seems to have changed around 1970, from one in which inflation was predominantly a monetary phenomenon to one in which structural elements played an increasingly important role.

Causes of Mexican Inflation

After a period of over fifteen years of relative price stability, the general price level in Mexico began to rise rapidly in the last quarter of 1972, increasing by approximately 30 percent by 1980. Explanations for the end of price stability are many.[2] (1) The government paid little attention to structural problems, permitting them to intensify and finally surface. (2) The government overreacted to the economic slowdown of 1971 with vastly expanded monetary and fiscal policies. (3) World inflation raised Mexican prices through more expensive imports, particularly foodstuffs. (4) The government's import substitution policy encouraged inefficient, high-cost production. (5) The Echeverría administration's attempt at social reform with a high level of economic growth resulted in large government deficits and severe debt service payments. A number of other sources are of course logically possible and at least not inconsistent with the country's overall economic patterns of growth and inflation.

General Patterns of Growth and Inflation

The actual record shows an average rate of real growth per annum in 1973–76 of 4.9 percent, compared with an average of 6.4 percent for the preceding six years of stability. The latter included a year of severe austerity (1971) with a low growth rate of 3.4 percent, when the government reduced the rate of public investment by over 23 percent in its attempt to dampen rising inflation.

During 1975, the government attempted to deal with inflation again, and it is possible that this was partly responsible for the fall in the rate of growth to 4.1 percent. In 1977, the effects of additional petroleum resources began to make themselves felt. The share of petroleum and its derivatives in GDP increased from 3.6 percent in 1973 to 5.0 percent in 1977 and to 6.3 percent in 1980. From 1977 to date, the new oil resources have added, directly or indirectly, possibly two percentage points to the rate of growth in GDP. Even with this lifting of the trend line, however, the average growth in the first four years of the López Portillo administration was only 6.4 percent, the same as for 1967–72.

In terms of overall patterns, prices were clearly more stable in 1960–70 than in the 1980s. Prices were also more stable relative to international prices and to U.S. prices during the 1960–70 period.

Conclusions about wages are more difficult to draw. Nominal urban minimum wages grew by 268 percent between 1970 and 1978. In real terms, the increase was 18.8 percent, deflating by the national consumer price index, and 18.4 percent deflating by the special consumer price index for low income families. Real wages in manufacturing industries rose by similar amounts.

It should be noted that in periods of high inflation, the annual changes in real wages fluctuate widely. Deflated by the national consumer price index, the real urban minimum 1971–78 shows four annual declines ranging from −0.9 percent to −6.2 percent and four annual increases ranging from 0.9 percent to 12.7 percent. In the same period, manufacturing wages were more stable, ranging from a decline of −3.1 percent in 1978 to increases of 0.3 percent to 9.0 percent in the other seven years.

Major Issues

Sorting out the relative importance of the potential causes of inflation is a difficult task but a necessary one since inflationary forces appear to be gathering strength, the productive expenditure of petroleum earnings will likely fuel excessive demand, and further spending will run afoul of severe supply inelasticities and / or bottlenecks.

After the failures in 1971 and 1975, Mexican authorities appear unwilling to risk impairing the rate of economic expansion as a means of controlling inflation. President López Portillo has noted on numerous occasions that the government must not reduce inflation by decelerating investment spending or general demand. As late as September 1980 and in the face of 30 percent inflation, the president outlined various anti-inflationary measures in his fourth State of the Nation Report, making clear that any conflicts between inflation and growth would be decided in favor of growth.

It is fair to say, however, that the ability of the Mexican government to come to grips with the nation's recent inflationary buildup will be one of the major factors determining the overall success of its new development programs and plans. In this connection, Leopoldo Solis warned in 1978 that inflation could cause exchange rate problems and thwart import substitution and export development, thereby hampering the goal of product diversification.[3]

Others have pointed out that Mexico is determined not to repeat the mistakes of Iran and Venezuela.[4] Venezuela has had reasonably stable prices, but petroleum income has not been used successfully to institute lasting developmental changes in the economy. Iran encountered high rates of inflation in the 1970s and failed to transform the structure of its internal production.

The nature of Mexican inflation and the course of inflation-related variables therefore merit considerable attention. The analysis below particularly emphasizes inflation in the 1970s and attempts to identify the type and source of the inflation experienced.

Theories of Inflation

The increase in the rate of inflation in the first half of the 1970s together with the government's seeming inability to stabilize the price level dramatized the need for a deeper understanding of the country's inflationary process. A debate over the precise cause of the rapidly accelerating price level has developed both within and outside of Mexico. For convenience, two extreme views on the country's inflationary process can be distinguished: the structuralist interpretation and the monetarist explanation.

The Structuralist Position

Structuralism was associated from the beginning with the more leftist writers in Mexico, together with a number of the leading technocrats in the Ministry of Planning. As developed in Mexico, structuralism seems largely concerned with potential and actual conflicts between growth, stabilization, and equity.[5]

Structuralism has always stressed disequilibrium and the notion that the country's inflation was inevitable once the government attempted rapid growth in the presence of structural bottlenecks or constraints. Therefore, the chief assumption has been that certain fundamental facets of the economic, institutional, and sociopolitical organization of the country in one way or another acted to inhibit economic expansion.[6]

One variant of the structuralist school suggests that the rapid industrial growth of the postwar years, far from being stable development, led to greater foreign penetration of the economy, worsening income distribution, and sectoral imbalance. These factors not only exacerbated social tensions but also led to economic stagnation.

From this perspective economic policy under Echeverría is seen largely as attempting to get the economy out of this impasse by further state intervention in heavy industry, wage support, and agrarian reform. In this, the Echeverría government is felt to have been frustrated by the world crisis of the 1970s and by opposition from both the domestic and foreign banking system. As Tello notes: "Critics forget that the deficiencies in economic policy were not in that which was implemented but rather in what was not: the restructuring of the financial, monetary and credit system so that it ceases to be the determinant factor in national economic development."[7]

The alleged structural constraints identified and analyzed by this theoretical school include the inelastic supply of foodstuffs, the infrastructure bottleneck, and the foreign exchange constraint.[8] In the structuralist view, inflation could not be stopped if these structural limitations were not eliminated. Distortions generated by the inflationary process itself generated further cumulative inflation. The main cumulative factors were distortions of the price system, mainly caused by the price control policies associated with inflation, and misallocation of resources, mainly investment funds.[9]

Along these lines many structuralists contend that Mexico's inflation was inevitable, given the country's phase of transition from an economy oriented outward and based on exports to one oriented inward and based on the domestic market. Such a transition, it was argued, required massive changes in the socioeconomic structure of the country. Price mechanisms, operating within very imperfect market structures and with limited resource mobility, were unable to achieve this. Given the imperfection of the system, attempts at major structural change simply produced shortages and disequilibrium on many fronts.

In particular, the employment problem is seen (in Tello and SPF) as clearly determined by the low demand for labor generated by an industry based on foreign technology, while the skewed income distribution produces a demand for luxury products based on this technology. Underemployment is seen, therefore, as a more critical problem than inflation.[10]

The attention to the composition of demand and the influence of industrial ownership means that this approach can be said to have made the transition from a Keynesian to a Kaleckian view of the world. This conclusion is strengthened by the recent detailed empirical attention to the process of price formation through "markups" on wages and imports by the CIDE group.

Many structuralists see the most serious threat to price stability over the next few years in severe supply bottlenecks. Lagging agricultural production and the short supply of skilled human capital are the two most pressing problems. Aluminum, cement, and oil refining capacities are reported to be full. Inadequate transportation and storage facilities may possibly be the most severe bottlenecks.

The railway system still relies heavily on telegraphic communications, employs old locomotives, and on a one-track system that limits the number of runs. According to the director of the national railway system complete rehabilitation of the rail tracks will take eighteen years and 65 billion pesos at current prices with 23 billion pesos programmed for 1980–82 to improve them. He indicated that the system is short 150 new diesel-electric locomotives and that 4,000 new cars will be needed each year.[11] Inadequate ports and rail transportation have led to an increase in highway use. In late 1979, in Baja California, merchandise was delayed over sixty days because truck operators balked at the prospect of an empty return run. Trucks waited for a month in Nuevo Laredo for import documents to be processed. At Coatzacoalcos government agencies and larger companies were paying double or triple the official trucking rates to hire trailers. Such gouging has led some producers such as pharmaceutical companies to withdraw some products from the market. Red tape limits the circulation of trucks to specific areas and means loads have to be switched, adding up to 60 percent to the cost.[12]

Critique of the Structuralist Approach

In this context, the term bottlenecks and the relationship of bottlenecks to inflation must be clarified. Structuralist analysis has often been criticized as unsound because there is no reason, at least in theory, why an increase in the price of one commodity (i.e., a bottleneck) should raise the general price level and provoke an inflationary spiral.[13] In an open economy, an increase in imports can keep prices constant. In a closed economy, neoclassical theory would predict that a rise in the relative price of one type of good (for example, beans) should shift demand to other goods and reallocate the factors of production, thus restoring equilibrium. But if the prices of manufactured goods are inflexible downward, a rise in food prices (with other prices constant) raises the average price level. In turn, if industrial wages are tied to consumer prices, they will rise leading to an upward movement in industrial prices. The change in relative prices may be insufficient to shift demand, and thus an inflationary spiral will develop.[14]

The Mexican inflation of the 1970s cannot be explained by structural factors alone. In addition, some sort of propagating mechanism had to be present to sustain price increases over such a long period of time. Here the structuralists are not particularly explicit. They mention a struggle among different economic groups to increase their shares of total income. This manifested itself to a certain extent in conflicts between wage earners and profit earners. Second, and probably more important, was the struggle between the private and public sectors to increase their share of real resources.

Barkin and Esteva have developed a sociological view along these lines that interprets the overall price level as determined by the conflict between different social classes over the economic surplus.[15] They see successive attempts to maintain or increase wage and profit levels rather than the money supply or growth problems as the prime cause of inflation. This line of argument is relatively novel in the Mexican context, but the authors' case seems weakened by the lack of formal specification in their model.[16] In particular, they do not specify the effects of fiscal structures, the stability or instability of business markups, and the influence of external price levels.

Sociology has contributed further to the inflation debate by analyzing entrepreneurial groups. Here some assumption must be made explicitly or implicitly about the strength of domestic industrial capital. The radical writers assume it to be a distorting influence, while the more orthodox structuralists argue that capital is incapable of further unaided industrialization. Unfortunately, there has been relatively little empirical research on this topic.

A Structuralist Two-Gap Inflationary Model

In sum, although a complete structuralist model has not previously been developed for Mexico, one can easily be constructed by incorporating a number of structural elements into a general Bruno-Chenery-Strout model. A structural inflationary process in the Mexican context could begin with a rapid expansion in economic activity stemming from oil-financed government investment in the industrial sector. Such an expansion should cut back underemployment generated over time by static conditions in the agricultural sector and a moderately high population growth.

In turn, increased incomes create an expanded demand for food, thus generating pressures in the agricultural sector. Due to the low price elasticity of supply in agriculture (a structural problem), however, substantial increases in relative prices in favor of the sector are necessary to clear the market. Food shortages (at relatively stable prices) are aggravated by the strain that oil-financed imports had already imposed on the country's port facilities and transport system. The result: while oil revenues are capable of financing imports of food and consumer products, these imports could not increase rapidly enough to augment domestic supplies, thus maintaining a relatively stable price level.

If unemployed resources could have been moved productively to the industrial sector, and if industrial prices had been flexible downward, a change in relative prices without inflation might have taken place. However, the low mobility of most domestic resources, and the inflexibility of industrial prices due to monopolistic positions encouraged by the import substitution industrial strategy, made monetary expansion the only means of generating prices high enough for the change in relative prices.

In short, a structuralist interpretation of Mexico's inflation would contend that domestic price increases stemmed largely from the inability of supply to adapt to a changing and growing level of demand. In the 1970s, this problem was characterized by inelasticity and instability in agricultural output together with an inadequate infrastructure, which precluded imports from aiding any adjustment to equilibrium at relatively stable prices.

With these mechanisms in mind, a structuralist two-gap model can be hypothesized for Mexico as follows.[17] If the Mexican authorities raised the rate of growth of real gross domestic product above the historic rate of 6 to 7 percent, the economy would generate a foreign trade gap due to the inelasticity of import demand, a structural problem, together with fixed export revenues. Imports must increase because additional amounts of raw materials and capital goods would be required by the industrial sector. The country's extremely underdeveloped tax system would not be capable of absorbing the excess liquidity from the expanding consumer sector. Given most individuals' low propensity to save, this would produce a gap between total domestic savings and investment greater than that between exports and imports. In these circumstances, inflation would most likely be the only mechanism capable of making the equilibrium adjustment between the domestic (savings-investment) and external (export-import) gaps. Inflation would increase savings by pricing individuals out of certain product markets, so that the domestic gap equaled the external gap.

Structuralists, therefore, view inflation as emerging in the process of making the two gaps equal after the fact. The actual adjustment is achieved through two struggles for the available consumer goods: that between wage earners and profit earners and that between the private sector and the public sector. The ultimate distribution of income will be determined by the relative strength of these groups.

Using this framework, it is possible to quantify the overall constraints on the country's growth during the period under consideration.

If imports are now defined to include net factor services, Y or gross national product is equal to:[18]

$$Y = C + I + (X - M) \tag{1}$$

Along with GNP, two additional identities can be created:

$$Y = C + S \qquad \text{and} \tag{2}$$

$$F = I - S \tag{3}$$

and from (1) with $Y = GNP$:

$$F = M - X$$

It is now possible to estimate an ex post savings function of the form:

$$S = a1 + b1Y + c1F$$

and an ex post import function of the form:

$$M = a2 + b2Y + c2F$$

Several possible constraints to the country's growth can now be identified within the context of the so-called two-gap analysis where GS equals the savings gap or

$(I - S)$, and GT equals the trade gap or $(M - X)$. If the trade gap had been a binding constraint on the country's growth during the period under consideration, an ex ante deficiency of (desired) foreign exchange would have existed, as an excess of required investment over potential savings for the level of income at the time. It can be shown that under these circumstances, the estimated coefficient $c1$ in equation (2) above would assume a value between -1 and 0. On the other hand, if the savings gap had been binding, foreign capital would have implemented rather than acted as a substitute for domestic savings.

In the equilibrating process, it is unlikely that adjustments reflecting ex ante deficiencies in the two gaps would have been alleviated by changes in exports. Actual exports could have fallen short of their potential only if the goods and services exported could have been consumed domestically in significant amounts, and some imports required for producing exports could be employed to produce goods for the internal market. The specialized nature of the oil industry and the limited areas to which the factors in this sector could be transferred in the short run precluded this type of adjustment in Mexico during the period under consideration.

The constraints on exports as an economic equilibrator made increases in imports over their desired level the likely mechanism of adjustment in those years in which the savings gap was constraining the expansion in income. During those periods actual and desired levels of savings would be equal, with the estimated value of $c1$ equaling zero.

Again, the theoretical literature has demonstrated that if in fact imports exceeded their minimum required levels in the presence of relatively abundant foreign exchange, estimates of $c2$ would be positive.

The above considerations can be used to derive a fairly precise method of identifying the macroeconomic constraints under which the Mexican economy operated during the 1951–82 period as a whole. Tests were also made for several subperiods to see if the importance of either the domestic or external constraints shifted. As the model is constructed, a value of $c1$ close to -1.0 together with a value of $c2$ not significantly different from 0.0 would imply that the trade gap posed the greatest hindrance on increased output. On the other hand, if estimates of $c1$ were close to 0.0 and $c2$ was significantly positive, it is likely that the savings gap had been binding. Finally, if estimates of $c1$ were significantly negative, but with an absolute value less than unity, while $c2$ was significantly positive, the country probably experienced periods of alternative savings and trade constraints, with neither dominating the period as a whole.

The results indicate that for the 1952–80 period the trade gap was binding with $c1 = 0.35$ and $c2$ small and insignificant. This pattern held fairly steadily during the various subperiods (1952–70; 1952–75; 1966–80; 1961–80) examined.

Apparently, the government's attempts at mobilizing savings were successful in alleviating any constraint from that source. On the other hand, an overvalued exchange rate combined with relatively high rates of income growth through most of the period to create a relative shortage of foreign exchange.

Cost Theories of Inflation

The structuralist approach is largely of interest because it provides a useful framework for developing an integrated view of Mexico's inflationary process. Because it relies on such concepts as relative inelasticity, the theory is always open to criticism: how inelastic does something have to be before it is relatively inelastic? However, several indirect tests such as the one above are possible, and with time a more complete empirical model will undoubtedly be constructed.

A discussion and quantitative assessment of the importance of cost factors is much more straightforward. However, any analysis of the cost-push origins of Mexican inflation will suffer from the limited availability of data and the existing data's limitations. There is no consistent time series for wages, nor is there an important price series. Further, the GDP deflator is so weighted by oil that it is of little value in analyzing the possible determinants of domestic price increases. There is a cost of living index and a wholesale price index, but both of these measures have serious defects. The cost of living index, based on a limited sample of goods and services purchased in Mexico City, does not therefore represent the consumption patterns of the majority of the rural population. The wholesale price index is heavily weighted toward imports.

Using the available data, the next section examines two cost factors—world prices and wages—as well as an empirical proxy for cost pressures—the effects on prices of deviations from the trend in real GDP. Taken in their entirety, the empirical results presented below cast doubt on the role of pure cost-push factors as a significant contributor to Mexico's inflation during the period under consideration. Admittedly, these may have been present in certain industries and at certain times, but their overall impact seems to have been minimal. While the following results are somewhat negative, they are of great value in that they narrow down the major inflationary pressures to those of a structural and/or monetary origin. In fact, the final inflationary equations estimated in the macroeconomic model presented in chapter 13 depict Mexican inflation as the result of essentially monetary causes.

Movements in World Prices

Given its size, it is safe to assume that Mexico's purchases and sales of nonoil goods in the world market had no effect on the prices of these goods. For all practical purposes, the prices of the country's nonoil exports and imports were determined by global demand and supply conditions. For purposes of analysis, therefore, the U.S. dollar export and import prices of these goods can be taken as exogenous variables. Given these international prices, the export and import prices in pesos were dependent on the peso/dollar rate.

There are two channels by which rising import prices might induce domestic inflation: the direct effect of rising prices in world markets, and an indirect effect of increased prices for imported raw materials, transmitted through the higher cost of domestic production for finished products. In the second channel, producers had little or no way of substituting for imported materials, which meant that there were few real possibilities (at least in modern industries) of switching from expensive imported goods to cheaper domestic sources of supply.

The data on external sources of inflation for this period are somewhat limited. Nevertheless, several patterns seem fairly clear. A close examination of the actual fluctuations in the rate of inflation in the 1970s suggests a fairly close link between domestic prices and the movement of international prices of food, raw materials, oil, and oil by-products. For example, the 1971–72 decline in the consumer price index appears to be linked in part to the reduction in international prices of foodstuffs and raw materials taking place at that time.

Similarly, the rise in the rate of inflation in 1973 and 1974 was taking place while the international prices of raw materials and intermediate goods were rising. The sharp increase in public sector prices and tariffs, particularly those on oil and oil by-products, no doubt added to the overall rise in domestic prices.

Of course, movements in international prices by themselves are not sufficient to explain the rising rate of Mexican inflation relative to the rates in other major countries. As internal sources of inflationary pressure, both the decline of agricultural production and the slowing down in oil production combined to accentuate the movements in international prices.

Specifically, the rapid rise in the import prices of basic foodstuffs in 1973–74 coincided with a fall in domestic production, thus increasing the import content of agricultural supplies and undermining the effectiveness of the government's agricultural prices policy, designed to neutralize the effect of imported inflation. The Middle East oil crisis in 1973–74 and the quadrupling of oil prices just happened to occur as the domestic oil industry was beginning to encounter difficulty meeting growing domestic demand.

Given available data, it is very difficult to make any clear distinction between external and internal sources of inflationary pressure for intermediate inputs into manufacturing and construction. There is surely a relationship between the import price of building materials, the rise in domestic wholesale prices, and the increase in the cost of housing and housing rentals. A similar pattern between import and domestic prices can be observed for textiles. For all of these items, it is apparent that both domestic and foreign sources of price increases contributed to the rise in Mexican wholesale and consumer prices. Domestic inflationary pressures corresponded generally in timing to the expansion of consumer incomes, and for building materials to the rapid expansion of expenditures in the construction sector.

At the aggregate level, recent empirical work on a large sample of countries suggests a possible relationship between the degree of national integration into the world economic system and inflation. In general, the more open countries have experienced less price inflation.[19] Presumably, openness serves as a kind of safety valve; domestic inflationary pressure spills over into the balance of payments in the open economy, thus necessitating less price inflation.

One way of testing for the effect of openness on domestic inflation is to test various formulations of a price equation, with measures reflecting the degree of contact with the world economy included as independent variables. Logical candidates in this regard are the country's import-income ratio, the rate of change in the import-income ratio, the country's terms of trade (the ratio of import prices to export prices), the rate of growth in the money supply, and the rate of growth of real gross domestic product.

Iyoha, the originator of this test, used imports / GDP as an independent variable, arguing that a negative correlation between these two variables could be interpreted as evidence in support of the hypothesis that in an open economy domestic inflationary pressures spill over into the balance of payments, thus resulting in less domestic inflation than otherwise would have been the case.[20]

It has been argued that this mechanism does not depict very accurately the processes at work in most developing countries, where foreign exchange shortages pose a severe limit to the possibility of absorbing potential inflationary pressures through increasing import surplus.[21] The typical developing country may, therefore, not really have a choice between its rate of domestic inflation and the magnitude of its balance of payments deficit. The rate of inflation may in part be determined by the foreign exchange constraint. Mexico's borrowing capacity in the international financial markets would seem to rule out this problem for most of the period under consideration.

Since there is no real consensus in the literature as to the best way of measuring openness, the simple ratio of nominal imports (in the national income accounts—*NAN*) to nominal gross domestic product, *GDPN* or $K = ZNAN/GDPN$, was used.

Another independent variable (suggested by Iyoha) is the terms of trade. Due to lack of import and export unit value figures for Mexico, the terms of trade effect (Q) was defined as the U.S. export unit value index (from International Monetary Fund Financial statistics) divided by the Mexican wholesale price index (*WPI*) or $Q = USEUV/WPI$.

Other independent variables included in the analysis were (1) the deviation of real GDP from its historical trend (*YDT*); (2) the rate of change of the terms of trade (*GQ*); (3) the growth of M2 money (*GM*2); (4) the growth in real GDP (*GGDPNP*); (5) the growth in M1 money and M1 lagged (*GM*1, *GM*1*L*); and (6) expected rate of inflation defined as last year's inflation minus that of the previous year (*INFF*), with inflation the rate of change in the gross domestic product deflator.

A number of different combinations were tried, with the best results (table 9.1) occurring when the various measures of openness were regressed simultaneously with the growth in the terms of trade (*GQ*), the rate of expected inflation (*INFE*), and the deviation from the trend (*YDT*). Regressions on the wholesale price increase gave consistently better but quite similar results to those of the consumer price index. Hence, only the results obtained from the regressions with the rate of change in wholesale prices are presented.

Table 9.1. Mexico: impact of openness on inflation, 1951–80

Dependent variable	Equation	Independent variables												
		GO	*GM1*	*GM1L*	*INFE*	*YDT*	K	*GGDPNP*	*GM2*	*RHO*	Intercept	r^2	*F*	*DW*
Rate of	(1)	−0.40	0.37	0.37						0.36	−4.02			
inflation		(−3.94)	(2.38)	(2.57)						(1.95)	(−1.63)	0.740	19.87	1.77
(Wholesale price index)	(2)	−0.38			0.26	0.05				0.65	6.61			
		(−4.22)			(3.15)	(3.62)				(4.40)	(4.39)	0.800	27.99	1.72
	(3)	−0.36			0.23		0140.16			0.871	−5.80			
		(−3.65)			(2.53)		(−1.74)			(9.03)	(−0.59)	0.774	23.87	1.97
	(4)	−0.55				0.04		0.24		0.72	4.29			
		(−7.10)				(2.49)		(1.73)		(5.28)	(1.77)	0.743	20.27	1.98
	(5)	−0.22			0.20			0.29	0.18	0.84	3.12			
		(−1.51)			(2.01)			(2.13)	(1.21)	(7.86)	(0.69)	0.786	18.32	2.09

Source: Compiled by the author.
Note: See text for definition of variables.

The value of K (the openness measure) is significant and has the expected negative sign (-1). Caution should be observed in interpreting these results, however, since the K measure is only slightly significant at the 95 percent level.

A plausible explanation of the negative relationship between GQ and the rate of inflation is that a substantial portion of imports during this period were required for industrialization. These imports did not represent a spillover effect "proper" from the domestic inflation. This type of import may have increased over time independently of changes in domestic prices. When a capacity constraint (YDT) was added to the regressions to take part of this effect into account, the GQ "t" value increased significantly. A possible explanation for this result is that, on the margin, additional imports did in fact represent a spillover great enough to overcome the positive effect of the price-inelastic imports.

This issue, while interesting and of some significance for policy design, was not pursued at length simply because several alternative (and somewhat competing) theories of the inflationary process in Mexico were found to be superior from both a statistical and a theoretical point of view.

Wage Increases

A second potential source of cost pressures during this period may have been excessive wage increases. Here it is wise to distinguish between changes in the minimum wage and other wage increases.

The Mexican constitution itself specifically recognizes the right of workers to receive a sufficient wage to ensure their basic needs and provide their children with the education to which they are entitled. Constitutional Article 123 instituted the country's minimum wage (the lowest amount a worker can be paid for a day's labor). According to Mario de la Cueva, the idea of the minimum wage is to establish the minimum level in the social scale below which life loses the dignity and essence belonging to the human person. With the aim of guaranteeing the minimum wage, the constitution provides that such earnings are not liable to discount, embargo, or compensation.[22]

Mexico's minimum wage refers to both general minimum wages and minimum professional wages, applied in skilled trades and fixed according to progress achieved in specific industrial branches, in commerce, professions, or special trades and activities. The level set for this second group of wages and salaries is obviously higher than the general minimum wage.

Because the cost of living tends to be considerably lower in rural areas than cities, the deputies drafting the constitution provided that a different scale be established for rural workers. Minimum wages are fixed by regional commissions made up of labor, management, and government representatives and require final approval by the National Minimum Wage Commission (set up along the same lines). Regional commissions are distributed throughout the country by socioeconomic zones. These zones are supposed to reflect natural, demographic, social, economic, and cultural features, each of which is taken into account in determining the minimum wage for that particular zone.[23]

In 1963, there were 111 zones established for minimum wage enforcement. In September 1974, the National Minimum Wage Commission's Council of Representatives, however, redistributed the zones more in keeping with recent economic, demographic, social, political, and administrative changes. This reform reduced the number of wage zones to 89, thereby simplifying the studies periodically carried out by the National Minimum Wage Commission, on cost of living, family budgeting, and other indicators.

In principle, the minimum wage is established after considering the results of these studies. The minimum wage should thus reflect the aggregate of goods and services that covers the basic material and cultural necessities of a worker and his family, the overall economic conditions of the country and of each zone in particular, the structure of activities in each zone, and the behavior of consumer markets.

In conformity with the constitutional guidelines, minimum wages should be remunerative, adequate, and fair. Consequently, minimum wages and those established in collective contracts were originally revised every two years.

One of the labor reform measures submitted to Congress in September 1974 argued that though the two-year period for wage revision is adequate in times of stability, it is far too long during periods of inflation. At that time, it was argued that most countries experiencing long periods of economic instability have created mechanisms to adjust wages frequently to the price level. Proponents of the reform also noted that wage increases in times of inflation had acted to maintain both social stability and business growth in a number of countries at a stage of development similar to that of Mexico. Finally, they pointed out that unless wage adjustments were made on an annual basis, there would be a marked inconsistency between the Echeverría administration's wage policy and its policy favoring the equitable distribution of income.

Based on these considerations, the federal labor law was amended on 30 September 1974, with the proviso that minimum wages be fixed annually, starting 1 January of the following year, and that collective contracts would be revised once a year as of 1 May 1975. All other collective contract clauses would continue to be renegotiated every two years.

The decree of 24 September 1974, amending the federal labor law, empowers workers, labor unions, special labor boards, permanent federal boards of conciliation, local boards of conciliation, and labor inspectors to denounce before the competent authorities any employer paying his workers less than the minimum wage or who shows receipts for larger amounts than those actually paid out. The decree established jail sentences of three weeks to two years in all cases and fines of up to two thousand pesos when the amount of the default does not exceed one month's minimum wages, five thousand pesos when the minimum has not been paid for two months, and ten thousand pesos when nonfulfillment extends over three months. However, if the employer pays back wages plus interest before the public prosecutor has reached a decision, punishment is limited to a fine.

Labor leaders have come to use the minimum wage as a base for collective bargaining demands. In addition, fringe benefits have become more and more liberal. Unionized workers have paid holidays, additional obligatory holidays such as May Day, a Christmas bonus of 15 days' pay, profit sharing, social security, housing benefits, and various services such as transport to work.

Many labor leaders privately concede, however, that up to 80 percent of rural workers and 50 percent of urban workers who should be receiving the minimum wage are not. Employers can easily ignore the law because of the tremendous demand for jobs, which has created a market overwhelmingly in their favor. There is no unemployment insurance in Mexico.

The actual trends in wages are difficult to analyze due to limitations in the data; only approximations are possible. As measured by all wages in a sample of firms, average real wages grew by about 7.5 percent per year from 1960 through 1964, by about 2.7 percent per year from 1965 through 1970, and by about 3.6 percent per year from 1971 through 1976. The annual rate for the period as a whole was about 4.2 percent.

The real minimum salary that some economists believe to be a more accurate measure of trends in average wages grew slightly faster: 4.9 percent per year over the period. Increases in fringe benefits further raised the real income of workers in the organized urban sector. Output per worker in manufacturing grew somewhat faster than wages, at 5 to 7 percent per year. This productivity growth, much faster than that observed in most countries, may be attributable mostly to the shift to more capital-intensive processes in a given sector. This shift itself results from distorted factor prices. A small part of the productivity growth is due to a shift toward more capital-intensive products.

Most of the increase in real wages during 1971–76 occurred in 1976. The annual increase had been under 2 percent through 1975, as measured by either the average wage in the same firms of average minimum wages. In 1976, the minimum wage rose 13 percent while average wages rose about 16 percent in real terms. All these estimates are based on annual data, and thus approximate midyear to midyear changes. The December-to-December increase in 1976 was even greater. From 1972 on, wages in Mexico rose relative to those in the United States, along with the increasing overvaluation of the peso. Devaluation in 1976 brought the relative wage back to the level of the late 1960s. For the 1968–79 period as a whole, real wages in Mexico seem to have risen by far more than in the United States. According to the Bank of Mexico figures, the real urban minimum in Mexico was 27.1 percent and the average real manufacturing wage 27.8 percent above the 1968 level by 1979; while in the United States the average real wage in private nonagricultural industries rose by only 8.7 percent in that time.[24] According to the monthly data of the General Statistical Department, the Mexican real urban minimum wage was 32.6 percent above the 1968 level on 1 January 1978, and 39.7 percent above the 1968 level on 1 January 1979. The U.S. real manufacturing wage on these dates was 9.6 and 8.1 percent, respectively, above the same base year.

These comparative data on wages point to an increase in the Mexican cost structure compared with that of the United States. The effort to keep up the purchasing power of wages appears to have led to excessive increases in money wages for those lucky enough to be employed, especially those protected by the minimum wage law and by the collective wage contracts negotiated by the trade unions.

The Mexican price level was changing rapidly, and relative prices were being distorted by uneven increases in the prices of individual goods and services, partly the result of the discriminatory system of price control. It becomes very difficult to measure the loss of international competitiveness under these conditions. It is easy to see, however, that the environment during the 1970s would certainly be conducive to increases in nominal wages and earnings, and possibly in real wages in key sectors where demand was also expanding rapidly.

Even though extensive price controls were being introduced by the early 1970s, these applied largely to basic foodstuffs, and not to the more dynamic manufacturing sectors. Hence, one would predict that wages and earnings would increase most rapidly in the sectors and industries in which employment was expanding most rapidly. Similarly, jobs requiring relatively higher levels of skill, given the relative shortage of trained manpower, should also have led in wage increases. Impressionistic evidence suggests that these patterns indeed dominated in the country's labor markets, where numerous accounts attest to the hindrance to growth posed by shortages of skilled labor.

On the wage side, the seventh-day payment, the 5 percent INFONAVIT contribution, the vacation bonus, the 1 percent education tax, the 9 to 12 percent social security tax, the year-end bonus, and the 8 percent levy of profit sharing all raised the cost of labor by as much as 50 percent. Moreover, the minimum wage itself tended to increase labor costs above a free market level. For workers earning the minimum salary, these charges were borne completely by the employer or by his customers if he could pass on the increased costs in the form of higher prices. For workers earning above the minimum salary, however, a part of these charges may have been reflected in lower nominal wages. The result of the increased labor charges and the subsidies to equipment purchasing was that the cost of labor relative to the cost of equipment was perhaps twice what it would have been in the absence of these measures.

Since these fringe benefits and the minimum wage were not available to many workers, distortions and inequities must have been created. Migration from rural to urban areas (always sensitive to wage differentials) was undoubtedly increased by the higher wages available in cities. On the other hand, the higher labor costs borne by larger firms that had to pay these fringe benefits may have protected many smaller, informal enterprises, which did not pay them and thus were better able to compete. This last effect may have been important even if the smaller enterprises did not produce the same products. Higher prices for products from larger enterprises may have shifted some consumption to other products or services produced by informal enterprises or by individuals with lower unit wage costs.

Despite the increased real wage rates in some areas, it seems that wage cost-push pressures did not dominate the inflationary process at this time. Wage increases clearly contributed to the general rise in production costs. Other costs were rising equally or more rapidly, however. Considerable reserves of unskilled labor existed both in the agricultural sector and as urban unemployment at the beginning of the period. It is hard to see, therefore, how increased labor costs could have been anything but one aspect of the heavy demands increased expenditures placed on all productive resources. There is little evidence to support the singling out of labor as a significant contributor to cost-push forces, not least because of the absence of strong labor unions.

In sum, while a case could perhaps be made for the existence of a wage cost-push mechanism in the manufacturing and construction sectors, it is difficult to see empirically how this effect could have dominated the inflationary process in these sectors, let alone in the economy as a whole.

Profit Sharing

A variant of the wage-cost mechanism is one involving potential increases in markups due to the country's profit-sharing formulas. The National Commission on Profit Sharing met for the first time in 1963. At that time, the commission ruled that the workers' share of net company profits, less deductions for income tax, "reasonable interest on capital," and "profit reinvestment," was 20 percent.

Experience in applying these guidelines together with changes taking place in the national economy during this time soon made it clear that a number of revisions in the original profit-sharing plan were necessary. The findings of a number of independent studies on the reforms made in fiscal and labor legislation also revealed an urgent need to update the profit-sharing system.

Accordingly, a second commission was created. On 14 October 1974, this commission calculated the workers' share at 8 percent of the net company profits, before the deductions stipulated in the earlier decree. The previous arrangement had reduced the share to 6 percent of profits before income tax payments.

A 1975 amendment to Mexico's labor legislation established federal norms for corporate compliance with profit sharing. The new law together with Mexico's tax law defines profits or taxable income in a broad way, excluding only pension fund earnings, dividends received from Mexican companies, and certain gains from the exchange or sale of corporate securities. Eight percent of all other income must be shared with employees.

Determining profit sharing on the basis of taxable income would seem to facilitate better control over the sums the workers actually receive and enable them to know and exercise their rights more directly. Presumably, the new rates leave sufficient margin for profit reinvestment, thereby stimulating the creation of new jobs while curbing the trend toward intensive use of capital encouraged by the previous system, which allowed larger deductions in sharable profits in proportion to capital intensity.

In fact, the 1974 commission ruled that the deductions provided in the previous system for "reasonable interest on capital" and "profit reinvestment" were technically unjustifiable, inasmuch as business and industrial enterprises do not earn interest but profits. The position of the commission appears to reflect the view that company growth rates are not dependent on profit reinvestment, since this type of expansion can be financed through the stock market, the issuing of industrial mortgage bonds, and bank credit.

The 8 percent of taxable profits to be shared is divided and then distributed in two equal parts. Fifty percent of the 8 percent lump sum is distributed among employees on the basis of the number of days worked by each during the year. The remaining 50 percent is distributed according to the salaries earned by each.

To administer profit sharing, the government has created a number of boards composed of an equal number of management and labor representatives. These bodies determine the specific profit share of each worker. Any dispute at the board level is referred to the area labor inspector. The final amounts determined by the boards (or inspectors) must be posted at each establishment and subsequently paid to employees no later than sixty days after the date on which annual income tax is due. Workers who object in any way to their allotments can submit a claim to Mexico's income tax authorities for federal review. Seldom, however, is this grievance procedure exercised or redress warranted. Thus, profit sharing is a long- and well-established practice in Mexico.

It should be noted that the right to share in corporate profits does not entitle workers to intervene in any way in the administration of their companies.

One major criticism of profit sharing centers on the program's inflationary impact. In fact, local businessmen report that the large periodic lump sum increases in purchasing power from profit sharing are usually spent on durable goods, appliances, automobiles, homes, etc. This effective demand for goods could presumably be sustained during inflationary periods despite the government's efforts to control price increases through tightening consumer credit.[25]

It would seem therefore that profit sharing would if anything affect inflation through some sort of demand-pull mechanism rather than through the cost-push pressures under consideration here.

Deviations from the Trend as a Measure of Inflationary Pressure

A proxy measure of the general level of bottlenecks, strains, and ultimately structural inflationary forces is some measure of the deviation of production from its long-run trend. This approach assumes that short-run deviations of output from its long-term trend are an adequate measure of inflationary pressure and that the monetary authorities either cannot or do not neutralize the impact of changes in holdings of foreign exchange on the money supply.[26]

As later analysis will show, the second assumption is open to some question. Setting aside those questions, however, several formulations of the general type:

$$INFW = YDT + WINF + INFWE + \text{other variables}$$

were estimated. Here *INFW* is a measure of domestic inflation (wholesale prices); *YDT* is a measure of the deviation of real production from its long-run trend; *WINF* is the rate of increase in world prices; and *INFWE* is a measure of price-induced expectations (the Harberger measure of expected inflation as the rate of inflation this year minus the inflation rate last year).

In direct contrast to a quantity of money-type price equations taking *Y* as given in the short run, this formulation incorporates a growing body of literature contending that the level of real output in developing countries, at least in the short run, is subject to the influence of domestic policy measures such as money supply changes.[27] Money supply changes are the measure of excess demand in a quantity-of-money equation at a given level of income. In contrast, the above formulation implies that shifts in money supply will affect prices only if they cause output to rise above its long-term trend.

Obviously, the major empirical issue in this approach is the ability of *YDT* to measure excess demand effectively. If *D* does not properly account for this factor, and because the various determinants of inflation tend to some degree to rise together, an undue share of the variation of the prices of home goods may be attributed to import prices and to the lagged price changes used in the expectations variable.

With these caveats in mind, a number of regressions of the above general form were run. As with the test of the openness inflation theory, regressions on the rate of increase in the wholesale price index gave somewhat better (but similar) statistical results when compared with results from the consumer price index.

Again, because the literature is not precise as to the best aggregate income measure to use in analyzing deviations from the trend, several different income series were tested. A logarithmic form was estimated along with the regular formulation (linear regression of real GDP in time).

Also tested was a measure computed as the difference between the observed growth rate in real GDP and the average growth rate (8.87) for the 1951–80 period as a whole (*GDT*).

The best statistical results were obtained with the measure of the deviation from the trend as that of the linear time trend (*YDT*). Using this measure, deviations from the trend (1951–80), world inflation (*WINF*), and the growth in *M*1 money (equation 9, table 9.2), an r^2 of over 0.90 was obtained.

As noted in the discussion of openness and inflation, all measures of openness were quite significant when regressed with *YDT*. These results are presented in that section.

Again, the rate of world inflation (*WINF*) is significant when regressed with *YDT* as is the growth in *M*2 and *M*1 measures of money and their lagged values. As in the test for openness, the expected rate of inflation, *INFWE*, was significant in each regression tested. Results with the rate of consumer price increases were similar (table 9.3) but not as satisfactory statistically.

While these results seem quite satisfactory, several conceptual difficulties warn

Table 9.2. Mexico: contribution of deviations from output trend to domestic inflation, 1951–80

Dependent variable	Equation	Independent variables												
		YDT	*INFWE*	*WINF*	*GM1*	*GM2*	*GM2L*	*GDT*	*GM1L*	*RHO*	Intercept	r^2	*F*	*DW*
Rate of	(1)	0.040	0.40		0.48					0.21	0.78			
inflation		(3.04)	(3.86)		(3.18)					(1.11)	(0.34)	0.774	23.96	1.3
(Wholesale	(2)	0.047	0.50							0.60	7.76			
price index)		(2.87)	(5.77)							(3.84)	(4.58)	0.639	19.51	1.7
	(3)	0.027			0.76					−0.08	−2.93			
		(2.09)			(4.99)					(−0.45)	(−1.28)	0.759	34.81	1.4
	(4)	0.038	0.47	0.30						0.55	6.13			
		(2.28)	(5.52)	(1.71)						(3.38)	(3.58)	0.684	15.15	1.6
	(5)	0.061								0.30				
		(3.44)								(1.64)	(5.65)	0.331	11.89	1.5
	(6)	0.038	0.025			0.39				0.28				
		(3.64)	(2.70)			(4.79)				(1.49)	1.09	0.836	35.71	1.4
	(7)	0.028	0.46			0.23	0.28			0.51	−0.23			
		(5.86)	(5.87)			(3.21)	(4.36)			(3.02)	(−0.17)	0.891	41.09	1.3
	(8)				0.75			0.28	0.35	0.04	−7.37			
					(4.61)			(1.47)	(2.08)	(0.20)	(−3.86)	0.768	23.23	1.8
	(9)	0.022		0.31		0.47				−0.08	−1.11			
		(2.78)		(3.54)		(8.04)				(−0.39)	(−1.07)	0.906	67.45	1.7

Source: Compiled by the author.
Note: See text for definition of variables.

Table 9.3. Mexico: influence of real factors on inflation, 1951–80

Dependent variable	Equation	Independent variables											
		YDT	*W1NF*	*1NFCE*	*GM1*	*GM1L*	*GDT*	*GM2*	*RHO*	Intercept	r^2	*F*	*DW*
Rate of	(1)	0.07	0.27	0.49					0.23	8.08			
inflation		(5.54)	(1.76)	(4.72)					(1.20)	(7.27)	0.786	25.84	1.4
(Consumer	(2)			0.47			0.31		0.93	17.66			
price index)				(5.74)			(1.98)		(12.77)	(1.81)	0.658	23.13	2.0
	(3)			0.50	0.35	0.45			0.60	−1.79			
				(5.52)	(2.24)	(2.94)			(3.93)	−0.50	0.691	15.63	1.6
	(4)	0.07		0.52					0.39	9.38			
		(5.49)		(5.46)					(2.17)	(8.53)	0.721	28.47	1.4
	(5)	0.06		0.41				0.22	0.23	5.83			
		(5.16)		(3.73)				(2.41)	(1.22)	(3.51)	0.807	29.35	1.5
	(6)	0.06		0.50	0.33				0.17	4.67			
		(4.87)		(4.99)	(2.26)				(0.85)	(2.12)	0.812	30.26	1.5
	(7)							0.51	0.48	1.78			
								(4.27)	(2.85)	(0.66)	0.422	18.24	1.6

Note: See text for definition of variables.

somewhat against accepting as accurate their depiction of the inflationary process in Mexico during this period. In general, at least three characteristics of the Mexican economy might limit the effectiveness of *YDT* as a measure of excess demand: the high proportion of agricultural products in both production and consumption, a fairly high rate of inflation, and an uneven growth of productive capacity.

The use of *YDT* as a measure of excess demand in the inflation equations implies that when the growth of output rose above its long-run trend the country's domestic productive capacity was being strained and that prices had to rise if output was to be increased any further. Clearly, this assumption is predicated on the existence of an upward sloping supply curve, whereby increasing prices stimulate further production. This situation is undoubtedly more likely in the more advanced economies where gross domestic product has a much higher proportion of industrial products. In general, there should be more scope for expanding the output of manufacturing and services in the short run than would be the case for agricultural products, particularly as in Mexico where most products were subject to a crop cycle or weather conditions. Even though import substitution industrialization was proceeding rapidly, GDP was still heavily concentrated on agricultural products, even in the 1970s. Given the rapid expansion in the consumption of food during this period, agriculture's output was probably more subject to fluctuations in domestic supply than in domestic demand. Conceivably, short-run deviations of agricultural production above its trend could result in lower rather than higher prices and vice versa, thus distorting the measure of excess demand captured by measuring the overall deviation from the trend.

A second limitation on the usefulness of *YDT* as a measure of excess demand is its implicit assumption that productive capacity grows at a fairly constant rate. While investment fluctuates from year to year in most advanced countries, Mexico's investment, particularly private investment, seems to have been especially volatile by any standards. Whether these fluctuations in capacity are high enough to invalidate the *YDT* measure of excess demand is difficult to assess. They do, however, cast serious doubts on the procedure.

Finally, using *YDT* as an accurate measure of demand pressure in Mexico is also questionable because of the country's high rates of inflation and money supply growth, particularly in the 1970s. Within a limited range, changes in short-run demand pressure could have resulted partially in higher industrial output and partially in price increases. Nevertheless, a point may have been reached in the early 1970s beyond which an increase in demand resulted only in higher prices. The high rates of money supply growth combined with a high proportion of output in agriculture may have been sufficient to reduce significantly the economy's short-run supply elasticity.

Conclusions

The structuralist interpretation of inflation would seem to be on sounder ground than that of the cost theory. In fact, it might even be argued that in the medium term, the development of industry through the country's import substitution strategy further added to domestic inflationary pressures. High levels of protection against world competition for new industries turned the domestic terms of trade sharply against agriculture in the 1960s and 1970s, thus reducing the rate of growth of agricultural output below what it would otherwise have been. The lack of investment in agriculture further exacerbated this problem.

It is also likely that the industrialization that did take place aggravated or even created a number of economic rigidities in the 1970s. Stepped-up government spending suddenly increased the demand for power and transport and made those infrastructures inadequate. Similarly, the short-term inadequacy of labor —both skilled labor and industrial entrepreneurs—was created by excessive industrial growth.

Ultimately, the tests outlined above, using proxies for structural factors, are statistically satisfactory but suffer from conceptual difficulties. Specifically, many of the underlying assumptions critical to validate measures of the deviation from the trend may not have been present in Mexico during the period examined. The real issue is whether or not, given the limitations of these theories and given the availability of direct data for testing, the quantity of money approach (or a version of it) might not give a better idea of the relative inflationary impact of external versus domestic factors.

Monetary elements also warrant more attention simply because in tests with structural factors the growth in money supply was always statistically significant.

This observation is important because the Mexican government's responses to inflation appear to have accepted implicitly the argument that its underlying causes were cost-related and not of monetary origins. As noted above, tests using monetary variables best explained the country's recent inflationary experience. Because of the weakness of cost elements in the Mexican inflationary process and the conceptual difficulties in identifying the exact magnitude of the structural sources of Mexican inflation, the macroeconomic model developed in chapter 13 incorporates equations depicting the country's inflationary process as essentially stemming from excess monetary demand—an excess supply of money in relation to the volume of real goods and services available.

10. Dynamics of the Fiscal System

Although the Mexican government's deficit had been increasing over the years without much academic or popular discussion, the mid-1970s saw the country's fiscal problems emerging as the central focus of the debate over the causes of the country's economic slowdown and its increasing internal and external disequilibrium.[1]

Increases in oil revenues have not alleviated the situation. The Mexican economy sustained its most severe downturn since World War II in the early 1980s and the country's public sector deficit increased to a record level—both in dollar magnitude and, more important, in relation to the overall volume of economic activity.

In fact, by late 1982 the $48 million a day earned by oil exports of 1.7 million barrels a day (about 90 percent of current exports) was used almost exclusively to finance the $35 million of daily interest payments on the public sector external debt of $60 billion. By late October 1982, about $10 million in repayments of principal had been frozen under a ninety-day moratorium. Bankers privately acknowledged that they had no option but to extend this moratorium until the end of 1983.[2]

The Wharton economic forecasting unit, which offers the most detailed macroeconomic reporting on Mexico, indicates one million new jobs were created in 1981, an increase of 5.4 percent.[3] Their forecasts indicated, however, that the employment rate would fall by 0.3 percent in 1982, a net loss of 65,000 jobs. Worse yet, the Wharton forecasts indicated the rate would fall by almost 1 percent in 1983.[4]

Mexico's short-lived boom financed by high oil prices and massive foreign borrowing created 4 million jobs between 1970 and 1981, giving the illusion of prosperity. The financial crisis of 1982 shattered that illusion.

The following sections examine several key issues surrounding the country's fiscal disequilibrium and offer some empirical estimates of the structure and responsiveness of the government's tax and revenue system.

As previous chapters have noted, the economic activities of the government have played a pivotal role in Mexico's changing development pattern. These activities were critical to the remarkably rapid process of expansion experienced by Mexico since World War II. As Fitzgerald notes, the growth of the public sector in the Mexican economy must also be seen as a source of the imbalance that has emerged over the last twenty years or so—an imbalance that itself led to accelerated growth in the public sector.[5] State intervention in the process of capital accumulation during the period of import-substituting industrialization is common to the experience of Latin America as a whole,[6] but in Mexico the scale and scope of this intervention appear to have been greater than elsewhere, generating an important debate over the size of the Mexican public sector.[7] The following sections examine the critical trends associated with the government's fiscal position and the savings effort of the private sector.

Savings

Mexico's overall national savings performance compares favorably with that of many countries at a similar stage of development.[8] Since 1970 Mexico's national savings have averaged around 19–24 percent of gross domestic product, a fairly high savings level by international standards. On the other hand, even during the postpetroleum period, the share of public savings has not increased markedly. Real public savings declined from a peak of 3.2 percent of gross domestic product in 1970 to − 0.5 percent in 1975, rising to 3.6 percent in 1979, only to fall again to 1.9 percent in 1981.

In spite of the poor public savings performance, public investment has grown at a markedly higher rate than private investment over the last decade, increasing its share of GDP from 7.3 percent in 1970 to 11.6 percent in 1981. Private investment increased its share of GDP from 12.3 to 13.6 percent during the same period (table 10.1).

The gap between public savings and public investment was financed by large increases in domestic and external borrowing and inflation. The balance of payments current account deficit increased markedly after 1970 reaching a peak of 4.4 percent of gross domestic product in 1975 (up from 3.2 in 1970), declining to 2.2 percent of gross domestic product in 1977, only to increase again to 3.7 percent by 1981. At the same time, the inflation tax became an important source of government financing. The inflation tax is defined as the rate of inflation multiplied by the real quantity of money, and represents the resources money holders must spend to keep constant the real value of their cash balances. It represented 1.6 percent of gross domestic product in 1975 and 2.2 percent of gross domestic product in 1976, peaking at 3.3 percent in 1977.

The following sections examine the causes of the relative decline in public savings, the implications of this trend, the nature and potential of private savings, and the implications for domestic savings of massive foreign borrowing.

Fiscal Trends

The relatively low tax ratio, the large increase in the general government's consumption expenditures, and the rapidly deteriorating financial situation of public enterprises are the major factors aggravating the already poor public savings performance in recent years.

Table 10.1. Mexico: trends in major macroeconomic aggregates, 1951–81 (percent of gross domestic product)

	1951	1960	1970	1975	1976	1977	1978	1979	1980	1981
Private consumption	84.9	79.5	71.8	68.7	68.1	66.3	66.0	64.4	62.0	62.0
Private investment	8.1	10.0	12.3	11.9	12.2	8.9	11.3	11.7	13.0	13.6
Private expenditures	93.0	89.5	84.1	80.6	80.3	75.2	77.3	76.1	75.0	75.6
Government consumption	4.2	5.1	7.8	10.3	11.0	10.8	10.9	10.9	10.8	10.8
Government investment	4.9	4.9	7.3	9.5	8.8	8.9	9.8	10.8	11.1	11.6
Government expenditure	9.1	10.0	15.1	19.8	19.8	19.7	20.7	21.7	21.9	22.4
Private savings	9.1	13.0	16.0	19.8	18.3	19.7	18.5	18.6	21.2	22.3
Government savings	0.9	1.4	3.2	−0.5	0.5	0.9	2.3	3.6	3.3	1.9
Total savings	10.0	14.4	19.2	19.3	18.8	20.6	20.8	22.2	24.4	24.5
Government current revenue	5.1	4.7	8.3	7.6	10.3	8.5	10.7	7.8	10.1	9.7
Government deficit	4.0	5.3	6.8	12.2	9.6	11.2	10.0	13.9	11.8	12.7
Total investment	13.0	16.7	22.4	23.7	22.3	22.8	23.6	25.9	28.1	28.2
Total consumption	89.1	84.6	79.6	79.0	79.1	77.1	76.9	75.3	17.4	72.8
Resource = external Gap	3.0	2.4	3.2	4.4	3.5	2.2	2.8	3.8	3.7	3.7
Private savings − private investment	1.0	3.0	3.7	7.9	6.1	10.8	7.2	6.9	8.2	8.9
Public savings − public investment	−4.0	−3.5	−4.1	−10.0	−8.3	−8.0	−7.5	−7.2	−7.8	−9.7
Net private, government savings − investment gap	−3.0	−0.5	−0.4	−2.1	−2.2	2.8	−0.3	−0.3	0.4	−0.8

Source: Bank of Mexico, *Informe Anual*, various issues.

Tax Revenues

Overall public sector savings have declined in spite of rapidly growing federal government revenues, particularly tax revenues. Mexico's development program during the 1950s and 1960s, emphasizing import substitution, undoubtedly had a negative impact on the generation of public resources through tax policy. This forced the government to rely increasingly upon the nontax financial sector—private savings and monetizing the deficit—for financing federal expenditures.[9] Writing in 1975, Escobedo noted that, "as the public financial requirements were increased mainly because of incapacity to increase tax revenues at the same rate as public expenditures . . . the Bank of Mexico had to tolerate greater increases in the money supply."[10] In fact, economists writing about the Mexican tax system have conveyed the impression that it has been seriously deficient both in providing revenue and in achieving desirable nonfiscal objectives, such as a more equal distribution of income and wealth. Although these generalizations contain a large measure of truth, they tend to mask the cumulative effects of the changes that have occurred over the years. Given the stable structure of the Mexican political system, it is easy to agree with the observation that "in Mexico there are no reforms of the tax system, only changes." Nevertheless, the structure of the tax system is substantially different from what it was in 1970. Furthermore, although double-digit inflation appears to have become a persistent problem, leading to the impression that the tax system is generating insufficient revenues, the revenues of the public sector in 1981 were much greater relative to gross domestic product than in 1970 (9.7 versus 12.6 percent), despite the lower inflation rate in the later year. Since 1970, the tax system has evolved in the direction of greater equity, as that term is generally employed in taxation. It is also apparent that the harmony of the tax system with economic development has greatly improved.[11]

Mexico's tax ratio has averaged around 11–13 percent of gross domestic product since 1975 (table 10.2). Two factors helping to keep it at this level are the inequality in the distribution in income and the very low ratio of imports to gross domestic product (less than 10 percent). The government has made significant efforts to increase the tax ratio and succeeded in achieving marginal rates of 25 percent on average for the period 1972–81.[12] It was anticipated that oil exports would increase the ratio to around 17 percent by the mid-1980s, but this target has been revised significantly downward in light of the worldwide oil glut.

Elasticity of the Revenue System

One way to evaluate the performance of Mexico's fiscal system is to examine the ability of the tax structure to generate proportionately higher revenues, both through discretionary action (tax rate and base changes, legislative action, improvement in collection techniques, and the like) and through revenue growth

Table 10.2. Mexico: trends in federal government revenue, 1951–81 (in percent)

	1951	1960	1970	1975	1976	1977	1978	1979	1980	1981
Percent of total revenue										
Current revenue	94.4	57.4	37.1	32.5	30.4	33.1	32.9	32.1	31.3	29.6
Income tax	(22.2)	(18.5)	(14.6)	(12.2)	(12.5)	(13.5)	(14.4)	(13.4)	(11.4)	(10.4)
Tax on production and trade	(13.9)	(8.7)	(6.2)	(7.6)	(5.9)	(6.9)	(6.1)	(5.3)	(2.9)	(1.8)
Sales tax	(11.1)	(5.6)	(4.0)	(5.9)	(5.8)	(5.9)	(5.7)	(5.8)	(5.4)	(5.2)
Import duties	(13.9)	(10.3)	(5.9)	(2.6)	(2.3)	(1.5)	(1.6)	(2.2)	(2.1)	(1.7)
Export duties	(13.9)	(5.6)	(0.9)	(0.7)	(0.5)	(2.2)	(2.3)	(2.8)	(6.3)	(6.8)
Other taxes	(5.6)	(—)	(2.4)	(1.6)	(1.5)	(1.4)	(1.5)	(1.4)	(1.9)	(2.1)
Nonfiscal revenue	(13.9)	(8.7)	(3.6)	(1.8)	(1.9)	(1.6)	(1.3)	(1.3)	(1.2)	(1.6)
Capital revenue	—	9.2	0.7	0.3	0.4	0.4	0.8	0.1	0.1	0.1
Financing	5.6	33.3	9.8	17.5	23.4	12.4	12.2	27.4	18.1	37.0
Internal	(2.2)	(15.4)	(7.9)	(13.3)	(18.3)	(9.1)	(8.9)	(23.7)	(15.9)	(35.0)
External	(2.8)	(18.5)	(2.0)	(4.2)	(5.1)	(3.3)	(3.3)	(3.7)	(2.3)	(1.9)
Income of state companies	—	—	52.2	49.7	45.7	54.1	54.1	40.4	50.5	33.4
Total revenue	100.	100.	100.	100.	100.	100.	100.	100.	100.	100.
Percent of gross domestic product										
Current revenue	9.1	7.2	9.7	11.9	11.7	12.4	12.9	13.5	15.8	12.6
Capital revenue	—	1.2	0.2	0.1	0.2	0.2	0.3	—	—	—
Borrowing	0.4	4.2	2.6	6.4	9.0	4.6	4.8	11.5	9.2	15.7
Income of state companies	—	—	13.6	18.2	17.6	20.3	21.2	17.0	25.6	14.2
Total revenue	9.2	12.5	26.1	36.7	38.5	37.4	39.3	42.1	50.7	42.5

Sources: Computed from Nacional Financiera, *La Economía Méxicana en Cifras* (Mexico City, 1981); Banamex, *Review of The Economic Situation of Mexico*, various issues.

(automatic with rising economic activity). In their study of Mexico's revenue system, Wilford and Wilford termed this measure "the revenue performance criterion," broadly defined as "the ability of the country's revenue structure to generate, from whatever sources, increased government revenues for current and capital expenditures during the process of economic growth."[13]

Along these lines it is clear that the pressure for increased revenues to finance GNP elastic demands for social goods and services requires that revenues increase at a higher rate than the growth in GDP. More specifically, the overall revenue GDP elasticity coefficient for a revenue structure must be elastic. The percentage change in revenue divided by the percentage change in GDP must be greater than one.

The advantage of the elasticity-type measure in a country such as Mexico, where relatively little is known about the complexity of the tax laws (exemptions, etc.), is that "one need not be concerned about the source of the alterations in tax yields (whether from national income-related or exogenous influences), but rather the overall ability of the source to stimulate proportionately higher revenues with economic development regardless of the factors stimulating that growth." Revenue performance can therefore be measured by the historic responsiveness of the tax source as GDP increases. This method permits evaluation of the government's effort to stimulate the development of additional resources under conditions of growth, unlike the much narrower measure of the responsiveness of yields solely to changes in GDP.

The elasticity of the various sources of government revenue (table 10.3) were estimated by regressing their logarithmic value on the logarithm of GDP for the period 1951–81 and also subperiods 1960–81 and 1965–81.[14] A Cochrane-Orchutt ordinary least squares estimation procedure was used in decreases. The results (tables 10.4 and 10.5) confirm that the overall system is elastic with the elasticity of current revenue not varying much for the different time periods (1.15 for 1951–81; 1.18 for 1960–81; and 1.16 for 1965–81).[15] There does not appear to be a marked difference over time in the elasticity of various taxes. This is consistent with the general observation that no significant reforms have been introduced in this area during the period under consideration.[16]

The elasticity of financing is somewhat above that of current revenue, 1.52 (1951–81) versus 1.15, yielding an elasticity of total revenue of 1.34, also considerably above that of current revenue.

In short, the country's deficit problems cannot be attributed exclusively to a deficient (inelastic) tax and revenue system but are clearly the result of an expenditure rate-public sector budget elasticity of 1.3 for 1951–81, considerably above that of current revenues.

In general, the results indicate that (1) the revenue source with the highest elasticity has been federal government borrowing; (2) the revenue structure in Mexico is much less income-responsive than one would desire for a country in its stage of development; (3) as larger shares of the national economy become dependent upon government infrastructure expenditures and the need for social

Table 10.3. Mexico: government revenue, expenditure elasticity, 1951–81

	Elasticity	T statistics	*RHO*	T statistics	r^2	*F*	*DW*
Current revenue	1.15	(32.37)	0.71	(5.54)	0.974	1,048.21	2.10
Income taxes	1.22	(38.94)	0.48	(3.02)	0.982	1,516.90	1.64
Tax on production and trade	0.42	(1.84)	0.95	(17.21)	0.108	3.39	1.50
Sales tax	1.35	(29.01)	0.64	(4.52)	0.967	841.41	1.90
Import duties	0.89	(17.34)	0.58	(3.93)	0.915	300.87	1.79
Export duties	2.33	5.46	0.95	(16.92)	0.516	29.87	2.49
Other taxes	1.28	(6.61)	0.34	(2.00)	0.610	43.82	2.27
Nonfiscal revenue	0.78	(21.74)	—	—	0.944	472.9	1.67
Capital revenue	0.26	(2.37)	—	—	0.167	5.62	1.93
Financing	1.52	(15.71)	0.36	(2.21)	0.898	246.83	2.18
Internal	1.71	(13.49)	0.42	(2.57)	0.866	182.03	2.08
External	1.18	(8.83)	—	—	0.736	78.02	2.04
Income of state companies (1965–81)	1.19	(63.78)	−0.90	(−8.15)	0.996	4,067.91	0.93
Total revenue	1.34	(15.26)	0.78	(6.89)	0.893	232.88	1.92
Government investment	1.21	(35.41)	0.54	(3.57)	0.978	1,254.35	2.08
Public sector budget	1.30	(13.54)	0.81	7.59	0.863	183.36	1.98
Government consumption	1.00	(10.86)	0.95	(16.77)	0.813	118.01	1.95
Government expenditure	1.19	(25.54)	0.78	(6.82)	0.959	652.35	2.05
Government revenue (national income accounts)	1.14	(25.68)	0.38	(2.25)	0.929	659.8	2.01

Source: computed by the author.
Note: Estimations of form: log $Y = a + b$ log *GDP* where Y = measure of revenue or expenditure. Estimations by ordinary least squares, Time Series Processor Version 3.5, Cochrane-Orcutt technique.

Table 10.4. Mexico: government revenue, expenditure elasticity, 1960–81

	Elasticity	*T* statistics	*RHO*	*T* statistic	r^2	*F*	*DW*
Current revenue	1.18	(58.59)	—	—	0.994	3,433.72	1.70
Income taxes	1.17	(26.11)	0.51	(2.68)	0.972	682.16	1.91
Tax on production and trade	0.20	(0.61)	0.96	(16.89)	0.021	0.03	1.46
Sales tax	1.31	(16.53)	0.66	(4.08)	0.935	273.39	1.94
Import duties	0.831	(11.64)	—	—			
Export duties	2.15	(5.58)	0.88	(8.50)	0.621	31.23	2.58
Other taxes	1.42	(10.57)	—	—	0.854	111.75	2.22
Nonfiscal revenue	0.86	(21.75)	—	—	0.961	473.26	1.77
Capital revenue	0.19	(1.02)			0.051	1.04	1.65
Financing	1.38	(16.76)	—	—	0.937	280.96	1.94
Internal	1.47	(17.90)	—	—	0.944	320.37	1.90
External	1.16	(6.06)	—	—	0.659	36.74	2.07
Income of state companies (1965–81)	1.19	(63.78)	−0.90	(−8.15)	0.997	4,067.91	0.94
Total revenue	1.24	(10.81)	0.76	(5.36)	0.861	116.93	1.81
Government expenditure (national income accounts)	1.16	(47.42)	0.38	(1.91)	0.992	2,249.29	2.21
Consumption	1.11	(25.81)	0.73	(4.95)	0.972	666.38	1.93
Investment	1.16	(51.99)	—	—	0.993	2,703.88	2.17
Government revenue (national income accounts)	1.08	(19.10)	—	—	0.950	364.81	2.13
Public sector budget	1.21	(9.99)	0.78	(−5.75)	0.840	99.92	1.89

Source: computed by the author.

Note: Estimations of form $Y = a + b \log GDP$ where Y = measure of revenue or expenditure. Estimations by ordinary least squares, Time Series Processor, Version 3.5, Cochrane-Orcutt technique.

Table 10.5. Mexico: government revenue, expenditure elasticity, 1965–81

	Elasticity	*T* statistics	*RHO*	*T* statistic	r^2	*F*	*DW*
Current revenue	1.16	(52.30)	—	—	0.995	2,735.81	1.96
Income taxes	1.08	(23.56)	0.57	(2.75)	0.975	555.46	1.39
Tax on production and trade	0.31	(1.09)	0.89	(7.91)	0.078	1.19	1.44
Sales tax	1.26	(10.72)	0.68	(3.74)	0.891	114.95	2.04
Import duties	0.77	(10.29)	—	—	0.883	105.89	1.70
Export duties	2.10	(6.95)	0.73	(4.27)	0.776	48.34	2.56
Other taxes	1.32	(8.01)	—	—	0.821	64.22	1.19
Nonfiscal revenue	0.81	(17.57)	—	—	0.954	308.89	1.68
Capital revenue	0.20	(0.81)	—	—	0.045	0.66	1.96
Financing	1.47	(17.74)	—	—	0.954	314.92	1.95
Internal	1.56	(16.91)	—	—	0.953	286.07	2.01
External	1.08	(6.90)	—	—	0.773	47.62	1.06
Income of state companies	1.19	(63.78)	−0.90	(−8.15)	0.996	4,067.91	0.93
Total revenue	1.22	(96.66)	—	—	0.998	9,343.47	1.66
Government expenditure (national income accounts)	1.15	(79.77)	—	—	0.998	6,363.34	1.98
Consumption	1.10	(23.95)	0.72	(4.81)	0.968	632.41	1.91
Investment	1.15	(55.68)	—	—	0.995	3,100.54	2.04
Government revenue (national income accounts)	1.07	(17.63)	—	—	0.942	307.91	2.07
Public sector budget	1.19	(44.88)	—	—	0.993	2,014.82	1.80

Source: computed by the author.
Note: Estimations by ordinary least squares, Time Series Processor, Version 3.5, Cochrane-Orcutt technique.

goods and services expands, the government with or without significantly increased oil revenues will face a tax structure that will finance a decreasing percentage of federal outlays; (4) a revenue structure that relies to such a heavy extent on income from state companies (around 20 percent) must ultimately encounter serious conflicts between the pricing of public services and the need for additional revenues; (5) to date, the tendency has been toward monetizing the debt with the resulting inflationary tax increasing in importance as a source of funds transferred to the government.

In view of the government's resource needs, the most important shortcoming of the tax system is its inability to generate the revenues required to meet the needs of rapidly growing expenditure programs. Indeed, much of the increase in revenue that has taken place is due to rate increases rather than an inherently elastic tax design. The main culprits here are the limited progressivity of the personal income tax and excise taxes, many of which until the introduction of the value-added tax (1980) were specific.[17]

The authorities are aware of the many deficiencies of the present tax system and have been working on alternative reform proposals over the past few years. The culmination of this effort was the enactment at the end of 1980 of various amendments to direct and indirect taxation. The changes cover different tax laws and include a new income tax law with important changes in tax jurisdiction, extent of the corporate income tax, taxation of business income of individuals, and taxation of income of nonresidents; amendments to the value-added tax introducing a zero rate for food and for some other items previously exempt from the tax; a "spiral tax on production and services," an excise tax that replaces previous taxes on soft drinks, alcoholic beverages, beer, gasoline, processed tobacco, life insurance, and telephone services; and other changes in the Customs Code, customs value, registration of vehicles, the tax on new cars, the tax on holding and use of vehicles, the tax on the acquisition of sugar, cacao, and other goods, the tax on urban unimproved land, and some other minor changes.[18]

These measures are positive modifications to the existing system. It is quite apparent, however, that strong political opposition together with the new petroleum riches may render an in-depth fiscal reform very difficult. The highly necessary reform of the special bases seems to be a particularly sensitive issue because it would affect strong interest groups such as transport, construction, and agriculture. However, a continued strengthening of the administrative process and a revision of indirect taxes will probably take place. Under the circumstances, this should be considered a minimum if the government wants to achieve its targets. On the positive side, the introduction of the value-added tax in 1980 seems to have eliminated the inefficient cascade aspects of the commercial receipts tax and to have improved internal controls.

Government Expenditures

Government current expenditure grew at an annual real rate of 14.9 percent during 1971–76, while its components of consumption, transfer, and interest payments were growing around 12 percent, 29 percent, and 15 percent per year, respectively.[19] For the period 1976–81, the rate of increase in real government consumption declined to an average annual rate of slightly over 7 percent, with its components growing more or less proportionately to their rates in the 1971–76 period. For the period as a whole, wages and salaries were the fastest growing component of consumption expenditures. This was the result of a rapid increase in the number of government employees and a somewhat more moderate increase in real wages. The number of public sector employees increased at more than 9 percent per year during this period while real wages and salaries increased at around 4 percent per year.

Federal government current transfers were the fastest growing component of current expenditures during most of this period and thus a major factor responsible for the public sector's poor savings performance. The enormous increase of transfers to trust funds in general and to agricultural financial entities in particular appears to be the main cause of the acceleration of extrasystem transfers.[20]

The emphasis on rationalization and the necessary fiscal restraints imposed by the stabilization program led to the relatively low growth of government consumption during the 1976–81 period. However, the government's commitment to launch an effective attack on poverty and to reduce the large gap between demand and supply for basic goods places continuous pressure on the authorities to return to the high rates of expenditure of the 1971–76 period.

Private Savings

Private sector savings have not only accounted for the great bulk of national savings but have averaged around 20 percent of GDP during the 1975–81 period. On the other hand, only around 10 percent of these funds are actually mobilized through the financial system. Little is known about the composition of these savings, but the evidence available suggests that a corporation's internal cash generation is its major component.[21] The only data readily available on the flow of funds of Mexican enterprises are from a Nacional Financiera (NAFINSA) study of the capital goods industry. According to this report, 30.3 percent of the financial requirements of these enterprises were financed from internal cash generation and equity during 1971–75, the other sources of financing being credit from other enterprises (23 percent), foreign credits (16 percent), and credit from the domestic banking system (16 percent).[22]

The limited role of domestic credit in financing Mexican enterprises simply reflects the relatively small share of total private savings channeled through the nation's financial markets. In addition, an important share of these funds are short-run deposits of enterprises. This situation combined with the almost complete absence of a securities market and other sources of domestic long-term financing tends to confirm the general belief that most of the private sector's investments are financed through internal cash generation, probably undistributed profits, and depreciation allowances.

In large part, the development strategy of the 1950s and 1960s reinforced these patterns. That strategy was based on a combination of high private sector profits and government supportive action. The former was supported by the protection available to industry through quantitative restrictions on imports during this period, the extremely favorable tax treatment on income from capital, and the inequality of income distribution. These factors contributed to abnormally high profit margins, which in turn provided the major source of private savings.

It is not at all obvious, however, that given the conditions in the 1980s—the increased importance of oil revenues together with the need to develop mass markets for industrial goods—that a genuine government policy shift in the direction of improved income distribution and more efficient industrial production would lead to reduced rates of investment, particularly if the authorities simultaneously worked to develop and strengthen the country's financial markets.

Contrary to common opinion, Mexico's financial markets are not highly developed. Financial intermediation in Mexico is in fact only slightly above the level of the average developing country. Mexico underwent a process of fairly rapid financial deepening through 1972 when the ratio of the combined assets of financial institutions to GDP reached a level somewhat in excess of 50 percent. Since then, this ratio has remained roughly constant, a fairly low ratio for an advanced developing country.

The Mexican financial system is relatively simple and is basically organized around banking-type institutions.[23] The securities market is the most underdeveloped sector of the Mexican financial market. Although securities trading in Mexico has increased very rapidly in the last two decades from an almost negligible base, the volume of all securities, both stocks and bonds, traded on the Mexican stock exchange remains quite low. The ratio of the value of shares traded to GDP is currently less than 1 percent, compared to ratios of 3 percent or more in developing countries where significant securities market development has taken place (such as Brazil and Korea).

Several factors are usually cited to explain the relative underdevelopment of the Mexican securities market.

First, until recently, finance companies and mortgage banks stood ready to repurchase their long-term bonds at par, allowing these institutions to pay long-term-bond rates of interest on what were basically sight deposits. This practice made private long-term corporate bonds relatively noncompetitive instruments. It also imposed a significant liquidity risk on these institutions, which resulted in serious institutional problems in 1976. As a result, these redeemable bonds have gradually been eliminated, thereby removing this obstacle to deeper bond market development.

Second, a portion of the interest paid to savers on bank deposits (called the *sobretasa*) is now exempt from tax, whereas all interest paid on debt securities is taxable. This subsidy to bank deposits, together with the authorities' unwillingness to authorize private short-term debt securities, has inhibited the growth of a short-term securities market.

Third, there is some evidence that the commercial banking system regards the development of a debt securities market as a competitive threat that would reduce the volume of financing conducted through the banking system as well as exert competitive pressures on bank profit margins. Bankers have acted in the past to impede securities market development. The banks also appear to believe that there is a high degree of substitutability over the short run between debt securities issues and bank deposits, and that large offerings of debt securities could lead to disruptive deposit withdrawals.

Finally, the main impediments to development of a share market are largely institutional. Rates of return on Mexican equity capital are high for shares registered on the stock exchange. However, the unwillingness of closely held firms to open their capital and to meet minimum disclosure requirements as well as the absence of a strong securities distribution system are probably the main impediments to stock exchange development.[24]

The reliance of the Mexican financial market on deposit liabilities has made the asset base on which domestic investment financing is built a very liquid one. The Mexican authorities are concerned about the lack of long maturities in the domestic financial market and have begun to stress the need for developing a long-term securities market of significant proportions. In 1977 PEMEX began issuing bonds (petro bonds) and more recently there have been several issues of new floating rate medium-term bond issues by major private corporations. While these are moves in the right direction, the current economic crisis is likely to halt major developments in the area for at least several years.

Loss of Instrument Effectiveness

As Leopoldo Solis and G. Ortiz observed, an important consequence of Mexico's inflationary experience, particularly after 1971, has been the loss of effectiveness of two of the main instruments of monetary control traditionally used by the Bank of Mexico: (1) changes in commercial bank reserve requirements, and (2) the setting of interest rates payable on savings deposits and other financial liabilities.[25]

Traditionally, the difference between the government's deficit and the flow of new foreign debt has determined the amount of internal finance required by the public sector. The Bank of Mexico has traditionally raised funds by imposing an increase in marginal reserve requirements on the banks. The reserves mobilized in this manner are used by the government for a large part of its expenditures. The domestic savings remaining in the banking system are then available to finance private sector activities.

During the stabilizing development period of the 1960s, the government's deficit fluctuated between 2.0 and 4.7 percent of GDP. About half of the deficit was financed with foreign savings. As a result, the ratio of foreign debt to GDP increased from 6.8 percent in 1960 to 9.8 percent in 1970. More important, the deficit was kept within reasonable limits and foreign debt was not used excessively.

Solis feels that the possibility of substituting domestic for foreign debt facilitated the use of reserve requirements as an effective instrument of monetary control during this period. It was only when the government's deficit exceeded the availability of foreign and domestic requirements and the excess debt became monetized that the usefulness of reserve requirements as a regulating instrument was nullified.

The acceleration of government spending, especially after 1972, did in fact result in deficits that could not be financed with noninflationary domestic resources, although foreign credit was liberally utilized. A good portion of deficits were directly monetized. The monetary base began to grow at more than twice its average 1960 rate. The resulting upsurge in inflationary pressures produced negative real interest rates. Apparently, as the environment became increasingly detrimental to financial savings, substitution between domestic and foreign credit became increasingly difficult. Reserve requirements were then of only limited usefulness as an instrument of monetary policy.

Under these conditions the Solis approach to policy would undoubtedly design new monetary instruments and attempt once again to gain control over the money supply and thus inflation.

Conclusions

Mexico's fiscal crisis can be viewed as the imbalance created by the acceleration in public sector accumulation and the inadequacy of its financing.[26] The resulting deficit produces a growing public sector borrowing requirement.

Clearly, the central issue in negotiations between Mexico and the International Monetary Fund over a $4.5 million dollar loan for stabilization purposes would continue to be the size of the country's public sector deficit, which in 1982 would reach a record 17 percent of gross domestic product.[27] The Mexican mission to the IMF has argued that a major factor behind the country's fifty-three years of stability is a high degree of deficit spending to meet basic social needs. Subsidies, mainly on basic foodstuffs, public transport, and energy, represented 14 percent of GDP in 1981.

The IMF wanted to reduce the budget deficit to 8 percent of GDP by the end of 1983. Mexican officials, on the other hand, contended that their target was the maximum permissible without causing a major economic contraction. In large part, the analysis above indicates that there is adequate scope for tax reform capable of making a significant contribution to the IMF's objective. Financial reforms would also be a key to enabling the country to solve its current fiscal crisis.

11. Macroeconomic Controversies: The Monetarist-Cambridge Interpretations of the Policy Environment

In recent years, an interest in the monetary approach to the balance of payments has resurfaced in Mexico. Keynesian orthodoxy dominated government circles during most of the 1950s and 1960s, which thus tended to view the balance of payments as a policy problem for government intervention. In contrast, the modern monetary approach sees the balance of payments as an automatic international adjustment mechanism.[1]

The monetary approach is organized around the supply and demand for money. The theory predicts that factors that increase the demand for money relative to the supply will subsequently cause a reserve inflow to restore equilibrium, while a relative excess supply of money will result in a reserve outflow and a balance of payments deficit. Once stock equilibrium is obtained in the country's money markets, reserve flows should cease, unless factors such as continued economic growth create ongoing pressures for readjustment.

Empirically, the debate among Mexican monetarists, Keynesians, and adherents to the Cambridge school of thought comes down to differences involving the degree to which movements in the country's balance of payments may be explained by monetary factors and the impact of government deficits on the economy (i.e., the applicability of the Cambridge analysis to the Mexican economy). The sections that follow attempt to resolve these issues or at least throw additional light on this ongoing debate about the nature of the Mexican development process. It is necessary to resolve these issues at least partly as a first step in the construction of a macroeconomic policy model capable of providing realistic insights into the options now available to the country's policymakers.

In general, the empirical analysis undertaken here and in the following chapter indicates that a Keynesian model containing monetary elements provides the most accurate picture of the major economic forces at work in the Mexican economy.

The Monetary Approach to the Balance of Payments

Any test of the relative merits of the Keynesian, monetary, or Cambridge models in describing the Mexican economy must implicitly take into account the fact that the periods considered by each model are somewhat different. Thus, it is not strictly valid to compare directly the explanatory power of each approach. The monetary approach emphasizes the long term, while the Keynesian and

Cambridge models emphasize shorter-run adjustments. Mussa notes that the monetary approach "explicitly raises the question of how long the very short run is" since the monetary approach is only relevant for policy if the long-run consequences are felt within a few years.[2]

Mussa also states that to have predictive power, the monetary approach assumes that the demand and supply of money are stable functions defined over a small number of variables:

> If money demand were passive (i.e. if the economy was in a liquidity trap), the monetary approach would have no predictive power. The cumulative balance of payments surplus would be whatever was dictated by exclusively non-monetary considerations, and the demand for money would simply adjust to that fact. A non-monetary approach to the balance of payments would not only be justified, it would be required.[3]

The monetary approach itself does not try to explain whether adjustments will occur primarily through the capital or current accounts, but only expects that an overall adjustment will result from the initial monetary supply-demand imbalance. The monetary approach has the distinct advantage of providing a unified theory of the country's entire balance of payments. As Kemp notes, "the great majority of models used in payments theory consider either the capital account or the current account separately."[4]

The Model

Since the basic proposition of the monetary model is that the balance of payments is a mechanism that restores equilibrium between the supply of and the demand for money, adoption of this approach to the Mexican case begins with the equilibrium relationship that money supply is equal to money demand:[5]

$$MS = MD \tag{1}$$

Assuming the money multiplier (the parameter that relates the supply of money to the monetary base or reserve money) to be fixed (and for convenience equal to one), equation (1) can be written in terms of the supply and demand for the monetary base as

$$MB = MD \tag{2}$$

where MD is equal to the monetary base. The monetary base in turn is defined as equal to the sum of net foreign, R, and domestic assets, DA, of the central bank. Therefore:

$$MB = R + DA \tag{3}$$

Assuming the demand for money to be a function of nominal income (given by the gross domestic product) and the interest rate i, MD can be written as:

$$MD = f(GDPN, i) \tag{4}$$

Equating (3) and (4), transforming from levels to changes and solving for the change in foreign reserves, *DR* yields:

$$\Delta R = -\Delta DA + a_1 \Delta GDPN + a_2 \Delta i \qquad (5)$$

The model asserts that causality runs from money demand to money supply. It follows that attempts by the authorities to increase the money supply (*MB*) above the quantity demanded by the public by changing the level of domestic assets will only result in an outflow of reserves. Similarly an increase in the demand for money will result in a reserve inflow. The model also predicts that Mexico will tend to gain international reserves as the country's real income and domestic price level (nominal income) rise, and lose international reserves as the authorities attempt to expand the money supply by increasing domestic assets and / or as the interest rate rises.

While Keynesian models often indicate that a rise in income will be associated with a similar reserve inflow, the mechanisms underlying the process are somewhat different. Keynesian models anticipate reserve inflows only when there is a shift in either export or import demand. The monetary model's results therefore appear paradoxical when viewed from a Keynesian perspective largely because they center on the demand for or supply of money. Monetary theory stresses the relationship whereby increases in real income induce a rise in the demand for money, while an increase in the interest rate reduces that demand. Furthermore, in the monetary approach, an increase in the price level reduces the real money supply and induces an inflow of reserves.[6]

The counterintuitive signs on the interest rate and price level variables associated with the monetary model follow from the assumption that, in monetary equilibrium, domestic inflation and interest rates are closely linked to and primarily determined by changes in the respective world rates.[7] It follows that reserve flows induced by price or interest rate differentials between Mexico and the rest the of the world, which the short-run Keynesian approaches stress, are absent in the monetarist framework concentrating on long-run equilibrium adjustments. The monetarist models remove price or interest rate differentials by assuming substitutability among the goods and securities of different countries. In the limiting case of perfect substitutability in the long run, interest rates and price levels should be fully equalized across nations.

Financial Institutions and the Monetary Approach

Given that a large share of Mexico's export earnings are now derived from oil revenues, it may be somewhat out of place to apply the monetary approach to the economy's adjustment mechanisms. Casual observation of Mexico's international payments in recent years might lead one to believe that the country's reserve flows are now determined almost exclusively by real variables (the price of oil, the volume of oil sales, etc.). If in fact this were the case, it is difficult to see how monetary factors would have much of an effect on movements in the balance of payments. On the other hand, when the balance of payments accounts are examined in their totality, rather than as individual components (such as the trade account), monetary variables appear to have continued to play an important role in the country's external adjustment process.

More specifically, the immediate cause of the bulk of reserve flows into Mexico after 1977 was in fact the rapid increase in oil exports beginning at that time. However, were there not a demand for the money created by these reserve flows, a compensating reserve outflow would have been necessary to balance the domestic supply and demand for money. This compensating outflow did not occur, at least initially, because at the time (the 1976–79 IMF stabilization period), the government's restrictions on the domestic component of the money supply allowed the foreign reserves generated by the oil exports to provide the desired liquidity for the domestic economy. In fact, increased oil revenues after 1977 initiated substantial increases in real income in Mexico. In part, the resulting increase in the demand for money has been met by the inflow of foreign reserves.

Two distinguishing features shape the determination of the supply of money in Mexico and the influence that the Bank of Mexico has over this process. First of all, the country has tended to be open, and consequently the flow of foreign reserves into and out of the country has been a major source of changes in the monetary base.[8] However, the importance of foreign reserves in the monetary base has declined dramatically, falling from well over 50 percent in the late 1950s and early 1960s to less than 20 percent since 1977 (table 11.1). Clearly, externally generated fluctuation in the balance of payments, associated with fluctuations in world demand for exports, was a major source of change in the money supply up to the mid-1960s, but has been much less so since that time.

Second, the thinness of Mexican capital markets precludes the Bank of Mexico from engaging in offsetting open market operations in government securities. Open market sales or purchases of securities by the Bank of Mexico to or from the nonbank public could, if substantial enough, help to offset these primary changes. However, the securities market is too narrow to permit such offsetting to be carried out to the extent necessary to sterilize completely the flow of foreign assets.

In sum, the monetary approach to the balance of payments appears to be consistent with the monetary institutions of the country during the 1950s and early 1960s but less so since then.[9] During the 1950s and early 1960s, the flow of foreign reserves was a major component of the monetary base and hence the money supply. These reserves must in the long run accommodate the needs of monetary equilibrium within the country. Sterilization of these reserve flows by the Bank of Mexico was precluded by the thinness of government securities markets.[10]

The monetarist model may apply less well to the Mexican economy in the late 1960s through the 1970s, however. The falling importance of foreign assets in the monetary base, the rapid expansion of domestic assets, and the increased influence of the government's budgetary decisions on the composition of the reserve base may well have reduced the ability of the monetarist model to explain this aspect of the country's macroeconomic dynamics.

Table 11.1. Mexico: determinants of money supply, 1951–81 (billions of pesos)

				Monetary Base						
	Foreign assets	Reserve money	Domestic assets	Domestic assets	Reserve assets	Money ($M1$)	Money multiplier ($M1$)	Quasi money QM	Money ($M2$)	Money multiplier ($M2$)
1951	2.57	4.96	1.93	38.9	61.0	6.97	1.41	1.49	8.46	1.71
1952	2.44	5.12	2.68	52.3	47.7	7.26	1.42	1.87	9.13	1.78
1953	2.16	5.46	3.30	60.4	39.6	8.05	1.47	2.05	10.10	1.85
1954	2.61	6.19	3.58	57.8	42.2	9.01	1.46	3.02	12.03	1.94
1955	5.51	7.08	1.57	22.2	77.8	10.77	1.52	3.36	14.13	2.00
1956	6.40	7.84	1.44	18.4	81.6	11.98	1.53	3.71	15.69	2.00
1957	5.95	8.04	2.09	26.0	74.0	12.78	1.59	4.65	17.43	2.17
1958	4.89	8.87	3.98	44.9	55.1	13.72	1.55	5.45	19.17	2.16
1960	5.52	10.43	4.91	47.1	52.9	17.35	1.66	5.40	22.75	2.18
1961	5.16	11.20	6.04	53.9	46.1	18.49	1.65	6.02	24.51	2.19
1962	5.34	12.44	7.10	57.1	42.9	20.93	1.68	6.63	27.56	2.22
1963	6.85	13.99	7.14	51.0	49.0	24.31	1.74	8.05	32.36	2.31
1964	7.34	16.15	8.81	54.6	45.4	28.59	1.77	9.23	37.82	2.34
1965	6.72	16.92	10.20	60.3	39.7	30.21	1.79	10.39	40.60	2.40
1966	7.23	18.82	11.59	61.6	38.4	33.89	1.80	11.81	45.70	2.43
1967	7.98	21.20	13.22	62.4	37.6	37.02	1.75	13.12	50.14	2.37
1968	8.55	24.49	15.94	65.1	34.9	42.26	1.73	14.79	57.04	2.33
1969	8.98	27.35	18.37	67.2	32.8	48.59	1.78	16.85	65.44	2.39
1970	10.33	29.30	18.97	64.2	35.8	53.80	1.84	18.26	72.00	2.46
1971	12.86	33.44	20.58	61.5	38.5	57.89	1.73	19.64	77.53	2.32
1972	16.80	57.58	40.78	70.8	29.2	68.24	1.19	22.91	91.15	1.58
1973	17.98	75.32	57.23	76.1	23.9	83.52	1.11	31.57	115.09	1.53
1974	18.81	105.32	86.51	82.1	17.9	100.77	0.96	38.39	139.16	1.32
1975	20.15	140.84	120.69	85.7	14.3	122.36	0.87	41.74	164.10	1.17
1976	28.16	130.95	102.79	78.5	21.5	157.97	1.21	85.02	242.99	1.86
1977	46.47	315.39	268.92	85.3	14.7	224.31	0.71	296.28	520.59	1.65
1978	54.37	397.90	343.53	86.3	13.7	285.79	0.72	394.86	680.65	1.71
1979	72.46	532.86	465.40	87.3	12.7	383.17	0.72	534.71	917.88	1.72
1980	95.50	346.50	651.00	81.2	12.8	508.70	0.68	754.20	1,262.90	1.69
1981	132.50	1,045.00	912.50	87.3	12.7	635.00	0.61	1,314.10	1,949.6	1.87

Source: International Monetary Fund, *International Financial Statistics*.

Empirical Results

To test the consistency of the monetary view with the financial movements experienced by Mexico during the 1951–81 period, the basic model presented above was estimated using annual data (table 11.1). Equation 5 does not require the separation of national income into price and real income components and was used for estimation purposes.

Since no acceptable interest rate data were available for Mexico, the U.S. short-term interest rate (the IMF series on the U.S. treasury bill rate) was used as a proxy for the opportunity cost of holding money. This approach is justified on the assumption of close linkage between national rates of return. Since this assumption might be considered questionable, regressions were also estimated with the interest rate term excluded.

The results (table 11.2) show that a high proportion of the variation in foreign assets is associated with fluctuations in domestic assets and gross domestic product. Interestingly, for the overall period 1951–81, the sign was positive for change in domestic assets, contrary to the predicted negative sign. For the 1951–70 and 1951–65 periods, however, the change in domestic assets is negative and highly significant when regressed on the change in foreign assets. Regressions for the 1960–81 period, however, again resulted in a positive sign for the change in domestic assets and a t value just barely significant at the 95 percent confidence level.

Clearly, one can conclude that the adjustment mechanisms stressed by the monetary approach were present and significant factors from at least 1951 through 1960. However, beginning some time in the 1960s this mechanism apparently began to lose its effectiveness in structuring the country's external position.

When changes in the government deficit, ΔGD ($GD = \Delta[GT - GE]$) where GT = current government revenues, and GE = current government expenditures) were regressed on the changes in foreign assets, a reverse pattern occurred. Changes in the deficit are highly significant in explaining changes in foreign assets for the period as a whole and for the 1960–81 period, but not for the earlier 1951–70 and 1951–65 periods.

Again, the results confirm the general hypothesis of a changing economic environment in which the economy became more and more insulated from external forces and the government increased its role and strength in shaping the country's broad economic movements.

An alternative test of this hypothesis was made by examining movements in the trade balance as defined by the national income accounts. Changes in the trade balance, ΔGAP (defined as change in exports minus imports minus net factor payments) were regressed on changes in GDP (ΔGDP), changes in the government deficit (ΔGD), defined the same as above, and changes in the private sector balance ΔPD (defined as the difference between private savings and private investment).

Table 11.2. Mexico: reserve flow estimations

	Independent variables								
	$\Delta BMDA$	ΔGDP	$\Delta USTB$	ΔGD	*RHO*	Intercept	Adjusted r^2	*F*	*DW*
(1951–81) $\Delta BMFA$ =	0.13 (20.80)					0.41 (0.98)	0.939	432.95	2.16
		0.02 (19.48)				−0.07 (−0.15)	0.931	379.82	1.96
	0.07 (2.49)	0.61 (2.38)				0.13 (0.28)	0.940	222.07	2.01
	0.07 (2.58)	0.02 (2.25)	−0.46 (−1.18)			0.20 (0.49)	0.947	162.29	2.10
				−0.12 (−8.51)		1.45 (1.27)	0.718	72.39	1.68
		0.02 (7.09)		−0.05 (−3.36)		−0.13 (−0.18)	0.899	125.91	1.50
		0.02 (7.08)	−0.34 (−0.81)	−0.05 (−3.29)		−0.08 (−0.11)	0.902	83.85	1.58
(1951–70) $\Delta BMFA$ =	−0.83 (−6.14)				0.69 (4.07)	1.41 (3.06)	0.684	37.82	1.98
	−0.76 (−5.13)	0.04 (2.44)				0.36 (1.00)	0.597	12.68	1.76
	−0.71 (−4.90)	0.04 (2.32)	0.22 (1.49)			0.32 (0.93)	0.627	9.04	1.74
				−0.07 (−1.02)		0.35 (1.30)	0.003	1.06	1.82

(1951–65)									
$\Delta BMFA =$	−0.97					0.92			
	(−7.13)					(3.85)	0.806	50.85	1.78
	−0.98	0.02				0.64			
	(−6.73)	(0.85)				(1.76)	0.784	22.79	1.76
				−0.09		0.26			
				(−0.87)		(0.73)	0.02	0.77	1.87
(1960–81)									
$\Delta BMFA =$	0.13					0.43			
	(17.71)					(0.76)	0.939	313.74	2.20
	0.07	0.02				0.08			
	(2.19)	(1.98)				(0.13)	0.940	158.12	2.04
	0.08	0.01	−0.73		−0.38	0.20			
	(2.46)	(1.82)	(−1.62)		(−1.85)	(0.38)	0.953	120.12	2.20
				−0.07	0.95	30.99			
				(−4.23)	(15.18)	(1.37)	0.458	17.98	1.11
		0.02		−0.04		−0.26			
		(6.03)		(−2.94)		(−0.25)	0.894	84.86	1.46
		0.02	−0.72	−0.05		−0.15			
		(6.23)	(−1.29)	(−3.09)		(−0.15)	0.902	55.24	1.55

Table 11.2. (continued)

	Independent variables								
	$\Delta BMDA$	ΔGDP	$\Delta USTB$	ΔGD	*RHO*	Intercept	Adjusted r^2	*F*	*DW*
(1965–81) $\Delta BMFA$ =									
	0.13 (14.56)					0.57 (0.73)	0.933	212.26	2.20
	0.07 (1.89)	0.01 (1.67)				0.13 (0.15)	0.932	96.58	2.03
	0.08 (2.18)	0.01 (1.48)	−0.82 (−1.55)		−0.42 (−1.84)	0.26 (0.37)	0.949	93.61	2.23
				−0.07 (−3.59)	0.94 (11.57)	32.32 (1.38)	0.443	12.95	1.11
		0.02 (5.05)		−0.05 (−2.51)		−0.32 (−0.22)	0.879	57.25	1.45
		0.02 (5.20)	−0.75 (−1.13)	−0.05 (−2.60)		−0.24 (−0.17)	0.888	40.61	1.54

Source: Computed by the author.

Note: $\Delta BMFA$ = Change in net foreign assets, Bank of Mexico
$\Delta BMDA$ = Change in net domestic assets, Bank of Mexico
ΔGDP = Change in nominal gross domestic product
$\Delta USTB$ = Change in United States Treasury Bill rate
ΔGD = Change in Government deficit

For the period as a whole (1951–81), the government deficit is strongly associated with movements in the balance of payments. The private sector balance is not significant when regressed by itself. For the subperiod 1951–70, the government deficit is less significant, increasing somewhat in the 1960–81 period. In all cases, the private sector deficit was not statistically significant when regressed individually.

The final results seem somewhat consistent with the Cambridge approach, which stresses that

> other than in the short term, the private sector shows a small and stable surplus (which implies that the public sector's budget deficit fully determines the current balance of payments: given the size of the budget deficit, changes in exports, imports prices, etc. make a lot of difference to real income and output, but none at all to the balance of payments however paradoxical this may at first sight appear.

In sum, at the present time the Keynesian or Cambridge models appear best to describe the Mexican economy, whereas in the 1950s and early 1960s a monetarist approach best described the more important mechanisms at work.

The Cambridge Analysis of the Mexican Economy

In April 1981 the Cambridge Policy Group released a paper drawing several major conclusions on Mexico's current economic problems.[12] Their first conclusion is that the Mexican economy is not "overheated," in the sense given by orthodox economists to this expression. "That is to say, the planned rate of economic growth is not too high relative to the country's productivity and consequently it is not generating inflation."[13]

In large part, this conclusion is derived from a survey that the Office of the Advisers of the President of the Republic made of business activity. In that survey, a large number of respondents indicated that from 1979 to 1980 "the constraints imposed by industrial plant and equipment in satisfying demand diminished very generally." This conclusion is based on answers of a qualitative nature regarding the adequacy of the individual producers' facilities for satisfying prospective demand in the year ahead.

In contrast to the more orthodox interpretation of Mexican inflation that stresses aggregate excess monetary supply, the Cambridge group attributes Mexican inflation largely to the behavior of costs (rather than to the expansion of demand). In the case of the rise of 25 percent in the price of manufacturing output in 1980, the report alleges that "7 percentage points of the rate of inflation were caused by an increase in gross profit margins. This is the key factor in the acceleration of the inflationary process in 1980."[14]

The second conclusion of the Cambridge report is that "given the existing foreign trade policy of Mexico, the present rate of expansion is leading to unstable increases" in the current deficit in the external accounts. "This is the central problem in the economy at present." And the remedy is "to introduce a strategy of direct and selective import controls." The aim is to reduce the annual rate of increase in imports from the 28 percent in 1980 to an average of 12 percent over the next three years, and thereafter gradually reduce the level further, once Mexican "productive capacity has been strengthened to a greater degree."

The group's major proposal is for import boards, which are to be "the central piece in the strategy of economic adjustment in the short run." The report recommends that some complementary measures in other fields be introduced. (1) A stricter policy of control over prices and incomes is necessary, with the granting of greater power to the responsible body in order to "prevent prices from rising higher than is justified by reference costs." (2) The value-added tax (VAT) should be reduced substantially on a wider range of consumer goods, and the loss of revenue recouped from taxes on medium and high incomes. (3) Interest rates should be reduced to narrow the gap between Mexican and U.S. rates from the level of 17.5 percentage points on one-year deposits to "the traditional level of 6 points." It was also regarded as indispensable that government should "establish limits to the active rates of interest over which at present no control whatever is exercised." (4) The Bank of Mexico "should suspend its policy of gradually depreciating the currency" and instead must "keep the exchange rate with the dollar stable, which it can do occasionally making both revaluations and devaluations, in each case keeping the changes small in accordance with the short term market conditions."

These proposals are important mostly because they articulate to a large degree the position taken in recent years by a number of President López Portillo's economic advisers. This analysis was an extension of an earlier study based on the Cambridge approach, which stressed that during the 1970s the economy progressively deteriorated in its capacity to finance the imports required by previous growth rates of production and employment. The earlier study attributed the rapid deterioration in the balance of payments to the exhaustion of the internal sources of finance needed for the model of industrialization followed in the 1960s, the slow development of domestic capital goods industry, the premature deterioration in the foreign trade surplus of the agricultural sector, and the consequent drying up of this source of finance for industrialization.[15]

This import-side view of the evolution of the industrial trade deficit stresses the pattern of structural change. Such a view contrasts sharply with the usual argument that blames Mexican manufacturing's failure to reduce its trade deficit largely on the damage that protection, as the main policy instrument to promote industrialization, has done to competitiveness and export capacity.

The earlier versions of the Cambridge Economic Policy Group models are capable of analyzing the Mexican economy. The Cambridge school's approach to economic policy in Mexico represents a novel theoretical innovation and, according to some observers, has had a notable effect on the government's budgetary policy. These developments are largely associated in Mexican policy circles with disenchantment with Keynesian demand management techniques: in particular, with the use of public expenditure as a regulator of aggregate demand, and with the practice of fine-tuning the components of demand in accordance with short-term economic forecasts. The Cambridge attack on the Keynesian macrosystem must be seen not only in the context of the ongoing (almost institutionalized) monetarist vs. Keynesian debate in Mexico, but also in the context of the reinterpretation of the Keynesian system by Leijonhufvud as well as its critical reappraisal in the light of contemporary conditions.[16]

Moreover the Cambridge analysis has emerged in a period of acute problems facing the Mexican authorities. This debate is of paramount importance given the apparent failure of Keynesian demand management techniques to maintain a steady noninflationary growth, the interdependent nature of the world economy, and the serious questioning of the conventional wisdom of a generation of post-Keynesian economic policymakers in Mexico.

Based largely on their analysis of the British economy, the Cambridge approach to economic policy proposes that the budget should be used to regulate the balance of payments, with the exchange rate adjusted to determine the level of domestic output and employment. The Cambridge critique of Mexican policymaking implies that the failure of economic management in Mexico in recent years stems from a reliance on short-term forecasting, which does not show the strength and implications of these relationships. This has, they claim, sustained the mistaken belief that the balance of payments is somehow more difficult to forecast and control than the level of domestic economic activity. The Cambridge group therefore contrasts their approach with Keynesian orthodoxy, which stresses the use of the budget to regulate the level of employment with the balance of payments determined in large part by the exchange rate. The Cambridge approach starts from the proposition that the simultaneous achievement of full employment and equilibrium in the balance of payments depends upon the balance between domestic expenditure and output, which leaves sufficient resources free for exports, and a degree of competitiveness that ensures that these resources will be employed. Since the balance of payments is defined as the difference between GNP and total domestic expenditure, balance of payments equilibrium depends upon total domestic expenditure being less than (or greater than) real national income by exactly the target surplus (or deficit) on current account.

The heart of the Cambridge approach is the assertion that, in the long run, the main source of imbalance between total domestic expenditure and real national income has been government's fiscal and monetary policy. According to the methodology upon which this assertion is based, the economy is composed of three sectors—the government (public), companies, and personal sectors; the new flow of funds into or out of the economy is by definition equal to the surplus or deficit on the balance of payments; the net acquisition of financial assets by the personal and companies sectors is small and fairly stable; and the public sector's budget deficit fully determines the current balance of payments. The sizes of the budget deficit, exports and imports, prices, etc., make a lot of difference to real income but none at all to the balance of payments.

This, then, is the basis of the Cambridge argument that the budget should be used to determine the balance of payments and that the latter is no harder to forecast and control than domestic economic activity. They conclude that, with only small and temporary exceptions, the government's fiscal policy should seek to ensure that total domestic expenditure is in line with national income, or different only to the extent required to effect long-term capital flows by an equivalent surplus or deficit on current account.

In fact, if internal leakages are zero, then indeed the exchange rate has no effect on the balance of trade, and changes in government spending cause equal and opposite changes in the balance of trade. When positive tax leakages are introduced, the trade balance can no longer be independent of the exchange rate. However, providing only that the marginal private propensity to spend is unity, change in the ex post government deficit causes equal and opposite changes in the trade balance. Finally, in a world of limited information in which the necessary action required to get to both external and internal balance is unknown, policymakers may for simplicity assign instruments to *targets*. If this is so, then the Cambridge assignment of the exchange rate to the level of income and the budget deficit to the balance of trade is appropriate as long as domestic leakages are less than foreign leakages.

It need hardly be said that there is a substantial political content at least implicit in the Cambridge school's approach. This is particularly so with regard to taxation policy. The Cambridge approach implies that by reducing the government's borrowing requirement through increased taxation, it is thereby possible to improve the balance of payments.

The assumptions of the Cambridge approach can be questioned in three broad areas: (1) the stability of the personal and company sectors financial surplus; (2) the mechanism whereby a country seeks to improve its position; and (3) the relative size of leakages consequent on an initial improvement in the balance of payments.

The second condition set out by the Cambridge school for the simultaneous achievement of full employment and a strong external position, via the relative competitive position of the country, is particularly open to question. In Keynesian orthodoxy, the exchange rate determines the balance of payments, since exchange rate changes imply changes in relative prices and therefore international competitiveness. According to this argument, the primary effect of the recent exchange rate devaluation will be to improve the external balance by increasing exports and reducing imports. By contrast, the Cambridge approach implies that the main effect of devaluation will be on the level of domestic activity—by increasing the level of economic activity through increased production by exporters and import substitution. Thus, the 1982 devaluations will simultaneously induce an expanded volume of imports, effectively negating any temporary improvement that may take place in the balance of payments.

Essentially, the disagreement between more orthodox Keynesian and the Cambridge group's policy recommendations in the current crisis hinges on the relative importance of the various leakages. The Cambridge approach stresses the overwhelming importance of the import leakage, asserting that while the improvement in the country's competitive position has increased the volume of exports and imports (and thereby raised the level of output and employment), it has not appreciably improved the current balance of payments. The econometric forecasting model developed below indicates that leakages other than imports—largely public sector leakages—made the increase in domestic activity considerably less than claimed by the Cambridge group and, thus, that the primary effect of the depreciation of the exchange rate will be on the current balance of payments.

Furthermore, the Cambridge approach appears to assume implicitly that monetary policy will facilitate fiscal policy and take no direct or indirect action to offset excessive external borrowing by the government, or to ensure through an appropriate monetary policy that the particular exchange rate regime is appropriate both to the desired level of domestic activity and the balance of payments objectives.

In contrast, the model developed below demonstrates that government deficits and the resulting need for credit (both internal and external) are the chief causes of inflationary pressures within the economy and thus ultimately the exchange rate and / or current account of the balance of payments.

One disquieting feature of the Cambridge approach is its lack of analysis on the role of inflation. This is somewhat unusual in a model that has been seriously proposed as a guide to Mexican economic policy. In a realistic policy model for Mexico, a reduction in the level of inflation is as important as the foreign balance of payments or maintaining full employment. The implications of the Cambridge approach in this area, particularly with regard to the international transmission of inflation in open economies, certainly require spelling out in more detail.

In summary, it is perhaps worth returning to the fundamental contention about the economic structure that has given rise to the Cambridge approach. The Cambridge position is that the financial balance of the private sector is quite stable, so that the marginal propensity to spend of the private sector is close to unity. There is a methodological point of some interest here. In focusing on how companies adjust their savings and investment plans in the face of changes in income, the Cambridge approach is essentially bringing in a super multiplier. In contrast, Keynesian models stress instability of expectations as the very basis of the doctrine that investment determines savings. In this view, savings adjust to whatever investment levels established by entrepreneurs in anticipation of changes in the level of economic activity. The Cambridge school appears to deny this. Both corporations and individuals are supposed either to adjust their investment plans either to changes in income or to the proportion of new income which they save. Further, they are supposed to do this almost completely whatever their new level of income. From this denial of the Keynesian doctrine, the

Cambridge approach derives its claim that fiscal policy should not attempt to compensate for short-term changes in private sector expenditure.

Conclusions

Keynesian doctrine has formed the basis of a number of forecasting models used over the years in Mexico. The Cambridge approach is asking us to abandon this tradition of empirical work, the methodological framework on which it rests, and the policy conclusions to which it has led. In contrast, the model developed in the next two chapters along Keynesian lines demonstrates that from an empirical point of view, many of the implicit assumptions underlying the Cambridge approach are not valid for Mexico. Furthermore, a Keynesian model incorporating monetary factors is not only capable of capturing the fundamental forces at work in the economy but is also capable of providing more realistic policy prescriptions than the Cambridge approach provides for the period of economic stabilization that Mexico now faces.

12. Impact of Fiscal Policy: A Critique of the Fitzgerald Thesis

Interest in the impacts associated with the Mexican government's finances and expenditures continues not only because of the government's current fiscal crisis, but because of the new insights this problem continues to provide into the fundamental economic relationships operating in the unique institutional environment that links the country's public, private, and financial sectors.[1]

One of the issues that has begun to attract attention is the manner in which the private sector responds to the forces created by the government's fiscal measures. The slowdown in private investment in the mid-1970s has been of particular concern. Does government spending displace a nearly equal amount of private spending? This notion, popularly known as the "crowding out" effect of government expenditures in the advanced countries, has recently gained increased attention in Mexico.[2] First, at the policy level, there is a feeling in some business circles that both continued deficits and the existence of a massive public debt has, and will continue to have, a negative effect on private capital expenditures.[3] Second, at the academic level, the perceived degree to which crowding out does or does not occur is at least one of the major issues that helps to distinguish between advocates of the major macroeconomic schools of thought: traditional Keynesians, the modern Cambridge school, and the monetarists.[4]

What follows focuses on crowding out more from an academic than practical (policy) point of view. It is written from largely a Keynesian perspective and is a critique of the recently developed and controversial Cambridge approach to the problem proposed in a series of papers by E. V. L. Fitzgerald.[5]

The empirical impact of the government's expenditures, taxes, and borrowing on various measures of private sector activity is examined through several different tests. Using ordinary least squares regressions, various components of government finance and expenditure are regressed on private savings, investment, and consumption. The impact of government fiscal actions on private sector aggregate over time is also estimated by several distributed lag formulations.

Alternative Interpretations of Crowding Out in the Mexican Context

Formally, the examination of possible crowding out of private sector activity by government fiscal actions should begin with the so-called government budget constraint.[6] Here, the fundamental identity underlying the analysis is that the total flow of government expenditure must equal the total flow of financing from all sources. The total flow of financing includes taxes, net government borrowing from the public, and the net amount of new money issued. Most important, this approach allows budget deficits or surpluses to be seen in a multidimensional context; i.e., they alter the size of public debt. Further, the method of financing such deficits or disposing of such surpluses affects the composition of private wealth. Clearly, these considerations imply that any discussion of the effects of fiscal policy actions should distinguish between the different monetary repercussions that result from alternative budgetary actions. Unfortunately, this has not always been done in the Mexican case. Instead, each school of thought has concentrated on one or two aspects of the process while assuming that the other impacts of fiscal policy on the private sector are either insignificant or for practical purposes can be treated as constant.

The different aspects of the crowding out effect can be best seen within a national account framework linking savings (S), investment (I), exports (X), and imports (Z), with $S - I = X - Z$.

Dividing savings and investment into that accounted for by the public and private sectors, with $GT =$ government revenue, and CG and IG for current government expenditure and investment, respectively, yields:

$$(GT - CG - IG) + SP - IP = X - Z, \text{ or}$$

$$GD + SP - IP = GAP$$

where the public account (GD) is defined as the difference between current public revenue and expenditure and the current account of the balance of payments is denoted by GAP.

The behavioral relationships between these variables are central to distinguishing the various schools of thought and their diverging policy orientations in the Mexican context. The logical extremes in behavioral relationships can be expressed in terms of three major theories.[7]

Conventional Crowding Out

Conventional crowding out occurs where changes in the fiscal deficit do not affect private savings (because these depend on aggregate income alone), or the external trade balance (which is determined by relative prices).[8] The major adjustment mechanism is a reduction in private investment as interest rates are forced up through declining bond prices (due to bonds' oversupply).[9]

The Monetary Approach to the Balance of Payments

The monetary approach focuses on the demand and supply of money, with interest rates determined in international financial markets. Private savings and investment are thus unaffected by movements in GD. Instead, the impact of an increased deficit would be felt mainly on the trade balance through an increased demand for foreign liabilities, with $GD = GAP$ (IP, SP constant).[10]

Keynesian Crowding Out

Keynesian crowding out takes place when the rise in aggregate demand resulting from the budget deficit produces increased private savings rather than consumption. Private investment and the trade balance are assumed to be largely unaffected in the short run; thus, $GD = -SP$.

Of course, some intermediate variation on these extreme versions is likely to transpire in practice. However, these three logical alternatives at least broadly delineate the major schools of thought.

In the Mexican context, conventional crowding out was the predominant view in the Banco de México and the Secretaria de Hacienda in the 1960s.[11] At that time, the orthodox position contended that financing fiscal deficits by imposing high marginal reserve requirements on the banking system and pegging interest rates to those on the New York money market would hold total credit down to the level of the monetary base, itself generated by the steady rise of financial asset acquisition by the private sector as a proportion of national income.[12]

A second approach has been termed the "new orthodoxy" of the Mexican view in the 1970s.[13] This approach stresses that changes in public sector deficits are met by directly expanding the money supply or by foreign borrowing.[14] Both methods have indirect and direct effects on the balance of payments. Financial asset acquisition by the private savings sector is determined by income (interest rates being exogenous). Investment would not suffer from credit restrictions under this mechanism, and variations in credit conditions would be reflected in the demand for foreign assets, that is, in capital outflows or increased imports.

Fitzgerald's thesis contends simply that for public sector capital accumulation to expand without an increase in taxation or destabilizing consequences, there must be a compensating increase in net private sector savings, whether forced or voluntary. He argues the first two positions, while not necessarily incorrect, err stressing in monetary stability, and that the third alternative (his) is not only more convincing in econometric terms but also contains greater insight into the actual interactions between the economy's key economic institutions.

Specifically for Mexico, the Fitzgerald thesis stems from several equations estimated by ordinary least squares techniques. These show that private savings as a percentage of gross domestic product is positively related to both private investment and the government deficit (GD) (as defined above to equal government current revenue minus government expenditures). In estimating several different import functions, Fitzgerald also found a positive relationship between imports and both the government deficit and government investment. These results from the national income accounts imply that during the period under consideration there was an offsetting one-to-one effect of government surpluses on private savings.[15]

From these results, Fitzgerald concludes that private consumption in Mexico has adjusted to provide that amount of private savings required to finance the domestic component of the public sector's borrowing requirements. On the other hand, the government used official external debt to finance an increased level of imports, generated by the increased average propensity to import stemming from changes in the composition of aggregate demand caused by the import substitution process. This interpretation is consistent with the observed fall in consumption as a percentage of GDP over the last thirty years.

The crowding out of consumption in Mexico appeared to be a Keynesian type of savings, but was not the result of a Keynesian process of expanded income and economic activity because of the high level of unemployment existing in the country during this period. Also, it was not a Keynesian mechanism relying on the bond coupon effect of higher public borrowing. Fitzgerald argues rather that interest rates are set to maintain balance with the U.S. rates.[16] He also argues that the Mexican patterns did not result from savings forced through inflation, again resulting from the effects of the budget deficit upon the real incomes of money holders. According to Fitzgerald, inflation rates in Mexico were low and in any case determined by prices in U.S. markets.

In Mexico, according to Fitzgerald, crowding out seems to have taken place through the capacity and willingness of the private banking system to reduce, directly or indirectly, the volume of consumer credit in response to increased state funding requirements. The crowding out of private consumption was, therefore, largely a result of the banking system's effect on the pattern of asset and liabilities acquisition by households.

The mechanism suggested by Fitzgerald, whereby private consumption is crowded out, is consistent with four relationships familiar from the earlier parts of the present study: (1) During the 1950s, 1960s, and 1970s, the monetary base, defined as private sector deposits in the banking system and purchases of financial intermediaries' obligations as well as notes and coin, expanded rapidly both in absolute terms and as a proportion of national income. (2) The main components of the demand for money are both functions of nominal GDP ($M1$ with a unitary elasticity and $M2$ with greater than unitary elasticity) rather than interest rates or expected inflation. According to Fitzgerald prices and interest rates are for the most part determined exogenously. (3) By imposing high marginal reserve requirements the Bank of Mexico achieved a large average reserve ratio in the 1960s and 1970s, thus providing a noninflationary source of fiscal resources. (4) Most important, for a given private gross savings rate, the higher the public sector borrowing requirement the lower the remaining credit for the private sector.

The Fitzgerald thesis breaks new ground with a number of somewhat conjectural assumptions about the motivations underlying government and bank action. According to Fitzgerald,

1. Contrary to popular belief, reserve requirements are simply imposed on banks, so that any public sector deficit could be financed.

2. The reduction in credit to the private sector does not necessarily reduce private investment.
3. The concentration of Mexican banking, in which the four major ownership groups control two-thirds of all private lending and also the center of major industrial conglomerates, assures the private sector of funds for investment.
4. Financial concentration enabled the banks to have considerable influence over the government itself. The banks could block not only attempts at tax reform in both 1962 and 1972 but also the expansion of the state itself in the 1970s.
5. In actuality, monetary policy, and particularly reserve ratios, are negotiated between the central bank, the treasury, and the private banks.
6. It follows that the banks in effect limited total public sector budget by constraining both the development of an efficient tax system and the borrowing powers of the government. The government's ability to borrow abroad was in turn limited by the IMF's stabilization program.
7. Savings are concentrated in the higher income groups where any distinction between savings and company profits is somewhat arbitrary.
8. Firms tend to rely heavily on self-finance, using retained profits to finance not only most fixed investment, but also a considerable proportion of their working capital.
9. Self-financing and the maintenance of a stable ratio of financial assets to fixed assets by firms means that credit tightening by banks will not affect investment directly from the funding side.
10. Unlike in most countries, bank credit is often used for working capital in Mexico. It is used to extend credit to consumers, either directly through hire purchase agreements or indirectly through credit to wholesalers, who then extend it to retailers and finally consumers.[17]

In sum, the Fitzgerald thesis argues that the Mexican economic system worked in a way fundamentally different from that envisaged in orthodox treatments of development finance. Such treatments incorrectly assumed that savings is a binding constraint on private investment and that the private industrial sector is in financial deficit even for fixed capital formation. In Mexico, on the other hand, the government's abstraction of funds from money markets (which link savers and investors) does not necessarily reduce private sector capital formation. The Mexican system works through determining private consumption and thus private savings as residuals, after the claims of both private investment and the fiscal deficit have been met.

The Cambridge mechanisms linking savings and investment are the critical link in the Fitzgerald interpretation of the government's role in recent Mexican economic growth, and differentiate his interpretation from the more orthodox interpretations.

However, Fitzgerald provides no statistical tests other than the one ordinary least squares regression result noted above (of private savings on the government deficit and private investment, all as a percentage of GDP), as to the validity of the Cambridge-type assertions concerning the savings-investment process. Essentially, he simply presents his interpretation as more or less consistent with what is known of the patterns of household savings, bank finance, and business profits in Mexico.

This study has no particular quarrel with the Fitzgerald interpretation of the savings-investment process in Mexico.[18] It does raise the possibility, however, that the more orthodox interpretations may in fact be on firmer empirical grounds and thus rely less on conjecture in describing the precise nature of government–private investor–consumer interactions.

Testing Alternative Models of Crowding Out: Short-Run Impacts

As a first step toward clearly identifying the impact of public sector fiscal actions on private sector activity, a number of functional equations commonly suggested as affecting private consumption, investment, and savings were estimated.

All estimates were for the 1951–81 period and were performed by ordinary least squares, using a Cochrane-Orcutt estimation procedure to correct for possible serial correlation.[19]

Private Consumption

Estimates (table 12.1) indicate that changes in private consumption (ΔPC) were largely a function of changes in GDP (ΔGDP) and increases in the price level (ΔCPI).

After these two variables the government's operations appear to have operated marginally, with increases in total government borrowing (ΔGBT), government internal borrowing (ΔGBI), and Bank of Mexico credit to the government ($\Delta BMGC$), all having positive impacts on private consumption. In particular, changes in the government deficit ΔGD were not significant (equation 6, table 12.1) when entered in the regression equation with GDP.

When entered separately, the government deficit ΔGD had, in contrast to the Fitzgerald result, a strong negative impact on the change in consumption (higher values of ΔGD mean greater government surplus).

These results (table 12.1) clearly indicate that the government's financing requirements have little direct financial crowding out effect on private consumption. Instead, their major impact is more likely to be indirect, through the Keynesian multiplier on GDP.

With regard to government expenditure separately, a somewhat different picture emerges. Government expenditures, together with inflation, have a strong negative relationship with private consumption. While the government expenditures may increase income and thus consumption, public expenditures may act as substitutes for private consumption. Thus, as the government has increased

Table 12.1 Mexico: incremental change in private consumption, 1951–81

	Independent variables										
	ΔGDP	$\Delta CP1$	ΔGBT	ΔGBI	$\Delta MSDC$	ΔGD	*RHO*	Intercept	r^2	*F*	*DW*
(1)	0.59							4.31			
	(115.46)							(2.13)	0.997	1,333.20	2.01
(2)	0.57		0.13					5.65			
	(61.52)		(4.93)					(1.80)	0.997	4,207.02	1.79
(3)	0.57			0.14				5.92			
	(60.84)			(5.11)				(1.83)	0.997	4,080.73	1.81
(4)	1.93	−16.54			1.23		0.97	1,317.50			
	(11.18)	(−5.39)			(3.87)		(22.08)	(2.46)	0.916	88.34	1.96
(5)	0.55				0.12			5.23			
	(22.82)				(2.01)			(2.62)	0.998	7,276.16	1.97
(6)	0.58					−0.13		4.31			
	(40.71)					(−1.34)		(1.90)	0.997	5,661.87	1.97

Source: Computed by the author.
Note: ΔGDP = Change in gross domestic product
$\Delta CP1$ = Change in consumer price index
ΔGBT = Change in total government borrowing
ΔGBI = Change in internal government borrowing
$\Delta MSDC$ = Change in monetary system domestic credit
ΔGD = Change in government deficit.

its role in the economy, especially in the 1970s, the private sector has accepted free publicly provided goods and services, reducing the demand for substitutes produced by the private sector and provided through the market place.

When the level of private consumption is regressed on various government fiscal variables, there is again no indication that on the financial side increased credit to the government sector or government deficits curtailed credit to the private sector in the sense that private sector consumption was reduced as the government increased its borrowing or absorbed more credit (*MSGC*) from the banking system. On the other hand, increased government current revenues (*GT*) tend to reduce private consumption as do increases in government savings (equations 5, 7, table 12.2). As with the change in consumption, increases in *GD* (an increase in the government's surplus) tend to result in a fall in private consumption (equation 6, table 12.2).

Private Savings

Private savings, like private consumption, were found to be largely related to income (GDP, ΔGDP). Several factors affected the incremental changes in private savings:

1. Contrary to Fitzgerald, the government deficit had a fairly strong negative impact (table 12.3). Increases in the government surplus, *GD*, increased private savings after changes in GDP had been taken into account.
2. On the other hand, increases in the government surplus by themselves had a negative impact on private savings.
3. Increases in government expenditure, *GENAN*, tended to reduce private savings (equations 2, 3, table 12.3).
4. Government borrowing, *GBT*, had a negative impact on the change in private savings.
5. Government taxes, ΔGT, tended to reduce private savings after income was taken into account.
6. Inflation tended to increase private savings as it had reduced private consumption.

For the level of private savings (table 12.4), more or less the same picture emerges:

1. Private savings are determined largely by the level of income, *GDP*.
2. Increases in the price level (ΔWPI) are strongly related to increases in private savings.
3. The government deficit, *GD*, has a minor negative effect on private savings (equations 1, 6, table 12.4).
4. Increases in government savings are negatively related to private savings.
5. Government borrowing is strongly related (equation 4, table 12.4) to increases in private savings.

Table 12.2. Mexico: government impact on private consumption, 1951–81 (current prices)

	Independent variables												
	GDP	*ΔCPI*	*GD*	*GT*	*SG*	*DUMEX*	*MSGC*	*GENAN*	*RHO*	Intercept	r^2	*F*	*DW*
(1)	0.60	−1.10	−0.14						0.95	116.17			
	(40.75)	(2.06)	(−1.61)						(16.45)	(2.24)	0.997	4,099.48	1.61
(2)	0.80	−2.19	0.63	−0.83					0.90	42.27			
	(9.23)	(−3.17)	(1.86)	(−2.32)					(11.23)	(1.45)	0.998	4,589.74	1.54
(3)	0.53					24.82	0.53		8.96	168.87			
	(33.87)					(2.86)	(5.80)		(19.47)	(30.44)	0.999	6,515.03	1.88
(4)	0.68	−2.39				19.28	0.56	−0.62	0.97	132.51			
	(11.90)	(−5.28)				(11.90)	(6.86)	(−2.72)	(20.22)	(2.66)	0.999	5,700.5	1.64
(5)	1.03	−1.88			−0.38	51.23		−1.77		−3.96			
	(24.36)	(−3.68)			(−2.55)	(4.50)		(−9.40)		(−0.85)	0.999	41,891.8	1.93
(6)	0.58		−0.19			23.22			0.90	79.63			
	(42.39)		(2.00)			(23.22)			(11.79)	(2.68)	0.998	4,675.01	2.01
(7)	0.61	−0.64			−0.38				0.97	176.66			
	(90.92)	(−2.02)			(−2.40)				(19.98)	(2.46)	0.998	4,064.18	1.85

Source: Computed by the author.
Note: *GDP* = Gross domestic product
ΔCPI = Change in consumer price index
GD = Government deficit
GT = Government current revenue (national income sense)
SG = Government saving
DUMEX = Dummy variable 0, 1951–76, 1, 1977–81
MSGC = Monetary system credit to the government
GENAN = Government expenditure (consumption plus investment).

Table 12.3. Mexico: change in private savings, 1951–81 (current prices)

	Independent variables													
	ΔGDP	*DUMEX*	$\Delta GENAN$	ΔGD	ΔGT	ΔWPI	ΔGBT	ΔSG	*IP*	*RHO*	Intercept	r^2	*F*	*DW*
(1)	0.27 (25.09)									0.39 (2.33)	−7.99 (−1.49)	0.958	629.48	1.98
(2)	0.47 (9.41)	−53.20 (−7.45)	−0.70 (−3.38)								−5.44 (−2.87)	0.992	1,070.85	2.05
(3)	0.46 (9.84)	−54.31 (−8.38)	−0.59 (−2.90)	0.15 (2.26)							−5.36 (−3.17)	0.994	1,028.89	2.06
(4)	0.22 (11.80)	−74.64 (−8.12)			0.18 (3.07)	1.68 (4.17)					−6.66 (−3.19)	0.993	804.68	1.97
(5)	0.31 (17.04)	−36.71 (−4.52)				0.98 (3.83)	−0.1 (−6.62)				0.96 (19.63)	0.977	257.48	1.63
(6)	0.32 (22.37)	−42.16 (−4.87)		0.20 (2.46)				−0.28 (−1.81)			−4.20 (−2.81)	0.994	1,139.44	2.23
(7)	0.41 (6.82)	−62.72 (−6.40)		0.27 (3.07)					−0.42 (−1.39)		−5.44 (−2.75)	0.992	827.45	2.10
(8)	0.33 (24.98)	−53.10 (−8.12)		0.24 (2.92)							−4.40 (−2.75)	0.993	1,290.76	2.24
(9)	0.27 (16.98)	−72.13 (−8.57)		0.19 (14.16)		1.61 (4.68)					−7.08 (−3.11)	0.992	773.91	1.94
(10)								−0.45 (−3.28)	1.71 (50.31)	−0.54 (−3.46)	0.30 (0.17)	0.991	1,462.06	2.51
(11)		−45.91 (−9.10)				3.21 (5.88)	−0.04 (−1.21)		1.03 (7.21)		6.41 (2.86)	0.991	692.81	2.02
(12)	0.34 (9.03)	−56.47 (−6.01)							−0.11 (−0.50)		−6.35 (−2.29)	0.991	692.81	2.02
(13)							−0.39 (−7.03)	−0.51 (−6.35)	2.19 (31.76)		−1.60 (−1.69)	0.977	2,980.46	1.78

Source: Computed by the author.
Note: See text for definition of variables.

Table 12.4. Mexico: determinants of private saving, 1951–81 (current prices)

	Independent variables												
	GDP	Δ*WPI*	*DUMEX*	*GD*	*GREV*	*GBI*	*IP*	*SG*	*RHO*	Intercept	r^2	*F*	*DW*
(1)	0.28	1.19	−56.32	0.27					0.97	−170.99			
	(21.34)	(3.94)	(−4.33)	(3.07)					(21.08)	(−2.11)	0.987	546.67	0.89
(2)	0.25	0.84	−36.82					−0.64	0.96	−112.10			
	(42.95)	(3.23)	(−3.42)					(−4.69)	(18.72)	(−2.10)	0.992	773.49	2.24
(3)	0.15	2.49	−47.36		0.37				−0.75	−7.08			
	(18.09)	(6.24)	(−4.43)		(8.90)				(−6.19)	(−3.45)	0.999	11,574.8	2.19
(4)	0.15	2.39	−42.67			0.37			−0.75	−7.20			
	(20.70)	(6.08)	(−3.95)			(9.09)			(−6.05)	(−3.59)	0.999	11,965.5	2.09
(5)	0.09	1.27	−40.54				1.02	−0.47	0.80	−17.96			
	(5.12)	(8.35)	(−40.54)				(9.00)	(−6.04)	(7.28)	(−2.92)	0.998	3,482.30	2.45
(6)	0.05	1.58	−47.83	0.07			1.25		0.51	−12.83			
	(1.90)	(6.35)	(−4.81)	(0.97)			(7.71)		(3.23)	(−2.93)	0.998	3,191.01	1.65
(7)		1.60	−28.98				1.59	−0.25	0.43	7.76			
		(6.85)	(−3.70)				(57.36)	(−2.53)	(2.37)	(−3.02)	0.998	6,704.15	1.92
(8)	0.03	1.60	−41.25				1.32		0.40	−10.22			
	(1.48)	(6.15)	(−4.46)				(8.43)		(2.32)	(−3.17)	0.999	5,860.21	1.72
(9)		1.60	−28.92				1.59	−0.25	0.40	−7.75			
		(6.85)	(−3.70)				(57.36)	(−2.53)	(2.37)	(−3.02)	0.998	6,704.15	1.92
(10)	0.09	2.10	−26.92				0.92	−0.46	0.85	−19.06			
	(4.82)	(7.86)	(−4.63)				(7.75)	(5.64)	(8.73)	(2.24)	0.998	2,694.8	2.04
(11)					0.10		1.44	−0.33		−5.45			
					(2.65)		(13.91)	(−3.17)		(−3.05)	0.999	11,528.2	1.99

Source: Computed by the author.
Note: See text for definition of variables.

Again, the picture that develops out of these results is one of little direct crowding out. Private savings appear largely undertaken to finance private investment. This is the "savings up" for investment motive often cited in the literature. While not tested directly by the above regressions, increased access to credit through the banking system seems, if anything, to stimulate increased savings and thus private investment. The only crowding out seems to be the forced savings effect on private consumption through increases in price stemming from the government's fiscal actions.

Private Investment

As with private consumption and private savings, private investment appears largely a function of changes in income (ΔGDP). In general, changes in price (ΔWPI) have reduced private capital formation, perhaps diverting funds into speculative activities. The government's financial actions do not appear to have been a significant element in crowding out private investment. Government credit from the banking system (*MSGC*) is even positively related to private investment (equation 3, table 12.5). When entered after changes in income, the government deficit has a positive impact (and *GD* or the government surplus has a negative impact) on private investment (equation 4, table 12.5). Individually, the government deficit also has a positive impact on private investment (equation 4, table 12.5). Government investment, *IG*, is strongly related to private investment (equations 6, 8, table 12.5) after income has been accounted for indicating the complementarity between government expenditures and private sector profitability.

In general, government activities on both the expenditure and financial side do not appear to have adversely affected private investment, other than through the adverse impact inflation may have had by diverting funds away from capital formation.

Alternative Impact Mechanisms

These three alternative policy mechanisms concerning impact of the government's fiscal operations on the major economic aggregates in general and private sector activity in particular over the 1951–81 period are summarized in the first column of table 12.6 where:

0 = right sign for coefficient, but not statistically significant when a relationship was predicted significant;
− = coefficient significant when theory predicted insignificant;
+ = sign as predicted and significant;
++ = sign as predicted and highly significant;
−− = sign as significant and opposite of what theory prdicted.

In general, the results do not overwhelmingly prove or disprove any one of the three major theories. Nevertheless, the conventional crowding out theory probably performed the worst of the three theories. The Keynesian model multiplier

Table 12.5. Mexico: determinants of private investment, 1951–81 (current prices)

	Independent variables												
	Δ*GDPN*	Δ*WPI*	*MSGC*	*GD*	*GT*	*IG*	Δ*GBT*	Δ*SG*	*RHO*	Intercept	r^2	*F*	*DW*
(1)	0.47									13.15			
	(58.60)									(4.00)	0.992	3,433.59	1.97
(2)	0.55	−1.55								16.00			
	(18.0)	(−2.57)								(4.08)	0.992	1,476.72	1.94
(3)	0.32	−1.92	0.45							17.32			
	(6.03)	(4.37)	(5.65)							(4.11)	0.993	1,140.48	1.86
(4)	0.39	−1.40		−0.33						14.18			
	(5.67)	(−2.49)		(−2.61)						(3.67)	0.993	1,062.15	1.92
(5)	0.30	−1.19			0.65				−0.39	8.98			
	(8.56)	(−3.69)			(6.86)				(−2.3)	(4.69)	0.998	1,467.69	1.69
(6)	0.14	−0.50				0.89			0.44	9.53			
	(2.73)	(−1.40)				(9.52)			(2.68)	(2.85)	0.996	2,034.00	1.80
(7)	0.52	−1.43					0.12		0.30	18.77			
	(14.75)	(−2.49)					(3.00)		(1.76)	(3.87)	0.990	800.12	2.09
(8)	0.13	−0.43				0.90		−0.29	0.40	10.59			
	(2.75)	(−1.32)				(10.45)		(−2.52)	(2.38)	(3.67)	0.997	2,088.38	2.16
(9)	0.34	2.04	0.34					−0.18	0.35	17.76			
	(5.79)	(−4.41)	(5.39)					(−1.03)	(2.03)	(4.48)	0.994	943.46	1.94

Source: Computed by the author.
Note: Δ*GDPN* = Change in gross domestic product
Δ*WPI* = Change in wholesale price index
MSGC = Monetary system credit to the government
GD = Government deficit
GT = Government current revenues (national accounting sense)
IG = Government investment
Δ*GBT* = Change in total government borrowing
Δ*SG* = Change in government saving.

Table 12.6. Mexico: summary of alternative crowding out theory performance

	Theoretical prediction	Empirical results				
		1951–81	1951–65	1951–70	1960–81	1965–81
Conventional crowding out	$\Delta SP \neq \Delta GD$	+	−	−	+	+
	$\Delta SP = \Delta GDP$	+	+?	+	+	+
	$\Delta GAP \neq \Delta GD$	−	−	−	−	−
	$IP = \Delta GD$	−	−	−	−	−
Monetarist approach	$\Delta SP \neq \Delta GD$	+	−	−	−	−
	$IP \neq \Delta GD$	+	+	+	+	+
	$\Delta GAP = \Delta GD$	+	+	+	+	+
	$\Delta GAP = \Delta PD$	+	−	−	+?	+?
Keynesian crowding out	$\Delta SP = -\Delta GD$	−	+	+	−	−
	$\Delta PCN \neq \Delta GD$	+	−	+?	+	+
	$IP \neq \Delta GD$	+	+	+	+	+
	$\Delta GAP \neq \Delta GD$	−	−	−	−	−
	$\Delta SP = \Delta GDP$	+	+?	+	+	+
	$\Delta PCN = \Delta GDP$	+	+	+	+	+
	$IP = \Delta GDP$	+	−	+?	+	+
	$\Delta GAP = -\Delta GDP$	+?	−	+	+?	+?

Source: Author.
Note: (+) = Econometric results consistent with theory predictions
(+?) = Econometric results partially consistent with theory predictions
(−) = Econometric results inconsistent with theory predictions

process as defined here (table 12.6) performed fairly well. At the same time, Fitzgerald's Keynesian variant, stressing increased private savings and reduced private consumption with increased government deficits, performed poorly. There is only limited evidence for the Fitzgerald thesis. Private savings actually increased with the government's revenue expenditure gap (*GD*), while private consumption seems only marginally affected by this variable. Similar results (tables 12.2 and 12.3) were obtained when regressions on the levels (rather than changes in) private consumption and savings were estimated. There is some evidence for forced savings with a positive sign obtained for regressions of the change in wholesale price index on private savings, together with negative signs for the change in the consumer price index regressed on private consumption.

Alternative Subperiods

With regard to the impact of the government fiscal position (*GD*), however, a much different picture emerges when several subperiods are examined separately (table 12.7), and only changes in the government's fiscal position and changes in GDP are included in the regression equations.

This formulation (table 12.7) brings out clearly that during the entire period (1951–81) changes in private savings (*SP*) were determined largely by changes in gross domestic product (the Keynesian hypothesis), with changes in *GD* providing no improvement in the r^2. Fitzgerald did not include GDP in his regressions of the government fiscal position on private savings. When only the government fiscal position is regressed, however, private savings are negative in sign (as predicted by Fitzgerald). For earlier periods, 1951–65 and 1951–70, changes in the government's fiscal position (*GD*) had a negative sign when regressed separately and with changes in GDP (in line with Fitzgerald). This pattern shifted in the latter periods (1960–81, 1965–81), with changes in the government fiscal position (ΔGD) yielding a positive (but statistically insignificant) sign when regressed on private savings changes in gross domestic product.

Private consumption (*PCN*) tended to increase with increases in the relative government surplus (*GD*) in 1951–65 and 1951–70 (as with Fitzgerald). On the other hand, increases in surplus tend to reduce private consumption in the later periods, 1960–81 and 1965–81, which is inconsistent with the Fitzgerald thesis. As with private savings, the government fiscal position (*GD*) does not in general provide a significant improvement in the r^2 after the change in gross domestic product.

The results for private investment (*IP*) indicate that changes in gross domestic product are clearly more important than changes in the government's fiscal position for all periods. If changes in the fiscal position have an impact on private investment, they were most likely to have been along Keynesian (accelerator) lines, with increases in the government surplus having a negative impact. If a factor, the negative demand impact of increases in the government position toward surplus would have most likely been present in the later time periods (1960–81, 1965–81).

Table 12.7. Mexico: impact of government deficits on private savings, consumption, and investment (current prices, billions of pesos)

Dependent variable:	ΔSP			ΔPCN			IP		
Independent variables:	ΔGD	ΔGDP	Adjusted r^2	ΔGD	ΔGDP	Adjusted r^2	ΔGD	ΔGDP	Adjusted r^2
1951–81	−1.78 (−14.33)		0.879	−4.33 (−19.86)		0.934	−3.44 (−18.12)		0.921
		0.26 (25.09)	0.957		0.59 (115.46)	0.998		0.47 (58.59)	0.992
	0.12 (1.57)	0.29 (18.69)	0.954	−0.13 (−1.34)	0.58 (40.71)	0.997	0.02 (0.16)	0.47 (23.00)	0.992
1951–65	−0.64 (−4.48)		0.614	1.18 (2.03)		0.207	0.09 (0.58)		0.058
		0.09 (0.94)	0.010		0.85 (6.07)	0.749		0.13 (1.64)	0.124
	−0.70 (−5.10)	0.13 (2.43)	0.689	1.03 (4.61)	0.76 (9.88)	0.916	0.15 (1.70)	0.14 (0.90)	0.112
1951–70	−0.51 (−3.22)		0.356	0.43 (1.14)		0.018	0.14 (1.06)		0.008
		0.14 (2.83)	0.292		0.68 (10.56)	0.867		0.11 (1.08)	0.010

	−0.76 (−5.88)	0.14 (5.70)	0.841	0.76 (3.74)	0.71 (15.60)	0.934	−0.20 (−0.44)	(8.93)	0.829
1960–81	−1.78 (−11.48)		0.867	−4.30 (−15.78)		0.925	−3.38 (−14.47)		0.912
		0.26 (20.74)	0.955		0.59 (95.48)	0.998		0.47 (54.31)	
	0.11 (1.32)	0.28 (15.57)	0.951	−0.13 (−1.06)	0.58 (33.35)	0.997	0.16 (0.31)	0.48 (19.08)	0.993
1965–81	−1.79 (−9.35)		0.852	−4.25 (−12.84)		0.921	−3.32 (−11.74)		0.901
		0.27 (17.67)	0.954		0.59 (86.58)	0.998		0.46 (47.89)	0.994
	0.12 (1.15)	0.29 (13.37)	0.948	−0.12 (−0.81)	0.58 (27.94)	0.997	0.10 (0.50)	0.48 (16.08)	0.993

Source: Computed by the author.
Note: ( ) = *T* statistic for above coefficient
ΔGD = Change in government deficit
ΔSP = Change in private savings
ΔGDP = Change in *GDP*
ΔPCN = Change in private consumption
IP = Private investment

Longer-Run Impacts

The major impacts of government actions—expenditures, borrowing, deficits, and taxes—on private sector activity may well only occur after a certain time lag. Fortunately, a number of econometric estimation procedures facilitate a direct determination of the impact of government activity on various private sector activities over time. One is not confined to a standard linear regression model that specifies a causal relation between the dependent and independent variables. This specification implies that a unit change of one of the independent variables causes a change in the dependent variable during the same period (and during that period alone). Particularly in examining the impact of government investment on private investment, this type of specification is too restrictive. For example, government expenditures on infrastructure may influence investment in various sectors of the economy over various periods, exerting some influence today, some next year, some the year after that, and so on. Such a causal spread over a period of time often is referred to in terms of distributed lags. The linear regression estimation procedure may be tailored to incorporate such effects.

For example, it can be demonstrated that an equation of the Koyck form:[20]

$$y = ax + byL + z \qquad \text{(a)}$$

implies an exponential decay, whereby the effect of a once and for all increase in government activity (ax) would influence private activity (y) not only during that period, but would also have a declining impact on their level in future years. It can be shown that this result stems directly from the inclusion of the government activity lagged by one year on the right-hand side of the equation.[21] Such impacts are easy to imagine in Mexico's case where the effects of government expenditures on consumption for instance, might be felt heavily during the first few periods, decaying gradually thereafter.

While a distinct improvement over the one period (year) impact formulation, it is not clear whether this specification is also too restrictive in analyzing the various impacts of government activities on the economy. In actuality, delays in planning, implementing, and the like may result in no appreciable effect of government investment on private investment, for example, for some time.

This type of situation can be approximated by adding another lagged term for the government activity (x) as in

$$y = ax + byL + cxL + z \qquad \text{(b)}$$

thus postponing the starting point for the exponential decay for one period (year). By including further lagged values of the independent variable (x) or oil exports, expenditures, and so on, the starting point of the exponential decay could be shifted to any value (year) in the future. Finally, if the government equation had been estimated as

$$y = byL + cxL + z \tag{c}$$

a special case of equation (b) can be shown to occur where exponential decay would begin to occur after even a further delay.

In short, formulations with one lagged dependent variable (impact) are capable of generating a variety of distributed lag schemes related to government impact. Such schemes can be easily estimated using standard econometric techniques. All these schemes are similar in that they exhibit exponential decay over some time range. More important, given Mexico's narrow markets in a number of areas, these formulations have the added advantage of generating impacts that make a priori sense, whose time profiles begin with an outburst followed by a gradual decay.

While the above formulations (equations a-c) are clearly significant improvements over the one period impact formulation, it is also easy to visualize government impacts as occurring gradually, reaching a peak after several years, and thereafter decaying. Such a scheme can be estimated by lagging the impact variable more than once:

$$y = byL + cxL + dyL2 + z \tag{d}$$

The time profile of the impact government-related effects would generate through this formulation is uniquely determined by the two parameters, c and d. A change in the values of c and d will vary the shape of the resulting unimodal time profile curve. As noted all curves of this type have the interesting property of gradually increasing their decay after reaching a peak year impact.

Each of the four basic formulations (a-d) above makes logical sense. Because there is little a priori basis for choosing one as superior in identifying a particular government-related impact on the private sector, all four were estimated. Satisfactory results were obtained only with specifications (a) and (c) above. Hence, these are the only estimates presented (tables 12.8, 12.9, and 12.10).

Government fiscal activities tested included *GENANP*, total real government expenditures (consumption and investment) from the national income accounts; *GFIP*, real government internal financing; *GDEFAP*, real government current revenues minus *GENANP*; *GDEFP*, total real government revenues (*GTP*) minus total government expenditures (*GENANP*); *GTFP*, total real government financing; *GCRTP*, current real government revenue; *GCTRP*, government total revenue; *GCNP*, real government consumption; *IGP*, real government investment; *GFEP*, real government external financing; and *GTP*, real government revenue.

For private savings (table 12.8) positive impacts of model (a) were given by: total government expenditures (*GENANP*); government current revenue (*GCRTP*); government total revenue (*GCTRP*); government consumption

(*GCNP*), and government investment (*IGP*). The government fiscal position (*GDEFT*), defined as government current revenue minus government expenditures, produced a negative impact. An increase in *GDEFT*—a reduction in the government deficit—would be expected over time to reduce private savings, a result quite contrary to the Fitzgerald thesis.

Specifications using model formulation (c) gave similar results or at least no markedly different effects over time than those identified by model (a).

The private investment (table 12.9) estimates show that this variable has a strong and positive relationship with government expenditures (*GENANP*) over time. One advantage of model (a) is that the estimated coefficients can be used to estimate both short- and long-term impacts of government activity on a variable such as private investment. Using the form for model (a) $y = a + bx + cyL$, it can be shown that $y = za + zbx + (1 - z)yL$, with the short-run adjustment zb and the long-run adjustment b.

This yields, for example, a short-run government expenditure (*GENANP*) impact of 0.52, while the long-run impact is 0.73 for government investment (*IGP*). The short-run impact on private investment is 0.65, with the long-run impact 0.83. More specifically, if government investment increased by one peso, private investment would increase by 0.65 peso the same year. Eventually private investors would adjust their plans so that private investment would increase by 0.83 peso.

The results for private consumption (table 12.10) showed no longer-run impacts stemming from the various government activities under consideration. Any impact on consumers would therefore most likely be fairly transitory, again somewhat contrary to the Fitzgerald thesis. In general, the longer-run impacts are consistent with those shown in the shorter term, with no markedly different results emerging from the analysis.

Conclusions

Mexico's fiscal crisis, according to Fitzgerald,[22] is simply the imbalance created by the acceleration in public sector accumulation and the inadequacy of its financing. By this reasoning, the resulting deficit is a growing public sector borrowing requirement, which stems largely from the refusal of the private sector to accede to higher taxes to pay for what are, after all, government activities designed to maintain and increase the profitability of its own activities.[23]

Interestingly, Fitzgerald does not seem necessarily to advocate tax reform in Mexico. He is obviously less concerned with monetary stability than Solis, and he seems to feel that with increased oil revenues for practical purposes there will be no real savings constraint on investment (either internal or external). Following this line of argument, "the problem of accumulation in the Mexican economy of the 1980s will not be demand management in the traditional sense, but rather

Table 12.8. Mexico: estimation of distributed impact of government variables on private savings, 1951–81 (constant 1975 prices)

Government variable	Coefficient of lagged private savings	Coefficient of government variable	Statistics			Coefficient of lagged private savings	Coefficient of lagged government variable	Statistics		
			r^2	F	DW			r^2	F	DW
GENANP	0.34 (1.48)	0.65 (4.29)	0.987	1,025.78	1.79	0.34 (1.70)	0.70 (3.84)	0.985	943.6	1.53
GFIP	1.03 (17.29)	0.16 (1.70)	0.979	671.14	2.05	0.92 (17.60)	0.53 (4.13)	0.987	995.19	1.53
GDEFAP	1.00 (6.58)	−0.24 (−0.78)	0.979	618.57	1.78	1.01 (8.40)	−0.26 (−0.90)	0.979	623.01	1.46
GDEFP	0.68 (7.55)	−0.62 (−4.89)	0.987	1,151.99	1.83	0.97 (0.48)	−0.22 (−0.99)	0.979	627.15	1.69
GTFP	1.01 (15.38)	0.18 (1.80)	0.980	678.32	2.07	0.92 (15.11)	0.46 (3.57)	0.985	896.45	1.50
GCRTP	0.72 (5.94)	0.54 (3.31)	0.984	855.78	1.54	0.58 (3.67)	0.77 (3.41)	0.985	871.96	1.79
GCTRP	0.70 (5.29)	0.17 (3.23)	0.984	842.96	1.72	0.61 (4.21)	0.22 (3.47)	0.985	881.45	1.57
GCNP	0.49 (2.02)	1.01 (2.58)	0.983	759.28	1.36	0.66 (2.83)	0.78 (1.90)	0.981	687.39	1.34
IGP	0.54 (4.09)	0.98 (4.41)	0.987	1,051.61	2.13	0.43 (2.98)	1.30 (4.78)	0.988	1,128.47	2.06
GFEP	1.10 (20.57)	0.11 (0.16)	0.978	605.29	1.64	1.14 (19.22)	−0.51 (−0.69)	0.978	615.57	1.71
GTP	1.20 (10.15)	−0.18 (−0.81)	0.978	619.63	1.61	0.96 (10.95)	0.34 (1.91)	0.981	688.23	1.55

Source: Computed by the author.
Note: See text for definition of variables.

Table 12.9. Mexico: estimation of distributed impact of government expenditures on private investment, 1951–81 (constant 1975 prices)

Government variable	Coefficient of lagged private investment	Coefficient of government variable	Statistics			Coefficient of lagged private investment	Coefficient of lagged government variable	Statistics		
			r^2	F	DW			r^2	F	DW
GENANP	0.52 (3.57)	0.29 (4.06)	0.980	648.11	2.00	0.37 (2.11)	0.40 (4.24)	0.969	417.6	1.83
GFIP	0.98 (20.91)	0.15 (3.17)	0.988	1,072.55	2.01	1.02 (15.77)	0.14 (1.50)	0.980	638.32	1.97
GDEFAP	0.96 (8.04)	−0.18 (−1.25)	0.977	557.39	1.97	0.96 (8.88)	−0.21 (−1.38)	0.970	432.69	1.89
GDEFP	0.84 (10.42)	−0.21 (−3.28)	0.987	1,016.58	1.92					
GTFP	0.96 (18.91)	0.15 (3.32)	0.988	1,092.83	1.99	1.02 (14.42)	0.10 (1.19)	0.978	586.22	1.96
GCRTP	0.75 (7.06)	0.29 (3.50)	0.981	707.61	1.88	0.53 (3.36)	0.48 (3.66)	0.975	516.50	1.90
GCNP	0.32 (1.86)	0.78 (4.51)	0.931	177.81	1.71	0.71 (3.55)	0.41 (2.01)	0.969	416.48	1.87
IGP	0.65 (6.48)	0.46 (4.71)	0.990	1,252.76	1.99	0.47 (3.98)	0.71 (5.39)	0.986	948.75	1.94
GFEP	1.20 (20.70)	0.03 (0.09)	0.961	319.52	2.05	1.13 (19.77)	−0.27 (−0.66)	0.973	468.97	1.95
GTRP						0.73 (4.65)	0.09 (2.41)	0.979	633.67	1.96
GTP	0.99 (8.81)	0.13 (1.07)	0.979	702.00	1.49	1.10 (10.56)	0.008 (0.06)	0.978	673.09	1.69

Source: Computed by the author.
Note: See text for definition of variables.

Table 12.10. Mexico: estimation of distributed impact of government variables on private consumption, 1951–81 (constant 1975 prices)

Government variable	Coefficient of lagged private consumption	Coefficient of government variable	Statistics		
			r^2	F	DW
GENANP	0.97 (18.24)	0.18 (1.39)	0.997	4,038.00	1.98
GFIP	1.02 (54.79)	0.15 (1.72)	0.997	4,240.32	2.00
GDEFAP	0.97 (23.20)	−0.45 (−1.77)	0.997	3,701.13	1.98
GDEFP	0.98 (28.58)	−0.24 (−1.71)	0.997	4,315.26	1.96
GTFP	1.01 (49.81)	0.15 (1.68)	0.997	4,094.07	1.99
GCRTP	1.01 (24.27)	0.13 (0.77)	0.996	4,270.40	1.95
GRTP	1.00 (24.53)	0.04 (0.95)	0.997	4,273.14	1.97
GCNP	0.98 (15.37)	0.32 (1.07)	0.997	3,751.45	1.95
IGP	0.98 (23.33)	0.32 1.54	0.997	4,398.86	1.99
GFEP	1.05 (53.24)	−0.28 (−0.38)	0.997	4,165.98	1.94
GTP	1.05 (25.34)	−0.05 (−0.22)	0.996	3,901.22	2.01

Source: Computed by the author.
Note: See text for definition of variables.

the planning of the composition of final demand itself and the income distribution that underlies it."[24]

The results obtained above, however, cast doubt on the validity of the Fitzgerald thesis. Fitzgerald's regression results were biased against the more orthodox Keynesian models by not including the gross domestic product. The more recent period, not included in Fitzgerald's analysis, appears to be a time most contrary to his proposed mechanism. The simple Keynesian mechanism linking movements in private activity to overall economic activity provides an explanation superior to that of Fitzgerald, who emphasizes (unmeasured) changes in income distribution as the most important elements in the savings-investment adjustment process.

A number of questions remain unanswered:

1. Income. What does the Mexican private sector regard as income? Is government spending on final goods and services seen as part of private income?

Free school milk, housing subsidies, and the like are examples of public expenditure constituting private income in kind. The negative relationship between government deficits and private consumption noted by Fitzgerald may in fact be due in part to replacement of private goods and services by public goods. Are government deficits excluded? Are current deficits (surpluses) viewed as equivalent to current taxes (transfers), and is public savings a perfect substitute for private savings? Certain kinds of taxes in Mexico are likely to compete directly with discretionary private savings: social security contributions and the state-run compulsory health insurance schemes are probably considered substitutes for voluntary private savings.

2. *Wealth.* What is regarded as wealth by the private sector? This is the capital account counterpart to the current account question asked above. If the private sector regards current deficits as equivalent to current taxes because the financing of the deficit is regarded as equivalent to taxation, then no matter what combination of high-powered money creation, new borrowing, and taxation is actually used to finance the deficit, government interest-bearing debt will not be counted as part of private net worth.

3. *Consumption.* What is regarded as consumption by the private sector? To what extent is public consumption a substitute for private consumption? Certain types of public consumption expenditure that compete directly with private consumption expenditure are public spending on education, law and order, health care, and care for the elderly. Again, rapid expansion of these government-provided services in recent years has simply been treated as a substitute for the private provision of such goods, thus accounting for some of the pattern noted by Fitzgerald.

4. *Investment.* What is regarded as investment by the private sector? To what extent is public investment a substitute for private investment? All indications are that public sector investment tends to improve the profitability of private investment, but these may be notable exceptions.

5. *Borrowing.* How closely do government securities substitute for corporate securities and other private securities in private portfolios?

This chapter has tried to throw some light on the crowding-out debate in Mexico. Ultimately, however, questions about the presence and strength of various forms of crowding out can only be resolved by a detailed analysis of the above five issues. All that has been attempted here is to indicate the range of theoretical possibilities and the econometrically estimated links at a high level of abstraction.

IV. Scope for Optimal Policymaking

Introduction

In recent years, scholars have found the techniques of optimal control theory, in particular Pontryagin's minimum principle, to be applicable to problems in economics. The first and most widespread application of control theory was in the area of economic growth, where the basic problem was to find an optimal allocation of output over time to consumption and investment. The theory has also been extended to similar quantitative models for development planning where the basic issue was the choice between consumption and investment.

But while economists have succeeded in applying optimal control theory to problems of limited scope, little attempt has been made to apply it to actual policy situations. This is, in part, because optimal control requires a linear model and long-term growth models are emphatically nonlinear.

However, short-term stabilization policy, whose econometric models are essentially linear or at least easily linearized, seems extremely amenable to optimal control assumptions. This final section of the book combines a linear econometric model of the Mexican economy with quadratic cost criteria to show how optimal control theory can function as a viable planning tool. The theory will be used, in chapter 13 to analyze the dynamic properties of the Mexican economy, in chapter 14 to formulate stabilization policies for the economy over the next several years, in chapter 15 to determine the impact of IMF-type stabilization programs on the economy, and in chapter 16 to understand better and quantitatively the trade-offs with which the Mexican policymaker is faced.

13. Optimal Stabilization Programs, 1975–81

The year 1978 represented the beginning of a period of rapid economic growth for the Mexican economy. Investment, consumption, and income started rising at impressive rates. This growth was a result of rising oil revenues; foreign loans and investments; an improvement in the stock of human capital; and the political stability provided by successive PRI administrations. However, by the early 1980s, the growth process was encountering more and more problems. A high and rising inflation, a low and declining productivity in all sectors, structural imbalances in most labor markets, and catastrophic rural emigration were but a few of the problems that culminated in the economic crisis of 1982, threatening to slow down and even stop the process of economic growth for the foreseeable future. To many observers the injection of massive oil income after 1977 had only exacerbated many of the long-standing problems facing the country.[1]

The relevant question at this juncture is whether a different set of government policies applied over the 1975–81 period could have produced the same expansion of economic growth minus the instability actually experienced. The optimal control exercises developed below show that a more prudent level of government expenditure, together with a stricter control of the money supply, was compatible with the income growth actually experienced over this period. More important, the model optimal control exercises show (albeit in retrospect) that a better coordination of monetary and fiscal policies during the 1975–81 period could have created an environment of price stability and a balance of payments equilibrium without any significant loss in overall economic expansion or private sector activity.

Alternative Explanations of the Current Crisis

Failures in Mexican economic growth have traditionally been analyzed in three more or less distinct manners. More radical economists such as Gonzales and Florescano (1979),[2] Ayala (1979),[3] de la Pena (1982),[4] Gonzalez and Casanova (1982),[5] and Harris and Barkin (1982)[6]—to name only a few—analyze Mexico as a typical example of dependent growth in which the center (the neocolonialist powers such as the United States) exploits the periphery (Mexico) with the cooperation of the bourgeois-comprador local elite, through mechanisms of unequal exchange.

At the other extreme, conservative economists such as Redvers Opie analyze the problem from a totally different point of view.[7] Generally speaking, they maintain that the economic growth process in Mexico deteriorated because of an increasing degree of government intervention in the economy.[8] They argue that this overwhelming (and misguided) government intervention distorted capital and labor markets, led to the creation of a large, inefficient, and heavily subsidized "modern" manufacturing sector at the expense of the more efficient "traditional" sector, crowded out private consumption and investment expenditures, and eventually strengthened the dual structure of the economy. This process then led to increased concentration of economic power in the hands of the government, which greatly increased both its incentives for and means of economic and political coercion, thus stifling the dynamic potential of the private sector.[9]

A middle or orthodox view encompasses the spectrum from monetarists such as Solis[10] to structuralists such as Tello[11] and Lustig,[12] to moderates like Reynolds,[13] to technocrats such as Beltran del Rio[14] and Looney.[15] With varying emphasis, these analysts contend that Mexico suffers from a number of structural problems, such as a low-quality labor force, an untrained entrepreneurial class, a low efficiency of the public administration, an underdeveloped capital market, and so on. These inefficiencies can be removed over time, but they require careful planning and allocation of resources by the government.

The analysis that follows is essentially in the technocratic tradition. It begins from the position that Mexico's current crisis is simply a temporary although very serious financial imbalance and that the government has the capability and sufficient viable options to set the economy on a high noninflationary growth path within the presidential term of Miguel de la Madrid (1982–87).

Analysis starts from the presumption that Mexico has sufficient oil to create problems but not enough, at least so far, to solve them. Since 1977 the central feature of its longer-run development policy has been the need to use petroleum export revenues in a manner capable of placing the economy on a high growth trajectory consistent with the government's long-standing income distributional objectives.

The second major problem, of shorter-term stabilization, is related to the rapid increases in government expenditure financed by oil revenues after 1976, together with the cutbacks in government allocations occasioned by the 1981–82 world oil glut. Both sets of problems and policies bear critically on the prospects for the country's eventual transformation into a modern industrial nation. The above two themes viewed in the aftermath of the late 1970s oil boom and the period after the 1981–82 oil glut form the subject of this chapter.

The Oil Economy Syndrome

The major adjustment problems faced by Mexico since the beginning of the oil boom can best be illustrated by considering the economy as divided into two major sectors: goods traded (agriculture, industry, oil, and other primary products), and nontradeables (construction, infrastructure, and certain services). As noted in chapter 4, in the pre-oil boom period, up to around 1976, external borrowing enabled domestic absorption of goods and services chronically to exceed domestic production.

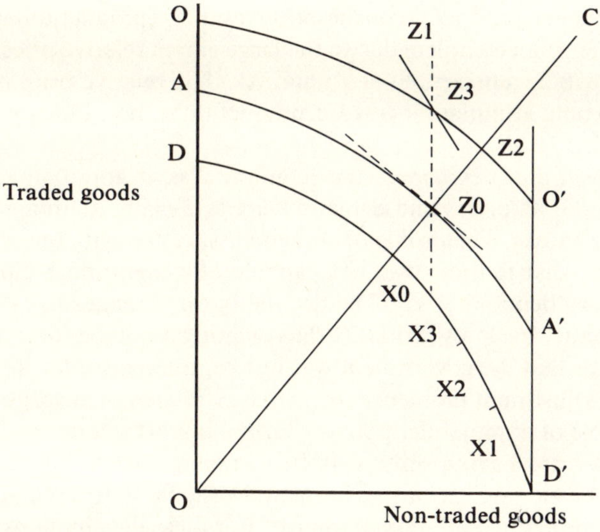

Figure 13.1.
1. DD′ = Domestic production frontier including both traded and nontraded goods.
2. AA′ = Absorption frontier including added goods provided domestically through external borrowing.

The process from 1976 to present can be depicted using the following diagram (figure 13.1)[16] where

DD′ = domestic production frontier (including both traded and non-traded goods;
AA′ = absorption frontier including added goods provided domestically through external borrowing; and
OC′ = consumption growth path (given the distribution of income) for relative prices of traded and nontraded goods).

Thus *OC* is the slope of DD′, AA′, or OO′ at the point of intersection with *OC*. Originally (1976) absorption is at Z_0 with production at X_0.

The post-1977 oil boom shifted the absorption frontier to OO′. This had several effects. Due to rigidities in supply, nontraded goods expand at a much slower rate. In the short run, demand for such goods shifts to Z_1 but supply remains at X_0. The resulting demand supply gap (X_0Z_1) was resolved largely through domestic inflation with the price of nontraded goods rising with regard to that of traded goods. By allowing the real exchange rate to appreciate through domestic inflation (holding the nominal rate constant after the 1976 devaluation), the profitability of goods produced in the nontraded sector increased. As their profitability improved, the production of nontraded goods began to increase at the expense of traded goods (largely agricultural and raw materials together with light manufactures and tourism).

Production and consumption adjust to the increase in incomes and relative prices of nontraded goods. Thus, movement begins from Z_1 toward Z_2 and X_0

toward X_2. Movement to Z_2 (consumption) and X_2 (production) in combination is partial rather than complete due to the large gap in relative prices of tradeables and nontradeables represented at Z_2 and X_2. The relative price ratio needed to achieve Z_2 would stimulate increased production of nontraded goods at the expense of traded goods.

When the oil glut developed, the economy was at approximately points Z_3, X_3. At these points prices and demand were artificially maintained by the augmented oil revenues. The profile of demand associated with the country's nonoil sector income distribution was not capable of generating a full employment noninflationary demand at Z_2. The decline in oil revenues has shifted the consumption frontier back toward DD′, thus creating a number of structural adjustment problems that the government was just beginning to address in late 1982.

Since the adjustment problems are primarily related to absorption levels, conventional tools of commercial policy—tariffs, import quotas, or differential exchange rates—are having only a limited impact, except insofar as they may influence domestic savings and investment decisions. In this regard, the devaluations in 1982 probably had limited impact. For these devaluations to be effective in restoring external balance, the government would have to significantly reduce expenditures. Given the high growth strategy of the López Portillo administration, fiscal strategy along these lines and of the magnitude required was postponed as long as possible. Nevertheless, such a strategy will most likely be forced on the government as part of an IMF stabilization program.

Modeling of the Economy

The econometric models developed below are intended to illustrate the options available to the government as it undertakes such a stabilization program over the next presidential term. In modeling the economy, this analysis developed a simultaneous equation macroeconomic model, to determine the various impacts governmental activity had on various sectors of the economy. A recursive variant of this model for a basis of comparison was also developed for the 1951–81 period. The simultaneous equation model was then modified to produce an optimal control policy model. The analysis used this optimal control model to examine the 1976–81 period for the purposes of identifying optimal stabilization paths, forecasting the optimal control's exogenous variables over the 1982–87 period, and developing several optimal control-generated stabilization programs for the 1982–87 period in light of the successes and failures experienced during the 1976–81 period.

All of the macroeconomic models are estimated from the national income identities and data for 1951–81 deflated by the gross domestic product deflator (1975 = 1.00). The financial variability, inflation, and U.S. figures are all taken from the International Monetary Fund's *International Financial Statistics*.

The Simultaneous Equation Model

The model was designed largely for the purpose of examining the impact of government fiscal activity on the private sector as part of an overall assessment of the Fitzgerald thesis begun in the previous chapter. Therefore, a relatively large number of public sector variables appear in the final estimated equations (table 13.1). More specifically, the problems examined by Fitzgerald, particularly the issue of crowding out, can best be analyzed within the context of a simultaneous macroeconomic model of this type.[17]

Since the analysis of crowding out in the previous chapter indicated Keynesian relationships to be more prevalent in Mexico than those hypothesized by the monetarists or Cambridge group, the model was constructed largely along Keynesian lines or is at least consistent with the Keynesian approach. For policy purposes government investment is assumed to be exogenous and controllable by the authorities for demand management. The other instrumental variable is Bank of Mexico credit to the government, which is assumed to be controlled by the central bank and acts as a credit rationing device. Along Keynesian lines the money supply is endogenously determined, and ultimately depends on the fiscal actions of the government.

Using the model, the actual issue of crowding out can be examined directly in the individual equations (by checking the sign of various government policy actions), and indirectly through the complete working of the simultaneous relationships, which in turn determine the overall direct and indirect impacts of the government's actions. The individual equations gave the following results:

1. *Private consumption.* Crowding out of private consumption occurs as a result of direct government expenditures (*GENANP*), consisting of real government consumption and investments. An alternative equation (1A) (table 13.1) indicates the negative impact of domestic credit (*MSDCP*) on private consumption.

While appearing to confirm the Fitzgerald thesis, the private consumption equations are more correctly interpreted as illustrating the long-run secular decline in private consumption as a share of GDP from 84.9 percent in 1951 to 62.0 percent in 1981. The contraction in private consumption took place as the government's share of GDP increased from 9.1 percent in 1951 to 22.4 percent over the same period. Along more orthodox lines, private consumption may have been indirectly crowded out by an inflation-induced forced savings mechanism (equation 35 showing the negative impact of changes in the consumer price index on private consumption).

2. *Private investment.* Private investment has been stimulated by direct government expenditure, and in particular by government investment (*IGP*). As

Table 13.1 Mexico: Keynesian simultaneous equation simulation model (two-stage least squares estimations)

Constant price national income block

Private consumption (*PCNP*)

(1) $$PCNP = \underset{(25.85)}{0.95GDPNP} - \underset{(-9.32)}{1.43GENANP} - \underset{(-0.05)}{0.39} \qquad DW = 1.63$$

(1A) $$PCNP = \underset{(52.52)}{0.73GDNP} - \underset{(-9.18)}{0.34MSDCP} + \underset{(5.78)}{31.46} \qquad DW = 1.17$$

Private investment (*IPP*)

(2) $$IPP = \underset{(17.41)}{1.20IGP} - \underset{(-1.89)}{1.42EXC} + \underset{(3.67)}{30.02} \qquad DW = 1.37$$

(2A) $$IPP = \underset{(3.70)}{0.32PSP} + \underset{(3.07)}{0.50IGP} + \underset{(4.91)}{12.16} \qquad DW = 1.50$$

(2B) $$IPP = \underset{(10.17)}{1.04IGP} + \underset{(2.03)}{1.28BMFAP} - \underset{(-2.33)}{1.80EXC} + \underset{(2.34)}{20.95} \qquad DW = 1.67$$

Private savings (*PSP*)

(3) $$PSP = \underset{(9.57)}{0.99IPP} - \underset{(-7.46)}{0.68GDEFP} + \underset{(0.12)}{0.40} \qquad DW = 2.42$$

(3A) $$PSP = \underset{(7.14)}{0.12GDPNP} - \underset{(-6.00)}{0.71GDEFP} - \underset{(-1.46)}{8.11} \qquad DW = 1.78$$

Government consumption (*GCNP*)

(4) $$GCNP = \underset{(4.12)}{42.29DUMPET} + \underset{(7.92)}{0.75GTP} + \underset{(1.61)}{7.42} \qquad DW = 2.67$$

(4A) $$GCNP = \underset{(3.05)}{0.45GTP} + \underset{(7.95)}{0.44BMGCP} + \underset{(3.29)}{10.56} \qquad DW = 1.66$$

Current government revenue (*GTP*)

(5) $$GTP = \underset{(3.51)}{0.08PENANP} + \underset{(2.51)}{0.42EP} - \underset{(-3.41)}{18.08} \qquad DW = 3.10$$

Imports (*ZP*)

(6) $$ZP = \underset{(-19.04)}{0.40TINP} - \underset{(-4.28)}{2.17EXC} + \underset{(1.57)}{8.02} \qquad DW = 1.11$$

Exports (*EP*)

(7) $$EP = \underset{(9.39)}{0.15E} + \underset{(10.34)}{0.05USYP} + \underset{(1.53)}{0.98EXC} - \underset{(-3.22)}{23.82} \qquad DW = 2.59$$

Bank of Mexico foreign assets (*BMFAP*)

(8) $$BMFAP = \underset{(3.61)}{0.12EP} - \underset{(-1.72)}{0.04GDEFP} + \underset{(6.63)}{8.11} \qquad DW = 0.99$$

Domestic credit (*MSDCP*)

(9) $$MSDCP = \underset{(12.06)}{3.17BMDAP} - \underset{(-5.04)}{1.35BMGCP} + \underset{(6.01)}{79.86DUMEX} + \underset{(3.26)}{12.10} \qquad DW = 1.49$$

Net factor pyaments (*NFPP*)

(10) $$NFPP = \underset{(-21.86)}{-0.27EP} + \underset{(6.42)}{6.44} \qquad DW = 1.92$$

Change in stocks (*ISNP*)

(11) $$ISNP = \underset{(9.14)}{0.033GDPNP} - \underset{(-3.35)}{9.91} \qquad DW = 1.63$$

Gross domestic product supply (*GDPNP*)

(12) $$GDPNP = \underset{(10.10)}{1.40TINP} + \underset{(19.12)}{0.08LAB} - \underset{(-15.35)}{597.54} \qquad DW = 1.36$$

Identities

Government expenditure (*GENANP*)

(13) $GENANP = IGP + GCNP$

Government deficit (*GDEFP*)

(14) $GDEFP = GTP - GENANP$

Total investment (*TINP*)

(15) $TINP = IGP + IPP$

Gross capital formation (*TINP*)

(16) $TINP = IGP + IPP + ISNP$

Private expenditures (*PENANP*)

(17) $PENANP = IPP + PCNP$

Government investment (*IGP*)

(18) $IGP = Exogenous$

Gross domestic product demand (*GDPNPD*)

(19) $GDPNPD = IPP + PCNP + GCNP + IGP + ISNP + EP + ZP$

Table 13.1 (continued)

Identities (continued)

Domestic absorption (*DAP*)

(20) $$DAP = PCNP + GCNP + IPP + IGP + ISNP$$

Gross national product (*GNPP*)

(21) $$GNPP = GDPNP + NFPP$$

Total savings (*STP*)

(22) $$STP = GNP - PCNP - GCNP$$

Domestic resource gap (*SIGAP*)

(23) $$SIGAP = STP$$

External resource gap (*EMGAP*)

(24) $$EMGAP = EP + ZP + NFPP$$

Nominal financial monetary block

Exports (*E*)

(25) $$E = \underset{(17.69)}{1.48 PETE} + \underset{(4.67)}{0.82 CPP} + \underset{(2.47)}{36.87 DUMPET} - \underset{(-1.67)}{15.27} \qquad DW = 2.32$$

Bank of Mexico domestic assets (*BMDA*)

(26) $$BMDA = \underset{(13.13)}{0.71 MSGC} + \underset{(7.62)}{0.24 MSPC} + \underset{(0.05)}{0.08} \qquad DW = 1.85$$

Bank of Mexico reserve money (*BMRM*)

(27) $$BMRM = \underset{(30.40)}{1.02 BMDA} + \underset{(3.49)}{0.12 BMGC} + \underset{(11.93)}{5.87} \qquad DW = 0.94$$

Government credit from monetary system (*MSGC*)

(28) $$MSGC = \underset{(119.78)}{1.00 BMGC} + \underset{(6.77)}{0.07 FGFI} + \underset{(4.59)}{3.05} \qquad DW = 1.09$$

Money supply (*M1*)

(29) $$M1 = \underset{(29.41)}{0.56 BMRM} + \underset{(3.71)}{42.10 DUMEX} + \underset{(7.01)}{20.84}$$

Price index block

Consumer price index (*CPI*)

(30) $$CPI = 746.27 EXCESS\,B + 0.34 USCPI - 17.88$$

(11.15) (1.81) (−2.21) $DW = 0.57$

(30A) $CPI = 0.39M1 + 0.48USCPI + 4.76$
(17.94) (4.48) (0.76) $DW = 0.65$

Wholesale price index (*WPI*)

(31) $WPI = 842.27EXCESS\ C + 2.46EXC - 29.17$
(28.54) (4.27) (−5.18) $DW = 0.78$

(31A) $WPI = 0.45M1 + 3.51EXC - 5.92$
(39.75) (9.02) (−1.30) $DW = 1.16$

Gross domestic product deflator (*DFGDP*)

(32) $DFGDP = 0.0049M1 + 0.013EXC + 0.18$
(37.01) (2.91) (3.73) $DW = 0.59$

(32A) $DFGDP = 0.0044M1 + 0.012EXC + 0.0023USCPI + 0.06$
(20.41) (2.77) (2.36) (0.86) $DW = 0.53$

Identities

Excess monetary demand (*EXCESS B*)

(33) $EXCESS\ B = M1/DAP$

Excess monetary demand (*EXCESS C*)

(34) $EXCESS\ C = M1/GDPNP$

Exogenous variables

MSPC = Private sector credit from monetary system
FGFI = Governmental domestic borrowing
EXC = Peso-dollar exchange rate
USYP = Real United States gross domestic product
USCPI = United States consumer price index
PETE = Mexican petroleum exports
CPP = Mexican crude petroleum production index (1975 = 100)
DUMPET = Dummy variable, increase in petroleum exports (0, 1951–74; 1, 1975–81)

DUMEX = Dummy variable, shift from fixed to flexible exchange rate (0, 1951–76; 1, 1977–81)

Recursive Version

Private consumption (*PCNP*)

(35) $PCNP = 0.84GDPNP - 1.30\Delta CPI - 0.78GENANP + 12.02$
(28.61) (−6.30) (−5.52) (2.17) $DW = 1.37$

Table 13.1 (continued)

Version (continued)

Private saving (*PSP*)

(36) $$PSP = \underset{(9.96)}{0.98IPP} - \underset{(-7.49)}{0.68GDEFP} + \underset{(0.13)}{0.44} \qquad DW = 2.42$$

Private investment (*IPP*)

(37) $$IPP = \underset{(6.41)}{0.63IPPL} + \underset{(4.89)}{0.54IGP} - \underset{(-1.58)}{0.76EXC} + 13.30 \qquad DW = 2.14$$

Gross domestic product (*GDPNP*)

(38) $$GDPNP = \underset{(7.84)}{0.63KPS} + \underset{(10.82)}{0.02LAB} - \underset{(-8.56)}{514.89}$$

Capital stock (*KPS*)

(39) $KPS = TINP + TINPL + TINPL2.$ Where $TINP = IGP$ (government investment + *IPP*, private investment, $TINPL$ = lagged one year, $TINPL2$ = lagged two years).

Imports (*ZP*)

(40) $$ZP = \underset{(-15.54)}{-0.35TINP} - \underset{(-5.16)}{2.06EXC} - \underset{(-3.76)}{0.19\Delta GDPNP} + \underset{(2.26)}{9.17} \qquad DW = 1.52$$

Government consumption (*GCNP*)

(41) $$GCNP = \underset{(3.25)}{14.51DUMPET} - \underset{(-13.65)}{0.52GDEFPL} + \underset{(17.30)}{0.59GTPL} - \underset{(-3.08)}{1.09EXC} + \underset{(3.52)}{13.62} \qquad DW = 1.66$$

Gross domestic product deflator (*DFGDP*)

(42) $$DFGDP = \underset{(4.11)}{0.51DFGDPL} + \underset{(2.58)}{3.52EXCESS\ C} - \underset{(-6.77)}{0.10} \qquad DW = 1.75$$

Source: Author.

Notes: Simultaneous model (equations 1–34 above) has 24 recursive equations, 10 simultaneous equations. Equations estimated over 1951–81 period by time series processor (*TSP*) version 3.5C, using two-stage least squares estimation procedure.

economic theory would predict, real private investment is negatively related to the peso-dollar exchange rate (*EXC*), indicating increased cost of capital goods imports associated with devaluation. It is also clear that private investment is facilitated by high levels of private savings (*PSP*) and the availability of foreign assets (*BMFAP*).

3. Private savings. Private savings do not follow the pattern suggested by Fitzgerald. Public sector deficits (*GDEFP*), defined as government current revenue minus government expenditure, were highly significant but contrary to the Fitzgerald thesis had a negative sign. This suggests a Keynesian-type relationship whereby the level of private savings is largely influenced by the overall level of economic activity (equation 3A), which in turn is modified through a multiplier associated with government fiscal policy.

4. Government consumption. As might be imagined, consumption by the government has been sharply modified by the oil boom. Statistically, this is evidenced by the significance of a dummy variable, *DUMPET*, which has a value of zero for the 1951–76 period and one for 1977–81, reflecting the jump in oil exports beginning in 1977. Increased government consumption in the wake of an oil boom is a common phenomenon and has been noted as ultimately a major contributing factor to the final crisis that inevitably follows the leveling off in oil revenues.

The other factors contributing to government consumption expenditure are current revenues (*GTP*) and credit from the Bank of Mexico (*BMGCP*). Simply put, the equations for government consumption indicate that the more the government has, the more it spends.

5. Government revenues. Government revenues are related to the tax base, depicted here by private expenditures (*PENANP*), consisting of private consumption and investment. The level of exports (*EP*) was also significant in the government revenue equation.

6. Imports. Imports were functionally related to the level of investment (*TINP*) and the exchange rate (*EXC*).

7. Exports. Real exports (*EP*) are set as a function of nominal exports (*E*), the level of real U.S. gross domestic product (*USYP*), and the peso-dollar exchange rate (*EXC*).

The sign of the exchange in the export and import equations indicates that a devaluation of the peso will increase exports and reduce imports. However, as will be noted later in the optimal control simulations, a devaluation of the peso will probably not aid in significantly improving the country's balance of payments, perhaps because oil exports are denominated in dollars, and imports are largely capital goods and other essential items whose price is probably fairly inelastic.

The remaining equations are straightforward and need little elaboration. The model is designed to examine the ex post adjustment of aggregate supply to demand. Therefore, gross domestic product is estimated as a supply concept, and as a simple linear function of the labor force and capital stock. Labor force figures were used simply because no reliable series on employment is available.

In the production function a proxy for capital stock, *KPS*, was used. This series was constructed as a sum of total current investment (*TINP*) plus that over the last two years: $KPS = TINP + TINPL + TINPL2$. Estimates using the capital stock series discussed in chapter 2 were found to yield slightly poorer statistical results than the proxy *KPS* used here. The term *LAB* is the International Labor Office estimate of the Mexican labor force. This series has the advantage of also being forecasted by the ILO and is thus used in the 1982–87 forecasts later in the chapter.

The inflation equations (30–32A) are of a monetary origin indicating that the price level is closely related to the ratio of money (*M*1) and GDP (*EXCESSC*) or real domestic absorption (*EXCESSB*). Increases in the ratio of money to real output or absorption result in inflationary pressures. To a lesser extent the rate of inflation is determined by the exchange rate (*EXC*) and the U.S. consumer price index (*USCPI*).

Similar results were obtained using either the constant with *EXCESSC* or simply *M*1. Hence, in the forecasts the *M*1 versions were used (equation 32).

These results are somewhat at variance with Fitzgerald, who contends that the price level in Mexico is very closely associated with that of the United States (*USCPI*). Prices are not exogenous, as he contends, with various government deficit measures clearly exerting upward pressure through their impact on the money supply.

The overall impact multipliers (tables 13.2 and 13.3) show that in general government investment has a strong positive effect on private investment and savings, but negligible influence on private consumption. The recursive version (table 13.4) does, however, indicate a slight reduction in private consumption—undoubtedly caused by government investment–government deficit–government borrowing–monetary base–money supply linkages.

With slight modification, the model was converted (table 13.5) into one more easily manipulated for forecasting and optimal control simulations of the economy.

The Optimal Control Forecasting Model

As with the simulation model, the optimal control model is based on the simple Keynesian theory of effective demand and income determination. It uses the basic income identity between ex post aggregate supply and aggregate demand. The model derives its structural relationships by means of two-stage least squares regression analysis. It has a built-on adjustment mechanism bringing ex ante supply and demand into balance in such a way that it generates consistent and internally compatible values for its endogenous variables.

The structure and estimation procedures of the model are designed for semi-developed economies and explicitly take into account Mexico's institutions and institutional constraints. It is constructed for planning and policymaking within the Mexican context.

Consistent with the Keynesian approach, the main economic policy variable of this model is government investment. In the case of the simultaneous equation model, government investment is considered exogenous to the system and is the chief instrument of the government's fiscal policy. The other instrumental variable is Bank of Mexico credit to the government, which the central bank regards as controllable. The rate of interest is not implicitly included in the model. However, given the levels of demand generated and the cutbacks in credit assumed necessary for any meaningful stabilization policy, the interest rate is assumed to act as a credit rationing variable. This necessarily implies the existence of excess demand for funds at official rates. The assumption of excess demand for funds implies that, since the interest rate will in actual practice be fixed at an official ceiling, there will be times when there are actually two interest rates: the official and the market rate. Obviously, the latter cannot be measured systematically. This is the major reason why interest rates are not introduced explicitly into the credit equations.

Model Linkages

The restrictions imposed on the model are largely the budget deficit and Bank of Mexico credit to the government. If the growth of GDP is to be promoted with a minimum of price and exchange rate instability, government expenditures will have to follow a rate of growth in line with the financial capabilities of the public sector. Failure to do this will necessarily affect not only the government's deficit, but more importantly will most likely make both domestic and foreign stability impossible. Therefore, the relevant endogenous variables responding to different policy shocks are private investment, GDP, taxes, imports, private consumption, domestic credit, and the money supply.

Implicit in the model is a channel through which government investment induces a multiplier process beginning with increased levels of private investment. Government investment is determined exogenously. Private investment depends on the infrastructure created by public investment, on foreign assets available for importing capital equipment, on the peso-dollar exchange rate, and on private savings. Private savings in turn respond to past investment needs and the government deficit.

Government investment has been part of an unbalanced Hirschman-type de-

Table 13.2. Mexico: simultaneous equation model: impact simulation, national income variables, 1981

	Simultaneous model						Recursive version (percentage change)	
			10 percent increase in government investment		10 percent devaluations			
	Actual values	Simulated values	Increase	Percent increase	Change	Percent change	Percentage increase in government investment	Percentage devaluation
Private investment (*IPP*)	223.4	220.2	235.6	7.0	218.0	−1.0	3.2	−0.1
Private consumption (*PCNP*)	1,018.0	1,026.6	1,026.5	—	1,023.7	−0.3	−0.8	—
Private expenditure (*PENANP*)	1,241.4	1,246.8	1,262.1	1.2	1,241.8	-0.4	-0.1	—
Private savings (*PSP*)	369.5	351.5	379.3	7.9	349.4	−0.6	5.6	−0.8
Government consumption (*GCNP*)	177.3	179.3	180.3	0.6	179.4	—	—	−1.1
Government investment	190.2	190.2	209.1	10.0	190.0	—	10.0	—
Government expenditure	367.3	369.5	389.4	5.4	369.6	—	5.1	−0.6
Government current revenue	159.6	170.8	172.1	0.8	170.9	—	—	—
Government deficit	−203.4	−198.7	−217.3	−9.4	198.6	—	−9.4	—
Exports	196.9	206.9	206.9	—	208.1	0.6	—	0.6
Imports	−213.4	−212.6	−223.9	5.3	−215.3	1.3	3.9	1.4
Net factor payments	−45.0	−49.3	−49.3	—	−49.6	0.6	—	0.6
Total investment	413.6	410.4	444.7	8.4	408.3	−0.5	5.9	—
Change in stocks	49.2	44.7	45.7	2.2	44.6	—	0.7	—
Gross domestic product − supply	1,641.0	1,637.2	1,667.0	1.8	1,634.2	−0.2	0.4	−0.05
Gross domestic product − demand	1,641.0	1,655.4	1,680.3	1.5	1,648.8	−0.4	0.4	—
Gross national product	1,596.0	1,587.8	1,617.7	1.9	1,584.5	−0.2	0.4	—
Total savings	400.7	381.9	410.9	7.6	381.5	—	4.0	—
Internal gap	−62.10	−73.2	−79.5	−8.6	−71.4	2.5	−17.4	3.8
External gap	−61.50	−54.9	−66.3	−20.8	−56.8	−3.5	−15.0	−3.5
GDP deflator	3.569	3.685	3.685	—	3.704	0.5	—	0.5

Source: Computed by the author.
Note: Derived for 1981 by individually increasing real government investment by 10 percent of its actual 1981 value, then devaluing the exchange rate by 10 percent over its 1981 value.

Table 13.3. Mexico: simultaneous equation model: impact simulation, monetary variables, 1981

	1981 Actual values	1981 Simulated values	Impact of a 10 percent increase in Bank of Mexico credit to government		Impact of a 10 percent increase in private sector credit	
			Value	Percentage	Value	Percentage
Bank of Mexico domestic assets	912.5	917.3	924.1	0.7	927.6	1.1
Bank of Mexico reserve money	1,045.0	1,049.8	1,060.9	1.1	1,060.3	1.0
Bank of Mexico government credit	850.7	850.7	935.7	10.0	850.7	—
Monetary system credit to government	907.4	906.8	917.4	1.2	906.8	—
Money supply	635.0	651.7	658.0	1.0	657.6	0.9
Goverment deficit	−742.1	−758.9	738.3	−0.8	−737.7	−0.8
Wholesale price index	367.0	369.9	373.8	0.9	373.6	0.8
Consumer price index	335.4	334.3	337.7	0.9	337.5	0.8
Gross domestic product deflator	3.57	3.68	3.715	0.8	3.713	0.8

Source: Computed by the author.

Note: Derived by individually increasing normal Bank of Mexico credit to the government by 10 percent over its 1981 value, then increasing the monetary system's credit to the private sector by 10 percent over its 1981 level. Roughly similar results (not shown here) were obtained by increasing government domestic borrowing by 10 percent over its 1981 value.

Table 13.4. Mexico: Keynesian macroeconomic forecasting model (two-stage least squares estimates)

Constant price national income block

Private consumption (*PCNP*)

(1) $$\underset{}{PCNP} = \underset{(25.85)}{0.95\Delta DPNP} - \underset{(9.32)}{1.41GENANP} - \underset{(-0.05)}{0.39} \qquad DW = 1.63$$

Private investment (*IPP*)

(2) $$IPP = \underset{(6.92)}{0.94IGPL} + \underset{(2.74)}{1.18BMFAPL} - \underset{(-2.52)}{1.28EXC} + \underset{(1.88)}{0.12PSPL} + \underset{(2.23)}{14.96} \qquad DW = 1.63$$

Private savings (*PSP*)

(3) $$PSP = \underset{(8.49)}{0.97IPPL} - \underset{(8.28)}{0.78GDEFP} + \underset{(0.50)}{1.91} \qquad DW = 2.62$$

Government consumption (*GCNP*)

(4) $$GCNP = \underset{(5.03)}{0.35GTP} + \underset{(7.95)}{0.49MSGCP} + \underset{(3.28)}{9.78} \qquad DW = 1.66$$

Current government revenue (*GTP*)

(5) $$GTP = \underset{(5.11)}{0.10GDPNP} + \underset{(2.04)}{0.55ZP} + \underset{(2.96)}{0.65EP} - \underset{(-3.87)}{14.94} \qquad DW = 2.04$$

Imports (*ZP*)

(6) $$ZP = \underset{(-11.05)}{-0.86IGP} - \underset{(-2.86)}{1.00BMFAPL} - \underset{(-1.79)}{9.95} \qquad DW = 1.11$$

Exports (*EP*)

(7) $$SP = \underset{(10.78)}{0.15E} + \underset{(8.88)}{0.049USYP} + \underset{(1.76)}{0.74EXC} - \underset{(-3.49)}{18.67} \qquad DW = 2.59$$

Bank of Mexico foreign assets (*BMFAP*)

(8) $$BMFAP = \underset{(2.35)}{0.08EP} + \underset{(2.54)}{0.10EPL} + \underset{(5.90)}{6.31} \qquad DW = 0.91$$

Net factor payments (*NFPP*)

(9) $$NFPP = \underset{(-21.86)}{-0.27EP} + \underset{(6.42)}{6.44} \qquad DW = 1.92$$

Change in stocks (*ISNP*)

(10) $$ISNP = \underset{(9.14)}{0.033GDPNP} - \underset{(-3.35)}{9.91} \qquad DW = 1.63$$

Gross domestic product – supply (*GDPNP*)

(11) $GDPNP = 0.63KPS + 0.07LAB - 514.87$

$(7.84) \quad (10.83) \quad (-8.56) \qquad DW = 1.18$

Identities

Government expenditure (*GENANP*)

(12) $GENANP = IGP + GCNP$

Government deficit (*GDEFP*)

(13) $GDEFP = GTP - GENANP$

Total investment (*TINP*)

(14) $TINP = IGP + IPP$

Capital Stock (*KPS*)

(15) $KPS = TINP + TINPL + TINPL2$

Gross capital formation (*TIP*)

(16) $TIP = IGP + IPP + ISNP$

Private expenditure (*PENANP*)

(17) $PENANP = IPP + PCNP$

Government investment (*IGP*)

(18) $IGP = Exogenous$

Gross domestic product – demand (*GDPNPD*)

(19) $GDPNPD = IPP + PCNP + IGP + GCNP + ISNP + EP + ZP$

Domestic absorption (*DAP*)

(20) $DAP = PCNP + GENP + IPP + IGP + ISNP$

Gross national product (*GNPP*)

(21) $GNPP = GDPNP + NFPP$

Total savings (*STP*)

(22) $STP = GNP - PCNP - GCNP$

Domestic resource gap (*SIGAP*)

(23) $SIGAP = STP$

External resource gap (*EMGAP*)

(24) $EMGAP = EP + ZP + NFPP$

Table 13.4 (continued)

Nominal financial-monetary block

Exports (*E*)

(25) $$E = 1.48PETE + 0.82CPP + 36.87DUMPET - 15.27$$
$$(17.69) \quad (4.67) \quad (2.47) \quad (-1.67) \qquad DW = 2.32$$

Bank of Mexico domestic assets (*BMDA*)

(26) $$BMDA = 0.71MSGC + 0.24MSPL + 0.08$$
$$(13.13) \quad (7.62) \quad (0.05) \qquad DW = 1.85$$

Bank of Mexico reserve money (*BMRM*)

(27) $$BMRM = 1.02BMDA + 0.12BMGC + 5.87$$
$$(30.40) \quad (3.49) \quad (11.93) \qquad DW = 0.94$$

Government credit from monetary system (*MSGC*)

(28) $$MSGC = 1.00BMGC + 0.07FGFI + 3.05$$
$$(119.78) \quad (6.77) \quad (4.59) \qquad DW = 1.09$$

Government domestic borrowing (*FGFI*)

(29) $$FGFI = 0.80BMGC - 14.84$$
$$(14.05) \quad (-1.17) \qquad DW = 1.33$$

Private sector credit from monetary system (*MSPL*)

(30) $$MSPC = 1.23BMGC - 8.86$$
$$(37.55) \quad (-1.22) \qquad DW = 0.25$$

Money supply (*M1*)

(31) $$M1 = 0.56BMRM + 42.10DUMEX + 20.84$$
$$(29.41) \quad (3.71) \quad (7.01) \qquad DW = 0.53$$

Bank of Mexico credit to government (*BMGC*)

(32) $BMGC$ = Exogenous

Peso-dollar exchange rate (*EXC*)

(33) EXC = Exogenous

United States real gross domestic product (*USYP*)

(34) $USYP$ = Exogenous

United States consumer price index (*USCPI*)

(35) $USCPI$ = Exogenous

Mexican petroleum exports (*PETE*)

(36) $PETE = \text{Exogenous}$

Mexican crude petroleum production index (*CPP*)

(37) $CPP = \text{Exogenous, } 1975 = 100.0$

Dummy variable, rise in petroleum exports (*DUMPET*)

(38) $DUMPET = 0, 1951\text{–}74; 1, 1975\text{–}81$

Dummy variable, shift from fixed to flexible exchange rate (*DUMEX*)

(39) $DUMEX = 0, 1951\text{–}76; 1, 1977\text{–}81$

Price index block

Consumer price index (*CPI*)

(40) $$CPI = \underset{(11.61)}{746.57 EXCESS\ B} + \underset{(1.82)}{0.34 USCPI} - \underset{(-2.21)}{17.84} \qquad DW = 0.57$$

Wholesale price index (*WPI*)

(41) $$WPI = \underset{(28.54)}{842.34 EXCESS\ C} + \underset{(4.26)}{2.54 EXC} - \underset{(-5.89)}{29.16} \qquad DW = 0.78$$

Gross domestic product deflator (*DFGDP*)

(42) $$DFGDP = \underset{(4.11)}{0.81 DFGDPL} + \underset{(2.58)}{3.52 EXCESS\ C} - \underset{(-6.27)}{0.10} \qquad DW = 1.75$$

Identities

Excess monetary demand (*EXCESS B*)

(43) $EXCESS\ B = M1/DAP$

Excess monetary demand (*EXCESS C*)

(44) $EXCESS\ C = M1/GDPNP$

Source: Author.

Notes: Estimated equations based on 1951–81 period; *L* at end of symbol indicates lagged one year; *L*2 at end of symbol indicates lagged two years; *P* at end of symbol indicates normal value deflated by the gross domestic product price deflator (*DFGDP*) with *GFGDP* = 1.00 for 1975. Estimates made with *TSP* version 3.5C, two-stage least squares estimation procedure.

Table 13.5. Mexico: optimal control stabilization program A, 1975–81 (billions of 1975 pesos)

	Actual		Model simulation	Model simulated values						Average annual growth, 1975–81	
	1975	1981	1975	1976	1977	1978	1979	1980	1981	Model	Actual
Private consumption (ex ante)	—	—	755.0	845.7	806.0	864.1	940.5	1,020.1	1,113.0	6.7	—
Private consumption (ex post)	755.9	1,017.0	755.0	845.7	806.0	864.1	940.5	997.8	1,072.8	6.0	5.1
Government consumption	113.5	177.3	113.5	138.4	138.6	120.7	100.5	109.4	110.0	−0.5	7.7
Total consumption (ex ante)	—	—	868.5	984.1	944.6	984.8	1,041.0	1,129.5	1,223.0	5.9	—
Total consumption (ex post)	869.4	1,194.3	868.5	984.1	944.6	984.8	1,041.0	1,107.2	1,182.8	5.3	5.4
Private savings	218.0	369.9	218.0	234.1	247.2	237.1	246.0	266.0	293.3	5.1	9.2
Private investment	131.1	223.4	131.0	144.5	134.1	143.4	163.9	192.0	211.2	8.3	9.3
Government investment	104.5	190.2	104.5	101.0	105.8	125.9	151.9	168.7	190.2	10.5	10.5
Change in stocks	25.0	49.2	25.0	31.4	30.2	32.4	35.3	39.3	43.7	9.8	11.9
Total investment	260.6	462.8	260.6	276.9	270.2	301.6	351.2	400.1	445.1	9.3	10.0
Exports	75.9	196.9	75.9	91.4	107.9	118.5	134.7	169.5	202.8	17.8	17.2
Net factor payments	−17.9	−45.0	−17.9	−18.2	−22.7	−25.6	−29.9	−39.3	−48.3	18.0	16.6
Imports (ex ante)	—	—	−105.8	−117.9	−122.2	−142.3	−167.2	−183.9	−206.9	11.8	—
Imports (ex post)	−105.8	−213.4	−105.8	−101.4	−106.0	−123.8	−156.5	−183.9	−206.9	11.8	12.4
Gross domestic product (supply)	1,100.0	1,641.2	1,100.0	1,250.9	1,216.8	1,281.2	1,370.3	1,492.7	1,623.8	6.7	6.9
Gross domestic product (demand)	1,100.0	1,641.2	1,100.0	1,234.4	1,200.6	1,262.7	1,359.6	1,515.1	1,664.0	7.1	6.9
Supply-demand gap	0.0	0.0	0.0	16.5	6.2	18.5	10.7	−22.4	−40.2	—	—

Gross domestic product (ex post)	1,100.0	1,641.2	1,100.0	1,250.9	1,216.8	1,281.2	1,370.3	1,492.7	1,623.8	6.7	6.9
Gross national product	1,082.1	1,596.2	1,082.1	1,232.7	1,194.1	1,255.7	1,340.4	1,453.4	1,575.5	6.5	6.7
Total savings	212.7	401.4	212.7	248.6	249.4	270.8	299.4	323.9	352.6	8.8	11.2
Domestic gap (ex ante)	—	—	−47.9	−28.3	−20.7	−30.8	−51.7	−76.1	−92.6	—	—
External gap (ex ante)	—	—	−47.8	−44.8	−36.9	−49.3	−62.4	−53.8	−52.4	—	—
Gap difference	0.0	0.0	0.1	−16.5	−16.2	−18.5	−10.7	22.3	40.2	—	—
Domestic = external gap (ex post)	−47.9	−219.3	−47.9	−28.3	−20.7	−30.8	−51.7	−53.8	−52.4	1.5	28.9
Government deficit	−134.7	−207.9	−134.7	−134.7	−134.7	−134.7	−134.7	−134.7	−134.7	7.5	0.0
GDP deflator	1.00	3.57	1.00	1.03	1.20	1.32	1.40	1.43	1.43	6.1	23.6
Rate of inflation	—	—	—	3.0	16.5	10.0	6.1	2.1	0.0	—	—

Source: Computed by the author.
Note: See text for assumptions used in model simulation.

velopment strategy. The government has used a deliberate tilting of the economy in favor of strategically selected industries as a means of accelerating growth. The government has apparently assigned major development priority to heavy industrialization. The government seems to believe that through government investment a big industrial push would stimulate a cluster of other activities whose benefits would soon trickle down to all lower social strata.

In this particular model, government expenditures will be financed in the first instance by revenue coming mainly from income and indirect taxes (*GTP*), which are endogenous to the system and a function of income (*GDPNP*), exports (*EP*), and imports (*ZP*). Four additional sources are considered for financing these expenditures: credit from the private banking system (*MSGCP*); credit from the central bank (*BMGCP*), which will be reflected in an increase in the money supply (*M*1) or in a reduction in the amount of credit discounted; foreign credit; and credit from the nonbanking sector.

Private bank credit to the government (*MSGC*), including that of private investment banks, depends on the legal reserve requirements, which by law are kept in some form of government debt instrument instead of non-interest-bearing reserves. This way of allocating public debt permits the central bank to rely less on an expansion in the stock of money. If controlled, this form of public debt should result in reduced inflationary pressures.

The amount of credit that the central bank grants the government (the level of treasury bills purchased) is assumed to be a policy variable and thus exogenous for the periods under examination. However, private credit, government credit from the banking system, and government domestic borrowing are endogenous, being ultimately determined by Bank of Mexico policy. To extend this credit, the central bank has to lower its discount rate to private banks, reduce its holding of international assets, or in turn increase the money supply.

Movements in the balance of payments produce changes in international reserves. The balance of payments is the difference between exogenously fixed exports and endogenously determined imports. Since changes in international reserves are endogenous, part of the monetary base also becomes endogenous. Thus, if the Bank of Mexico increases its financing of government deficits, it will simultaneously need to reduce the amount of credit available to private banks to avoid fueling inflation by creating new money in excess of the trend.

In sum, the main real endogenous variables in the system are private investment, imports, taxes, government consumption, private savings, and foreign assets. All are determined mainly by the behavior of GDP, which in turn is heavily dependent on government investment.

Nature of Optimum Control

The macro model is the key element in the optimum control exercises.[18] The literature on optimum control is highly technical, yet the concept itself is straightforward. The essential idea of optimal control is precisely to derive the optimal policy in order to steer the economy to the specified targets. A necessary step in applying control theory is to specify an objective function or a welfare loss function by which the outcome associated with the optimal policy or its alternatives can be evaluated. Given the welfare loss function and a dynamic model, a policy sequence can be found to minimize the expectation of the welfare loss for a given period. In the present case, where the welfare loss function is quadratic and the dynamic system is linear, the solution takes the form of a linear feedback control equation. That is to say, the optimal policy is a linear function of lagged endogenous variables and the exogenous factors, including the target values of the target variables.

Once the objective function is determined, the programming model can be used together with the objective functions to derive the optimal policy.[19] The optimal policy so derived does not require any further consistency check as required in the conventional programming exercises that usually do not make use of a well-defined objective function and a simultaneous equation model.

These calculations do not include many particularly political elements, which are nevertheless imperative in making a policy decision. Nevertheless, policies derived within the framework of optimal control have the merit of logical consistency and compatability.

The welfare loss function is specified in quadratic form as:

$$W = \tfrac{1}{2} \sum_{t=1}^{n} (Y_t - Y_t^x)^1 K_t (Y_t - Y_t^*)$$

where Y_t^x indicates the target values of Y_t; K_y is a diagonal matrix of rank q, with q indicating the number of targets, and n is the specified period. The elements in the K matrix indicate the weights of penalty, which are attached to the squared deviations between the actual values and the target values of the target variables. The deterministic optimal control problem for Mexico is therefore to find the X_y that minimizes the welfare loss functions, given the macroeconomic relationships depicting the country's main economic linkages.

It should be noted that in most of the exercises described below, there was equality between the number of targets and the number of control variables, so that the optimal policy solution was unique. This solution did not depend on the K matrix, given that the targets selected were compatible for the given set of control variables and that the control variables were independently and indefinitely variable.

Two-Gap Estimates

Throughout, these forecasts include two distinct estimates of the so-called foreign resources gap, the difference between savings and investment, and exports and imports—net factor payments.[20] Prima facie, there might appear to be something inconsistent in producing two different estimates—that of the savings-investment gap and that of the foreign exchange gap—if ex post the two are equal to each other. One way of justifying the estimation procedure is simply to argue that two estimates of the same magnitude could provide a check on the accuracy of the estimation procedure. This interpretation is not necessarily incorrect, but it certainly is not the one underlying the method of this study, nor does it justify the statistical effort required by the dual estimation procedure.

The real significance of the dual procedure lies elsewhere. Valuable information about the character of Mexico's development process can be derived from the comparison of the alternative estimates. What is probably more important, significant policy implications for the next six years can be derived from that comparison. If, for example, during the post-1982 stabilization period a single gap were considered, and that gap happened to be the smaller of the two, then policies designed to reduce the country's foreign resource requirements through a change on one of the two aggregates determining that particular gap (savings or investment, or alternatively exports or imports) might turn out to be completely ineffective. What is worse, such policies might frustrate the country's recovery effort in several respects.

The gap evaluations cannot be taken merely as the different estimates of the same statistic because the actual foreign resource gap in each year over the forecast period (1982–87) is determined by both short- and long-run forces. The gap estimates as produced in this study, on the other hand, depend only on long-run forces. There is no reason why the many different long-run determinants should work out exactly to an equality of the two statistics. Entirely different factors and economic agents (decision makers) act upon the four central aggregates—savings, investment, exports, and imports. Finally, in a simple Keynesian model, equality of ex ante savings and investment is a sufficient condition of equilibrium, whereas this is not so for an ex ante equality between the savings-investment and the foreign exchange gaps. In the latter situation, the equality is a necessary but not a sufficient condition. Sufficiency requires, in addition, that the two gaps be equal to the foreign resources actually forthcoming.

This study, however, is concerned not so much with the condition of equilibrium as with correctly estimating necessary foreign resources, the level of income, and the rate of growth. In particular, it is important to structure short-run adjustments so that equality of the two gaps does not violate the assumptions on which the individual equation estimates are based and, specifically, that it does not frustrate the overall growth generated by the model.

The crucial problem in the gap analysis is that of compressibility. Given the overall rate of growth and the development structure postulated for the projection period (1982–87), total investments and imports of capital and intermediate goods and services will most likely be inelastic or noncompressible. Likewise, exports of domestic capital or intermediate goods cannot be expanded in the short run without frustrating development. All these inelasticities are purely technological. Change in any of the aggregates or subaggregates mentioned would always necessarily alter the development process somewhere in the economy, either for lack of capital goods or for lack of intermediate products.

The only instances where such a technological conflict is absent are savings, imports of consumer goods, and exports of consumer goods. But there can be other conflicts—social, political, institutional, and such conflicts (as with exports) are entirely beyond the control of the country itself—limiting alterations of these aggregates. In the forecasts that follow, therefore, adjustments of the resource gaps from ex ante to ex post are made through either downward movements in either private consumption (if the savings-investment gap is the larger of the two gaps) or imports (if the export-import gap is the larger).

Analysis of the 1975–81 Period

To determine the scope for policy action and the impact of a severe stabilization program on the economy, the 1975–81 period was recreated with exogenous variables assigned their actual values. The first run (table 13.2)—Stabilization Program A—optimized real gross domestic product subject to the proviso that the government deficit would not exceed its 1975 level, 134.7 billion pesos. Bank of Mexico credit to the government was minimized. Interestingly, the model generated only a slight reduction in GDP from its actual (1981) value—1623.8 billion pesos vs. the 1641.2 attained in 1981. On the other hand, the model reduces inflation to zero by that date (compared with an actual figure of 26.7 percent).

For the early period the external gap exports-imports-net factor income exceeded the domestic gap, savings-investment. This was reversed in 1980 and 1981 as oil revenues began to take hold. Adjustments to ex post values were made in the simulation through reduced imports (when the external gap was larger) and reductions in private consumption (when the savings-investment gap was the larger of the two). It should be noted that for all years the adjustments from ex ante to ex post were not large, however.

Overall most real variables experienced higher values under the simulated stabilization program than actually occurred. It appears therefore that the rapidly increasing government deficits that characterized the period provided few if any positive growth-inducing forces.

Although Bank of Mexico credit to the government (*BMGC*) was minimized in Stabilization Program A, it still increased from 127.5 billion pesos in 1975 to 155.7 in 1981 (compared to actual values of 127.5 and 850.7, respectively).

The second optimal control simulation—Stabilization Program B—was structured along much different lines. To determine the technical limits and trade-offs associated with policy action in Mexico, the target for 1981 for Program B (table 13.6) was to achieve a rate of inflation in line with the long-run U.S. rate (around 6 percent). As part of the optimal control procedures, the banking system's credit to the government was maximized (given the inflation target), the government deficit was unconstrained, and Bank of Mexico credit to the government was used as the policy instrument.

Significantly (table 13.6), most of the real macroeconomic variables achieved 1981 levels similar to those reached in Stabilization Program A with little loss in real output (GDP) from its actual 1981 value (1625.1 billion pesos versus 1641.2 billion). The government deficit did increase (after an initial decline) from its

Table 13.6. Mexico: optimal control stabilization program B, 1975–81 (billions of 1975 pesos)

	Model simulated values							Average annual rate of growth, 1975–81	
	1975	1976	1977	1978	1979	1980	1981	Model	Actual
Private consumption (ex ante)	755.0	877.2	846.4	875.9	913.9	987.4	1,066.3	5.9	—
Private consumption (ex post)	755.0	877.2	846.4	875.9	913.9	973.1	1,038.6	5.5	5.1
Government consumption	113.5	116.8	109.5	110.4	116.6	131.1	143.5	4.0	7.7
Total consumption (ex ante)	868.5	994.0	955.9	986.3	1,030.5	1,118.5	1,209.8	5.7	—
Total consumption (ex post)	868.5	994.0	955.9	986.3	1,030.5	1,104.2	1,182.1	5.3	5.4
Private savings	218.0	217.2	224.6	227.3	256.3	281.9	320.5	6.6	9.2
Private investment	131.0	144.5	132.1	140.6	162.8	193.3	213.1	8.4	9.3
Government investment	104.5	101.0	105.8	125.9	151.9	168.7	190.2	10.5	10.5
Change in stocks	25.0	31.4	30.2	32.2	35.2	39.3	43.7	9.8	11.9
Total investment	260.6	276.9	268.1	298.8	349.9	401.3	447.1	9.4	10.0
Exports	75.9	91.4	107.9	118.5	134.7	169.6	202.8	17.8	17.2
Net factor payments	−17.9	−18.2	−22.7	−25.6	−29.9	−39.3	−48.3	18.0	16.6
Imports (ex ante)	−105.8	−117.9	−122.2	−142.3	−167.2	−184.0	−206.9	11.8	—
Imports (ex post)	−105.8	−110.6	−116.6	−125.5	−148.5	−184.0	−206.9	11.8	12.4
Gross domestic product (supply)	1,100.0	1,251.7	1,215.5	1,278.2	1,366.6	1,491.0	1,625.1	6.7	6.9
Gross domestic product (demand)	1,100.1	1,244.5	1,209.8	1,261.4	1,347.9	1,505.3	1,652.8	7.0	6.9
Supply-demand gap	0.0	7.2	5.7	16.8	18.7	−14.3	−27.7	—	—

Gross domestic product (ex post)	1,100.0	1,251.7	1,215.5	1,278.2	1,366.6	1,491.0	1,625.1	6.7	6.9
Gross national product	1,082.1	1,233.5	1,192.8	1,252.7	1,336.7	1,451.7	1,576.8	6.5	6.7
Total savings	212.7	239.4	236.8	266.3	306.2	333.2	367.0	9.5	11.2
Domestic gap (ex ante)	−47.9	−37.5	−31.3	−32.5	−43.7	−68.1	−80.1	8.9	—
External gap (ex ante)	−47.8	−44.8	−36.9	−49.3	−62.4	−53.8	−52.4	1.5	—
Gap difference	0.0	−7.3	−5.6	−16.8	−18.7	14.3	27.7	—	—
Domestic = external gap (ex post)	−47.9	−37.5	−31.3	−32.5	−43.7	−53.8	−52.4	1.5	28.9
Government deficit	−134.7	−113.1	−105.7	−124.7	−151.2	−156.6	−168.0	3.8	7.5
GDP deflator	1.00	1.04	1.20	1.35	1.48	1.60	1.70	9.2	23.6
Rate of inflation	—	4.0	15.4	12.5	9.6	8.1	6.3	—	—

Source: Computed by the author.
Notes: See text for assumptions used in model simulation.

initial 134.7 billion peso figure to 168.0 by 1981 but remained within a feasible range of the government's borrowing capabilities.

Government consumption assumes most of the burden of stabilization in both programs A and B, falling by −0.5 percent per annum in program A and by 4.0 percent in program B versus an actual average annual rate of increase of 7.7 percent for the period. Private investment falls slightly in program B, but not enough to warrant concern.

Due to the depressing effect of government expenditures on private consumption, such consumption (equation 1, table 13.1) actually expands somewhat in both programs over its historical 5.1 percent annual increase. On the other hand, in both program A and program B, private savings was somewhat below the rates actually obtained during this period.

Conclusions

All in all, the country appears to have little real growth or investment to show for the rapid increase in government deficits, money supply, and inflation experienced in the post-1975 period. The optimal control simulations show that under reasonable assumptions, comparable rates of real growth and private sector activity were possible under conditions of fiscal restraint and price stability.

These results are encouraging. They indicate in a preliminary sort of way that the fairly harsh stabilization program implemented toward the end of 1982 would not necessarily result in a large-scale and prolonged contraction of economic activity. The private sector seems resilient enough, given fairly high levels of government investment, to withstand a sizable reduction in the rate of growth of government consumption, the public deficit, and domestic credit. With this factor in mind, several stabilization programs were designed for the 1982–87 optimal control exercises that follow.

14. Scope for Optimal Policy in an Oil-Based Economy, 1982–87

Signals of Mexico's current economic crisis started to break in mid-1981 when it became clear that the government's projections were being completely invalidated by a soaring balance of payments deficit.[1] The government ordered public spending to be cut by 10 percent. Failing to impose this spending cut, however, in February 1982 the peso was devalued by 40 percent following a massive outflow of capital. Next a rash of ill-considered wage increases were made (with the presidential elections obviously in mind), setting off a classic wage-price spiral. Finally, in April, the government announced a new and more determined round of spending cuts, this time backed by presidential decree. After years of rapid growth, Mexico faced the prospect of little more than stagnation over the next two or three years. The bitter irony, of course, is that the country's oil wealth is at the heart of its current troubles.

Prospects and Policies

Gains from the terms of trade over 1978–80 were equivalent to about 6.3 percent of Mexican GDP. By 1980 petroleum represented 45 percent of merchandise exports and 30 percent of federal revenue.

Even though the recent crisis was brought on by the 1981–82 worldwide oil glut, in any case Mexico would have had to reformulate its extraction, accumulation, portfolio, and development policies. Even in 1980, after two booming years marked by import expansion at 31 percent annually, the country had seen its real exchange rate appreciate as inflation rose to 30 percent annually. Capital flowed into Mexico in response to the country's enhanced creditworthiness, undermined attempts to contract credit, and permitted increased absorption. Appreciation reduced incentives for private investment in manufacturing and undoubtedly encouraged considerable substitution of cheap imported capital goods for domestic labor.

What adjustment policies are open to the country and which seem most promising? The remainder of this chapter presents some thoughts on this topic without, however, analyzing in any great detail their political feasibility. This discussion assumes, as a fundamental policy objective, the desire to increase absorption and the long-term rate of nonoil economic growth, rather than to cut oil output, accumulate reserves, and / or significantly reduce the country's outstanding external debt.

The Oil Syndrome

The dynamic issues facing the Mexican economy after 1975 reflected policy options at a number of levels. Considering the country as an international price taker and abstracting from institutional constraints on the level of production, the prime decisions facing Mexico related to the petroleum extraction profile over time, the split of income into consumption and accumulation, and the division of investment into real domestic capital formation and the accumulation of claims on foreign countries. All of these choices may be summarized as fundamental savings and portfolio decisions.[2]

As shown in the previous chapter, the subsequent level of policy and institutional choice concerned distribution, consumption, savings, investment, and production patterns in the nonoil economy. The nonoil sectors were subsequently subject to stress arising from changes in the intensity of demand and its sectoral pattern and shifts in relative prices.

Medium-term adjustment has been heavily influenced by the limited linkages between the oil sector and the domestic economy, and the taxation of petroleum rents by the government. Both factors have combined to limit the primary impact of the oil revenues to changes in public sector revenues. Oil revenues accrue in foreign currency, while the bulk of government spending is on nontraded goods—construction, infrastructure, and services. Thus, even potential budget surpluses might prove inflationary because an increase in the foreign component of the monetary base would be only partially offset by decreased claims of the banking system on the federal government.

A secondary albeit considerably smaller increase in government revenues was also generated from taxes levied on the post-1977 expanded volume of imports. The net shift in the distribution of national income in favor of the public sector increased demands (largely urban) for nontradeables, especially construction and service activities. Finally, increased public spending began straining the country's administrative capacity.

The resulting inflationary forces set off a complex sequence of events. First, the real purchasing position of the public sector itself eroded, because that sector was a net exporter. The resulting relaxation of domestic revenue-raising efforts produced a tendency for real revenues to fall short of those reasonably anticipated on the basis of the country's level of income and industrial development. Following an initial increase in 1977, the public sector savings performance consequently deteriorated steadily, while adherence to expanded real investment targets led to government deficits greater than before the oil boom, despite a massive increase in nominal and real government revenues.

Because private savings did not increase relative to private investment, larger deficits developed on the trade and current balance of payments accounts. The unexpected magnitude of the deficits, and the difficulties created for the manufacturing and nonoil primary sectors by real appreciation, eventually shifted government policy toward contraction of credit and spending. This adjustment tended at first to "overshoot" policy goals, rather than proceeding smoothly. The government's contractionary credit policies and controls, intended to slow inflation and correct the country's external imbalance, inhibited private expenditures, which were effectively crowded out by the public sector. In addition, there is some indication that the increase in domestic demand (from multiplier effects out of government spending) may not be capable of significantly increasing capacity in the productive trade sectors unless policies become more specifically focused. Finally, even without overshooting, private investment outside the construction and service sectors may have been inhibited somewhat by the real appreciation of the exchange rate.

The latter effects have tended to operate through several mechanisms: through higher wages and / or reduced factor supplies in factor markets, through increased costs of intermediate goods and of the nontraded component of investment relative to product prices, and through decreased efficiency due to bottlenecks in the surrounding economy. These stresses were somewhat greater than those experienced by most of the other less developed oil-producing countries due to the large share of domestic goods in the Mexican economy's consumption and intermediate flows.

In addition, the government's desire to raise absorption rapidly in line with rising revenues biased further the composition of public spending. Obviously, it was difficult to double or treble certain categories of expenditure in a few years. Primary expenditure decisions made by a relatively limited number of individuals tended naturally to emphasize large capital-intensive projects that required relatively little in the way of domestic human resources or institutional changes. Public investment therefore tended to be biased heavily in favor of infrastructure, which became a leading sector, rather than responding to the demands established by the private commodity-producing sectors.

Foreign exchange reserves were accumulated following the initial post-1976 increases in revenues. However, the absorption-sterilizing impact of reserve accumulation was offset by the induced inflow of capital attracted by the enhanced creditworthiness of the country. Monetary policy proved particularly ineffectual due to the free mobility of capital. Emphasis was placed on fiscal policy, but the government's decision to opt for a high growth strategy (thus absorbing the oil revenues as fast as possible) greatly constrained the scope for policy fine-tuning.

Preliminary forecasts using the simultaneous equation model (table 13.4) indicate that continuation of an unconstrained high growth–oriented strategy (table 13.5) would lead (table 14.1) to continued high rates of inflation—a 22.2 percent average annual rate over the 1981–87 period, a rapidly increasing government deficit—7.6 percent average annual growth rate between 1981–87, and despite high annual oil exports (15 percent) a growing excess of the external gap over the internal gap.

Thus, it is apparent that even if it was feasible to continue the policies pursued during most of the post-1976 period (if external funds were still plentiful and available), this would only aggravate further the country's debt and inflationary difficulties.

On the basis of this preliminary assessment, the following optimal control simulations were designed to see if politically feasible modifications of past government policy could not only resolve the country's post-oil glut crisis, but, more important, return the economy to stable noninflationary growth.

Analysis of the 1981–87 Period

For the optimal control analysis of the 1981–82 period, the model's exogenous variables were set at the following rates (largely reflective of historical movements):

1. the exchange rate (*EXC*), 90 pesos per dollar—more or less the average rate as of October 1982;
2. crude petroleum production index (*CPP*), 6 percent—down from the rate of the previous few years, reflecting the worldwide oil glut;[3]
3. crude petroleum exports (*PETE*), 6 percent—again down from the 1978–81 period, reflecting the oil glut;
4. real U.S. gross domestic product (*USYP*), 2.5 percent;
5. the U.S. consumer price index (*USCIP*), 6 percent—reflecting U.S. monetary policies and governmental priorities.

The Exchange Rate

The setting of the exchange rate at a constant level (at 90 pesos to the U.S. dollar) needs some explanation. The exchange policy to be adopted in the future is of course closely connected with the inflation objectives of the government. A fixed exchange rate would require accepting the U.S. inflation rate. A gliding parity, on the other hand, would permit the Mexican domestic inflation rate to exceed that of the United States by the amount of the depreciation of the exchange rate, while a floating rate is in theory consistent with any inflation target. A basic question in the design of an appropriate combination of monetary and exchange policy is, how much inflation should the Mexican authorities accept?[4]

It is a truism that the optimal exchange rate policy allows for the greatest increase in real output and maximizes short-term destabilizing capital flows and fluctuations in the domestic price level.[5] On the other hand, it is not clear which type of rate is capable of meeting these objectives simultaneously; exchange rate measures aimed in one direction frequently produce undesired effects with respect to a second objective. The main challenge facing the Mexican authorities in designing current exchange rate policy is to reconcile the short-term objective of exchange rate stability with the long-run requirement of a realistically valued rate.[6]

It is difficult to exaggerate the importance of maintaining a correct alignment of the exchange rate. An overvalued exchange rate would reduce the tradeable goods sector of the economy, reducing exports, raising imports, and augmenting the dependence of the economy on the petroleum industry. The financial affluence resulting from oil revenues would only aggravate the problem since the necessary adjustments could be postponed indefinitely. At the same time, given that Mexico's manufacturing exports tend to be labor intensive, there would be a conflict between the goals of employment creation and the target rate of income growth.[7]

A flexible or semiflexible rate may not produce a satisfactory solution either. For example, after the devaluation of September 1976 and during the first few months of 1977, during which time the exchange rate showed substantial fluctuations, speculative short-run capital flows were quite large. When the Bank of Mexico intervened more actively in the foreign exchange market, capital flows were considerably smoothed. It appears that small, unannounced depreciations of the exchange rate triggered destabilizing capital flows.[8]

A related problem that seems to be associated with a fluctuating (and depreciating) exchange rate is that of dollarization, or a faster increase in deposits denominated in foreign currency—mostly the U.S. dollar—than in peso-denominated deposits. Currency substitution of this type is quantitatively quite important in Mexico. Thus, any attempt to achieve monetary independence through flexible or semiflexible rates may undermine any advantage associated with floating rates.[9]

Some observers have gone so far as to argue that exchange rate uncertainty may be destabilizing in Mexico's case. They have suggested that the problem might degenerate from a simple one of individuals wanting to hold a diversified currency portfolio (producing controlled shifts into dollars) into an all-or-nothing crisis. If a decline in the value of the peso was anticipated, for example, it is conceivable that massive shifts into dollars would completely destabilize the currency.[10]

The problems presented by dollarization in Mexico are easy to illustrate. Probably the best measure of the degree of dollarization is the dollar-to-peso ratio of various money aggregates. By this indicator, the proportion of dollar-denominated financial claims rose from 5.2 percent in 1975 to 19.4 percent in December 1976. The ratio of foreign to domestic currency deposits in Mexican banks in July 1979 was such that nearly 20 percent of the total deposits held by the public were in foreign currency.

In short, the real size of the banking system was reduced during this period because of a lack of confidence in the economy and stability of the peso brought about by rising inflation. The result was that investment fell off drastically because peso credit was scarce, while at the same time dollar credits were considered too risky.[11]

Table 14.1. Mexico: preliminary simulations, national income accounts, 1981–87 (billions of 1975 pesos)

	Actual value	Recursive model simulation		1982 forecast		Simultaneous model forecast					Average annual growth
	1981	1980	1981	Recursive model	Simultaneous model	1983	1984	1985	1986	1987	1981–87
Private consumption (ex ante)	—	947.1	1,005.9	1,161.8	963.1	1,032.1	1,104.3	1,179.5	1,259.2	1,341.9	—
Private consumption (ex post)	1,018.0	941.3	1,018.0	1,161.8	963.1	1,032.1	1,104.3	1,179.5	1,259.2	1,341.9	4.7
Private investment	223.4	189.9	220.2	190.6	152.5	177.6	205.1	234.9	268.7	305.2	5.3
Private savings	369.9	315.5	354.7	274.1	294.2	330.4	370.1	413.2	461.9	514.5	5.7
Government consumption	177.3	168.2	182.7	193.7	196.5	208.9	222.4	237.4	253.9	272.2	7.4
Government investment	190.2	168.7	190.2	209.3	209.3	230.3	253.3	278.3	306.5	337.0	10.0
Government revenue	159.6	147.4	169.5	213.1	193.6	209.9	227.7	247.4	269.2	293.3	10.7
Government deficit	−203.4	−189.5	−203.4	−189.9	−212.3	−229.3	−248.0	−268.3	−291.2	−315.9	7.6
Total investment	413.6	358.6	410.4	399.9	361.7	407.9	458.4	513.3	575.2	642.2	7.6
Change in stock	49.2	40.2	45.0	48.5	44.3	48.4	52.8	57.4	62.5	67.8	5.5
Total gross capital formation	462.8	398.8	455.4	448.4	406.0	456.3	511.2	570.7	637.7	710.0	7.4
Exports	196.9	173.4	206.9	287.0	287.0	307.5	330.6	357.0	386.9	421.1	13.5
Imports (ex ante)	—	−183.2	−213.2	−346.8	−313.3	−349.6	−369.8	−391.7	−416.5	−443.2	—
Imports (ex post)	−213.4	−205.1	−213.4	−278.6	−209.8	−256.8	−289.5	−326.4	−368.4	−415.3	11.7
Net factor payments	−45.0	−40.3	−49.3	−70.9	−70.9	−76.4	−82.7	−89.8	−97.8	−107.0	15.5

Gross domestic product supply	1,641.0	1,502.8	1,644.8	1,749.8	1,625.1	1,747.9	1,878.9	2,018.2	2,169.5	2,329.9	6.0
Gross domestic product demand (ex ante)	—	1,499.9	1,641.4	1,681.6	1,521.5	1,655.1	1,798.7	1,952.9	2,121.3	2,302.1	—
Gross domestic product demand (ex post)	1,641.0	1,502.8	1,644.8	1,749.8	1,625.1	1,747.9	1,878.9	2,018.2	2,169.5	2,329.9	6.0
Gross national product	1,596.0	1,462.6	1,595.4	1,678.9	1,554.2	1,671.5	1,796.3	1,928.4	2,071.6	2,222.9	5.7
Total savings	400.3	351.6	402.3	385.8	394.5	430.5	469.5	511.6	558.5	608.8	7.2
Internal gap (ex ante)	—	−47.2	−52.2	−62.5	−11.6	−25.8	−41.6	−59.2	−79.2	−101.2	—
External gap (ex ante)	—	−50.1	−55.6	−130.7	−115.1	−118.6	−121.9	−124.5	−127.3	−129.1	—
Internal = external gap (ex post)	−62.1	−50.1	−55.6	−62.5	−11.6	−25.8	−41.6	−59.2	−79.2	−101.2	8.5
Gross domestic product deflator	3.56	2.72	3.58	4.36	5.18	6.00	7.03	8.30	9.90	11.89	22.2

Source: Computed by the author.

Notes: Assumes exogenous rates of growth 1982–87; (a) real government investment = 10 percent; crude petroleum production = 15 percent; crude oil exports = 15 percent; private sector credit = 30 percent; Bank of Mexico credit to government = 20 percent; monetary system credit to government = 20 percent; United States GDP growth = 2.5 percent; U.S. inflation = 6.0 percent; government internal borrowing = 30 percent.

Dollarization in Mexico is, therefore, clearly associated with exchange rate uncertainty. Apparently, this problem cannot be overcome through forward markets due to their thinness and high cost of transactions. Therefore, in the absence of working futures markets and their potentially stabilizing role, the peso would probably continue to fluctuate if the exchange rate were floating. The experience since 1976 indicates that currency substitution can be traced directly to exchange rate uncertainty, associated with attempts of clean floating.

In any case, the practice of a managed float of the peso since late 1976 amounted to an actual peg to the dollar, and it reinforced Mexico's dependence on the United States. Mexico cannot gain much short-run stimulus from any peso depreciation vis-à-vis Germany, Japan, or Switzerland, for example, because of her relatively small export markets in those countries.[12] Furthermore, since oil exports are denominated in dollars, at least one-half of the country's exports would not be affected by a devaluation. A final point is that simulations of the economy with a rapidly falling exchange rate indicate that private investment would be severely affected (and thus the overall rate of growth reduced).

Based on these considerations, a fixed peso exchange rate (that of October 1982) was used in the forecasts. This required in addition, of course, that the Mexican inflation rate had to be held close to that of the U.S. (6 percent) to avoid overvaluation.

Optimal Control Simulations

The initial run (table 13.5) represents a nonoptimized solution, with the exogenous values set at the rates given above, and the policy variables of real government investment (IGP) and Bank of Mexico (*BMGC*) nominal credit to the government arbitrarily set at 4.9 and 20 percent, respectively.

This run establishes a bench mark for comparison. It also demonstrates the ramifications of relatively slow government investment growth rates; private investment expands at an average rate of 1.8, while GDP increases at 4.7 percent—both considerably below their 1975–81 values of 9.3 and 6.9 percent, respectively.

In this and the other exercises two distinct gaps are generated: internal (savings minus investment) and external (exports minus imports, net factor payments). These gaps are equal to the difference between aggregate demand and supply. Since aggregate supply must control, demand is adjusted to supply. In adjusting aggregate demand, either private consumption or imports was adjusted from its ex ante forecasted level to an ex post figure (thus equalizing the two gaps). Two types of adjustments of the ex ante to ex post values for these gaps were considered: adjustment from the estimated to the minimum dominant gap, that is, to whichever of the two gaps was the larger to that of the size of the smaller, and adjustment of the smaller minimum gap to the larger.

If, for example, the savings-investment gap exceeds the external gap, savings could be increased and private consumption reduced. Such an adjustment depends, as is noted in chapter 11, on additional flexibility in the tax structure over and above the way the tax structure underlies (or is implicit in) the estimated savings function. Presumably, this additional flexibility could be tapped through appropriate policy measures in order to minimize the export-import gap.

The second adjustment—allowing the smaller of the ex ante gaps to adjust up to the larger—was not adopted largely for two reasons. The stabilization environment likely to prevail throughout most of the forecast period discouraged such adjustment. Second, given the government's current $82 billion external gap, the authorities might not be able to finance the larger gap in any case.

In the nonoptimal run, therefore, supply exceeded demand and the domestic gap exceeded the external. Adjustment was made through reducing consumption instead of increasing imports (table 14.2).

It is easy to demonstrate the problems associated with the alternative adjustment mechanism, allowing the trade gap to expand up to the size of the ex ante savings-investment gap. Where the savings-investment gap is the larger and determines the minimum consistent requirement of foreign resources, the proper policy often recommended is to relax import restrictions on nonessential—presumably mostly consumer—products. If the market for foreign exchanges were perfectly unimpeded, as might possibly be the case if oil revenues pick up dramatically, a case could even be made for a currency appreciation or for a reduction in import duties. Alternatively, exports of some products that could be readily consumed at home could be reduced through an appropriate policy. Clearly, these measures would run counter to the country's stabilization and debt repayment efforts.

Furthermore, given that imports of capital goods and intermediate products are currently controlled along with other imports through quantitative restrictions and the August 1982 exchange controls, then a relaxation of such controls would be undesirable. Such a policy change would lead, at least in the short run, to increased investment, and thus the binding gap would be increased. In this event, external financing might fall short of the minimum requirement consistent with increased capital formation and growth.

The other adjustment alternative—neglect of the gap disparity and reliance on autonomous forces of adjustment by the authorities—also appears undesirable. Given the excess of the ex ante savings-investment gap over the import-export gap, there will be as noted above an excess of effective demand over effective supply in the economy during this period. Either undesired inventory or reduction of inflationary pressures would have to produce the ex post adjustment. In the former case, total ex post investment will be smaller than the intended investment, that necessary to generate the assumed rate of growth, depending on the amount of involuntary inventory reduction. In this case, the adjustment would take place via a reduction in the dominant savings-investment gap to the level of the export-import gap. The growth process would not, however, be altered because the productive or growth investment will have been realized. However, with a reduced demand for investment credit and a reduced savings-investment gap, the reduction of inventories would most likely be matched by an equivalent accumulation of foreign exchange. Actually, under the above policy

Table 14.2. Mexico: nonoptimal stabilization program, 1982–87 (billions of 1975 pesos)

	Model simulation 1981	Forecasted values						Average annual rate of growth, 1981–87
		1982	1983	1984	1985	1986	1987	
Private consumption (ex ante)	1,009.6	1,100.0	1,097.7	1,138.8	1,219.2	1,292.9	1,371.3	5.2
Private consumption (ex post)	1,013.0	1,098.6	1,084.5	1,126.1	1,201.0	1,271.1	1,344.4	4.8
Government consumption	182.7	211.2	207.1	207.2	211.6	216.5	222.0	3.3
Total consumption (ex ante)	1,009.6	1,100.0	1,097.7	1,138.8	1,219.2	1,292.9	1,371.3	5.2
Total consumption (ex post)	1,195.7	1,309.8	1,291.6	1,333.3	1,412.6	1,487.6	1,566.4	4.6
Private savings	354.7	363.3	314.7	347.1	361.4	381.1	399.7	2.0
Private investment	220.2	161.2	189.0	200.3	215.6	229.7	245.5	1.8
Government investment	190.3	200.0	209.0	219.0	230.0	242.0	254.0	4.9
Change in stocks	45.0	48.7	48.9	50.8	54.4	57.8	61.4	5.3
Total investment	455.4	410.0	446.9	470.2	500.0	529.5	560.9	3.5
Exports	206.9	273.3	282.2	291.7	301.6	312.0	323.0	7.7
Imports (ex ante)	−213.2	−215.9	−238.6	−254.5	−265.6	−277.7	−289.8	5.3
Imports (ex post)	−213.2	−215.9	−238.6	−254.5	−265.6	−277.7	−289.8	5.3
Gross domestic product (supply)	1,644.8	1,777.4	1,782.2	1,840.7	1,948.5	2,051.5	2,160.4	4.7
Gross domestic product (demand)	1,641.1	1,778.7	1,795.4	1,853.4	1,966.8	2,073.2	2,187.3	4.9
Supply-demand gap	—	−1.3	−13.2	−12.7	−18.3	−21.7	−26.9	—
Gross domestic product (ex post)	1,644.8	1,777.4	1,782.2	1,840.7	1,948.5	2,051.5	2,160.4	4.7

Gross national product	1,595.4	1,710.0	1,712.4	1,768.4	1,873.5	1,973.4	2,079.6	4.5
Total savings	403.2	398.8	407.7	422.4	442.7	464.3	486.3	3.2
Domestic gap (ex ante)	−52.2	−11.2	−39.3	−47.8	−57.2	−65.2	−74.5	6.1
External gap (ex ante)	−55.6	−9.9	−26.1	−35.1	−39.0	−43.4	−47.6	−2.6
Gap difference	−3.4	1.4	13.2	12.7	18.2	21.80	26.9	—
Domestic = external gap (ex post)	−55.6	−9.9	−26.1	−35.1	−39.0	−43.4	−47.6	−2.6
Government deficit	−203.4	−189.5	−200.6	−207.4	−211.7	−218.1	−224.4	1.7
GDP deflator	3.57	4.34	5.29	6.40	7.65	9.08	10.76	20.2
Rate of inflation	—	21.6	21.9	21.0	19.5	18.7	18.5	—

Source: Computed by the author.

of import liberalization, this amount of foreign exchange would permit the replenishment of inventories to a nominal level from foreign sources.

Of course market-oriented adjustments of this type could never be lasting. In the long run, with limited inventories market forces would necessarily lead to inflation, thus running counter to the main objective of stabilizing price increases, in line with those in the United States. Furthermore, inflation might tend to reduce exports either through a transfer of productive resources to nontraded goods or from increased competition by domestic buyers. As a result, the temporarily accumulated foreign exchange reserves would tend to return to their original level, and the export-import gap would tend to adjust to the initially larger savings-investment gap. Adjustments would be produced through a trade contraction rather than through a trade expansion. Note that over the forecast period a policy of import liberalization would have expanded trade, whereas in the absence of any policy exports would be contracted. In fact, with prices rising relative to those in the United States, not only would exports have been reduced but importers' rent (or quasi-rent) would have increased. The end result would be equivalent to increased commercial protection—definitely undesirable from the point of view of increased efficiency and thus the country's long-run growth potential. In short, reducing consumption—as opposed to allowing the external gap to increase up to the size of the savings-investment gap—can be easily defended, given the country's currently dual problems of rapidly rising inflation and external debt.

Starting from the base established in the nonoptimal run, Stabilization Program I specifies:

1. real government investment ≤ 8 percent; and
   8 percent; and
2. the target—real GDP (*GDPNP*) be optimized in 1978.

The improvement (table 14.3) in output levels over the nonoptimal result (table 14.2) is marked, with private investment increasing to 4.4 percent average annual growth and gross domestic product to 5.6 percent.

While optimal under the constraints imposed, the run is not particularly desirable because in it inflation persists at around 17 to 18 percent. In addition, under the model's assumptions, the government's deficit increases from 203.4 billion pesos in 1981 to 265.4 billion pesos by 1987.

To counteract the inflation problem, Stabilization Program II was designed with:

1. government investment ≤ 8 percent;
2. government deficit constant at 203.4 billion pesos;
3. minimization of banking system credit to government; and
4. maximization of real gross domestic product in 1987.

As a result of the optimal control program (table 14.4), inflation fell to 0.2 percent per annum by 1987, with only a 1 percent drop in the annual rate of growth in gross domestic product—to 5.6 percent per year, and an increase in private investment, stabilizing above a 4 percent average annual rate of growth.

The one disadvantage of this program appears to be the negative 3.6 percent annual growth in real government consumption. The problems associated with government consumption lead to the design of Stabilization Program III, which assumes:

1. optimizing real GDP in 1987;
2. reaching a target rate of growth of 6 percent rate of inflation in 1987;
3. maximizing banking system credit to the government;
4. real government investment $\leq$ 8 percent.

The results (table 14.5) of program III are distinctly superior to those of program II. Under this program, private investment reached 4.4 average annual growth. The government deficit was not overly excessive, with an average annual increase of 4.8 percent, lower than the GDP increase at 5.6 percent. Inflation occurred at an acceptable target rate. The internal-external ex ante gaps are quite close and in a range where financing should not be difficult. Government consumption increases at 2.6 percent per annum—in line with a good stabilization program. Program III was therefore considered the most desirable strategy for the government to attempt. It is not only feasible but should not result in the severe dislocation entailed by program II or similar programs.

As a basis of comparison, one additional program is presented. In Stabilization Program IV the exchange rate was gradually devalued from 20 pesos to 90 by 1987. The result of these assumptions closely resembles the outcome of program I. Compared with program I, private investment has a lower overall growth (table 14.5), although the initial shock of the massive devaluation is avoided.

There is little evidence that a staged devaluation over the six-year period to 1988 would be in any way superior to the once-and-for-all 1982 devaluation actually in effect.

Comparison with program I shows that nearly all of program IV's output levels are lower. In particular, the drag of the increased cost of capital imports on private investment seems most severe. Finally, in contrast to programs I through III where the ex ante savings-investment gap dominates throughout most of the forecast period, program IV is characterized by the ex ante dominance of the external (export-import) gap. In this case, policies allowing the smaller savings-investment gap to adjust upward to the trade gap would definitely undermine any stabilization effort. One line of action usually recommended when the savings-investment gap is smaller is that of reducing savings through reduced taxation of one sort or another. On the other hand, it is clear that it would be inappropriate to try to further stimulate productive investment. First, this would invalidate the underlying growth assumption. GDP would increase, and, more important, import requirements would be liable to increase significantly. The import equation used in the simulations is heavily weighted by investment. In fact, whenever investment projects cannot be undertaken without some foreign inputs, it would

Table 14.3. Mexico: optimal control stabilization program I, 1982–87 (billions of 1975 pesos)

	Actual 1981	Model simulation 1981	Forecasted values 1982	1983	1984	1985	1986	1987	Average annual rate of growth: Model 1981–87	Actual 1975–81
Private consumption (ex ante)	—	1,009.6	1,132.4	1,094.8	1,144.5	1,239.2	1,329.1	1,431.1	6.0	—
Private consumption (ex post)	1,017.5	1,013.0	1,132.4	1,091.5	1,144.5	1,235.7	1,324.6	1,411.2	5.7	5.1
Government consumption	177.3	182.7	213.0	206.7	206.6	211.5	217.2	225.1	3.5	7.7
Total consumption (ex ante)	—	1,192.3	1,345.4	1,301.5	1,351.1	1,450.7	1,546.3	1,656.2	5.6	—
Total consumption (ex post)	1,194.8	1,195.7	1,345.4	1,298.2	1,351.1	1,447.2	1,546.3	1,636.3	5.4	5.4
Private savings	369.9	354.7	367.3	326.9	371.8	400.2	435.9	461.1	4.5	9.2
Private investment	223.4	220.2	161.2	194.5	213.0	237.0	260.0	285.3	4.4	9.3
Government investment	190.3	190.3	205.3	200.9	238.7	257.3	277.4	287.8	7.1	10.5
Change in stocks	49.2	45.0	50.2	49.4	52.0	56.4	60.8	65.3	6.4	11.9
Total investment	462.8	455.4	416.7	464.8	503.6	550.7	598.2	638.4	5.8	10.0
Exports	169.9	206.9	273.3	282.2	291.7	301.6	312.0	323.0	7.7	17.2
Net factor payments	−45.0	−49.3	−67.3	−69.8	−72.3	−75.0	−77.8	−80.8	8.6	—
Imports (ex ante)	—	−213.2	−215.9	−238.6	−254.5	−265.6	−277.8	−289.8	5.3	—
Imports (ex post)	—	−213.2	−208.8	−238.6	254.1	−265.6	−277.8	−289.8	5.3	12.4

Gross domestic product (supply)	1,641.2	1,644.8	1,822.2	1,796.5	1,875.4	2,010.6	2,143.9	2,278.9	5.6	6.9
Gross domestic product (demand)	1,641.2	1,641.4	1,815.1	1,799.7	1,875.0	2,014.0	2,148.4	2,298.8	5.8	6.9
Supply-demand gap	—	3.4	7.1	−3.2	0.4	−3.4	−4.5	−19.9	—	—
Gross domestic product (ex post)	1,641.2	1,644.8	1,822.2	1,796.5	1,875.4	2,010.6	2,143.9	2,278.9	5.6	6.9
Gross national product	1,596.2	1,595.4	1,754.8	1,726.7	1,803.1	1,935.6	2,066.1	2,198.1	5.5	6.7
Total savings	401.4	403.2	409.4	425.2	451.9	484.8	519.9	541.9	5.1	11.2
Domestic gap (ex ante)	—	−52.2	−7.4	−39.6	−51.6	−65.9	−78.4	−96.5	10.8	—
External gap (ex ante)	—	−55.6	−14.5	−36.3	−52.0	−62.4	−73.9	−76.6	5.5	—
Gap difference	—	−3.4	−7.1	3.3	−0.4	3.5	4.5	19.9	—	—
Domestic = external gap (ex post)	—	−55.6	−7.4	−39.6	−51.6	−65.9	−78.4	−96.5	9.6	28.9
Governemnt deficit	−207.9	−203.4	−194.7	−216.3	−232.4	−245.6	−261.8	−265.4	4.5	7.5
GDP deflator	3.57	3.57	4.30	5.25	6.32	7.50	8.84	10.38	19.5	23.6
Rate of inflation	26.7	26.7	20.5	22.1	20.4	18.7	17.9	17.4	—	—

Source: Computed by the author.

Table 14.4. Mexico: optimal control stabilization program II, 1982–87 (billions of 1975 pesos)

	Model simulation 1981	Forecasted values						Average annual rate of growth
		1982	1983	1984	1985	1986	1987	1981–87
Private consumption (ex ante)	1,009.6	1,117.5	1,112.9	1,184.8	1,296.9	1,407.8	1,526.1	7.1
Private consumption (ex post)	1,013.0	1,117.5	1,103.1	1,174.1	1,277.8	1,382.3	1,492.5	6.7
Government consumption	182.7	221.7	194.5	177.9	169.5	158.1	146.7	−3.6
Total consumption (ex ante)	1,192.3	1,339.2	1,307.4	1,362.7	1,466.4	1,565.9	1,672.8	5.8
Total consumption (ex post)	1,195.7	1,339.2	1,297.6	1,352.0	1,447.3	1,540.4	1,642.2	5.4
Private investment	220.2	161.2	195.1	211.3	234.1	255.5	279.6	4.1
Government investment	190.3	205.1	220.4	238.4	256.9	277.4	298.9	7.8
Change in stocks	45.0	50.1	49.4	51.9	56.3	60.6	65.3	6.4
Total investment	455.4	416.5	465.0	501.8	547.4	593.6	643.7	5.9
Exports	206.9	273.3	282.2	291.7	301.6	312.0	323.0	7.7
Net factor payments	−49.3	−67.3	−70.0	−72.3	−74.9	−77.8	−80.8	8.6
Imports (ex ante)	−213.2	−220.3	−248.4	−271.2	−288.8	−308.2	−328.4	7.5
Imports (ex post)	−209.8	−209.7	−248.4	−271.2	−288.8	−308.2	−328.4	7.5
Gross domestic product (supply)	1,644.8	1,819.3	1,796.5	1,814.3	2,007.5	2,138.0	2,277.5	5.6
Gross domestic product (demand)	1,641.4	1,808.7	1,806.2	1,884.9	2,026.7	2,163.4	2,311.1	5.9
Supply-demand gap	3.4	10.6	−9.7	−10.6	−19.2	−25.4	−33.6	—

Gross domestic product (ex post)	1,644.8	1,819.3	1,796.5	1,874.3	2,007.5	2,138.0	2,277.5	—
Gross national product	1,595.4	1,752.0	1,726.8	1,801.9	1,932.5	2,060.2	2,196.7	5.5
Total savings	403.2	412.7	419.4	439.2	466.1	494.3	523.9	4.5
Domestic gap (ex ante)	−52.2	−3.8	−45.7	−62.5	−81.3	−99.4	−119.8	14.9
External gap (ex ante)	−55.6	−14.4	−35.9	−51.8	−62.2	−73.9	−86.2	7.6
Gap difference	−3.4	−10.6	9.8	10.7	19.1	25.5	33.6	—
Domestic = external gap (ex post)	−55.6	−3.8	−35.9	−51.8	−62.2	−73.9	−86.2	—
Government deficit	−203.4	−203.4	−203.4	−203.4	−203.4	−203.4	−203.4	0.0
GDP deflator	3.57	4.07	4.51	4.82	5.00	5.09	5.10	6.12
Rate of inflation	26.7	14.0	10.8	6.9	3.7	1.8	0.2	—

Source: Computed by the author.

Table 14.5. Mexico: optimal control stabilization program IV, 1982–87 (billions of 1975 pesos)

	Model simulation	Forecasted values						Average annual rate of growth	
	1981	1982	1983	1984	1985	1986	1987	Model 1981–87	Actual 1975–81
Private consumption (ex ante)	1,009.6	1,148.1	1,131.9	1,173.0	1,230.3	1,292.2	1,358.2	5.1	—
Private consumption (ex post)	1,009.6	1,148.1	1,131.9	1,173.0	1,230.3	1,292.2	1,358.2	5.1	5.1
Government consumption	182.7	202.0	200.4	203.4	208.3	213.7	219.8	3.1	7.7
Total consumption (ex ante)	1,192.3	1,350.1	1,332.3	1,376.4	1,438.6	1,505.9	1,578.0	4.8	—
Total consumption (ex post)	1,192.3	1,350.1	1,332.3	1,376.4	1,438.6	1,505.9	1,578.0	4.8	5.4
Private savings	354.7	383.2	374.9	385.8	400.8	416.4	435.8	3.5	9.2
Private investment	220.1	200.0	202.1	207.1	212.9	220.8	229.7	0.7	9.3
Government investment	190.3	205.2	220.5	238.4	256.9	277.4	298.9	7.8	10.5
Change in stocks	45.0	50.2	50.3	52.8	55.9	59.4	63.0	5.8	11.9
Total investment	455.4	455.3	472.9	498.3	525.8	557.6	591.6	4.5	10.0
Exports	206.9	224.8	243.5	262.6	282.2	302.3	323.0	7.7	17.2
Imports (ex ante)	−213.2	−220.3	−244.6	−263.2	−282.6	−303.7	−325.7	7.3	—
Imports (ex post)	−209.8	−208.4	−223.3	−237.0	−250.8	−265.8	−281.8	5.0	12.4

Gross domestic product (supply)	1,644.8	1,821.8	1,825.3	1,900.3	1,995.8	2,100.0	2,210.8	5.1	6.9
Gross domestic product (demand)	1,641.4	1,809.9	1,804.0	1,874.2	1,964.0	2,062.1	2,166.9	4.7	6.9
Supply-demand gap	3.4	11.9	21.3	26.1	31.8	37.9	43.9	—	—
Gross domestic product (ex post)	1,644.8	1,821.8	1,825.3	1,900.3	1,995.8	2,100.0	2,210.8	5.1	6.9
Gross national product	1,595.4	1,767.6	1,766.0	1,835.9	1,926.0	2,024.8	2,130.0	4.9	6.7
Total savings	403.2	417.5	433.8	459.4	481.4	518.9	552.0	5.4	11.2
Domestic gap (ex ante)	−52.2	−37.9	−39.1	−38.9	−38.3	−38.7	−39.6	−4.5	—
External gap (ex post)	−55.6	−49.8	−60.4	−65.1	−70.1	−76.6	−83.5	7.0	—
Gap difference	−3.4	−11.9	−21.3	−26.2	−31.8	−37.9	−43.9	53.2	—
Domestic = external gap (ex post)	52.2	37.9	39.1	38.9	38.3	38.7	39.6	−4.5	28.9
Government deficit	203.4	214.9	229.5	240.9	252.6	266.7	281.7	5.6	7.5
GDP deflator	3.57	4.30	5.22	6.27	7.48	8.88	10.51	19.7	23.6
Rate of inflation	26.7	20.4	21.4	20.1	19.3	18.7	18.4	—	—

Source: Computed by the author.

be impossible to adjust the investment-savings gap to the larger trade gap through increased investment.

Assuming the authorities are capable of raising the external funds equal to the external gap, they could neglect the gap disparity altogether and rely entirely on autonomous economic adjustment, that is, an adjustment through free market forces. However, then another type of problem might develop. If prices are inflexible, or if the current rigid inflationary trend persisted, undesired inventories could accumulate. This in turn would reduce economic activity and produce an excess of existing capacity, or a reduced impetus to invest. Given the decline in private investment forecast (from 220.2 billion pesos in 1981 to 161.2 in 1982) (table 14.6), the added inventory accumulation would only contribute to the private sector's adjustment difficulties. While a further decline in private investment would most likely reduce the foreign resource requirements, the long-run economic development and growth of the country would be bound to suffer.

Even if prices were perfectly flexible, or if prevailing inflationary trends could respond readily to deficiencies of effective demand, the deflationary environment implied by the ex ante savings-investment gap being less than the exports-imports gap could affect entrepreneurs' confidence and expectations. Without policy interference, this could lead again to a reduced investment effort and subsequent decline in the overall rate of growth.

From the monetary ramifications (table 14.7) of the four programs (program IV is identical to I), it is clear that program II (constant government deficit) would be too extreme, with actual declines in a number of the major credit and monetary items. Even program III, selected as optimal on the basis of the trends in real expenditure items, would be severe. This program permitted only a 10.5 percent increase in the money supply, together with a slight fall in real private sector credit.[13]

Implications for Policy

The above results point out that the imbalance between domestic resources supplied and demanded stems primarily from the public sector. Limits or pseudo-market forces must therefore be introduced via a centralized planning framework, to ensure that the independent decisions of public sector agencies do not culminate in excessive levels of domestic absorption, particularly with regard to consumption.

Current expenditures should be monitored not only because of absorption difficulties but also because they strain markets for skilled labor. A detailed domestic-foreign breakdown of public expenditures and revenues would be a valuable planning tool. It would also indicate the slackening of domestic revenue-raising efforts. Some flexibility is vital in plan formulation. Obviously, as in 1976–77, it will be necessary to curb the demand of public agencies for foreign loans.

It may be more feasible to raise the efficiency of much of the country's existing infrastructure rather than to embark on grandiose (however tempting) projects that absorb domestic resources. Old ports could run more efficiently (perhaps with new imported equipment and expertise), and old roads could be upgraded. The payoff for policies of improved efficiency is exceptionally large for oil exporters, since foreign resources complementary to domestic ones should abound once the current oil glut has passed.[14]

Given the initial drop in private investment projected in all of the stabilization programs, a considerable effort needs to be made to channel resources toward private sector agriculture and manufacturing (assuming that the roas ahead does not lead to a state-owned economy).[15] This is no easy task, especially given the nationalized banking system and general lack of confidence in the peso.

Furthermore, the tradeoffs involved in helping one or the other sector should be recognized. Limiting cheap food imports may protect agriculture, but it fosters increased domestic wage demands that make it harder for Mexican industries to compete with imports.

The optimal control analysis does not deal with one major concern, the undesirably large migration within the country stemming from a combination of rural neglect and accelerated urban spending. This, together with equity considerations, argues for substantial real revenues to be spent in the rural sector and for the maintenance of adequate producer prices. Rural spending should cover infrastructure, technical assistance, and perhaps promotion of nonfarm industry. Inadequate organization may limit the expansion rate of rural spending. The unused rural allocation should then be saved or used to retire the government's outstanding external debt rather than being diverted to uses that will harm the rural sector through inducing real appreciation of the exchange rate.

Appropriate industrial policy for Mexico—a topic hotly debated within the country—should be formulated with the country's medium-term comparative advantage in mind.[16] This study argues against indiscriminate protection of domestic industry but also against a noninterventionist free trade policy. The prime need seems to be to foster the acquisition of industrial management and technical and organizational skills. Even the remarkable Far Eastern examples suggest that this is a slow process.

A suitable strategy might be to pick a range of strategic industries and provide them with incentives—production subsidies, training grants, tariff protection, and export subsidies—fairly uniformly. Incentives should not discriminate strongly in favor of capital or of domestic sales, although a limited bias toward import substitution may be necessary.

The Korean experience argues rather for export-focused incentives because of the technical benefits accruing from international competition.[17] Brazil, too, has forced exports from the private sector in exchange for government concessions. Incentives should also be conditional on steady improvements in total factor productivity toward internationally competitive levels, and possibly on limited

Table 14.6. Mexico: optimal control stabilization program III, 1982–87 (billions of 1975 pesos)

	Model simulation	Forecasted values						Average annual rate of growth
	1981	1982	1983	1984	1985	1986	1987	1981–87
Private consumption (ex ante)	1,009.6	1,135.0	1,103.6	1,150.5	1,241.5	1,330.6	1,437.7	6.1
Private consumption (ex post)	1,013.0	1,135.0	1,097.5	1,149.5	1,237.2	1,325.9	1,427.4	5.9
Government consumption	182.7	211.1	200.6	201.7	208.9	214.8	213.3	2.6
Total consumption (ex ante)	1,192.3	1,346.1	1,304.2	1,352.2	1,450.4	1,545.4	1,651.0	5.6
Total consumption (ex post)	1,195.7	1,346.1	1,298.1	1,351.2	1,446.1	1,540.7	1,640.7	5.4
Private savings	354.7	365.7	321.8	367.5	396.9	433.6	463.4	4.6
Private investment	220.2	161.2	194.1	211.9	236.2	259.3	285.1	4.4
Government investment	190.3	205.1	220.5	238.4	256.9	277.4	298.9	7.8
Change in stocks	45.0	50.2	49.4	51.9	56.4	60.8	65.5	6.5
Total investment	455.4	416.6	464.0	502.3	549.6	597.5	649.5	6.1
Exports	206.9	273.3	282.3	291.7	301.6	312.0	323.0	7.7
Net factor payments	−49.3	−67.4	−69.8	−72.3	−74.9	−77.8	−80.8	8.6
Imports (ex ante)	−213.2	−220.3	−248.4	−271.2	−288.8	−308.2	−328.4	7.5
Imports (ex post)	−213.2	−214.2	−248.4	−271.2	−288.8	−308.2	−328.4	7.5
Gross domestic product (supply)	1,644.8	1,821.7	1,795.9	1,874.0	2,008.0	2,142.0	2,284.7	5.6
Gross domestic product (demand)	1,641.4	1,815.6	1,802.0	1,875.0	2,012.8	2,146.8	2,295.0	5.7
Supply-demand gap	3.4	6.1	−6.1	−1.0	−4.2	−4.8	−10.3	—
Gross domestic product (ex post)	1,644.8	1,821.7	1,795.9	1,874.0	2,008.6	2,142.0	2,284.7	5.6

Gross national product	1,595.4	1,754.3	1,726.1	1,801.7	1,933.6	2,064.2	2,203.9	5.5
Total savings	403.2	408.3	422.0	449.4	483.1	518.8	552.9	5.4
Domestic gap (ex ante)	−52.2	−8.3	−42.0	−52.9	−66.5	−78.7	−96.5	10.8
External gap (ex ante)	−55.6	−14.4	−35.9	−51.9	−62.2	−74.0	−86.2	7.6
Gap difference	−3.4	−6.1	6.1	1.0	4.3	4.7	10.3	—
Domestic = external gap (ex post)	−55.6	−8.3	−35.9	−51.9	−62.2	−74.0	−86.2	−7.6
Government deficit	−203.4	−192.6	−209.6	−227.2	−242.8	−260.0	−269.3	4.8
GDP deflator	3.57	4.21	4.89	5.58	6.25	6.88	7.30	12.7
Rate of inflation	26.7	17.9	16.2	14.1	12.0	10.1	6.1	—

Source: Computed by the author.

Table 14.7. Mexico: optimal control simulations, monetary component, 1981–87

	Actual values		Model simulation	Forecasted values 1987			Actual	Average annual growth model, 1981–87		
				Model						
	1975	1981	1981	I and IV	II	III	1975–81	I and IV	II	III
(billions of current pesos)										
Bank of Mexico										
Credit to government	127.5	850.7	850.7	2,540.2	940.8	1,669.6	37.2	20.0	1.7	11.9
Reserve money	140.8	1,045.0	1,049.8	3,722.0	1,131.9	2,005.1	39.7	23.5	1.3	11.4
Domestic assets	120.7	912.5	917.4	3,344.4	993.3	1,763.6	40.1	24.1	1.3	11.5
Monetary system										
Private credit	53.0	1,079.4	1,069.4	5,161.8	1,148.4	2,044.7	65.3	30.0	1.2	11.4
Government credit	129.8	907.4	906.8	2,725.3	995.6	1,765.1	38.3	20.1	1.6	11.7
Government domestic borrowing	53.6	870.9	870.9	2,600.5	737.9	1,320.8	59.1	20.0	−2.7	7.2
Money supply (1975 = 100.0)	122.4	635.0	651.7	2,147.2	696.8	1,185.8	31.6	22.0	1.1	10.5
Gross domestic product deflator	1.00	3.57	3.57	10.38	5.10	7.30	23.6	19.5	6.1	12.7
Wholesale price index	100.0	367.0	369.0	985.0	449.1	628.5	24.2	17.8	3.3	9.3
Consumer price index	100.0	335.4	333.5	760.4	286.3	446.6	22.3	14.7	−2.5	5.0
(billions of 1975 pesos)										
Bank of Mexico										
Credit to government	127.5	238.4	238.4	244.8	184.6	228.7	11.0	0.4	−4.1	−0.7
Foreign assets	20.1	37.1	33.9	63.4	63.3	63.4	10.8	11.0	11.0	11.0
Domestic assets	120.7	255.7	257.0	322.4	194.9	241.6	13.3	3.8	−4.5	−1.0
Reserve money	140.8	292.8	294.2	358.8	222.1	274.7	13.0	3.4	−4.6	−1.1
Monetary system										
Government credit	129.8	254.3	254.1	262.7	195.3	241.8	11.9	0.6	−4.3	−0.8
Domestic credit	197.1	597.9	493.0	733.3	410.5	499.1	20.3	6.8	−3.0	0.8
Private credit	53.0	299.7	299.6	497.5	225.3	280.1	33.5	8.8	−4.6	−1.1

Source: Computed by the author.

increases in the average wage bill per employee in assisted industrial units. The Indonesian experience suggests that without such provisions government assistance might lead to highly dualistic industrial labor markets.[18]

At the beginning of the process, the selected industries might be fairly import-intensive, to reduce strain on domestic resources. The construction component of manufacturing investment is fortunately less than that of infrastructure. There may be little point in trying immediately to expand the domestic capital goods industry by restricting imports; natural barriers to building up domestic resources are surely challenging enough. Early attempts to move ahead rapidly without capital goods might prove to be counterproductive in the longer run.

Given most forecasts for world oil demand and prices, the government understandably decided to use its oil resources to transform the country rapidly into a major industrial power. The prospects were indeed dazzling. With the best collateral in the world, the Mexican government was able to secure however much it needed from the international banking system, both to bring its new oil resources to market and also to underwrite investments in ports, iron and steel complexes, and petrochemicals on a grand scale. From 1978–81 with annual growth rates in excess of 8 percent, the country was enjoying the world's most rapid progress matched only by the handful of newly industrialized countries in southeast Asia.

Yet one year after the peak in oil revenues (1981), Mexico faced the imperative of raising $500 million every seven days, week in and week out. Mexico has leaped into the lead as the world's largest borrower. With zero growth and inflation around 70 percent, it will take some time before stability can be restored.

In a speech on 6 October 1982, President López Portillo predicted: "I estimate that in one or two years the equilibrium will have been restored, unless the international situation definitely deteriorates. This is the problem that I hope, I assure you, will be transitory because recovery, given the country's vitality, is assured."[19] The analysis in this chapter tends to confirm this belief, although in somewhat less optimistic terms than the president's.

15. Optimal IMF-Type Stabilization Programs during the de la Madrid Presidency, 1983–87

On 10 November 1982, the Mexican government announced it had reached a long-awaited agreement with the International Monetary Fund on an austerity program aimed at easing the crisis caused by the nation's huge foreign debt. Under the agreement, Mexico may receive $3.84 billion worth of credit from the IMF over the next three years, but the government must drastically reduce its deficit, raise taxes, and curb imports to qualify for the funds.[1]

The main purpose of the analysis below is to examine the feasibility and ramifications of various IMF-type stabilization programs on the Mexican economy during the de la Madrid presidency (1982–87).

Since economic policy enacted in Mexico has a variety of objectives, it seems useful for the purposes of this study to distinguish different levels for the systematic evaluation of the stabilization policies and of their impact on inflation and economic growth. This chapter will explore four such levels. On the basis of several optimal control macroeconomic simulations of the economy, an attempt will be made first to evaluate the IMF program in accordance with its own internal logic. This analysis centers on the relative efficiency of stabilizing instruments and especially of government deficit control.

Second, the policies will be evaluated according to the degree of consistency between the instruments used and the economic situation to which they are applied. This will produce an assessment of the technical consistency of the policy package for Mexico. In particular, the analysis will examine the ability of the IMF's policies to adjust to the economy's underlying economic trends in a manner consistent with the attainment of the highest rate of growth feasible during the period under consideration.

Third, the relationship of the stabilization policies to the country's external borrowing requirements will be explored, with reference both to the trend in required capital inflows and the changing level of borrowing consistent with optimal growth. The stabilization policies may bring about structural change and as a result cause conflicts that show the austerity measures to be too harsh, causing a loss in employment-generating expenditures.

Fourth, we shall consider the relationship between the instruments used in the stabilization process and the objective of bringing about a rapid redistribution of economic surplus toward the private capitalist sector. In this context we will evaluate the trade-off between economic stabilization, growth, and capital formation.

The IMF Letter of Intent

The "letter of intent" represents only the first step in a lengthy negotiating process to arrive at a final IMF loan package. It outlined a proposed three-year economic adjustment program for Mexico. In late August 1982, access to $1 billion of a $1.85 billion emergency credit was granted by the Bank for International Settlements conditional upon Mexico's reaching an agreement with the IMF. Mexican officials had also agreed not to request a new moratorium on principal payments or seek new credits from commercial banks until the fund had approved the austerity program.

The proposed program focuses on the projected size of Mexico's public sector deficit, which in 1982 was approximately the equivalent of 16.5 percent of the country's gross national product, the highest ratio in the country's history. Mexican officials had hoped that the fund would accept a 10 percent deficit in 1983, but the fund's preference for stronger austerity measures apparently prevailed. The letter of intent promises deficits of 8.5 percent in 1983, 5.5 percent in 1984, and only 3.5 in 1985, all of which imply a sharp cut in public expenditures.

Mexico's only other specific commitment was that its public sector debt, which stood at about $60 billion, should not increase by more than $5 billion in 1983, including the first $1.28 billion received from the IMF credit. Although Mexico expected to earn $15 billion from oil exports in 1983, much of this revenue would be on interest payments, with the result that tight import controls would be maintained.

Mexico was able to resist policies that would use a deep recession as a corrective measure. The IMF accepted many of Mexico's proposals concerning wages, interest rates, and exchange rates. More specifically, the government successfully defended its exchange controls, including its current three-tier exchange rate, and did not agree to raise domestic interest rates, all of which policies the fund sought to change. Instead, the government promised only to maintain an exchange rate to stimulate exports and discourage both imports and the flight of capital.

Because of widespread opposition to an IMF agreement from labor and political parties, the letter of intent sought to reassure the public that the austerity program would be guided "by a criterion of social equity and protection of lesser income groups" and would include wage increases "to protect the standard of living of the working class." Nevertheless, the document specified price increases for public service, new direct and indirect taxes, and the reduction of many of the huge subsidies that have swollen budget deficits in recent years. Upon signing the agreement, the Secretary of Finance and Public Credit noted that the country's economy, which expanded by 8.5 percent in 1981, would grow only by 1 percent in 1982. He suggested that a contraction in 1983 was unavoidable.

To determine whether a program as suggested by the IMF letter would work in Mexico without serious and immediate contraction of the economy in the near term, several simulations of the economy were performed using the model and optimal control procedure developed in chapters 13 and 14 above.

Analysis of the 1981–87 Period

For optimal control analysis of the 1981–87 period, the model's exogenous variables were set at the following rates (largely reflective of historical movements):

1. the exchange rate (*EXC*), 70 pesos per dollar—more or less the average rate as of October 1982;
2. crude petroleum production index (*CPP*), 6 percent—down from the rate achieved in the 1978–80 period, reflecting the worldwide oil glut;
3. crude petroleum exports (*PETE*), 6 percent—again down from the 1978–81 period, reflecting the oil glut;
4. real U.S. gross domestic product (*USYP*), 2.5 percent;
5. the U.S. consumer price index (*USCPI*), 6 percent—reflecting U.S. monetary policies and governmental priorities.

Optimal Control Simulations

A series of optimal control simulations of the economy were performed to determine the sensitivity of the economy to alternative stabilization packages. In all cases, the exogenous variables were assumed to take the values noted above.

Non-IMF "Mild" Stabilization Program

The initial run (table 15.1) represents a non-IMF simulation, in that government deficits are not reduced in accordance with those specified in the letter of intent. The only objective specified is the maximization of real GDP by 1987, consistent with a gradual reduction of inflation to 20 percent per annum by that year. This program probably depicts the mildest stabilization program open to the government. In addition to the values for the exogenous variables specified above, government internal borrowing (*GFI*) was set at a 20 percent average annual rate of increase, as was Bank of Mexico credit to the government (*BMGC*). Private sector credit from the banking system (*MSPC*) was allowed to increase at 30 percent per annum. Real government investment (the design variable) was largely unconstrained.

The results (table 15.1) show largely a continuation of past growth rates, with real gross domestic product increasing at an annual average rate of 5.9 percent. The rates of inflation quickly came down to the 20 percent range, the first indication that the government would with a little effort be even more successful in this area.

On the other hand, both the internal and external gap increase rapidly (14.3 and 7.1 percent annually, respectively). Even if the government were successful in equalizing the gaps through reducing private consumption, it is likely that the projected size of the export gap (eventually reaching 84.1 billion pesos in 1987) could be covered by foreign capital inflows in light of the country's existing debt. Without a stricter stabilization effort, the likely outcome of this strategy would be a considerable reduction in the growth rate of all major aggregates.

The IMF Stabilization Program I

The IMF Stabilization Program I represents a fairly severe stabilization effort. Government internal borrowing and Bank of Mexico credit to the government and private sector from the monetary system are all set at a 5 percent average annual increase for the 1982–87 period. The major constraint is that outlined by the November 1982 letter of agreement: government deficits as a percentage of GNP are fixed at 8.5 percent, 5.5 percent, and 3.5 percent for 1983, 1984, and 1985–87, respectively. Inflation is set at 10 percent or less for 1987. Given these constraints, government investment is designed to maximize the level of real gross domestic product in 1987.

The results (table 15.2) generally indicate that a program along these lines would give a severe shock to the economy. In particular, GDP would expand at an average annual growth rate of only 2.3 percent, real private investment at 4.6 percent, total national savings would contract at 3.9 percent, and total investment would decline at 3.0 percent. If the domestic gap is brought into line with the external gap through programs reducing private consumption, Mexico quickly becomes a capital exporter (1.2 billion pesos by 1984). In light of this, such a program would impose a severe burden on the economy and would be overkill as a means of bringing the country's resource gaps into a range where external financing considerations posed no particular constraints.

The IMF Stabilization Program II

The IMF Stabilization Program II attempts to determine the extent to which the government deficit/GNP ratio could be reduced, given the constraint that inflation reach 10 percent by 1987 and that Mexico achieve a positive rate of GDP growth each year during the 1982–87 period. All other assumptions are as in IMF program II.

The results (table 15.3) indicate that it is impossible to reduce the government deficit/GDP ratio below 7.5 percent in 1987, and that while it is an improvement over the current ratio, it is still a long way from the targets set by the IMF. In the simulation, the ex ante domestic gap increases at an annual rate of 8.3 percent, requiring a fairly significant reduction in private consumption in order to equate it ex post with the (smaller) external resource gap.

Table 15.1. Mexico: non-IMF stabilization effort (optimal solution), 1982–87 (billions of 1975 pesos)

	1981	1982	1983	1984	1985	1986	1987	Average annual rate of growth 1981–87
Private consumption (ex ante)	—	1,161.1	1,126.7	1,190.4	1,283.9	1,375.0	1,476.7	—
Private consumption (ex post)	1,009.6	1,166.2	1,117.7	1,181.2	1,272.3	1,360.5	1,444.4	6.2
Government consumption	182.7	210.5	204.8	206.5	211.8	217.6	226.1	3.6
Total consumption (ex ante)	—	1,376.6	1,331.5	1,396.9	1,495.7	1,590.6	1,702.8	—
Total consumption (ex post)	1,192.3	1,376.7	1,322.5	1,387.7	1,484.1	1,578.1	1,670.5	5.8
Private savings	354.7	372.5	357.8	399.4	429.5	464.5	486.3	5.4
Private investment	220.2	186.8	2,187.2	2,387.6	2,614.6	2,846.0	310.0	5.9
Government investment	190.3	205.1	221.6	238.3	256.9	277.1	283.9	6.9
Change in stocks	45.0	51.3	50.4	53.6	58.0	62.4	66.7	4.5
Total investment	455.4	443.2	490.7	530.6	576.3	624.1	660.7	6.4
Exports	206.9	253.9	262.8	272.2	282.2	292.6	303.6	6.6
Net factor payments	−49.3	−62.1	−64.5	−67.1	−69.9	−72.6	−75.5	7.4
Imports (ex ante)	−213.2	−220.3	−247.8	−267.6	−285.3	−304.4	−312.1	6.6
Imports (ex post)	−213.2	−220.3	−247.8	−267.6	−285.3	−304.4	−312.1	6.6

Gross domestic product (supply)	1,644.8	1,853.6	1,828.2	1,923.1	2,057.4	2,190.5	2,322.6	5.9
Gross domestic product (demand)	1,641.4	1,853.4	1,837.2	1,932.2	2,069.0	2,203.0	2,355.0	6.2
Supply-demand gap	3.4	0.2	−9.0	−9.1	−11.6	−12.5	−32.4	—
Gross domestic product (ex post)	1,641.4	1,853.6	1,828.2	1,923.1	2,057.4	2,190.5	2,322.6	5.9
Gross national product	1,595.4	1,791.5	1,763.6	1,856.0	1,987.6	2,117.9	2,247.1	5.9
Total savings	403.2	414.0	432.2	459.0	491.3	527.3	544.3	5.1
Domestic gap (ex ante)	−52.2	−28.4	−58.5	−71.6	−84.4	−96.9	−116.4	14.3
External gap (ex ante)	−55.6	−28.5	−49.5	−62.4	−72.8	−84.4	−84.1	7.1
Gap difference	−3.4	−0.1	9.0	9.2	11.6	12.5	32.3	—
Domestic = external gap (ex post)	−52.2	−28.4	−49.5	−62.4	−72.8	−84.4	−84.1	8.3
Government current revenue	169.5	214.3	202.4	207.2	217.3	226.9	243.0	6.2
Government deficit	−203.4	−201.4	−223.9	−237.7	−251.3	−267.9	−267.0	4.6
Government deficit/GNP	12.75	11.24	12.70	12.81	12.64	12.65	11.50	−1.7
Rate of inflation	—	19.8	21.4	19.9	18.4	17.6	17.4	—

Source: Computed by the author.
Note: See text for model and forecast assumptions.

Table 15.2. Mexico: IMF stabilization program I (optimal solution), 1981–87 (billions of 1975 pesos)

	1981	1982	1983	1984	1985	1986	1987	Average annual rate of growth 1981–87
Private consumption (ex ante)	—	1,049.2	1,195.4	1,259.4	1,306.7	1,305.1	1,328.6	4.7
Private consumption (ex post)	1,009.6	1,035.4	1,126.5	1,251.3	1,214.7	1,224.5	1,244.4	3.5
Government consumption	182.7	191.7	177.3	164.1	154.9	157.1	160.9	−2.1
Total consumption (ex ante)	—	1,240.9	1,372.7	1,423.5	1,461.6	1,462.2	1,489.5	3.8
Total consumption (ex post)	1,192.3	1,227.1	1,303.8	1,415.4	1,369.6	1,381.6	1,405.3	2.8
Private savings	354.7	367.2	293.6	286.5	238.7	223.3	209.5	−8.4
Private investment	220.2	186.8	215.8	194.3	178.4	163.1	166.2	−4.1
Government investment	190.3	202.7	182.4	164.3	152.0	154.9	159.9	−2.9
Change in stocks	44.9	46.1	49.5	50.2	50.7	50.9	52.2	2.5
Total investment	455.4	435.7	447.8	408.8	381.1	369.0	378.3	−3.0
Exports	206.9	253.9	262.8	272.2	282.2	292.6	303.6	6.6
Net factor payments	−49.3	−62.1	−64.5	−67.1	−69.8	−72.6	−75.5	7.4
Imports (ex ante)	−213.2	−218.2	−214.2	−204.0	−195.1	−199.3	−205.5	−0.6
Imports (ex post)	−213.2	−218.2	−214.2	−204.0	−195.1	−199.3	−205.5	−0.6

Gross domestic product (supply)	1,644.8	1,698.5	1,800.2	1,820.5	1,837.9	1,844.0	1,882.0	2.3
Gross domestic product (demand)	1,641.4	1,712.2	1,869.1	1,900.6	1,929.9	1,924.6	1,966.0	3.1
Supply-demand gap	3.4	−13.7	−68.9	−80.1	−92.0	−80.6	−84.0	—
Gross domestic product (ex post)	1,644.8	1,698.5	1,800.2	1,820.5	1,837.9	1,844.0	1,882.0	2.3
Gross national product	1,595.4	1,636.4	1,735.7	1,753.4	1,768.2	1,771.4	1,806.4	2.1
Total savings	403.1	395.5	363.0	329.9	306.6	309.2	316.9	−3.9
Domestic gap (ex ante)	−52.2	−40.2	−84.8	−78.9	−74.6	−59.9	−61.5	2.8
External gap (ex ante)	−55.6	−26.4	−15.9	1.2	17.4	20.7	22.7	—
Gap difference	−3.4	13.8	68.9	80.1	92.0	80.6	84.2	—
Domestic = external gap (ex post)	−52.2	−26.4	−15.9	1.2	17.4	20.7	22.7	
Government current revenue	169.5	200.0	218.1	231.9	245.0	250.0	257.6	7.2
Government deficit	−203.4	−194.5	−141.6	−96.5	−61.9	−62.0	−63.2	−17.7
Government deficit/GNP	12.75	11.89	8.16	5.55	3.50	3.50	3.50	−19.4
Rate of inflation	—	17.5	11.6	9.4	8.0	7.1	6.0	—

Source: Computed by the author.
Note: See text for model and forecast assumptions.

Table 15.3. Mexico: IMF stabilization program II (optimal solution), 1982–87 (billions of 1975 pesos)

	1981	1982	1983	1984	1985	1986	1987	Average annual rate of growth 1981–87
Private consumption (ex ante)	—	1,133.9	1,155.8	1,197.7	1,206.3	1,337.7	1,401.7	5.6
Private consumption (ex post)	1,009.6	1,108.6	1,121.7	1,161.2	1,161.5	1,279.4	1,337.1	4.8
Government consumption	182.7	185.7	188.7	191.3	194.4	194.5	196.3	1.2
Total consumption (ex ante)	—	1,319.6	1,344.5	1,389.0	1,400.7	1,532.2	1,598.0	5.0
Total consumption (ex post)	1,192.3	1,293.7	1,310.4	1,352.5	1,355.9	1,473.9	1,533.4	4.3
Private savings	354.7	347.7	320.0	339.0	341.7	339.8	339.6	−0.7
Private investment	220.2	186.8	205.6	212.0	220.4	226.9	228.9	0.7
Government investment	190.3	194.4	197.9	203.3	206.6	206.9	209.2	1.6
Change in stocks	44.9	48.4	49.4	51.3	54.0	56.5	58.9	4.6
Total investment	455.3	430.0	453.0	465.6	481.1	490.3	497.7	1.5
Exports	206.9	253.8	262.8	272.7	282.2	292.6	303.6	6.6
Net factor payments	-49.3	−62.1	−64.5	−67.1	−69.8	−72.6	−75.5	7.4
Imports (ex ante)	−213.2	−211.0	−227.5	−236.7	−242.1	−243.9	−247.9	2.5
Imports (ex post)	−213.2	−211.0	−227.5	−236.7	−242.1	−243.9	−247.9	2.5

Gross domestic product (supply)	1,644.8	1,766.1	1,798.3	1,853.7	1,937.3	2,012.8	2,086.3	4.0
Gross domestic product (demand)	1,641.4	1,792.0	1,832.4	1,890.3	1,982.1	2,071.2	2,150.9	4.6
Supply-demand gap	3.1	−25.9	−34.1	−36.6	−44.8	−58.4	−64.6	—
Gross domestic product (ex post)	1,644.5	1,766.1	1,798.3	1,853.7	1,937.3	2,012.8	2,086.3	4.0
Gross national product	1,595.4	1,704.0	1,733.8	1,786.6	1,867.5	1,940.2	2,010.8	3.9
Total savings	403.2	384.4	389.7	397.6	406.6	407.9	412.8	0.4
Domestic gap (ex ante)	169.5	210.6	210.6	217.2	229.1	242.4	254.7	7.0
External gap (ex ante)	−52.2	−45.2	−63.3	−68.0	−74.4	−82.2	−84.4	8.3
Gap difference	−55.6	−19.3	−29.3	−31.5	−29.6	−23.9	−19.8	−15.8
Domestic = external gap (ex post)	−3.4	25.9	34.1	36.5	44.8	58.3	64.6	—
Government current revenue	52.2	−19.3	−29.2	−31.5	−29.6	−23.9	−19.8	−15.8
Government deficit	−203.4	−169.4	−175.5	−176.4	−179.5	−159.0	−150.8	−4.9
Government deficit/GNP	12.75	9.94	10.12	9.52	9.20	9.64	7.50	−8.5
Rate of inflation	—	16.8	12.0	9.1	6.8	5.3	4.3	8.8

Source: Computed by the author.
Note: See text for model and forecast assumptions.

Table 15.4. Mexico: IMF stabilization program III (optimal solution), 1981–87 (billions of 1975 pesos)

	1981	1982	1983	1984	1985	1986	1987	Average annual rate of growth 1981–87
Private consumption (ex ante)	—	1,149.8	1,178.7	1,181.1	1,221.6	1,276.9	1,398.0	5.6
Private consumption (ex post)	1,009.6	1,119.0	1,124.5	1,150.7	1,200.7	1,259.2	1,337.7	4.8
Government consumption	182.7	183.4	178.0	188.8	199.7	210.3	202.7	1.8
Total consumption (ex ante)	—	1,333.2	1,356.7	1,369.9	1,421.3	1,487.2	1,600.7	5.0
Total consumption (ex post)	1,192.3	1,302.4	1,302.5	1,339.5	1,400.4	1,469.5	1,540.4	4.4
Private savings	354.7	349.7	274.9	262.9	238.4	250.5	225.5	−7.3
Private investment	220.2	186.8	202.8	193.3	207.8	221.3	239.1	1.4
Government investment	190.3	191.2	183.7	198.6	213.9	229.0	218.0	2.3
Change in stocks	45.0	48.7	49.0	50.4	53.1	56.3	59.6	4.8
Total investment	455.4	426.7	435.6	442.2	474.8	506.6	516.6	2.1
Exports	206.9	253.9	262.8	272.3	282.2	292.6	303.6	6.6
Net factor payments	−49.3	−62.1	−64.5	−67.1	−69.8	−72.6	−75.6	7.4
Imports (ex ante)	—	−208.3	−215.3	−233.5	−248.3	−263.0	−255.4	3.1
Imports (ex post)	−213.2	−208.3	−215.3	−233.5	−248.3	−263.0	−255.4	3.1

Gross domestic product (supply)	1,644.8	1,774.6	1,785.6	1,826.8	1,909.0	2,005.7	2,105.2	4.2
Gross domestic product (demand)	1,641.4	1,805.4	1,839.8	1,850.9	1,930.0	2,023.3	2,165.5	4.7
Supply-demand gap	3.40	−30.8	−54.2	−24.0	−21.0	−17.6	−60.3	—
Gross domestic product (ex post)	1,644.8	1,774.6	1,785.6	1,826.8	1,909.0	2,005.7	2,105.2	4.2
Gross national product	1,595.4	1,712.5	1,721.0	1,759.7	1,839.2	1,933.1	2,029.7	4.1
Total savings	403.2	397.3	364.4	389.8	417.9	445.9	429.0	1.0
Domestic gap (ex ante)	−52.2	−47.4	−71.2	−52.4	−56.8	−60.6	−87.6	9.0
External gap (ex ante)	−55.6	−16.6	−17.0	−28.3	−35.9	−42.9	−27.3	−11.2
Gap difference	−3.4	30.8	54.2	24.1	20.9	17.7	60.3	—
Domestic = external gap (ex post)	−52.2	−16.6	−17.0	−28.3	−35.9	−42.9	−27.3	−11.2
Government current revenue	169.5	203.3	244.1	305.1	350.8	378.9	409.2	15.8
Government deficit	−203.4	−171.2	−117.6	−82.3	−62.8	−60.3	−11.5	−38.0
Government deficit/GNP	12.75	9.81	6.59	4.51	3.29	3.01	0.57	−40.4
Rate of inflation	—	15.8	12.3	11.0	7.1	5.2	3.9	—

Source: Computed by the author.
Note: See text for model and forecast assumptions.

Table 15.5. Mexico: IMF stabilization program IIIA (optimal solution), 1981–87 (billions of 1975 pesos)

	1981	1982	1983	1984	1985	1986	1987	Average annual rate of growth 1981–87
Private consumption (ex ante)	—	1,154.7	1,158.8	1,176.5	1,242.9	1,291.6	1,385.1	—
Private consumption (ex post)	1,009.6	1,123.0	1,121.8	1,155.9	1,214.8	1,276.9	1,343.5	3.2
Government consumption	182.7	182.9	185.4	195.2	200.6	212.6	212.7	2.6
Total consumption (ex ante)	—	1,337.0	1,344.2	1,371.7	1,443.5	1,504.2	1,597.8	—
Total consumption (ex post)	1,192.3	1,305.9	1,307.2	1,351.1	1,415.4	1,489.5	1,556.2	4.5
Private savings	354.7	348.2	288.7	274.3	251.3	264.6	247.0	−5.9
Private investment	220.2	186.8	202.2	204.6	217.7	224.3	244.0	1.7
Government investment	190.3	190.6	194.0	207.7	215.5	232.5	232.7	3.4
Change in stocks	45.0	48.7	49.2	51.0	54.0	57.1	60.3	5.0
Total investment	455.4	426.2	445.4	463.3	487.1	513.8	537.1	2.8
Exports	206.9	253.9	262.8	272.3	282.2	292.6	303.6	6.6
Net factor payments	−49.3	−62.1	−64.5	−67.0	−70.0	−72.5	−75.5	7.4
Imports (ex ante)	−213.1	−207.8	−224.1	−241.3	−250.0	−265.9	−268.0	3.9
Imports (ex post)	−213.1	−207.8	−221.1	−241.3	−250.0	−265.9	−268.0	3.9

Gross domestic product (supply)	1,644.8	1,778.3	1,791.3	1,845.4	1,935.2	2,029.9	2,128.9	4.4
Gross domestic product (demand)	1,641.4	1,810.0	1,828.3	1,866.0	1,963.3	2,044.6	2,170.5	4.8
Supply-demand gap	3.4	−31.7	−37.0	−20.6	−28.1	−14.7	−41.6	—
Gross domestic product (ex post)	1,641.4	1,778.3	1,791.3	1,845.4	1,935.2	2,029.9	2,128.9	4.4
Gross national product	1,595.4	1,716.2	1,726.7	1,718.3	1,865.4	1,957.3	2,053.4	4.3
Total savings	403.2	378.5	382.6	406.5	421.8	453.2	455.5	2.1
Domestic gap (ex ante)	−52.2	−47.7	−62.8	−56.7	−65.4	−60.6	−81.6	7.7
External gap (ex ante)	−55.6	−16.0	−25.8	−36.1	−37.2	−45.9	−40.0	−5.3
Gap difference	−3.4	31.0	37.0	20.6	28.2	14.7	41.6	—
Domestic = external gap (ex post)	−52.2	−16.0	−25.8	−36.1	−37.2	−45.9	−40.0	−4.3
Government current revenue	169.5	203.3	244.0	305.1	350.8	378.9	409.2	15.8
Government deficit	−203.4	−170.2	−135.3	−98.0	−65.3	−66.1	−36.2	−25.0
Government deficit/GNP	12.75	9.92	7.8	5.5	3.5	3.4	1.8	−27.8
Rate of inflation	—	15.7	12.2	9.3	6.8	5.1	3.8	

Source: Computed by the author.
Note: See text for model and forecast assumptions.

If the necessary reduction in consumption could be achieved, Mexico's external financing requests stabilize at between 19.3 and 31.5 billion pesos, compared to 52.2 billion in 1981. These levels of capital inflow seem within the country's reach and indicate perhaps that the IMF targets for the government's deficit may be too stringent and costly in terms of foregone increases in real output. Real GNP is projected to grow at 4.0 percent annually, with private investment growing at nearly 1 percent per annum by 1987 (compared to a 2.3 percent increase in GDP and −4.1 percent decline in private investment under IMF Program I).

Given the insistence of the IMF on an extreme reduction in the size of the deficit, however, IMF Program II may not be a viable compromise between the non-IMF program outlined above and IMF Program I.

The IMF Stabilization Program III

One way for the government to reduce the burden of the IMF government deficit targets would be to undertake a major tax reform, so that all of the deficit adjustment would not be placed on expenditures and thus demand. While the government has made significant strides in recent years to increase nonoil revenues, most authorities acknowledge that considerable scope for fiscal reform still exists. Assuming that the authorities have the political will to reform the tax structure, government current revenues (*GTP*) were forecast to increase at an annual average rate of 15 percent over the 1982–87 period. The exogenous growth rates are as in IMF programs I and II, with real GDP maximized for 1987 (given the IMF government deficit/ratio yearly targets for 1983–87).

The results (table 15.4) indicate that government efforts would pay off very well in the tax area. Specifically, private investment expands at an annual average of 1.4 percent, real GDP grows at 4.2 percent, with overall investment expanding at 2.1 percent and inflation reduced to 3.9 percent by 1987. Importantly, the external gap declines at an annual rate of 11.2 percent, reaching 27.3 billion pesos by 1987. Furthermore, the program is consistent with increases in the standard of living as ex post private consumption expands at an average rate of 4.8 percent.

As a check on the sensitivity of the results to the choice of objective functions, IMF Stabilization Program III-A was run with the same assumptions as program III except that the terminal capital stock rather than real GDP was maximized in 1987. As the results show (table 15.5), it makes little difference to the success of this type of program whether real GDP or terminal capital stock are optimized.

Conclusions

In retrospect, the Mexican crisis of August 1982 was an old-fashioned financial panic dominated by a sharp shift in expectations.[2] It was facilitated by a convertible currency—a rarity among developing countries—and its dimensions went far beyond what the economic conditions justified. Indeed, with imports down by 25 percent in the first four months of 1982, and 1981 exports modestly higher, Mexico's external deficit promised to be smaller in 1982 than in 1981, running at perhaps $8 billion. The peso had been devalued, and austerity measures, although inadequate, were at least begun. Moreover, Mexico's crisis was a cash flow problem more than a fundamental economic problem—a case of illiquidity rather than insolvency. It remains to be seen whether Mexico and the world financial system will emerge from the episode relatively unscathed.

In any case, stabilization will require restricting government expenditure. This is particularly true for current (operating) expenditures. The optimal control analysis developed above clearly indicates that it is also extremely important to treat investment outlays with care. Substantial and indiscriminate reductions risk jeopardizing the longer-term growth of the economy. Thus, the government must ensure that investment projects are authorized according to a strict order of priority. Whatever form the stabilization program takes, the GDP growth rate in 1982 and 1983 should fall significantly below its recent trend. The recent wage increases and the higher cost (in local currency) of the external debt service will require a cutback in the investment expenditures of the public and private sectors. A slight recovery in exports and a reduction in imports are expected to lead to an improvement in the trade balance.

One of the characteristics of the Mexican tax system until quite recently was that tax collection had an almost unitary elasticity, so that tax revenues fluctuated only slightly above the nominal GDP. Recent reforms have attempted to increase the rate of tax collection more rapidly than the growth rate of the nominal national product, in order to strengthen the effect of taxes as an automatic stabilizer. Our analysis above indicates that the government's ability to increase tax revenues will ultimately determine to a large degree whether the period of stabilization will be painful and contractionary or simply austere, with a quick return to high growth assured.

16. The Policy-making Dilemma

Postdevaluation (1982) Mexican fiscal policy will require restricting government expenditure. This is particularly true for current (operating) expenditures. It is also extremely important to treat investment outlays with care. Substantial and indiscriminate reductions risk jeopardizing the longer-term growth of the economy. Thus, the government must ensure that investment projects are authorized according to a strict order of priority.

One of the characteristics of the Mexican tax system until quite recently was that tax collection had an almost unitary elasticity, so that tax revenues fluctuated only slightly above the nominal GDP. Recent reforms have attempted to increase the rate of tax collection more rapidly than the growth rate of the nominal national product, in order to strengthen its effect as an automatic stabilizer. This should give the authorities greater scope and ability to reduce inflationary pressures while providing funds to meet the priorities of the national budget.

Policy Options

Realistically, the quantitative forecasts presented in the previous chapter on the evolution of the Mexican economy in the near future are somewhat problematical. Accurate assessments concerning the country's medium-term prospects will be possible only after the new administration has a year or so to outline its modifications in the country's development strategy and when the confusion generated by the recent exchange rate adjustments is dissipated.

However, the Mexican economy will probably evolve along one of three possible courses in the coming years: variable inflation, with slow growth and fluctuations of the "stop-go" type; recession, with declining inflation and increasing unemployment; and moderate growth, with stable or perhaps even declining inflation.[1] The third alternative is obviously the government's choice, and one shown in the previous chapter to be feasible. The second course is more or less the current state of affairs and is the presumed result of a relatively strict International Monetary Fund–type program. This latter option can be rejected more or less out of hand as a likely outcome simply because experience has shown that more often than not this policy mix has led to strong social tensions that in time become uncontainable and produce drastic policy changes. The net result is often an unstable path such as the first alternative above (the "stop-go" type). In choosing voluntary deflation, countries apparently condemn themselves to inflation. In both cases, forces are unleashed that make it necessary to redirect economic policy and thus destabilize both the policy and its impacts. Interestingly, in Latin America at least, successive corrections generally occur within increasingly short periods of time and thus destabilize the economic indicators on which companies and investors must base decisions. Clearly, the problem becomes serious when changes of direction take place before the economic system adapts to the previously established set of conditions, making an unstable situation of the "stop-go" type increasingly likely.

The pattern Mexico seems to be following currently, but that the new administration must make every possible attempt to avoid, is one where credit and public expenditures rise, thus increasing the real demand pressure upon resources, accelerating the rate of price increases, and increasing the balance of payments deficit. The deficit in turn eventually forces reductions in credit and public expenditures, but only after the situation has degenerated so far that nothing less than extreme contractions in expenditure will reverse the process. This in turn reduces economic activity, and the process begins again in what seems to be a vicious cycle.

A series of conflicts are currently developing in Mexico over the foreign debt, wages and other domestic income, and in general over national purchasing power. All of these conflicts threaten to set off the self-perpetuating "stop-go" instability outlined above. Such conflicts may arise because the "stop-go" process is clearly operating by modifying the consumers' real income, altering the surpluses available for export, and reducing investment. In other words, current economic policies in Mexico are in real danger of undermining their own continuity. Obviously, unless reversed, the resulting instability will lower rates of private investment and decelerate any long-run potential real GDP growth.

Whatever shortcomings "stabilizing development" had as an economic policy in its heyday between 1955 and 1970, it was a coherent strategy, enabling the private sector to adapt to the prevailing conditions. This sector responded by undertaking long-term projects that probably would have been impossible in the presence of a "stop-go" instability.

The Mexican economic situation in 1982 approximated the second alternative above. Under such circumstances, it is urgently necessary to reduce any incompatibility between the balance of payments and the growth of real GDP. To achieve this, two associated conditions are necessary:[2] First, the peso must not be overvalued, especially for long periods of time. Second, the level of wages and other domestic incomes must not be separated from the conditions that prevail in the markets for labor, capital, and other factors of production. The previous chapter indicated that a new economic policy, to fulfill these conditions and establish a pattern of growth capable of overcoming the limitations of the 1971–81 period of stop-go inflationary growth, is quite feasible if the government has the political will to implement it.

Incompatibilities in Policy Objectives

Examination of Mexico's major economic objectives has revealed a number of additional potential incompatibilities.[3] In large part the apparent trade-offs inherent in the country's development generate the ongoing debate within Mexico on economic and social development in general and on trade in particular. Growth rates of 8 percent per year have shown a tendency to raise Mexican inflation significantly above the U.S. level, undermining both income distribution and manufacturing export goals (because of an increasingly overvalued peso). Mexico's inflation rate was around 30 percent in 1981 and exceeded 100 percent in 1982, due to the devaluation of the peso. Supply constraints, bottlenecks, and lack of monetary controls have thus closely linked high rates of growth to rapid increases in inflation.

Rapid growth has also hampered the development of a domestic capital goods industry. The overvaluation of the peso resulting from growth-induced inflation made imports of capital goods relatively attractive. Similarly, the inflationary and exchange rate effects of rapid growth significantly reduced the attractiveness of Mexican manufactured goods exports. Mexico thus begins to look like a mono-export economy.[4]

Even as late as early 1984, the trade-off among industry and agriculture implicit in the Global Development Plan (GDP), the National Industrial Development Plan (NIDP), and the Mexican Food System (SAM) had not yet become fully apparent.[5] The NIDP was drawn up without much emphasis on agriculture. On the other hand, SAM and the GDP did not fully integrate planning in all sectors when reemphasizing agriculture. It is clear upon a careful reading of the plans, however, that they combine the different views of several ministries without truly integrating these views into one general perspective.

One apparent trade-off between industry and agriculture in the NIDP is a gap in projected productivity between the two sectors, with agriculture lagging significantly behind industry. This discrepancy has been addressed to some extent by the subsequent publication of the GDP and the Mexican Food System (SAM) plans.

Both the GDP and SAM emphasize agriculture. Rates of growth 4 percent higher than that projected in the NIDP are now the official targets for the sector. Self-sufficiency in corn and beans by 1982 was a major target. An increase in agricultural investment over the period 1980–82, sufficient to bring the sector's allocation up to 22 percent of total public investment, became a major objective. Self-sufficiency in other basic foods by the end of the 1980s is also an explicit government objective. Finally, significant reforms in food prices, credit, packaging, transportation, and tractor production are anticipated.

The resolution of priorities and the means best suited to attain the country's development objectives will sooner or later force the government to define more clearly its view of the future structure of Mexican society, the country's relationship with the United States, and its role in the international economic system.[6] Mexico may opt for a model of independent nationalist development, or for one of full integration into the international economic system.

The nationalist/internationalist debate stems directly from the general ideological tendencies and divisions of the Mexican political system.[7] In very general terms, Mexican nationalists tend to emphasize petroleum conservation, diversification of markets away from the United States, continued use of nontariff protection methods (anti-GATT), development of basic foods rather than export agriculture, a relatively large government role in the economy, and heavy expenditure on social programs. In sharp contrast, Mexican internationalists tend to stress high levels of petroleum production, expansion rather than diversification of markets, closer relationships with the United States, opening of the economy more rapidly to import competition as the best way of developing competitive industries (pro-GATT), encouraging comparative advantage forces in agriculture, reliance on the private sector for continued growth, and trickle-down theories of income distribution. The internationalist position is a composite of views. The complete set of policies outlined above is not advocated by any one person or group but is rather the general attitude of many leading technocrats in the government. In practice, policy as of 1984 combined these two themes, but leaned somewhat toward the nationalist side.

Final Observations

Under the best of circumstances, it will take several years for the Mexican economy to get on track again. Private investment will most likely fall below its 1981 level for several years, with possibly even larger declines in the living standards of wide segments of the population. Also, under the best of circumstances, it would be difficult for a president in the Mexican political system to endure the costs of keeping harsh economic policies in force for several years in a row. Clearly, keeping up such policies is much more difficult when these unpopular reforms are being resisted by influential groups from within and demanded from abroad by unpopular foreign powers (the IMF).

Mexico would do well to achieve even zero real growth in 1984. While Stabilization Program II indicates that positive rates of growth were possible in 1983 and 1984, it is clear that if the unpopular reforms facing President de la Madrid were delayed, watered down, or ignored, Mexico's monetary crisis would become a long-term economic crisis. It is still unclear what effects Mexico's financial difficulties will have on popular action. In the United States, newspaper and television documentaries have forecast convulsive, even revolutionary political events. Such predictions seem based on a misunderstanding of Mexico. Mexico may be a country of nationalists, but it is also a country of patriots. Unlike the intellectuals who attempt to speak for them, the common people of Mexico and even much of the middle class are quite conservative. As one observer has recently noted:

> No one has made money for many decades by betting against the Mexican political elite's instinct for self-preservation. If a political change does arrive, it ...ore likely to come through a change of sentiment than a change in leaders. ... a history of great disappointments. An interruption of the rise to ... may be among the most unnecessary of these, but it would ...ne most bitter.[8]

Table A.1. Mexico: Gross domestic comparison, selected countries

	Newly industrializing countries				Developing countries			
	Mexico	Brazil	Singapore	Korea	Cameroon	Tunisia	Sri Lanka	Philippines
GNP per capita, 1979 (in dollars)	1,640	1,780	3,830	1,480	560	1,120	230	600
GNP per capita growth, 1960–79	2.7	4.8	7.4	7.1	2.5	4.8	2.2	2.6
Growth in GDP								
1960–70	7.2	5.4	8.8	8.6	3.7	4.7	4.6	5.1
1970–79	5.1	8.7	8.4	10.3	5.4	7.6	3.8	6.2
Growth in agriculture								
1960–70	3.8	—	5.0	4.4	—	2.0	3.0	4.3
1970–79	2.2	5.0	1.7	4.8	3.5	5.1	2.6	4.9
Growth in industry								
1960–70	9.1	—	12.5	17.2	—	8.2	6.6	6.0
1970–79	6.4	9.6	8.6	16.5	6.5	8.6	3.6	8.4
Growth in manufacturing								
1960–70	9.4	—	13.0	17.6	—	7.8	6.3	6.7
1970–79	6.4	10.9	9.3	17.8	5.4	10.6	1.7	6.7
Growth in services								
1960–70	6.9	—	7.7	8.9	—	4.5	4.6	5.2
1970–79	4.7	8.7	8.5	8.8	6.3	8.1	4.5	5.4

Percent GDP in agriculture								
1960	16	16	4	37	—	24	32	26
1979	10	11	2	20	32	16	27	24
Percent GDP in industry								
1960	29	35	18	20	—	18	20	28
1979	38	38	36	39	16	33	31	35
Percent GDP in manufacturing								
1960	23	26	12	14	—	8	15	20
1979	39	28	28	27	9	12	21	24
Percent GDP in services								
1960	55	49	78	43	—	58	48	46
1979	52	51	62	41	52	51	42	41
Average annual rate of inflation								
1960–70	3.6	46.1	1.1	17.5	4.2	3.7	1.8	5.8
1970–79	18.3	32.4	5.5	19.5	10.3	7.5	12.3	13.3

Source: Compiled from World Bank, *World Development Report*, 1981.

Table A.2. Mexico: comparison of industrialization, selected countries

	Newly industrializing countries				Developing countries			
	Mexico	Brazil	Singapore	Korea	Cameroon	Tunisia	Sri Lanka	Philippines
Distribution of manufacturing value added (percent 1975 prices)								
Food and agriculture (1978)	22	14	6	19	37	26	38	38
Textiles and clothing (1978)	11	10	5	20	15	16	15	11
Machinery and transport equipment (1978)	17	28	43	19	2	7	—	8
Chemicals (1978)	14	11	5	11	8	17	4	10
Other manufacturing (1978)	36	37	41	31	38	34	43	33
Value added in manufacturing (millions of 1975 dollars)								
1970	15,416	17,852	827	2,346	201	222	556	2,805
1978	24,856	37,685	1,815	9,064	312	538	644	4,761
Gross manufacturing output per capita (1975 dollars)								
1970	—	410	1,628	182	—	174	—	192
1977	—	—	2,874	567	—	298	—	541

Source: Compiled from World Bank, *World Development Report*, 1981.

Notes

Preface

1. See accounts by Juan Vasquez, "Behind the Burnout of Mexico," *San Francisco Chronicle* (24 August 1982), p. 10; Alan Riding, "The Crisis in Mexico," *New York Times* (23 August 1982), p. 1; William Chislett, "Lopez Portillo Plays for High Economic Stakes," *Financial Times* (23 February 1982), p. 2; Alan Riding, "Mexico's Road to Trouble is Coated with Oil," *New York Times* (21 February 1982), p. E3; Alan Riding, "Mexico's Mood is Pessimistic," *San Francisco Chronicle* (15 February 1982), p. 16; Alan Riding, "Mexico's Economy: Need for Sacrifice is Stressed," *New York Times* (25 May 1982), p. 33; and Basil Caplan, "Mexico—The World's New Biggest Borrower," *The Banker* (July 1982), pp. 33–44.

2. Quoted in Alan Riding, "Mexicans Gloomy Over Peso," *New York Times* (12 April 1982), p. 23.

3. See Leroy O. Laney, "How Contagious is 'Dutch Disease'?," Federal Reserve Bank of Dallas, *Economic Review* (March 1982), pp. 3–12.

4. Quoted in Alan Riding, "Dramatic Shift in Mexican Mood," *San Francisco Chronicle* (14 April 1982), p. 26.

5. William R. Cline, "Mexico's Crisis, The World's Peril," *Foreign Policy* (Winter 1982–83), p. 118.

Introduction to Part I

1. Obviously, all classifications of this type are somewhat arbitrary, but, based on the country's level of industrial output and per capita income, the standard references on the subject all place Mexico in this category. See Anthony Edwards, *The Newly Industrial Countries and Their Impact on Western Manufacturing* (London: The Economist Intelligence Unit, December 1979); "OECD and the NICSs: The Current Trade Pattern," *OECD Observer* (November 1981), pp. 12–13; Bela Balassa, *The Newly Industrializing Countries in the World Economy* (Elmsford, N.Y.: Pergamon Press, 1981); and Louis Turner et al., *Living with the Newly Industrializing Countries* (London: Royal Institute of International Affairs, 1980).

2. Unless otherwise specified, the comparative statistics used in this report are taken from The World Bank, *World Development Report 1981* (New York: Oxford University Press, 1981).

1. An Overview of the Mexican Economy

1. See Robert Looney, *Mexico's Economy: A Policy Analysis with Forecasts to 1990* (Boulder, Colo.: Westview Press, 1978); Robert Looney, *Development Alternatives of Mexico beyond the 1980s* (New York: Praeger Publishers, 1982); Leopoldo Solis, *Economic Policy Reform in Mexico: A Case Study for Developing Countries* (Elmsford, N.Y.: Pergamon Press, 1981); and Clark Reynolds, *The Mexican Economy* (New Haven: Yale University Press, 1970).

2. Unless otherwise specified all data prior to 1950 are taken from Nacional Financiera, *La Economía Méxicana en Cifras* (Mexico City: Mexico Nacional Financeria, 1981).

3. The World Bank, *World Tables 1976* (Baltimore: Johns Hopkins University Press, 1976).

4. See in particular Richard Harris and David Barkin, "The Political Economy in the Eighties," *Latin American Perspectives* (Winter 1982), pp. 2–19; Pablo Gonzalez Casanova, "The Economic Development of Mexico," in *Economic Development* (San Francisco: W. H. Freeman, 1980), pp. 98–107; Carlos Tello, *La Política Económica en México: 1970–1976* (Mexico City: Siglo XXI, 1979); and Carlos Perzabel, "Characteristics de la Crisis en México," *Historia y Sociedad* (1978), pp. 41–60.

5. Based on Menno Vellinga, *Economic Development and the Dynamics of Class: Industrialization, Power and Control in Monterrey, Mexico* (Assen, The Netherlands: Van Gorcum, 1979), ch. 2.

6. See P. Lamartine Yates, *Mexico's Agricultural Dilemma* (Tucson: University of Arizona Press, 1981), ch. 11, for an elaboration of these points.

7. John Freivalds, "Mexico: The Agricultural and Livestock Sectors," *Bank of London and South America Review* (August 1975), pp. 440–47.

8. Chandra Hardy, "Mexico's Development Strategy for the 1980s," *World Development* (June 1982), pp. 503–5.

9. See Cynthia Hewitt de Alcamtara, *Modernizing Mexican Agriculture: Socioeconomic Implications of Technological Change, 1940–1970* (Geneva: United Nations Research Institute for Social Development, 1976), for a summary of these views.

10. The following data on agriculture are taken from World Bank, *Special Study of the Mexican Economy: Major Policy Issues and Prospects*, (Washington: IBRD, 30 May 1979), Report No. 2307–ME, (confidential).

11. Based on the analysis presented in A. Nowick et al., *Mexico: Manufacturing Sector: Situation, Prospects and Policies* (Washington, D.C.: The World Bank, 1979), annex III.

12. An excellent survey is given in Antonio Aspra, "Import Substitution in Mexico: Past and Present," *World Development* (January 1977), pp. 111–24.

13. Unless otherwise noted, population data are taken from Francisco Alba, *The Population of Mexico* (London: Transaction Books, 1982).

14. Clark W. Reynolds, "Labor Market Projections for the United States and Mexico and Current Migration Controversies," *Food Research Institute Studies* (1979).

15. Gerald Boon, *Technology and Sector Choice in Economic Development* (Alphen den Rijn, 1978).

16. Leopoldo Solis, "Industrial Priorities in Mexico," in United Nations Industrial Development Organization, *Industrial Priorities in Developing Countries* (New York: United Nations, 1979), pp. 96–97.

17. Boon, *Technology and Sector Choice.*

18. E. V. K. Fitzgerald, "A Note on State Capital and Industrialization," in Jean Carrière, ed., *Industrialization and the State in Latin America* (Amsterdam: CEDLA, 1979), p. 64.

19. As outlined in Secretaria de Patrimonio y Fomento, *Plan Nacional de Desarrollo Industrial, 1979–82* (Mexico City, 1979).

20. As discussed in general terms in World Bank, *Special Study of the Mexican Economy: Major Policy Issues and Prospects.*

21. The English edition is *Mexico: National Industrial Development Plan*, vol. I (London: Graham and Trotman, 1979).

2. Mechanisms of Mexican Economic Growth

1. Chandra Hardy, "Mexico's Development Strategy for the 1980s," *World Development* (June 1982), p. 510.

2. E. Denison, "How to Raise the High Employment Growth Rate by One Percentage Point," *American Economic Review* (May 1962).

3. Following Clark Reynolds, *A Shift-Share Analysis of Regional and Sectoral Productivity Growth in Contemporary Mexico* (Laxenburg, Austria: International Institute for Applied Systems Analysis, 1980), p. 4.

4. Henry Bruton, "Productivity Growth in Latin America," *American Economic Review* (December 1967), p. 1105.

5. Reynolds, *Shift-Share Analysis*, p. 5.

6. Ibid., p. 6.

7. Bruton, "Productivity Growth."

8. Clark Reynolds, *The Mexican Economy* (New Haven: Yale University Press); see also Clark Reynolds, "Growth Distribution and Structural Change in Mexico: Recent Trends and Future Prospects," in L. E. Koslow, ed., *The Future of Mexico* (Tempe: Arizona State University Press, 1977); and Clark Reynolds, "Why Mexico's 'Stabilizing Development' Was Actually Destabilizing (with Some Implications for the Future)," *World Development* (June–September 1978).

9. Marcelo Selowsky, "Education and Economic Growth: Some International Comparisons," cited in Organization of American States, *Domestic Efforts and the Needs for External Financing for Development in Mexico*, OEA I Ser-H/XIV, CIAP/562, 28 August 1972, p. 85 (confidential).

3. External Sources of Instability

1. The following section is based on an analysis of data presented in Bank of Mexico, *Informe Anual*, various issues; International Monetary Fund, *Balance of Payments Year Book*, various issues; and International Monetary Fund, *Direction of Trade*, various issues.

2. Computed from Dirección General de Estadistica, Secretaria de Industria y Comercio, *Anuario estadistico del Comercio exterior* (Mexico City: Talleres Graficos de la Nacion), various issues.

3. John Purcell, "Trade Conflicts and U.S.-Mexican Relations," Program in United States-Mexican Studies, University of California, San Diego, *Working Papers in U.S.-Mexican Studies, No. 38* (1982), pp. 38–39.

4. Guillermo Teutli Otero, "Positive Results for the Maquiladora Program," in John Christman, ed., *Business Mexico* (Mexico City: American Chamber of Commerce of Mexico, 1981), pp. 149–54.

5. Bank of Mexico, *Informe Anual*, 1981.

6. A point elaborated on in Guillermo Ortiz and Leopoldo Solis, "Financial Structure and Exchange Rate Experience: Mexico, 1954–1977," *Journal of Development Economics* (December 1979), pp. 515–48; and Leroy Laney, "Currency Substitution: The Mexican Case," *Voice of the Federal Reserve Bank of Dallas* (January 1981), pp. 1–10.

7. Juan Vasquez, "Behind the Burnout of Mexico," *San Francisco Chronicle* (24 August 1982), p. 10.

8. Clark Reynolds, "The Mexican Economy, 1982–87: Key Economic Issues, Policy Alternatives, and Implications for International Business," in Alice B. Lentz, *Country Risk Analysis: Mexico* (San Francisco: Council of Americas, 1982), p. 22.

9. Basil Caplan, "Mexico—The World's New Biggest Borrower," *The Banker* (July 1982), pp. 33–44.

10. Alan Riding, "Mexico's Road to Trouble Is Coated with Oil," *New York Times* (21 February 1982), p. E3; Alan Riding, "Mexico's Economic Imbalances," *New York Times* (6 April 1981), p. 23; William Chislett, "Lopez Portillo Plays for High Economic Stakes," *Financial Times* (23 February 1982), p. 3; and Alan Riding, "Mexico's Mood Is Pessimistic," *San Francisco Chronicle* (15 February 1982), p. 52.

11. William Chislett, "The Oil Miracle Turns Sour," *Financial Times* (27 April 1982), p. 16; and Dan Dorfman, "Downhill in Mexico," *San Francisco Examiner* (27 June 1982), p. D1.

12. William R. Cline, "Mexico's Crisis, the World's Peril," *Foreign Policy* (Winter 1982–83), pp. 108–9.

13. Alan Riding, "Mexican Outlook—Banks are Wary," *New York Times* (17 August 1982), p. 29.

14. Alan Riding, "Mexico Reopens Exchanges with High Rate for the Dollar," *New York Times* (20 August 1982), p. 46.

15. "How Long Can Bankers Pull Rabbits Out of a Sombrero?" *The Economist* (28 August 1982), pp. 59–60.

4. Policymaking during the Echeverría Administration, 1971–76

1. Sidney Weintraub, "Case Study of Economic Stabilization: Mexico," in William Cline and Sidney Weintraub, eds., *Economic Stabilization in Developing Countries* (Washington, D.C.: Brookings Institution, 1981), pp. 272–75.

2. See Robert Looney, *Mexico's Economy: A Policy Analysis with Forecasts to 1990* (Boulder, Colo.: Westview Press, 1978), ch. 5.

3. Travier Marquez, "La Economia Méxicana en 1977 y su Futuro," Madrid, 25 October 1977 (mimeo).

4. A fascinating inside account of this episode is provided in Leopoldo Solis, *Economic Policy Reform in Mexico: A Case Study for Developing Countries* (Elmsford, N.Y.: Pergamon Press, 1981), ch. 3.

5. Quoted in Carlos Vidali Carbajal, "Politica Tributaria," in *Política Hacendaria y Financiera en México, 1971–1976*, Suplemento de Comercio Exterior (August 1976), pp. 24–25.

6. See Robert Looney, "Mexico's Fiscal Crisis: A Critique of the Fitzgerald Thesis," paper presented at the Eighth Annual Eastern Economic Association meetings, Philadelphia, 28 April 1981, pp. 7–9.

7. Leroy Laney, "Currency Substitution: The Mexican Case," *Voice of the Federal Reserve Bank of Dallas* (January 1981), pp. 1–10, gives an excellent analysis of this process.

8. Weintraub, "Case Study," pp. 281–83.

9. A detailed account of industrial policy during this period is given in World Bank, *Mexico: Manufacturing Sector—Situation, Prospects and Policies* (Washington, D.C.: IBRD, 1979). The following section draws heavily on this report.

10. The long-run problems caused by the underdevelopment of the capital goods sector are documented in Leopoldo Solis, "Industrial Priorities in Mexico," in United Nations Industrial Development

Organization, *Industrial Priorities in Developing Countries* (New York: United Nations, 1979), pp. 106–7. See also Adriaan ten Kate and Robert Bruce Wallace, *Protection and Economic Development in Mexico* (New York: St. Martin's Press, 1980), ch. 3.

11. ten Kate and Wallace, *Protection and Economic Development*, pp. 118–19.

12. Centro de Investigación y Docencia Económicas, "The Mexican Economy: Recent Development and Future Prospects," *Cambridge Journal of Economics* (June 1980), pp. 178–79.

13. Eduardo Venezian and William Gamble, *The Agricultural Development of Mexico* (New York: Praeger Publishers, 1969), pp. 63–64.

14. Solis, *Economic Policy Reform*, pp. 12–13.

15. Centro de Investigación y Docencia Económicas, "Mexican Economy," p. 180.

16. See Looney, *Mexico's Economy*, ch. 8, for a detailed account of the events immediately prior to the devaluation.

17. David Gordon, "Mexico: A Survey," *The Economist* (22 April 1978), p. 18.

18. The mechanism originally identified in John Koehler, *Economic Policy Making with Limited Information: The Process of Macro-Control in Mexico* (Santa Monica: The Rand Corporation, 1968).

19. Solis, *Economic Policy Reform*, p. 34.

5. Policymaking in the Early López Portillo Years: Devaluation and Stabilization

1. *El Heraldo* (Mexico City), 21 November 1977.

2. Clark Reynolds, "Why Mexico's 'Stabilizing Development' Was Actually Destabilizing," *World Development* (July–August 1978), p. 1014.

3. See E. V. K. Fitzgerald, "Stabilization Policy in Mexico: The Fiscal Deficit and Macroeconomic Equilibrium, 1960–77," in Rosemary Thorp and Laurence Whitehead, eds., *Inflation and Stabilisation in Latin America* (New York: Holmes and Meier, 1979), pp. 47–49.

4. Following the detailed account provided by Sidney Weintraub, "Case Study of Economic Stabilization: Mexico," in William Cline and Sidney Weintraub, eds., *Economic Stabilization in Developing Countries* (Washington, D.C.: Brookings Institution, 1981), pp. 285–89.

5. Organization of American States, *Short Term Economic Reports: Mexico* (Washington, D.C.: OAS, 1980), pp. 33–34.

6. Ibid.

7. The following account is based on facts obtained from the annual editions of *La Economía Méxicana* (Mexico City: Publicaciónes Ejecutivas de México) for 1976–80.

8. Luis R. Luis, "Stabilization Policy, Employment and the Balance of Payments: The Recent Mexican Experience," paper presented at the Eighth Annual Eastern Economic Association meetings, Philadelphia, 9–11 April 1981.

9. Ibid., pp. 27–29.

10. See Jaime Ros, "Pricing in the Mexican Manufacturing Sector," *Cambridge Journal of Economics* (September 1980), pp. 211–32.

11. James Schlagheck, *The Political, Economic, and Labor Climate in Mexico*, rev. ed. (Philadelphia: The Wharton School, 1980), pp. 103–5.

12. The following labor developments are based on facts culled from the annual editions of *La Economía Méxicana*.

13. Weintraub, "Case Study," pp. 289–90.

14. Recent analysis, however, confirms the expected deterioration in the distribution of income. See Michael Twomey, "Exchange Rate Devaluations and Income Distribution in Latin America," paper presented at the Western Economics Association meetings, San Francisco, 2 July 1981.

15. William Chislett, "Critical Year for Economy after Peso Devaluation," *Financial Times* (22 March 1982), p. II. For an excellent assessment of postdevaluation policy, see Abel Beltran del Rio, "Mexico's Troubled Economy: Peso Prognosis," *Wharton Magazine* (Winter 1977), pp. 55–56.

6. Industrial Policy under López Portillo

1. A critique of this line of argument is given in Nora Lustig, "Characteristics of Mexican Economic Growth," *Journal of Development Economics* (June 1982), pp. 355–76.

2. See Sam Lanframco, "Mexican Oil, Export-Led Development and Agricultural Neglect," *Journal of Development Economics* (July 1981), pp. 125–52.

3. Calvin Blair, "Economic Development Policy in Mexico: A New Penchant for Planning," Institute of Latin American Studies, University of Texas, *Technical Papers Series, No. 26* (Austin, 1980).

4. William Glade, "Prospects for Mexico's Socioeconomic Growth," *Texas Business Review* (March–April 1979), pp. 47–50.

5. Summaries are given in James Street, "Prospects for Mexico's Industrial Development Plan in the 1980s," *Texas Business Review* (May–June 1980), pp. 125–32; and E. V. K. Fitzgerald, "Oil and Mexico's Industrial Development Plan," *Texas Business Review* (May–June 1980), pp. 133–37.

6. See also Nathan Warman, "Industrial Development Policy," in John Christman, ed., *Business Mexico* (Mexico City: American Chamber of Commerce of Mexico, 1981), pp. 77–88.

7. Edward Wygard and Bill Kryzda, "The National Industrial Development Plan: Goals and Incentives," in Christman, ed., *Business Mexico*, pp. 89–96.

8. The following sections summarize the plan as it is presented in Secretaria de Patrimonio, *Mexico Industrial Development Plan*, vol. 1 (London: Graham and Trotman, 1979), ch. 1. An excellent and detailed critical commentary is given in Redvers Opie, *Mexican Industrialization and Petroleum* (Mexico City: ECANAL, 1979).

9. John F. H. Purcell, "Trade Conflicts and U.S.-Mexican Relations," Program in United States–Mexican Studies, University of California San Diego, *Working Papers in U.S.-Mexican Studies, No. 38* (1982), pp. 47–48.

10. Based on Leopoldo Solis, *Economic Policy Reform in Mexico* (Elmsford, N.Y.: Pergamon Press, 1981), pp. 98–105.

11. William Chislett, "Mexicans Debate GATT Membership," *Financial Times* (14 December 1979), p. 3.

12. Alan Robinson, "Letter from Mexico," *Journal of Commerce* (3 April 1980), p. 5.

13. Ibid.

14. Chislett, "Mexicans Debate GATT Membership."

15. Summarized in Robinson, "Letter from Mexico."

16. Ibid.

17. Alan Riding, "Mexico Bets on Industry to Make the Most of Its Oil Boom," *New York Times* (9 December 1979), p. 7.

18. Robinson, "Letter from Mexico."

19. See James Schlagheck, *The Political, Economic, and Labor Climate in Mexico* (Philadelphia: The Wharton School, 1980), ch. 4.

20. An excellent account is given in Menno Vellinga, *Economic Development and the Dynamics of Class: Industrialization, Power and Control in Monterrey, Mexico* (Assen, The Netherlands: Van Gorcum, 1979).

21. See, for example, Solis, *Economic Policy Reform*; Robert Looney, *Mexico's Economy: A Policy Analysis with Forecasts to 1990* (Boulder, Colo.: Westview Press, 1978); World Bank, *Special Study of the Mexican Economy: Major Policy Issues and Prospects* (Washington, D.C.: IBRD, 30 May 1979), Report 2307-ME (confidential); and Miguel Wionczek, "Incomplete Formal Planning: Mexico," in E. Hagen, ed., *Planning Economic Development* (Homewood, Ill.: Richard D. Irwin, 1963), pp. 150–82.

7. Fiscal Policy under López Portillo: Prelude to the 1982 Crisis

1. As summarized in American Chamber of Commerce of Mexico, *Quarterly Economic Report, Exchange Controls* (October 1982), pp. 1–4.

2. The following sections are based on data derived from the annual budget documents and annual presidential *Informes*, 1973–81.

3. Basil Caplan, "Mexico—the World's New Biggest Borrower," *The Banker* (July 1982), pp. 40–43.

8. Policymaking in López Portillo's Final Year: The 1982 Devaluations and Aftermath

1. See American Chamber of Commerce of Mexico, "Devaluation of the Peso," *Quarterly Economic Report* (March 1982); William Chislett, "The Oil Miracle Turns Sour," *Financial Times* (27 April 1982), p. 3; Alan Riding, "Mexico's Economy: Need for Sacrifice Is Stressed," *New York Times* (25 May 1982), p. 33; Alan Riding, "Dramatic Shift in Mexican Mood," *San Francisco Chronicle* (14 April 1982), p. 26; Alan Riding, "Mexicans Gloomy over Peso," *New York Times* (12 April 1982), p. 23; William Chislett, "Anxiety over Mexican Spending," *Financial Times* (23 March 1982), p. 4; Alan

Riding, "Mexico's Road to Trouble Is Coated with Oil," *New York Times* (21 February 1982), p. E3; Alan Riding, "Mexico's Mood Is Pessimistic," *San Francisco Chronicle* (15 February 1982), p. 16; and William Chislett, "Lopez Portillo Plays for High Economic Stakes," *Financial Times* (23 February 1982), p. 4.

2. Isabel Zamorano, "Finance Minister Discusses Austerity Measures," *Excelsior* (Mexico City) (20 February 1982), pp. 1A, 8-12-A.

3. Ibid.

4. J. Jesus Rangel, "Oteyza Announces 12 Point Economic Program," *Excelsior* (Mexico City) (25 March 1982), p. 1-A.

5. Ibid., pp. 12-A, 27-A.

6. Ibid., p. 3-A.

7. "PRI 1982-88 Basic Plan and Platform Summarized," *El Dia* (Mexico City) (4 November 1981), supp. 2–11.

8. Ibid., p. 3.

9. Carlos Ramirez, "Resignation of Finance Minister Analyzed," *Procesco* (Mexico City) (22 March 1982), p. 6.

10. Ibid., pp. 7–10.

11. Chislett, "Oil Miracle Turns Sour," p. 16.

12. "Mexico," *Bank of London & South America Review* (August 1982), p. 138.

13. Ibid.

14. Chislett, "Oil Miracle Turns Sour," p. 16; Dan Dorfman, "Downhill in Mexico," *San Francisco Examiner* (27 June 1982), p. D1.

15. Alan Riding, "Mexico Reopens Exchanges with High Rate for the Dollar," *New York Times* (20 August 1982), p. 6.

16. "How Long Can Bankers Pull Rabbits Out of a Sombrero?" *The Economist* (28 August 1982), pp. 59–60.

17. Alan Riding, "Mexico Seizing Banks to Curtail Flight of Capital," *New York Times* (2 September 1982), p. 1.

18. William R. Cline, "Mexico's Crisis, the World's Peril," *Foreign Policy* (Winter 1982–83), pp. 110–11.

19. Based on Alan Riding, "Mexico to Accept Strict IMF Terms for Major Credit," *New York Times* (11 November 1982), p. 1.

9. Scope for Anti-Inflationary Policy

1. Brian Griffiths, *Inflation: The Price of Prosperity* (New York: Holmes and Meier, 1976), p. 3.

2. C. Richard Bath, John Evans, and Dilmus James, "Dependency, Inflation, and the Allocation of Mexico's Petroleum Reserves," *Texas Business Review* (September–October 1981), pp. 198–99.

3. Leopoldo Solis, "The Petroleum Boom in Mexico: An Opportunity for Correcting the Pattern of Economic Development," paper presented to the North American Economic Studies Association, December 1978.

4. For example, Geraldo M. Bueno, "Desarrollo y Petróleo: La Experiencia de los Paises Exportadores," *Trimestre Economico* (1980), pp. 283–301; Leroy O. Laney, "How Contagious is 'Dutch Disease'?," Federal Reserve Bank of Dallas, *Economic Review* (March 1982), pp. 10–11.

5. See C. Tello, *La Política Económica en México, 1970–1976* (Mexico, D.F.: Siglo XXI, 1979); Centro de Investigación y Docencia Económícas, *Economía Méxicana* (Mexico, D.F.: C.I.D.E., 1979).

6. E. V. K. Fitzgerald, "Recent Writing on the Mexican Economy," *Latin American Research Review* (1981), p. 238.

7. Tello, *La Política Económica*, p. 207.

8. From P. Gonzalez and E. Florescano, eds., *México Hoy* (Mexico, D.F.: Siglo XXI, 1979).

9. Marnie Mueller, "Structural Inflation and the Mexican Experience," *Yale Economic Essays* (Spring 1965), pp. 150–53.

10. Fitzgerald, "Recent Writing," p. 238.

11. Bath et al., "Dependency, Inflation, and Allocation," p. 193.

12. Ibid.

13. C. H. Kirkpatrick and F. I. Nixson, "The Origins of Inflation in Less Developed Countries: A Selective Review," in Michael Parkin and George Zis, eds., *Inflation in Open Economies* (Manchester: Manchester University Press, 1976), p. 132.

14. Ibid.

15. D. Barkin and G. Esteva, *Inflación y denogracia el caso de México* (Mexico, D. F.: Siglo XXI, 1979); a similar account is given in David Barkin and Gustavo Esteva, "Social Conflict and Inflation in Mexico," *Latin American Perspectives* (Winter 1982), pp. 48–64.

16. Fitzgerald, "Recent Writing," p. 240.

17. See H. Chenery, "The Structuralist Approach to Development Policy," *American Economic Review* (May 1975), pp. 310–16.

18. A complete specification of the model is given in Luis Landau, "Saving Functions in Latin America," in Hollis Chenery, ed., *Studies in Development Planning* (Cambridge, Mass.: Harvard University Press, 1971), pp. 299–321.

19. See Milton Iyoha, "Inflation and Openness in Less Developed Economies: A Cross Country Analysis," *Economic Development and Cultural Change* (October 1973), pp. 31–38. See, however, criticisms of this study in M. A. Akhtar, "An Empirical Note on Inflation and Openness in Less Developed Economies," *The Philippine Economic Journal* (1976), pp. 636–49; and Kirkpatrick and Nixson, "Origins of Inflation," pp. 158–59.

20. Iyoha, "Inflation and Openness," p. 33.

21. Kirkpatrick and Nixson, "Origins of Inflation," p. 158.

22. James Schlagheck, *The Political, Economic and Labor Climate in Mexico*, rev. ed. (Philadelphia: The Wharton School, 1980), pp. 89–90.

23. Ibid., pp. 101–2.

24. Bank of Mexico, *Informe Anual*, various issues.

25. Schlagheck, *Political, Economic and Labor Climate*, pp. 94–95.

26. See Ichiro Otani, "Inflation in an Open Economy: A Case Study of the Philippines," International Monetary Fund, *Staff Papers* (1975), pp. 750–74.

27. Summarized in E. J. Sheehey, "On the Measurement of Imported Inflation in Developing Countries," *Weltwirtschaftliches Archiv* (1979), pp. 68–79.

10. Dynamics of the Fiscal System

1. See Leopoldo Solis, "A Monetary Will-O'-the-Wisp: Pursuit of Equity through Deficit Spending," Princeton University, Woodrow Wilson School, *Discussion Paper No. 77* (1977); E. V. K. Fitzgerald, "The Fiscal Crisis of the Latin American State," in J. F. J. Toye, ed., *Taxation and Economic Development* (London: Frank Cass, 1978); Clark Reynolds, "Why Mexico's 'Stabilizing Development' Was Actually Destabilizing (with Some Implications for the Future)," *World Development* (June-September 1978); C. Tello, *La Política Económica en México* (Mexico City: Siglo XXI, 1979); and E. V. K. Fitzgerald, "Stabilization Policy in Mexico: The Fiscal Deficit and Macroeconomic Equilibrium, 1960–1977," in Rosemary Thorp and Laurence Whitehead, eds., *Inflation and Stabilisation in Latin America* (New York: Holmes and Meier, 1979), pp. 23–64.

2. William Chislett, "Bitter Dose of Austerity," *Financial Times* (2 November 1982), p. 17.

3. Wharton, EFA, *Mexico*, various reports.

4. Apparently, the Wharton forecasts were the first to identify many of the country's oil-related development problems. See Abel Beltran del Rio, "The Mexican Oil Syndrome: Early Symptoms, Preventive Efforts and Prognosis," in Werner Baer and Malcolm Gillis, eds., *Export Diversification and the New Protectionism* (Champaign: University of Illinois Press, 1981), pp. 115–30.

5. E. V. K. Fitzgerald, "The New International Division of Labour and the Relative Autonomy of the State: Notes for a Reappraisal of Classical Dependency," *Bulletin of Latin American Research* (October 1981), pp. 1–12. See also E. V. K. Fitzgerald, "A Note on State Capital and Industrialization in Mexico," in Jean Carrière, ed., *Industrialization and the State in Latin America* (Amsterdam: CEDLA, 1979), pp. 49–72.

6. E. V. K. Fitzgerald, "Some Aspects of the Political Economy of the Latin American State," *Development and Change* (1976).

7. E. V. K. Fitzgerald, "The State and Capital Accumulation in Mexico," *Journal of Latin American Studies* (1978), p. 263.

8. An excellent comparative analysis is given in Vito Tanzi, "Disequilibrium in the Fiscal Sector of Developing Countries," paper presented at the American Economic Association meetings, Washington, D.C., 28–30 December 1981.

9. D. Sykes Wilford and Walton Wilford, "Fiscal Revenues in Mexico: A Measure of Performance, 1950–1973," *Public Finance/Finances Publiques* (1976), p. 103.

10. Gilberto Escobedo, "Ahorroy Desarrollo Económico," Bank of Mexico, *Working Paper* (1975), p. 73.

11. See John Evans, "The Evolution of the Mexican Tax System since 1970," University of Texas, Institute of Latin American Studies, *Technical Papers Series No. 34* (1982).

12. Pedro Massone, "The Mexican Income Tax (1980)," International Bureau of Fiscal Documentation, *Bulletin* (1981), pp. 389–90.

13. Wilford and Wilford, "Fiscal Revenues in Mexico."

14. Past measurements of elasticity have stirred up an ongoing debate over methodological problems associated with the underlying data sources. In addition to the Wilford and Wilford article cited above, see Arthur J. Mann, "Mexican Fiscal Revenue and Performance, 1950–1977: A Revisit," *Public Finance/Finances Publiques* (1978), pp. 378–85, and D. Sykes Wilford and Walton Wilford, "Comment on 'Mexican Fiscal Revenue Performance, 1950–77: A Revisit,'" *Public Finance/Finances Publiques* (1979), pp. 134–37.

15. Roughly similar results were obtained by Wilford and Wilford, "Fiscal Revenues in Mexico."

16. Leopoldo Solis, *Economic Policy Reform in Mexico: A Case Study for Developing Countries* (Elmsford, N.Y.: Pergamon Press, 1981).

17. Mann finds the tax system more or less proportional. See Arthur Mann, "The Mexican Tax Burden by Family Income Class," *Public Finance Quarterly* (July 1982), pp. 305–31.

18. Massone, "Mexican Income Tax (1980)," pp. 389–90.

19. Other components are given in Arthur Mann, "Wagner's Law: An Econometric Test for Mexico: 1975–76," *National Tax Journal* (1980), pp. 189–201.

20. E. V. K. Fitzgerald, "Patterns of Public Sector Income and Expenditure in Mexico," University of Texas, Institute of Latin American Studies, *Technical Papers Series No. 17* (1978).

21. E. V. K. Fitzgerald, "Patterns of Savings and Investment in Mexico: 1939–76," Cambridge University Centre of Latin American Studies, *Working Papers No. 30* (1977).

22. NAFINSA-UNIDO, *México: Una Estrategia para el Desarrollo de la Industria de Bienes de Capital* (Mexico City: NAFINSA, 1977), table VI-14, p. 342.

23. See Gustavo Romero Kolbeck, "Public Sector Banking," and Federico Carrera Cortez, "The Commercial Banking System and Investment Opportunities," in John Christman, ed., *Business Mexico* (Mexico City: American Chamber of Commerce of Mexico, 1981), pp. 105–22.

24. Based in part on John Rhoads, "The Mexican Stock Exchange," in Christman, ed., *Business Mexico*, pp. 137–44.

25. Guillermo Ortiz and Leopoldo Solis, "Financial Structure and Exchange Rate Experience: Mexico, 1954–1977," *Journal of Development Economics* (December 1979), pp. 515–48.

26. E. V. K. Fitzgerald, "The Fiscal Deficit and Development Finance: A Note on the Accumulation Balance in Mexico," Cambridge University, Centre of Latin American Studies, *Working Papers No. 35* (April 1979), pp. 16–17.

27. Chislett, "Bitter Dose of Austerity."

11. Macroeconomic Controversies: The Monetarist-Cambridge Interpretations of the Policy Environment

1. H. G. Johnson, "The Monetary Approach to the Balance of Payments Theory," in H. G. Johnson, ed., *Further Essays in Monetary Economics* (Cambridge, Mass.: Harvard University Press, 1973), p. 231.

2. M. Mussa, "A Monetary Approach to Balance of Payments Analysis," *Journal of Money, Credit and Banking* (August 1974), p. 338.

3. Ibid., p. 336.

4. D. S. Kemp, "The Monetary View of the Balance of Payments," Federal Reserve Bank of St. Louis, *Review* (April 1975), p. 14.

5. The model shown here is based on the derivation found in Johnson, "Monetary Approach."

6. See R. M. Stern, *The Balance of Payments: Theory and Economic Policy* (Chicago: Aldine, 1973), chs. 6 and 10.

7. R. Zecher, "Monetary Equilibrium and International Reserve Flows in Australia," *Journal of Finance* (December 1974), pp. 1525–26.

8. B. Griffiths, *Mexican Monetary Policy and Economic Development* (New York: Praeger Publishers, 1972), ch. 4.

9. Perhaps explaining why earlier studies tended to confirm the theory while this one finds less support. See D. Sykes Wilford and J. Richard Zecher, "Monetary Policy and the Balance of Payments in Mexico, 1955–75," *Journal of Money, Credit and Banking* (August 1979), pp. 340–438, for evidence in support of the approach. See also Mike Farrell, "International Impact of U.S. Money Supply: The Case of Mexico," *A Mexican Economic Review* (June 1980), pp. 433–43, and Mario Blejer and Leonardo Leiderman, "Inflation and Relative Price Variability in the Open Economy," *European Economic Review* (1982), pp. 387–402, for a partial confirmation of the monetary theory under the period of relatively fixed exchange rates, from 1951 to 1976. D. Sykes Wilford, "Price Levels, Interest Rates, Open Economies, and a Fixed Exchange Rate: The Mexican Case, 1954–74," *Review of Business and Economic Research* (Spring 1977), pp. 52–65, found evidence of the validity of the unified goods market hypothesis for Mexico, confirming in part the monetary approach to the balance of payments. However, Francis Ahking, "Mexico: The Open Economy—A Note," *Review of Business and Economic Research* (1978), pp. 103–7, finds that the results obtained using a more refined estimation procedure cast doubt on the applicability of the unified goods theory for Mexico.

10. Gilberto Escobedo, "The Response of the Mexican Economy to Policy Actions," Federal Reserve Bank of St. Louis, *Review* (June 1973), p. 21. See also Gilberto Escobedo, "Formulation of a Model of the Mexican Economy," Federal Reserve Bank of St. Louis, *Review* (July 1973), pp. 8–19, for a comparison of Keynesian and monetarist models of the Mexican economy.

11. T. F. Cripps, M. J. Fetherston, and W. A. H. Godley, "Simulations with the Cambridge Economic Policy Group Model," in Michael Posner, ed., *Demand Management* (London: Heinemann, 1978), pp. 10–11.

12. John Eatwell and A. Singh, "Se Encuentra 'Sobrecalentada' la Economía Méxicana—Un Analisis de los Problemas a Corto y Mediano Plazo," Mexico City, April 1981 (mimeo).

13. Ibid., p. 3.

14. Ibid., p. 5.

15. Centro de Investigación y Docencia Económicas, "The Mexican Economy: Recent Development and Future Prospects," *Cambridge Journal of Economics* (June 1980), pp. 177–97.

16. See A. Leijonhufvud, *On Keynesian Economics and the Economics of Keynes* (New York: Oxford University Press, 1968); J. R. Hicks, *The Crisis in Keynesian Economics* (New York: Oxford University Press, 1974).

12. Impact of Fiscal Policy: A Critique of the Fitzgerald Thesis

1. An earlier version of this chapter was presented at the Southern Economic Association meetings, Atlanta, 12 November 1982. I am particularly thankful for the constructive comments provided by George Feiwel and Richard Wood.

2. See E. V. K. Fitzgerald, "The Fiscal Deficit and Development Finance: A Note on the Accumulation Balance in Mexico," Cambridge University, Centre of Latin American Studies, *Working Papers No. 35* (April 1979); and E. V. K. Fitzgerald, "A Note on Capital Accumulation in Mexico: The Budget Deficit and Investment Finance," *Development and Change* (June 1980), pp. 391–417.

3. See particularly the views of Redvers Opie expressed in his *Mexican Industrialization and Petroleum* (Mexico City: ECANAL, August 1979), *The Overall Development Plan 1980–82: An Appraisal* (Mexico City: ECANAL, August 1980), and especially his *The 1981 Report of the Bank of Mexico: A Disastrous and Tragic Decade of Economic Policy* (Mexico City: ECANAL, May 1982). On a more popular level, see Luis Pazos, *Devaluación y Estatismo en México* (Mexico City: Editorial Diana, 1976).

4. Willem Buiter, "Crowding Out and the Effectiveness of Fiscal Policy," *Journal of Public Economics* (1977), pp. 309–10.

5. In addition to the references contained in n. 2 to this chapter, see Fitzgerald's "The New International Division of Labour and the Relative Autonomy of the State: Notes for a Reappraisal of Classical Dependency," *Bulletin of Latin American Research* (October 1981), pp. 1–12; "Stabilization Policy in Mexico: The Fiscal Deficit and Macroeconomic Equilibrium, 1960–77," in Rosemary Thorp and Laurence Whitehead, eds., *Inflation and Stabilisation in Latin America* (New York: Holmes and Meier, 1979); "The Fiscal Crisis of the Latin American State," in J. F. J. Toye, ed., *Taxation and Economic Development* (London: Frank Cass, 1978); "The State and Capital Accumulation in Mexico," *Journal of Latin American Studies* (1978), pp. 263–82; "The Public Investment Criterion and the Role of the State," *Journal of Development Studies* (July 1977), pp. 365–72; and "A Note on State Capital and

Industrialization in Mexico," in J. Carrière, ed., *Industrialization and the State in Latin America* (Amsterdam: CEDLA, 1979).

6. Based on the Fitzgerald citations given in notes 2 and 5 above.

7. In particular, see Clark Reynolds, "Why Mexico's 'Stabilizing Development' Was Actually Destabilizing (with Some Implications for the Future)," *World Development* (June 1978); R. Villarreal, *El Desequilibrio Externo en la Industrializacion de México, 1929–75* (Mexico City: Fondo de Cultura Economica, 1976); and C. Tello, *La Política Económica en México* (Mexico, D.F.: Siglo XXI, 1979).

8. This summary is based on Fitzgerald's interpretation and exposition. See his "Fiscal Deficit and Development Finance," pp. 4–6.

9. A. S. Blinder and R. M. Solo, "Analytical Foundations of Fiscal Policy," in A. S. Blinder, R. M. Solo, et al., eds., *The Economics of Public Finance* (Washington, D.C.: The Brookings Institution, 1973), pp. 3–119.

10. Rodger Spencer and William Yohe, "The Crowding Out of Private Expenditures by Fiscal Actions," Federal Reserve Bank of St. Louis, *Review* (October 1970), pp. 12–24.

11. Fitzgerald, "Fiscal Deficit and Development Finance," p. 6.

12. As articulated in D. Brothers and Leopoldo Solis, *Mexican Financial Development* (Austin: University of Texas Press, 1966).

13. Fitzgerald, "Fiscal Deficit and Development Finance," p. 6.

14. See Leopoldo Solis, "A Monetary Will-O'-the-Wisp: Pursuit of Equity through Deficit Spending," Princeton University, Woodrow Wilson School, *Discussion Paper No. 77* (1977); Guillermo Ortiz and Leopoldo Solis, "Financial Structure and Exchange Rate Experience: Mexico, 1954–1977," *Journal of Development Economics* (December 1979).

15. Fitzgerald, "Fiscal Deficit and Development Finance," pp. 8–9.

16. Ibid., pp. 14–15.

17. Fitzgerald, "Note on Capital Accumulation in Mexico," pp. 399–405.

18. One critic is Maryann Keating. See her paper on "The Fiscal Crisis in Mexico," presented at the annual meetings of the Atlantic Economics Association, Washington, D.C., October 1979; and her paper on "The Fiscal Crisis in Mexico, Peru and Chile: A Review Essay of the Cambridge School," prepared for the annual meeting of the Midwestern Economics Association, Chicago, December 1980.

19. Estimates were made using ordinary least squares with a Cochrane-Orcutt procedure to correct for serial correlation. The program used in all analysis in the study is Bronwyn Hall and Robert E. Hall, *Time Series Processor, Version 3.5* (Stanford, Calif., April 1980).

20. L. M. Koyck, *Distributed Lags and Investment Analysis* (Amsterdam: North Holland, 1954).

21. See Z. Griliches, "Distributed Lags: A Survey," *Econometrica* (1967), pp. 16–49; M. Nerlou, "Lags in Economic Behavior," *Econometrica* (1972), pp. 221–51.

22. Fitzgerald, "Fiscal Deficit and Development Finance," pp. 16–17.

23. Ibid., p. 18.

24. Ibid., p. 21.

13. Optimal Stabilization Programs, 1975–81

1. See Alan Riding, "The Mixed Blessing of Mexico's Oil," *New York Times Magazine* (11 January 1981), pp. 22–59; Alan Friedman, "A Colossal Mountain of Debt," *Financial Times* (20 August 1982), p. 13; and Dan Dorfman, "Downhill in Mexico," *San Francisco Examiner* (27 June 1982), p. D1.

2. P. Gonzales and E. Florescano, eds., *México hoy* (Mexico City: Siglo XXI, 1979).

3. P. Ayala et al., "La Crisis económica: evolución y perspectivas," in Gonzales and Florescano, *México hoy*.

4. Sergio de la Pena, "Proletarian Power and State Monopoly Capitalism in Mexico," *Latin American Perspectives* (Winter 1982), pp. 20–35.

5. Pablo Gonzalez Casanova, "Mexico: The Most Probable Course of Development," *Latin American Perspectives* (Winter 1982), pp. 78–88.

6. Richard Harris and David Barkin, "The Political Economy of Mexico in the Eighties," *Latin American Perspectives* (Winter 1982), pp. 2–19.

7. In particular, see his *Analisis del Presupuesto Méxicano Pova 1979* (Mexico City: ECANAL, January 1979); *The Last Informe of President Echeverría: Inflation and Devaluation* (Mexico City: American Chamber of Commerce of Mexico, September 1976); and *Mexican Industrialization and Petroleum* (Mexico City: ECANAL, August 1979).

8. Redvers Opie, *The 1981 Report of the Bank of Mexico: A Disastrous and Tragic Decade of Economic Policy* (Mexico City: ECANAL, 1982), p. 53.

9. Redvers Opie, *Report on Mexico—May to August 1982* (Mexico City: ECANAL, 1982), pp. 11–12.

10. Leopoldo Solis, *Economic Policy Reform in Mexico: A Case Study for Developing Countries* (Elmsford, N.Y.: Pergamon Press, 1981).

11. C. Tello, *La Política económica en México, 1970–76* (Mexico City: Siglo XXI, 1979).

12. Nora Lustig, "Characteristics of Mexican Economic Growth," *Journal of Development Economics* (June 1982), pp. 355–76.

13. Clark Reynolds, *The Mexican Economy* (New Haven: Yale University Press, 1970); and Clark Reynolds, "The Mexican Economy, 1982–1987: Key Issues, Policy Alternatives, and Implications for International Business," in Alice Lentz, ed., *Country Risk Analysis: Mexico* (San Francisco: FMME, 1982).

14. Abel Beltran del Rio, "Mexico's Troubled Economy: Peso Prognosis," *Wharton Magazine* (Winter 1977), pp. 55–56; "Econometric Forecasting for Mexico: An Analysis of Errors in Prediction," in J. Behrman and J. Hanson, eds., *Short Term Macroeconomic Policy in Latin America* (Cambridge, Mass.: Ballinger, 1979); and "The Mexican Oil Syndrome: Early Symptoms, Preventive Efforts and Prognosis," in W. Braer and M. Gillis, *Export Diversification and the New Protectionism: The Experiences of Latin America* (Urbana-Champaign, Ill.: Bureau of Economic and Business Research, 1981), pp. 115–30.

15. Robert Looney, *Mexico's Economy: A Policy Analysis with Forecasts to 1990* (Boulder, Colo.: Westview Press, 1978).

16. A similar approach is given in Alan Gelb, "Capital Importing Oil Exporters: Adjustment Issues and Policy Choices," World Bank, *World Bank Staff Working Paper, No. 475* (August 1981).

17. E. V. K. Fitzgerald, "The Fiscal Deficit and Development Finance: A Note on the Accumulation Balance in Mexico," Cambridge University, Centre of Latin American Studies, *Working Papers No. 35* (April 1979).

18. The program used for the optimal control exercises is a modified version of that developed by G. Vanderplaats at the Naval Postgraduate School, Monterey, Calif. See his "COPES—A Fortran Control Program for Engineering Synthesis" (mimeo), no date, and "The Computer for Design and Optimization," paper presented at the ASME annual winter meeting, New York, December 1976.

19. See, for example, Gregory Chow, *Analysis and Control of Dynamic Economic Systems* (New York: John Wiley, 1975); Robert Pindyck, *Optimal Planning for Economic Stabilization: The Application of Control Theory to Stabilization Policy* (Amsterdam: North Holland Publishers, 1973).

20. See Lance Taylor, *Macro Models for Developing Countries* (New York: McGraw-Hill, 1979), ch. 8.

14. Scope for Optimal Policy in an Oil-Based Economy, 1982–87

1. Basil Caplan, "Mexico—The World's New Biggest Borrower," *The Banker* (July 1982), p. 33.

2. See Francisco Carrada-Bravo, *Oil, Money and the Mexican Economy: A Macroeconomic Analysis* (Boulder, Colo.: Westview Press, 1982), for a recent macroeconomic analysis touching on several of these issues.

3. Compare with Jesus-Agustin Velasco, "Mexico in the World Oil Market: Opportunities and Dangers for Mexican Development," Harvard University, John F. Kennedy School of Government, *Discussion Paper E-80-07* (October 1980); and David Ronfeldt, Richard Nehring, and Arturo Gandara, *Mexico's Petroleum and U.S. Policy: Implications for the 1980s* (Santa Monica: The Rand Corporation, 1980), p. 81.

4. Guillermo Ortiz and Leopoldo Solis, "Financial Structure and Exchange Rate Experience: Mexico, 1954–1977," *Journal of Development Economics* (December 1979), p. 538.

5. A stable rate is also said to reduce investor uncertainty and facilitate investment and trade. See James R. Dempsey, "Pesos or Dollars in Mexico?," *Euromoney* (June 1978), pp. 147–64, and James R. Dempsey, "The Mexican Back to Back Loan," *Euromoney* (May 1978), pp. 69–75, for an excellent account of how fluctuating rates complicate business decision making.

6. Abel Beltran del Rio, "Mexico's Troubled Economy: Peso Prognosis," *Wharton Magazine* (Winter 1977), p. 56.

7. Leroy O. Laney, "Oil Inflation and the Mexican Peso," *Voice of the Federal Reserve Bank of Dallas* (September 1979), p. 3.

8. Leopoldo Solis, *Economic Policy Reform in Mexico: A Case Study for Developing Countries* (Elmsford, N.Y.: Pergamon Press, 1981), p. 119.

9. See Guillermo Calvo and Carlos Alfredo Rodriguez, "A Model of Exchange Rate Determination under Currency Substitution and Rational Expectations," *Journal of Political Economy* (June 1977); and Arturo Brillenbourg and Susan Schadler, "A Model of Currency Substitution in Exchange Rate Determination, 1973–78," International Monetary Fund, *Staff Papers* (September 1979).

10. Leroy O. Laney, "Currency Substitution: The Mexican Case," *Voice of the Federal Reserve Bank of Dallas* (January 1981), p. 8.

11. Solis, *Economic Policy Reform*, pp. 119–20.

12. Calvin Blair, "Economic Development Policy in Mexico: A New Penchant for Planning," Office for Public Sector Studies, Institute of Latin American Studies, The University of Texas at Austin, *Technical Papers Series No. 26* (1980), p. 15.

13. The program advocated here is one of credit constraint and is not a "monetarist" policy. The ramifications of the monetarist approach are well known and can probably be avoided in Mexico's case. An excellent critique of the difficulties associated with monetarist programming is given in David Felix, "Latin American Monetarism in Crisis," *IDS Bulletin* (1 December 1981), pp. 6–13.

14. See Edward Williams, "Petroleum and Political Change," in Jorge Dominguez, *Mexico's Political Economy* (Beverly Hills: Sage Publications, 1982), for an excellent summary of developments in the oil and gas sector.

15. Chandra Hardy, "Mexico's Development Strategy for the 1980s," *World Development* (June 1982), p. 510.

16. See Ernesto Marcos, "Design of a Development Policy for Mexico: Industry and Oil," in William Baumol, ed., *Public and Private Enterprise in a Mixed Economy* (New York: St. Martin's Press, 1980), pp. 57–66, and "Discussion of Dr. Marcos' Paper," ibid., pp. 66–68; C. Richard Bath, John Evans, and Dilmus James, "Dependency, Inflation and the Allocation of Mexico's Petroleum Reserves," *Texas Business Review* (September-October 1981), pp. 196–202; and E. V. K. Fitzgerald, "Oil and Mexico's Industrial Development Plan," *Texas Business Review* (May–June 1980), pp. 133–37.

17. Bela Balassa, "The Process of Industrial Development and Alternative Development Strategies," in Bela Balassa, *The Newly Industrializing Countries in the World Economy* (Elmsford, N.Y.: Pergamon Press, 1981), pp. 1–28.

18. Ibid.

19. "Mexico to Recover in Two Years," *Monterey Peninsula Herald* (7 October 1982), p. 8.

15. Optimal IMF-Type Stabilization Programs during the de la Madrid Presidency, 1983–87

1. This discussion is based on accounts of the IMF Stabilization Program for 1983–85, given in Art Pine, "IMF Is About to Confront Mexico's Debt Mountain," *Wall Street Journal* (27 September 1982), p. 1; Federal Reserve Bank of Chicago, *International Letter* (17 December 1982), pp. 1–4; American Chamber of Commerce of Mexico, *Mexico Update* (27 December 1982), pp. 1–2; and *IMF Survey* (5 January 1983), pp. 1–2.

2. William R. Cline, "Mexico's Crisis, the World's Peril," *Foreign Policy* (Winter 1982–83), pp. 107–8.

16. The Policymaking Dilemma

1. A similar assessment was made by Leopoldo Solis for the period following the 1976 devaluation and stabilization program. See his "The External Sector of the Mexican Economy," in Joseph Grunwald, ed., *Latin America and the World Economy: A Changing International Order* (Beverly Hills: Sage Publications, 1978), pp. 133–46.

2. Further elaboration on these points is contained in Robert Looney, "The Oil Question and Policy Optimization in Mexico," paper presented at the Eighth Annual Eastern Economic Association meetings, Washington, D.C., April 29, 1982.

3. See also Sidney Weintraub, "Case Study of Economic Stabilization: Mexico," in William R. Cline and Sidney Weintraub, eds., *Economic Stabilization in Developing Countries* (Washington: Brookings Institution, 1981), pp. 272–95; Laurence Whitehead, "Mexico From Bust to Boom: A Politi-

cal Evaluation of the 1976–79 Stabilization Programme," *World Development* (November 1980); and Leopoldo Solis, "The Petroleum Boom in Mexico: An Opportunity for Correcting the Pattern of Economic Development," paper presented at the North American Economic Association meetings, Mexico City, December 28, 1978.

4. Similar to the process described in Jahangir Amuzegar, "Oil Wealth: A Very Mixed Blessing," *Foreign Affairs* (Spring 1982), pp. 814–35.

5. See Calvin Blair, "Economic Development Policy in Mexico: A New Penchant for Planning," Institute of Latin American Studies, University of Texas at Austin, *Technical Papers Series No. 26* (1980).

6. Carlos Benito, "Policies for Food Production and Consumption in Underdevelopment: The Case of Mexico," *Journal of Policy Modeling* (1979), pp. 383–98.

7. See E. V. K. Fitzgerald, "Recent Writings on the Mexican Economy," *Latin American Research Review* (1981), pp. 236–44, for a summary of this debate.

8. Nick Eberstadt, "La Crisis," *New Republic* (18 October 1982), p. 21.

Bibliography

Ahking, Francis. "Mexico: The Open Economy—A Note." *Review of Business and Economic Research* (1978): 103–7.

Akhtar, M. A. "An Empirical Note on Inflation and Openness in Less Developed Countries." *The Philippine Economic Journal* (1976): 636–49.

Alisky, Marvin. "Population and Migration Problems in Mexico." *Current History* (November 1981): 365–69.

American Chamber of Commerce of Mexico. "Devaluation of the Peso." *Quarterly Economic Report* (March 1982).

Amuzegar, Jahangir. "Oil Wealth: A Very Mixed Blessing." *Foreign Affairs* (Spring 1982): 814–35.

Aspra, Antonio. "Import Substitution in Mexico: Past and Present." *World Development* (January 1977): 111–24.

Ayala, P., et al. "La Crisis económica: evolución y perspectivas." In P. Gonzalez et al., *México Hoy*. Mexico, D.F.: Siglo XXI, 1979.

Bailey, John. "Agrarian Reform in Mexico." *Current History* (November 1981): 357–58.

Balassa, Bela. *The Newly Industrializing Countries in the World Economy*. Elmsford, N.Y.: Pergamon Press, 1981.

Bank of Mexico. *Informe Anual*.

Baranson, Jack. *North-South Technology Transfer: Financing and Institution Building*, 55–56. Mt. Airy, Md.: Lomond Publications, 1981.

Barkin, David, and Gustavo Esteva. *Inflación y denogracia: el caso de México*. Mexico, D.F.: Siglo XXI, 1979.

———. "Social Conflict and Inflation in Mexico." *Latin American Perspectives* (Winter 1982): 48–64.

Bath, C. Richard, John Evans, and Dilmus James. "Dependency, Inflation, and the Allocation of Mexico's Petroleum Reserves." *Texas Business Review* 1 (September–October 1981): 198–99.

Beltran del Rio, Abel. "Econometric Forecasting for Mexico: An Analysis of Errors in Prediction." In Jere Behrman and James Hanson, eds., *Short-Term Macroeconomic Policy in Latin America*. Cambridge, Mass.: Ballinger, 1979.

———. "Mexico's Troubled Economy: Peso Prognosis." *Wharton Magazine* (Winter 1977): 55–56.

———. "The Mexican Oil Syndrome: Early Symptoms, Preventive Efforts and Prognosis." In W. Braer and M. Gillis, eds., *Export Diversification and the New Protectionism: The Experiences of Latin America*, 115–30. Urbana-Champaign: Bureau of Economic and Business Research, 1981.

Benito, Carlos. "Policies for Food Production and Consumption in Underdevelopment: The Case of Mexico." *Journal of Policy Making* (1979): 383–98.

Benoit, Emile. *Defense and Economic Growth in Developing Countries*. Lexington, Mass.: Lexington Books, 1973.

———. "Growth and Defense in Developing Countries." *Economic Development and Cultural Change* (January 1978): 271–80.

Bergsman, Joel. "Income Distribution and Poverty in Mexico." In World Bank, *Staff Working Paper No. 395* (June 1980).

Best, Brinley. *Mexico: The Next Ten Years*. London: Euromoney Publications, 1981.

Bizzarro, Salvatore. "Mexico's Poor." *Current History* (November 1981): 370–73.

Blair, Calvin. "Economic Development Policy in Mexico: A New Penchant for Planning." In Institute of Latin American Studies, University of Texas at Austin, *Technical Papers Series No. 26* (1980).

Blejer, Mario, and Leonardo Leiderman. "Inflation and Relative Price Variability in the Open Economy." *European Economic Review* (1982): 387–402.

Blinder, A. S., and R. M. Solo. "Analytical Foundations of Fiscal Policy." In A. S. Blinder et al., eds., *The Economics of Public Finance*, 3–119. Washington, D.C.: Brookings Institution, 1973.

Brothers, D., and Leopoldo Solis. *Mexican Financial Development*. Austin: University of Texas Press, 1966.

Bruton, Henry. "Productivity Growth in Latin America." *American Economic Review* (December 1967): 1105.

Bueno, Geraldo M. "Desarrollo y Petróleo: La Experiencia de los Paises Exportadores." *Trimestre Económico* (1980): 283–301.

———. "The Structure of Protection in Mexico." In Bela Balassa et al., eds., *The Structure of Protection in Developing Countries*, 169–202. Baltimore: Johns Hopkins University Press, 1971.

Buira, A. "Causas Principales y Efectos Internos de la Inflación." In E. Fernandez, ed., *Cincuenta Años de Banca Central*. Mexico City: Fondo de Cultura Económica, 1976.

Buiter, William. "Crowding Out and the Effectiveness of Fiscal Policy." *Journal of Public Economics* (1977): 309–10.

Caplan, Basil. "Mexico—The World's New Biggest Borrower." *The Banker* (July 1982): 33–44.

Carlson, Keith, and Rodger Spencer. "Crowding Out and Its Critics." Federal Reserve Bank of St. Louis, *Review* (December 1975): 2–17.

Carrera Cortez, Federico. "The Commercial Banking System and Investment Opportunities." In John Christman, ed., *Business Mexico*, 105–22. Mexico City: American Chamber of Commerce of Mexico, 1981.

Centro de Investigación y Docencia Económicas. "The Mexican Economy: Recent Development and Future Prospects." *Cambridge Journal of Economics* (June 1980): 177–97.

Chenery, H. et al., *Redistribution with Growth*. New York: Oxford University Press, 1974.

———. "The Structuralist Approach to Development Policy." *American Economic Review* (May 1975): 310–16.

Chislett, William. "Alfa Trapped in a Vicious Circle." *Financial Times* (25 May 1982): 19.

———. "Anxiety over Mexican Spending." *Financial Times* (23 March 1982): 4.

———. "Critical Year for Economy after Peso Devaluation." *Financial Times* (22 March 1982): II.

———. "Lopez Portillo Plays for High Economic Stakes." *Financial Times* (23 February 1982): 4.

———. "Mexicans Debate GATT Membership." *Financial Times* (14 December 1979): 3.

———. "Military Eye on Central America." *Financial Times* (22 March 1982): 111.

———. "The Oil Miracle Turns Sour." *Financial Times* (27 April 1982): 3.

Chow, Gregory. *Analysis and Control of Dynamic Economic Systems*. New York: John Wiley, 1975.

Coale, Ansley. "Population and Growth and Economic Development: The Case of Mexico." *Foreign Affairs* (January 1978): 427–29.

Cripps, T. F., M. J. Fetherston, and W. A. H. Godley. "Simulations with the Cambridge Economic Policy Group Model." In Michael Posner, ed., *Demand Management*, 10–11. London: Heinemann, 1978.

Cuthbertson, Keith. *Macroeconomic Policy: The New Cambridge, Keynesian and Monetarist Controversies*, ch. 3. London: Macmillan, 1979.

de la Pena, Sergio. "Proletarian Power and State Monopoly Capitalism in Mexico." *Latin American Perspectives* (Winter 1982): 20–35.

Denison, E. "How to Raise the High Employment Growth Rate by One Percentage Point." *American Economic Review* (May 1962).

Dirección General de Estadistica, Secretaria de Industria y Comercio. *Anuario estadistico del Comercio exterior*, various issues. Mexico City: Talleres Graficos de la Nacion.

Dominguez, Jorge. "International Reverberations of a Dynamic Political Economy." In Jorge Dominguez, ed., *Mexico's Political Economy*. Beverly Hills: Sage Publications, 1982.

______. "Introduction." In Jorge Dominguez, ed., *Mexico's Political Economy: Challenges at Home and Abroad*, p. 13. Beverly Hills: Sage Publications, 1982.

Dorfman, Dan. "Downhill in Mexico." *San Francisco Examiner* (27 June 1982): D1.

Eatwell, John, and A. Singh. "Se Encuentra 'Sobrecalentada' la Economía Méxicana: Un Analisis de los Problemas a Corto y Mediano Plazo." Mexico City, April 1981 (mimeo).

Eberstadt, Nick. "La Crisis." *New Republic* (18 October 1982): 21.

Edwards, Anthony. *The New Industrial Countries and Their Impact on Western Manufacturing*. London: The Economist Intelligence Unit, December 1979.

Escobedo, Gilberto. "Ahorroy Desarrollo Económico." Bank of Mexico, *Working Paper* (1975): 73.

______. "Formulation of a Model of the Mexican Economy." Federal Reserve Bank of St. Louis, *Review* (July 1973): 8–19.

______. "The Response of the Mexican Economy to Policy Actions." Federal Reserve Bank of St. Louis, *Review* (June 1973): 21.

Evans, John. "The Evolution of the Mexican Tax System Since 1970." Institute of Latin American Studies, University of Texas at Austin, *Technical Papers Series No. 34* (1982).

Farrell, Mike. "International Impact of U.S. Money Supply: The Case of Mexico." *A Mexican Economic Review* (June 1980): 433–43.

Feliz, David. "Income Inequality in Mexico." *Current History* (March 1977): 111.

Fitzgerald, E. V. K. "A Note on Capital Accumulation in Mexico: The Budget Deficit and Investment Finance." *Development and Change* (June 1980): 391–417.

______. "A Note on State Capital and Industrialization in Mexico." In J. Carrière, ed., *Industrialisation and the State in Latin America*. Amsterdam: CEDLA, 1979.

______. "Mexico: A New Direction in Economic Policy?" *Bank of London and South American Review* (1979).

______. "Oil and Mexico's Industrial Development Plan." *Texas Business Review* (May-June 1980): 133–37.

______. "Patterns of Public Sector Income and Expenditure in Mexico." Institute of Latin American Studies, University of Texas at Austin, *Technical Papers Series No. 17* (1978).

______. "Patterns of Savings and Investment in Mexico: 1939–76." Centre of Latin American Studies, Cambridge University, *Working Papers No. 30* (1977).

______. "Recent Writings on the Mexican Economy." *Latin American Research Review* (1981): 236–44.

———. "Some Aspects of the Political Economy of the Latin American State." *Development and Change* (1976).

———. "Stabilization Policy in Mexico: The Fiscal Deficit and Macroeconomic Equilibrium 1960–77." In Rosemary Thorp and Laurence Whitehead, eds., *Inflation and Stabilisation in Latin America*. New York: Holmes and Meier, 1979.

———. "The Fiscal Crisis of the Latin American Stage." In J. F. J. Toye, ed., *Taxation and Economic Development*. London: Frank Cass, 1978.

———. "The Fiscal Deficit and Development Finance: A Note on the Accumulation Balance in Mexico." Centre of Latin American Studies, Cambridge University, *Working Papers No. 35* (April 1979).

———. "The New International Division of Labour and the Relative Autonomy of the State: Notes for a Reappraisal of Classical Dependency." *Bulletin of Latin American Research* (October 1981): 1–12.

———. "The Public Investment Criterion and the Role of the State." *Journal of Development Studies* (July 1977): 365–72.

———. "The State and Capital Accumulation in Mexico." *Journal of Latin American Studies* (1978): 263–82.

Freivalds, John. "Mexico: The Agricultural and Livestock Sectors." *Bank of London and South America Review* (August 1975): 440–47.

Friedman, Alan. "A Colossal Mountain of Debt." *Financial Times* (20 August 1982): 13.

Gallagher, Charles F. "Population, Petroleum and Politics: Mexico at the Crossroads." Part I and part II, American Universities Field Staff *Reports No. 19, 42* (1980).

Gelb, Alan. "Capital Importing Oil Exporters: Adjustment Issues and Policy Choices." In World Bank, *World Bank Staff Working Paper, No. 475* (August 1981).

Glade, William. "Prospects for Mexico's Socioeconomic Growth." *Texas Business Review* (March-April 1979): 47–50.

Gollas, M. *Ciencia y Desarrollo* (May-June 1978).

Gonzalez Casanova, Pablo. "The Economic Development of Mexico." In *Economic Development*, 98–107. San Francisco: W. H. Freeman, 1980.

Gonzalez, P. and E. Florescano, eds. *México Hoy*. Mexico, D. F.: Siglo XXI, 1979.

Gordon, David. "Mexico: A Survey." *The Economist* (22 April 1978): 18.

Griffiths, Brian. *Inflation: The Price of Prosperity*, p. 3. New York: Holmes and Meier, 1976.

———. *Mexican Monetary Policy and Economic Development*, ch. 4. New York: Praeger Publishers, 1972.

Griliches, Z. "Distributed Lags: A Survey." *Econometrica* (1967): 16–49.

Hall, Bronwyn, and Robert E. Hall. *Time Series Processor, Version 3.5*. Stanford, Calif., April 1980.

Hansen, Rodger D. *The Politics of Mexican Development*, chs. 2 and 8. Baltimore: Johns Hopkins University Press, 1971.

Hardy, Chandra. "Mexico's Development Strategy for the 1980s." *World Development* (June 1982): 503–5.

Harris, Richard, and David Barkin. "The Political Economy of Mexico in the Eighties." *Latin American Perspectives* (Winter 1982): 2–19.

———. *Analisis del Presupuesto Méxicano Pova 1979*. Mexico City: ECANAL, January 1979.

———. *The Last Informe of President Echeverría: Inflation and Devaluation*. Mexico City: American Chamber of Commerce of Mexico, September 1976.

———. *Mexican Industrialization and Petroleum.* Mexico City: ECANAL, August 1979.

Hernandez Laos, Enrique, and Jorge Cordova Chavez. "Estructura de la Distribución del Ingreso en México." *Comercio Exterior* 29, no. 5 (1979).

Hewitt de Alcamtara, Cynthia. *Modernizing Mexican Agriculture: Socioeconomic Implications of Technological Change 1940–1970.* Geneva: United Nations Research Institute for Social Development, 1976.

Hicks, J. R. *The Crisis in Keynesian Economics.* New York: Basic Books, 1974.

Higgins, Benjamin. *Economic Development*, p.638. New York: Norton, 1968.

International Bank for Reconstruction and Development / World Bank. *World Development Report, 1980.* New York: Oxford University Press, 1980.

International Monetary Fund. *Balance of Payments Year Book*, various issues.

———. *Direction of Trade*, various issues.

Iyoha, Milton. "Inflation and Openness in Less Developed Economies: A Cross Country Analysis." *Economic Development and Cultural Change* (October 1973): 31–38.

Johnson, H. "The Monetary Approach to the Balance of Payments Theory." In H. Johnson, ed., *Further Essays in Monetary Economics*, p. 231. Cambridge, Mass.: Harvard University Press, 1973.

Jolly, Richard. "Objectives and Means for Linking Disarmament to Development." In Richard Jolly, ed., *Disarmament and World Development, 105–12.* London: Pergamon Press, 1978.

Kaldor, Mary. *"The Military in Development." World Development* (June 1976).

Keating, Maryann. "The Fiscal Crisis in Mexico." Paper presented at the annual meetings of the Atlantic Economics Association. Washington, D.C., October 1979.

———. "The Fiscal Crisis in Mexico, Peru and Chile: A Review Essay of the Cambridge School." Paper prepared for the annual meeting of the Midwestern Economics Association. Chicago, December 1980.

Kemp, D. S. "The Monetary View of the Balance of Payments." Federal Reserve Bank of St. Louis, *Review* (April 1975): 14.

Kennedy, G. *The Military in the Third World.* London: Duckworth, 1974.

Kirkpatrick, C. H., and F. I. Nixson. "The Origins of Inflation in Less Developed Countries: A Selective Review." In Michael Parkin and George Zis, eds., *Inflation in the World Economy*, 132. Manchester: Manchester University Press, 1976.

Koehler, John. *Economic Policy Making with Limited Information: The Process of Macro-Control in Mexico.* Santa Monica: Rand Corporation, 1968.

———. "Economic Policy Making with Little Information and Few Instruments: The Process of Macro-Control in Mexico." *Rand Papers No. 4764.* Santa Monica Rand Corporation (1972).

Kolbeck, Gustavo Romero. "Public Sector Banking." In John Christman, ed., *Business Mexico*, 105–22. Mexico City: American Chamber of Commerce of Mexico, 1981.

Koyck, L. M. *Distributed Lags and Investment Analysis.* Amsterdam: North Holland, 1954.

La Economía Méxicana. Mexico City: Publicaciones Ejecutivas de Mexico, 1976–1980.

Lamadrid, A. "Industrial Location Policy in Mexico." In United Nations Industrial Development Organization, *Industrial Location and Regional Development*, 563–65. New York: United Nations, 1971.

Landau, Luis. "Saving Functions in Latin America." In Hollis Chenery, ed., *Studies in Development Planning*, 299–321. Cambridge, Mass.: Harvard University Press, 1971.

Laney, Leroy. "Currency Substitution: The Mexican Case." *Voice of the Federal Reserve Bank of Dallas* (January 1981): 1–10.

——— "How Contagious Is 'Dutch Disease'?" Federal Reserve Bank of Dallas, *Economic Review* (March 1982): 10–11.

Lanframco, Sam. "Mexican Oil, Export-Led Development and Agricultural Neglect." *Journal of Economic Development* (July 1981): 125–52.

Lavell, A. M. "Regional Industrialization in Mexico: Some Policy Considerations." *Regional Studies* (1972): 343–63.

Leijonhufvud, A. *On Keynesian Economics and the Economics of Keynes*. New York: Oxford University Press, 1968.

Looney, Robert. *Development Alternatives of Mexico Beyond the 1980s*. New York: Praeger Publishers, 1982.

——— *Economic Origins of the Iranian Revolution*, ch. 13. Elmsford, N.Y.: Pergamon Press, 1982.

——— *Mexico's Economy: A Policy Analysis with Forecasts to 1990*. Boulder, Colo.: Westview Press, 1978.

——— "Mexico's Fiscal Crisis: A Critique of the Fitzgerald Thesis," 7–9. Paper presented at the eighth annual Eastern Economic Association meetings, Philadelphia, 28 April 1981.

——— "The Oil Question and Policy Optimization in Mexico." Paper presented at the eighth annual convention of the Eastern Economic Association. Washington, D.C., 29 April 1982.

Luis, Luis R. "Stabilization Policy, Employment and the Balance of Payments: The Recent Mexican Experience." Paper presented at the eighth annual convention of the Eastern Economic Association. Philadelphia, 9–11 April 1981.

Lustig, Nora. "Characteristics of Mexican Economic Growth." *Journal of Development Economics* (1982): 355–76.

Madrigal Hidalgo, Chavez. "Recopilación Sobre el Consumo de Nutrientes on Diferentes Zonas de México." In *La Denutrición y la Salud en Mexico*. Mexico City: INN, 1976.

Mann, Arthur. "The Mexican Tax Burden by Family Income Class." *Public Finance Quarterly* (July 1982): 305–31.

——— "Mexican Fiscal Revenue and Performance, 1950–1977: A Revisit." *Public Finance/Finances Publiques* (1978): 378–85.

——— "Wagner's Law: An Econometric Test for Mexico: 1975–76." *National Tax Journal* (1980): 189–201.

Marquez, Travier. "La Economía Méxicana en 1977 y su Futuro." Madrid, 25 October 1977 (mimeo).

Massone, Pedro. "The Mexican Income Tax (1980)." International Bureau of Fiscal Documentation, *Bulletin* (1981): 389–90.

Mendoza-Berrueta, Elisco. "Regional Implications of Mexico's Economic Growth." *Weltwirtschaftliches Archiv* (1968): 87–123.

Mexico: National Industrial Development Plan, vol. 1. London: Graham and Trotman, 1979.

Mueller, Marnie. "Structural Inflation and the Mexican Experience." *Yale Economic Essays* (Spring 1965): 150–53.

Mussa, M. "A Monetary Approach to Balance of Payments Analysis." *Journal of Money, Credit and Banking* (August 1974): 338.

Nacional Financiera. *La Economía Méxicana en Cifras*. Mexico City: Nacional Financiera, 1981.

NAFINSA-UNIDO. *Mexico: Una Estrategia para el Desarrollo de la Industria de Bienes de Capital*, 342, table VI-14. Mexico City: NAFINSA, 1977.

Nerlou, M. "Lags in Economic Behavior." *Econometrica* (1972): 221–51.

Nowick, A. et al. *Mexico: Manufacturing Sector: Situation, Prospects and Policies*, annex III. Washington, D.C.: World Bank, 1979.

Nugent, J. "Momentum for Development and Development Disequilibria." *Journal of Development Economics* (July 1977): 49.

Opie, Redvers. *Mexican Industrialization and Petroleum*. Mexico City: ECANAL, August 1979.

______. *The Overall Development Plan 1980–82: An Appraisal*. Mexico City: ECANAL, August 1980.

______. *The 1981 Report of the Bank of Mexico: A Disastrous and Tragic Decade of Economic Policy*. Mexico City: ECANAL, May 1982.

______. *Report on Mexico—May to August 1982*, 11–12. Mexico City: ECANAL, 1982.

Organization of American States. *Short Term Economic Reports: Mexico*, 33–34. Washington: OAS, 1980.

Ortiz, Guillermo, and Leopoldo Solis. "Financial Structure and Exchange Rate Experience: Mexico 1954–1977." *Journal of Development Economics* (December 1979).

Otani, Ichiro. "Inflation in an Open Economy: A Case Study of the Philippines." International Monetary Fund, *Staff Papers* (1975): 750–74.

Otero, Guillermo Teutli. "Positive Results for the Maquiladora Program." In John Christman, ed., *Business Mexico*, pp. 149–54. Mexico City: American Chamber of Commerce of Mexico, 1981.

Pazos, Luis. *Devaluación y Estatismo en México*. Mexico City: Editorial Diana, 1976.

Perez Mendoza, Vincente Ernesto. *The Role of the Armed Forces in the Mexican Economy in the 1980s*, 7–8. Masters thesis, Naval Postgraduate School, Monterey, Calif. (June 1981).

Perzabel, Carlos. "Characteristics de la Crisis en México." *Historia y Sociedad* (1978): 41–60.

Pindyck, Robert. *Optimal Planning for Economic Stabilization: The Application of Control Theory to Stabilization Policy*. Amsterdam: North Holland Publishers, 1973.

Poister, T. H. *Public Program Analysis*, 540. Baltimore: University Park Press, 1978.

Purcell, John F. H. "Mexican Social Issues." In Susan Kaufman Purcell, ed., *Mexico-United States Relations*, 51. New York: Praeger Publishers, 1981.

______. "Trade Conflicts and U.S. Mexican Relations," 38–48. Program in United States–Mexican Studies, University of California, San Diego, *Working Papers in U.S. Mexican Studies, No. 38* (1982).

Ramirez, Carlos. "Resignation of Finance Minister Analyzed." Mexico City, *Procesco* (22 March 1982): 6.

Ramirez Izquierdo, V. *Revista Méxicana del Trabajo* (January–March 1972).

Rangel, J. Jesus. "Oteyza Announces 12 Point Economic Program." Mexico City *Excelsior* (March 25, 1982): 1-A, 12-A, 27-A.

Rao, Potluri, and Roger Miller. *Applied Econometrics*, ch. 7. Belmont, Calif.: Wadsworth, 1971.

Reynolds, Clark. "Growth Distribution and Structural Change in Mexico: Recent Trends and Future Prospects." In L. E. Koslow, ed., *The Future of Mexico*. Tempe: Arizona State University Press, 1977.

______. "Labor Market Projections for the United States and Mexico and Current Migration Controversies." *Food Research Institute Studies* (1979): 129.

______. *The Mexican Economy*. New Haven: Yale University Press, 1970.

______. "The Mexican Economy 1982–87: Key Economic Issues, Policy Alternatives, and Implications for International Business." In Alice B. Lentz, ed., *Country Risk Analysis: Mexico*, 22. San Francisco: Council of Americas, 1982.

———. *A Shift-Share Analysis of Regional and Sectoral Productivity Growth in Contemporary Mexico*, 4. Laxenburg, Austria: International Institute for Applied Systems Analysis, 1980.

———. "Why Mexico's 'Stabilizing Development' Was Actually Destabilizing." *World Development* (July 1976): 1005–18.

———. "Why Mexico's 'Stabilizing Development' Was Actually Destabilizing (with Some Implications for the Future)." *World Development* (June-September 1978).

Rhoads, John. "The Mexican Stock Exchange." In John Christman, ed., *Business Mexico*, 137–44. Mexico City: American Chamber of Commerce of Mexico, 1981.

Riding, Alan. "Mexico's Economic Imbalances." *New York Times* (6 April 1981): 7.

———. "Mexico Bets on Industry to Make the Most of Its Oil Boom." *New York Times* (9 December 1979): 7.

———. "Mexico's Economy: Need for Sacrifice Is Stressed," *New York Times* (25 May 1982): 33.

———. "Dramatic Shift in Mexican Mood." *San Francisco Chronicle* (14 April 1982): 26.

———. "Mexico's Road to Trouble Is Coated with Oil." *New York Times* (21 February 1982): 3.

———. "Mexico's Mood is Pessimistic." *San Francisco Chronicle* (15 February 1982): 16.

———. "The Mixed Blessing of Mexico's Oil." *New York Times Magazine* (11 January 1981): 22–59.

Robinson, Alan. "Letter from Mexico." *Journal of Commerce* (April 3, 1980): 5.

Ros, Jaime. "Pricing in the Mexican Manufacturing Sector." *Cambridge Journal of Economics* (September 1980): 211–32.

Sanders, Thomas. "Mexico in 1975." *American Universities Field Staff Reports* (September 1975): 4–7.

Schlagheck, James. *The Political, Economic, and Labor Climate in Mexico*, rev. ed. ch. 4. Philadelphia: Wharton School, 1980.

Secretaria de Patrimonio. *Mexico Industrial Development Plan*, vol. 1, ch. 1. London: Graham and Trotman, 1979.

Secretaria de Patrimonio y Fomento. *Plan Nacional de Desarrollo Industrial, 1979–82*. Mexico City, 1979.

Selowsky, Marcelo. "Education and Economic Growth: Some International Comparisons." In Organization of American States, *Domestic Efforts and the Needs for External Financing for Development in Mexico*, 85. OEA 1 Ser-H/XIV, CIAP/562, 28 August 1972 (confidential).

Sheehey, E. J. "On the Measurement of Imported Inflation in Developing Countries." *Weltwirtschaftliches Archiv* (1979): 68–79.

Singer, Morris. *Growth Equality and the Mexican Experience*, chs. 3–4. Austin: University of Texas Press, 1969.

Smithies, Arthur. *The Economic Potential of the Arab Countries*, 22–25. Santa Monica: Rand Corporation, 1978.

Solis, Leopoldo. "A Monetary Will-O'-the-Wisp: Pursuit of Equity Through Deficit Spending." Woodrow Wilson School, Princeton University, *Discussion Paper No.* 77 (1977).

———. *Economic Policy Reform in Mexico: A Case Study for Developing Countries*. Elmsford, N.Y.: Pergamon Press, 1981.

———. "Industrial Priorities in Mexico." In United Nations Industrial Development Organization, *Industrial Priorities in Developing Countries*, 48–112. New York: United Nations, 1979.

———. "The External Sector of the Mexican Economy." In Joseph Grunwald, ed., *Latin*

America and World Economy: A Changing International Order, 133–46. Beverly Hills: Sage Publications, 1978.

______. "The Financial System in the Economic Development of Mexico." *Weltwirtschaftliches Archiv* (1968): 36–68.

______. "The Petroleum Boom in Mexico: An Opportunity for Correcting the Pattern of Economic Development." Paper presented at the North American Economic Studies Association meetings. Mexico City, 28 December 1978.

Spencer, Rodger, and William Yohe. "The Crowding Out of Private Expenditures by Fiscal Actions." Federal Reserve Bank of St. Louis, *Review* (October 1970): 12–24.

Statistical Analysis System. *SAS User's Guide, 1979 Edition*, 157–62. Cary, N.C.: SAS Institute, 1979.

Stern, R. M. *The Balance of Payments: Theory and Economic Policy*, chs. 6 and 10. Chicago: Aldine, 1973.

Street, James. "Prospects for Mexico's Industrial Development Plan in the 1980s." *Texas Business Review* (May-June 1980): 125–32.

Tanzi, Vito. "Disequilibrium in the Fiscal Sector of Developing Countries." Paper presented at the 1981 American Economic Association meetings. Washington, D.C., 28–30 December 1981.

Taylor, Lance. *Macro Models for Developing Countries*, ch. 8. New York: McGraw-Hill, 1979.

Tello, C. *La Política Económica en México, 1970–1976*. Mexico, D.F.: Siglo XXI, 1979.

______. *Economía Méxicana*. Mexico, D.F.: Centro de Investigación y Docencia Económicas, 1979.

ten Kate, Adriaan, and Robert Bruce Wallace. *Protection and Economic Development in Mexico*, ch. 3. New York: St. Martin's Press, 1980.

Trejo Reyes, Saul. "Comments." In William Cline and Sidney Weintraub, eds., *Economic Stabilization in Developing Countries*, 293. Washington, D.C.: Brookings Institution, 1981.

______. "Desempleo y Subocupación en México." *Comercio Exterior* (May 1972).

______. *El Trimestre Económico* (1975, No. 167).

Turner, Louis, et al. *Living with the Newly Industrializing Countries*. London: Royal Institute of International Affairs, 1980.

Twomey, Michael. "Exchange Rate Devaluations and Income Distribution in Latin America." Paper presented at the Western Economics Association meetings. San Francisco, 2 July 1981.

U.S. Arms Control and Disarmament Agency. *World Military Expenditures and Arms Transfers: 1967–1976*. Washington, D.C.: U.S. ACDA, 1978.

Urguidi, Victor. "An Overview of Mexican Economic Development." *Weltwirtschaftliches Archiv* (1968): 10–11.

Van Ginneken, Woulter. *Socio-Economic Groups and Income Distribution in Mexico*, chs. 1 and 3. London: Croom Helm, 1980.

Vanderplaats, G. "COPES—A Fortran Control Program for Engineering Synthesis." No place, no date (mimeo).

______. "The Computer for Design and Optimization." Paper presented at the ASME annual winter meeting. New York, December 1976.

Vasquez, Juan. "Behind the Burnout of Mexico." *San Francisco Chronicle* (24 August 1982): 10.

Vellinga, Menno. *Economic Development and the Dynamics of Class: Industrialization, Power and Control in Monterrey, Mexico*. Assen, The Netherlands: Van Gorcum, 1979.

Venezian, Eduardo, and William Gamble. *The Agricultural Development of Mexico*, 63–64. New York: Praeger Publishers, 1969.

Vidali Carbajal, Carlos. "Politica Tributaria." In *Política Hacendaria y Financiera en México, 1971–1976*, 24–25. Suplemento de Comercio Exterior (August 1976).

Villarreal, R. *El Desequilibrio Externo en la Industrialización de México, 1929–75*. Mexico City: Fondo de Cultura Económica, 1976.

Warman, Nathan. "Industrial Development Policy." In John Christman, ed., *Business Mexico*, 77–88. Mexico City: American Chamber of Commerce of Mexico, 1981.

Weintraub, Sidney. "Case Study of Economic Stabilization: Mexico." In William Cline and Sidney Weintraub, eds., *Economic Stabilization in Developing Countries*, 272–95. Washington, D.C.: Brookings Institution, 1981.

Whitehead, Laurence. "Mexico from Bust to Boom: A Political Evaluation of the 1976–79 Stabilization Programme." *World Development* (November 1980).

Whynes, David. *The Economics of Third World Military Expenditure*. Austin: University of Texas Press, 1979.

Wilford, D. Sykes. *Monetary Policy and the Open Economy: Mexico's Experience*, 65. New York: Praeger Publishers, 1977.

______. "Price Levels, Interest Rates, Open Economies, and a Fixed Exchange Rate: The Mexican Case, 1954–74." *Review of Business and Economic Research* (Spring 1977): 52–65.

______ and Walton T. Wilford. "Comment on 'Mexican Fiscal Revenue Performance, 1950–77: A Revisit.'" *Public Finance/Finances Publiques* (1979): 134–37.

______. "Fiscal Revenues in Mexico: A Measure of Performance, 1950–1973." *Public Finance/Finances Publiques* (1976): 103.

______. "The Revenue-Income Elasticity Coefficient: Performance and Stability Criteria." *Public Finance/Finances Publiques* (1976): 103–15.

______. "The Revenue-Income Elasticity Coefficient: Performance and Stability Criteria." *Review of Business and Economic Research* (Winter 1976): 90–93.

______ and J. Richard Zecher. "Monetary Policy and the Balance of Payments in Mexico, 1955–75." *Journal of Money, Credit and Banking* (August 1979): 340–438.

Wilkie, James. *The Mexican Revolution: Federal Expenditure and Social Change Since 1910*, 2d ed. chs. 4 and 6. Berkeley: University of California Press, 1970.

Wionczek, Miguel. "Incomplete Formal Planning: Mexico." In E. Hagen, ed., *Planning Economic Development*, 150–82. Homewood, Ill.: Richard D. Irwin, 1963.

World Bank. *Special Study on the Mexican Economy: Major Policy Issues and Prospects*, vol. I, main report. Washington, D.C.: IBRD, 30 May 1979, report No. 2307-ME (confidential).

______. *World Development Report, 1980*, 118–19.

______. *World Development Report, 1981*. New York: Oxford University Press, 1981.

______. *World Tables, 1976*. Baltimore: Johns Hopkins University Press, 1976.

Wygard, Edward, and Bill Kryzda. "The National Industrial Development Plan: Goals and Incentives." In John Christman, ed., *Business Mexico*, 89–96. Mexico City: American Chamber of Commerce of Mexico, 1981.

Yates, P. Lamartine. *Mexico's Agricultural Dilemma*, ch. 11. Tucson: University of Arizona Press, 1981.

Zamorano, Isabel. "Finance Minister Discusses Austerity Measures." Mexico City, *Excelsior* (20 February 1982): 1-A, 8-A, 12-A.

Zecher, R. "Monetary Equilibrium and International Reserve Flows in Australia." *Journal of Finance* (December 1974): 1525–26.

Index

About the author
Robert E. Looney is Associate Professor of National Security Affairs at the Naval Postgraduate School, Monterey, California.
Among his recent books are *Saudi Arabia's Growth Potential*, *Economic Causes of the Iranian Revolution*, and *Economic Policy Making in Saudi Arabia*.